AL-FIQH AL-ISLĀMĪ

الفقه الإسلامي

AL-FIQH AL-ISLĀMĪ

ACCORDING TO THE ḤANAFĪ MADHHAB

VOLUME 2

ZAKĀT, FASTING AND ḤAJJ

SHAYKH MOHAMMAD AKRAM NADWI

AL-FIQH AL-ISLĀMĪ Vol.2

ISBN: 978-0-9555779-4-9

British Library Cataloguing in Publication Data
A catalogue record of this book is available from The British Library

Editors: Susanne Thackray, Syed Tohel Ahmed, Junaid Ahmed, Shafiur Rahman.

Cover Design: Syed Nuh

Printed by: Imak Offset Print, Istanbul, Turkey

Typsetting: Abdassamad Clarke

Angelwing Media
www.angelwingmedia.net

DISTRIBUTORS
UK
Blackstone
96 Whitechapel Road
London, E1 1JQ
Tel: 020 7247 0373
Email: wholesale@blackstonedirect.com
www.blackstonedirect.com

USA & Canada
Al-Rashad Books
www.al-rashad.com
email: orders@al-rashad.com
Tel: +1 (330) 203-1522

Fiji and New Zealand
Iqra Academy (Iqra Islamic Trust)
info@iqrafiji.org
www.iqrafiji.org

بسم الله الرحمن الرحيم

CONTENTS

Dedication from the Author and Publisher

We dedicate this book to our respective parents (Hafiz Tajammul Husain & Munawwar Jahan, Taiyabur Rahman & Rabia Khanom, Bashir Uddin & Anwara Begum and Syed Abdul Latif & Renwara Khanam). It was our parents who firmly laid the foundation of Imān in our hearts. May Allāh forgive them for any shortcomings and envelope them in His Infinite Mercy.

"Your Lord has decreed that you worship none but Him, and that you be kind to parents. Whether one or more attain old age in your life, say not to them a word of contempt, nor repel them, but address them in terms of honour. And out of kindness, lower to them the wing of humility, and say, "my Lord! Bestow on them Your Mercy, even as they cherished me in childhood." (*Isrā'*: 23–24)

KEY TO TRANSLITERATION

ا	*alif*
ب	*bā*
ت	*tā*
ث	*thā*
ج	*jīm*
ح	*ḥā*
خ	*khā*
د	*dāl*
ذ	*dhāl*
ر	*rā*
ز	*zā*
س	*sīn*
ش	*shīn*
ص	*ṣād*
ض	*ḍād*
ط	*ṭā*
ظ	*ẓā*
ع	*ʿayn* (indicated with a ʿ)
غ	*ghayn*
ف	*fā*
ق	*qāf*
ك	*kāf*
ل	*lām*
م	*mīm*
ن	*nūn*
ه	*hā*
و	*waw*
ي	*yā*
٫	*hamzah* (indicated with a ')

Longer vowels are indicated by a stroke over the letter, e.g. *ā, ī, ū* and *Ā, Ī, Ū*.

كتاب الزكاة

THE BOOK OF ZAKĀH

Introduction

The principle and practice of charity is recognised in every religious tradition — to my knowledge, without exception. It is related to the virtues of kindness (also expressed in courtesy and civility) and generosity (also expressed as hospitality to visitors and benevolence with strangers, travellers, etc).

The distinguishing feature of charity is that, unlike other acts of giving, it expects no return for the gift from the person(s) to whom it was given. Charity is for the other; it entails permanently dispossessing oneself of something in order to benefit the other(s).

In some traditions, charity is understood to be a moral obligation, a duty of the individual to help others who are in need of assistance. Those in need can be more efficiently helped if the resources needed are pooled and centrally distributed and therefore charitable organisations which do this are a common feature of most societies.

In some societies, certain needs are managed through state controlled taxation; a proportion of one's wealth is taken by government, pooled with others, and then spent on providing for those in society unable to provide for themselves (the sick, disabled, unemployed, widows, orphans, elderly, etc.). Expenditures from this type of highly centralised and organised 'public welfare' programme are legally restricted to the society in which the tax has been collected. Plainly, this way of managing needs is very different from charity – tax-payers are 'giving' to the system in the expectation of 'getting back' from the system at some future date.

Also, because state expenditures are wholly impersonal, people receiving 'public welfare' rarely feel that they have been in receipt of some human kindness; on the contrary, such payments are presented and perceived as 'legal rights or statutory obligations'. Generally speaking, however, if such a system is run fairly, it appears to be efficient at meeting people's needs.

So, if the needs of people can efficiently be met without charity, what is the point of charity? One answer is that all needs can never be met; there remain needy people, within society, and outside it, whom the state system cannot identify as legally qualified for assistance because, for example, they are foreigners or they do not have a fixed address, or some other bureaucratic reason. So charity is still needed to make up for the failures or limitations of 'public welfare'. But what if the failures or limitations could be greatly reduced or even eliminated? What then?

A much better answer to the question "What is the point of charity?" can be found by reflecting on the meaning and intent of two terms in the Islamic tradition, either of which can be correctly translated as charity. The two terms are *ṣadaqah* and zakāh.

The two terms are blurred (though not quite interchangeable) in the Qur'ān and Prophetic ḥadīth (e.g. the command to take *ṣadaqah* from the believers; the command to pay *ṣadaqat al-fiṭr*). The root meaning of *ṣadaqah* (to prove oneself, true, credible) is to behave as a believer is supposed to behave – someone who is kind and generous and can be trusted not to hurt others by act or speech, because he truly does (as he claims) fear God. Thus, *ṣadaqah* is the more general term: it is not only about giving from one's wealth. It is the disposition and act of kindness arising from fear of God and expecting reward from only God: to greet a neighbour cheerfully is *ṣadaqah*; to clear a public footpath of hindrances is *ṣadaqah*; for one unable to be positively kind, not harming one's neighbour is accepted as *ṣadaqah* – provided this is done out of fear of God.

Whereas *ṣadaqah* is not necessarily related to one's wealth, zakāh is. As implemented by the Prophet (peace be upon him), zakāh is a calculated amount of one's wealth which one has a religious and legal duty to pay. The root meanings of zakāh connect it to the idea of (1) purifying, or cleansing oneself of the taints of avarice, thus freeing oneself from being trapped (or owned) by the things one owns. And (2) growing, prospering: zakāh lifts a burden from the soul, so that it can grow in goodness. In the same way as a stone can obstruct a plant's growth, and removing it allows the plant to benefit from light and hence flourish. Not recognising the duty of zakāh can obstruct one's wealth from bringing good to oneself and one's community.

Zakāh is a legal duty, yet it is not a tax in the same way as other state-imposed taxes.

(1) Though it is a collective duty to gather zakāh, it is better that this duty is done at local levels, where people's incomes and needs are better understood.

(2) The proceeds of zakāh must, whenever possible, be disbursed locally.

(3) The expenditures from zakāh are strictly defined by the Qur'ān. Only if there is no outlet to spend zakāh on one or more of these heads of expenditure locally is it allowed to send the funds to a neighbouring or other locality where there is need. (For emergencies abroad, there is *ṣadaqah*.)

Zakāh is designed and intended primarily to relieve owners of wealth from the burdens and potential ills of wealth – therefore, it is not dependent on the existence of need in a society or locality. Rather, it is dependent on the amount of wealth one has. Zakāh becomes obligatory when one's wealth reaches the point of *niṣāb* (the minimum that necessitates payment of zakāh). Zakāh, therefore, must be collected and paid, regardless of need.

Ultimately, *ṣadaqah* and zakāh are both expressions of faith, both are acts of worship. Together, their function in society is to keep the levels of kindness and benevolence in a society relatively high, and to maintain kindness and benevolence as the defining norm of relationships between human beings. In practice this means that people working for a living, consider work to be both a means of livelihood and a means of pleasing God. It means that the moral constraints that govern human exchange and relationship also govern economic transactions and relationship.

The norm in functioning Islamic communities is for one to try and not be so poor as to require zakāh, because it is better to be a zakāh-payer than a receiver. But even the poorest can do *ṣadaqah* in the form of acts of kindness, such as being cheerful with others.

Chapter 1: The Importance of Zakāh

Zakāh, as mentioned above, means 'purity' and increase. In the legal context it refers to the payment by a Muslim of what is due to Allāh and is payable to the poor; it is called 'zakāh' because it purifies the rest of a believer's wealth and causes it to increase. Allāh, Exalted is He, says: "*Take zakāh from their wealth to purify and cleanse them*".[1]

Zakāh is linked with *ṣalāh*

Zakāh is only next to *ṣalāh* in importance. It has been mentioned together with *ṣalāh* in 82 verses of the Qur'ān. Some of these verses are mentioned below to show how much emphasis the Qur'ān has put on zakāh. Allāh, Exalted is He says: "*Establish ṣalāh and pay zakāh*".[2] "*Those who believe in the unseen observe the ṣalāh, and from our provisions to them, they give to charity*". [3] "*You shall observe the ṣalāh and give zakāh, and bow down with those who bow down*".[4] "*You shall observe the ṣalāh and give the zakāh. Any good you send forth on behalf of your souls, you will find it with Allāh. Allāh is seer of everything you do*".[5] "*Righteousness is not turning your faces towards the east or the west. Righteous are those who believe in Allāh, the Last Day, the angels, the scripture, and the prophets; and they give the money, cheerfully, to the relatives, the orphans, the needy, the travellers, the beggars, and to free the slaves; and they observe ṣalāh and give the zakāh; and they keep their word whenever they make a promise; and they steadfastly persevere in the face of persecution, hardship, and war. These are the truthful; these are the righteous*".[6] "*Those who believe and lead a righteous life, and observe ṣalāh, and give the zakāh, they receive their recompense from their Lord; they will have nothing to fear, nor will*

1 *al-Barā' ah* 103.
2 *al-Nūr* 56.
3 *al- Baqarah* 3.
4 *al-Baqarah* 43.
5 *al-Baqarah* 110.
6 *al-Baqarah* 177.

they grieve".[7] *"As for those among them who are well founded in knowledge, and the believers, they believe in what was revealed to you, and in what was revealed before you. They are observers of the ṣalāh, and givers of the zakāh; they are believers in Allāh and the Last Day. We grant these a great recompense".*[8] *"Your real allies are Allāh and His Messenger, and the believers who observe the ṣalāh, and give the zakāh, and they bow down".*[9] *"The believing men and women are allies of one another. They command righteousness and forbid evil, they observe the ṣalāh and give the zakāh, and they obey Allāh and His Messenger. These will be showered by Allāh's mercy. Allāh is Almighty, Most Wise".*[10]

Zakāh as a pillar of Islam

Furthermore, the Prophet ﷺ has affirmed zakāh as one of the five pillars of Islam. ʿAbdullāh ibn ʿUmar narrated from the Prophet ﷺ who said: "Islam is built upon [the following] five pillars: testifying that there is no god except Allāh and that Muḥammad is His Messenger, the establishment of the prayer, the giving of zakāh, the fast of Ramaḍān and the pilgrimage to Makkah".[11]

The objectives of zakāh

While discussing the objectives of zakāh, Shāh Walīullāh al-Dihlawī remarks: "Know that there are two main objectives of zakāh. One is the disciplining of the self because there is a relation between subliminal human consciousness and avarice. Avarice is the worst of moral attributes which can lead to unbound infelicity in the Hereafter. A greedy man's heart will remain attached to worldly possessions even during the last moments of his life and hence be punished severely in the future existence. But if he is accustomed to paying zakāh his infatuation for wealth will be softened and it will be a source of advantage to him in the end. In the Hereafter the most superior moral virtue, after the love and fear of Allāh, is generosity. Just as devoutness, prayer, supplication and repentance are instrumental in forging an identity with the Celestial

7 *al-Baqarah* 277.

8 *al-Nisā'* 162.

9 *al-Mā'idah* 55.

10 *al-Barā' ah* 71.

11 al-Bukhārī, *k. al-īmān, b. duʿā'ukum īmānukum;* Muslim, *k. al-īmān, b. bayān arkān al-islām wa daʿā'imihi al-ʿiẓām.*

World; generosity goes a long way to demolish the narrow, mean and debased patterns of worldly existence, for it is the very antithesis of vulgarity and beastliness. The real aim is that the celestial attributes acquire the upper hand and the animal attributes are subdued or, rather, evolve into the class of human qualities to which the celestial attributes belong. The way to realise that is to spend from one's own wealth even if one needs it, also to forgive the oppressor, and to bear trials and hardships with steadfast patience; in this way, with faith in the Hereafter, the vicissitudes of this world are more easily borne. The Prophet ﷺ has enjoined all these things upon us and prescribed their proper limits. Included among them is the spending of wealth to which a number of conditions are attached and which commands so much importance that it has been mentioned, repeatedly in the Qur'ān side by side with faith and worship. '*They will say: 'We were not of those who prayed nor did we feed the hungry. We used to wade in vain pursuits like all waders'.*[12]

The other purpose is related to living in cities, where the weak and the indigent also live and if their needs are not taken care of they may starve. Moreover, the administration of the town is dependent on revenue and those who are entrusted with the defence and administration of the city are not free to earn a private income. They, too, have to depend for their livelihood on state-revenue. Collective expenses cannot easily, if at all, be borne by particular individuals. For these reasons, necessarily, it is a legitimate, established practice to levy money from the people (as a whole.)"[13]

Zakāh is not like taxation

Zakāh is an act of worship; it is not like a worldly tax. It is solely for Allāh, like *ṣalāh* and other acts of worship. Shaykh Abū al-Ḥasan ʿAlī Nadwī says affirming this point: "There are many factors which distinguish zakāh from worldly taxes and other imposts. These special features have imparted to it a unique character of religious sanctity and endued it with the power to make its influence felt in every sphere of life and morality. This cannot be said of any other form of taxation however fair and legitimate it may be. The most outstanding characteristic of zakāh

12 *al-Muddaththir* 43-5.

13 Shāh Walīullah, *Ḥujjatullāh al-bālighah,* ii. 60-61.

is the spirit of *īmān* (belief) and *iḥtisāb* (expectation of reward only from Allāh) which makes it a unique institution of its kind. None of the traditional taxes or economic systems can lay a claim to it. On the other hand, an element of reluctance and rancour is present in all of them. This is so because the payer is not moved by the conviction that the levy is from Allāh who is going to recompense him for it. Furthermore, he knows that those who have imposed the taxes are mere mortals like himself, and, perhaps, of a lower moral and intellectual calibre, and a large part of the revenue thus collected is going to be spent on vain luxury and ostentation and for the benefit of a few privileged sections of the society only".[14]

Warnings against those who do not give charity

There are clear and severe warnings against those who love their wealth so much as to prevent them from giving zakāh. These warnings are mentioned in both the Qur'ān and the Sunnah. For example, Allāh says: "*O you who believe. Most surely many of the experts of law and the monks eat away the property of men falsely and turn them from Allāh's way; and as for those who hoard treasures of gold and silver and do not spend them for the sake of Allāh – warn them of grievous sufferings. On the Day when that [hoarded wealth] shall be heated in the Fires of Hell and their foreheads and their sides and their backs branded with it, [it will be said to them:] 'These are the treasures which you have hoarded for yourselves. Now taste of what you used to accumulate*".[15] "*And they should not think – they who cling to all that Allāh has granted them out of His bounty – that this is good for them. No, it is bad for them, for that which they hoard will be hung about their necks on the Day of Judgement*".[16] "*Have you seen the one who rejects the Day of Judgement? He is the one who drives away the orphans with harshness. And does not encourage the feeding of the poor. So woe to those who observe the ṣalāh, but are heedless of their ṣalāh. They only show off. And they refuse help to the needy*".[17]

Abū Hurayrah reported from Allāh's Messenger ﷺ who said: "If any owner of gold or silver does not pay what is due on him, when the Day of Resurrection comes, plates of fire will be beaten out for him; these will

14 Abū al-Ḥasan ʿAlī Nadwī, *The Four Pillars of Islam*, p. 106.

15 *al-Barā'ah* 34-35.

16 *Āl-ʿImrān* 180.

17 *al-Māʿūn* 1-7.

then be heated in the fire of Hell and his sides, his forehead and his back will be cauterised with them. Whenever these cool down, (the process is) repeated during a day the extent of which will be 50 thousand years, until judgement is pronounced among servants, and he sees whether his path is to take him to Paradise or to Hell".

It was said: 'Messenger of Allāh, what about the camel?' He (the Prophet ﷺ) replied: 'If any owner of camels does not pay what is due on him....when the Day of Resurrection comes a soft sandy plain will be set for him, as extensive as possible, (he will find) that not a single young one is missing, and they will trample him with their hoofs and bite him with their mouths. As often as the first of them passes him, the last of them will be made to return during a day the extent of which will be 50 thousand years, until judgement is pronounced among servants and he sees whether his path is to take him to Paradise or to Hell'.

It was (again) said: 'Messenger of Allāh, what about cows (cattle) and sheep?' He said: 'If any owner of the cattle and sheep does not pay what is due on them, when the Day of Resurrection comes a soft sandy plain will be spread for them, he will find none of them missing, with twisted horns, without horns or with a broken horn, and they will gore him with their horns and trample him with their hoofs. As often as the first of them passes him the last of them will be made to return to him during a day the extent of which will be fifty thousand years, until judgement will be pronounced among the servants. And he will be shown his path leading him to Paradise or to Hell'.

It was said: 'Messenger of Allāh, what about the horse?' Upon this he said: 'The horses are of three types. To one man (these are) a burden, and to another man (these are) a covering, and still to another man (these are) a source of reward. The one for whom these are a burden is the person who rears them in order to show off, for vainglory and for opposing the Muslims; so they are a burden for him. The one for whom these are a covering is the person who rears them for the sake of Allāh but does not forget the right of Allāh concerning their backs and their necks, and so they are a covering for him. As for those which bring reward (these refer to) the person who rears them for the sake of Allāh to be used for Muslims and he puts them in the meadow and field. And whatever they eat from that meadow and field will be recorded on his behalf as good deeds, as will also the amount of their dung and urine. And these will not break their halter and prance a course or two without having had recorded the amount of their hoof marks and their dung as a good deed on his behalf (on behalf of their owner). And their master does not bring them past a river from which they drink, though he did not intend to quench their thirst, but Allāh will record for him the amount of what they drink on his behalf as deeds'. It was said: 'Messenger of Allāh, what about the asses?,' Upon this he said: 'Nothing has been revealed to me with regard to the asses (in particular) except this one verse of a comprehensive nature: "*He who does an atom's weight of good will see it, and he who does an atom's weight of evil will see it'.*"[18]

Abū Hurayrah also narrated that the Prophet ﷺ said: "On the Day of Resurrection camels will come to their owner in the best state of health they have ever been (in the world), and if he had not paid their zakāh (in the world) then they will tread on him with their feet; and similarly, sheep will come to their owner in the best state of health they have ever been and if he had not paid their zakāh, then they will tread on him with their hooves and will butt him with their horns". The Prophet ﷺ added: "One of their rights is that they should be milked while water is kept in front of them". The Prophet ﷺ added: "I do not want anyone of you to come to me on the Day of Resurrection, carrying over his neck a sheep that will be bleating. Such a person will (then) say: 'O Muḥammad (please intercede for me,) I will say to him: 'I can't help you, for I conveyed Allāh's message to you'. Similarly, I do not want anyone of you to come to me carrying over his neck a camel that will be grunting. Such a person (then) will say: 'O Muḥammad (please intercede for me)'. I will say to him: 'I can't help you for I conveyed Allāh's message to you'."[19]

Jābir ibn ᶜAbdullāh al-Anṣārī reported that Allāh's Messenger ﷺ said: "The owner of a camel who does not pay what is due on it will be punished (in this way) on the Day of Resurrection. Many more camels (along with his camel) will come and the owner will be made to sit on a soft sandy ground and they will trample on him with their feet and hooves. And no owner of the cattle who does not pay what is due on them (will be spared the punishment) but on the Day of Resurrection, many more will come and he (the owner) will be made to sit on the soft sandy ground and will be gored by their horns and trampled under

18 Muslim, *k. al-zakāh, b. ithm mānīᶜ al-zakāh.* The verse quoted in the ḥadīth is from *al-Zilzal* 7-8.

19 al-Bukhārī, *k. al-zakāh, b. ithm mānīᶜ al-zakāh.*

their feet. And no owner of goats and sheep who does not pay what is due on them (will be spared the punishment) but many more will come on the Day of Resurrection and he (the owner) will be made to sit on a soft sandy ground and they will gore him with their horns and trample on him with their hooves. And there will be more (among this flock of sheep and goat) without horns or with broken horns. And no owner of treasures who does not pay its due but his treasure will come on the Day of Resurrection like a bald snake and will pursue him with its mouth open, and when it will come near he will run away from it, and it will be said to him thus: 'Take your treasure which you concealed, for I do not need it'. When he finds no way out he will put his hand in its mouth and it will gnaw it like a he-camel. Abū Hurayrah narrated that the Messenger of Allāh ﷺ said: "Whoever is made wealthy by Allāh and does not pay the zakāh of his wealth, on the Day of Resurrection his wealth will be turned into a bald-headed poisonous male snake with two black spots over the eyes. The snake will encircle his neck and bite his cheeks and say: 'I am your wealth, I am your treasure'."[20]

Al-Aḥnaf ibn Qays narrated: "While I was sitting with some people from the Quraysh, a man with very rough hair, clothes, and appearance came and stood in front of us, greeted us and said: 'Inform those who hoard wealth, that a stone will be heated in the Hell-Fire and be put on the nipples of their breasts until it comes out from the bones of their shoulders and then put on the bones of their shoulders until it comes through the nipples of their breasts the stone will be moving and hitting'. After saying that, the person retreated and sat by the side of a pillar. I followed him and sat beside him, and I did not know who he was. I said to him: 'I think the people disliked what you said'. He said: 'These people do not understand anything, although my friend told me (this)'. I asked: 'Who is your friend?' He replied: 'The Prophet ﷺ said to me: 'O Abū Dharr, do you see the Mountain of Uḥud?' And on that I started looking towards the sun to judge how much remained of the day as I thought that the Messenger of Allāh ﷺ wanted to send me to do something for him and I said: 'Yes'. He said: 'I do not love to have gold equal to the Mountain of Uḥud unless I spend it all (in Allāh's cause) except three *dīnārs*'. These people do not understand and (so they) collect worldly wealth. No, by Allāh, neither I (Abū Dharr) ask them for

20 al-Bukhārī, *k. al-zakāh, b. ithm mānic al-zakāh.*

worldly benefits nor am I in need of their religious advice until I meet Allāh, The Honourable, The Majestic'."[21]

ʿAdī ibn Ḥātim narrated: "While I was sitting with the Messenger of Allāh ﷺ peace be upon him, two people came to him; one of them complained about his poverty and the other complained about the prevalence of robberies. The Messenger of Allāh ﷺ said: 'As regards stealing and robberies, there will shortly come a time when a caravan will go to Makkah from Madīnah without any guard. And regarding poverty, The Hour (Day of Judgement) will not be established until one of you wanders about with his object of charity and will not find anybody to accept it. And (no doubt) each one of you will stand in front of Allāh and there will be neither a curtain nor an interpreter between him and Allāh, and Allāh will ask him: 'Did I not give you wealth?' He will reply in the affirmative. Allāh will further ask: 'Did I not send a Messenger to you?' Again that person will reply in the affirmative. Then the person will look to his right and will see nothing but Hell-Fire, and then he will look to his left and will see nothing but Hell-Fire. And so, any (each one) of you should save himself from the Fire even by giving half of a date-fruit (in charity). If you do not find half date-fruit, then (you can do it through saying) a good pleasant word (to your brethren)'."[22]

21 al-Bukhārī, *k. al-zakāh, b. mā uddiya zakātuhū laysa bi kanz.*

22 al-Bukhārī, *k. al-zakāh, b. al-ṣadaqah qabl al-radd;* Muslim, *k. al-zakāh, b. al-ḥathth ʿalā al-ṣadaqah wa law bishiqqi tamrah.*

Chapter 2: The Obligation of Zakāh

According to the Qur'ān, zakāh, like *ṣalāh,* was decreed on the earlier prophets and their followers: "*We made them* (*Ibrāhīm and his descendants*) *imāms who guided in accordance with Our commandments, and we taught them how to work righteousness, and how to observe the ṣalāh and the zakāh. To us, they were devoted worshipers*".[23]

Charity existed in Islam from the very beginning and was considered as a pious act, like *ṣalāh.* Both types of charity, obligatory and optional, were introduced in Makkah and people used to spend their money in the path of Allāh. The exact details concerning the obligation of zakāh and its payment were not revealed at that time; rather it was left to the consciousness of believers. It was only in the second year of *hijrah* (migration) that zakāh was defined properly and became part of the legal system. One purpose behind establishing zakāh as an obligatory act was that one who receives it does not feel a burden, but rather that there is a sense of thankfulness and gratitude on the part of the giver, since he has been enabled by the recipient to discharge his obligation.

THE EVIDENCE FOR IT BEING OBLIGATORY

Zakāh's obligatory status is based on the Book of Allāh, the Sunnah of His Messenger, and the consensus of the Companions.

Besides the verses mentioned earlier, there are others which includes: "*You shall give the due alms to the relatives; the needy, the poor, and the travelling alien, but do not be excessive, extravagant. The extravagant are brethren of the devils, and the devil is unappreciative of his Lord. Even if you have to turn away from them, as you pursue the mercy of your Lord, you shall treat them in the nicest manner. You shall not keep your hand stingily tied to your neck, nor shall you foolishly open it up, lest you end up blamed and sorry*".[24] "*My Mercy encompasses all things. I will decree it for those who lead a righteous life, give the zakāh, and*

23 *al-Anbiyā'* 73.

24 *al-Isrā'* 26-29.

believe in our revelations".[25] "*O you who believe, you shall give to charity from the provisions we have given to you, before a day comes where there is no trade, no nepotism, and no intercession. The disbelievers are the unjust*".[26] "*O you who believe, you shall give to charity from the good things you earn, and from what We have produced for you from the earth. Do not pick out the bad therein to give away, when you yourselves do not accept unless your eyes are closed. You should know that Allāh is Rich, Praiseworthy*".[27]

ʿAbdullāh ibn ʿAbbās has narrated that when Allāh's Apostle ﷺ sent Muʿādh ibn Jabal to Yemen, he said to him: "You are going to people of a Book. First of all, invite them to worship Allāh and when they come to know Allāh, inform them that Allāh has enjoined on them five prayers in every day and night; and if they start offering these prayers, inform them that Allāh has enjoined on them the zakāh. And it is to be taken from the rich amongst them and given to the poor amongst them; and if they obey you in that, take zakāh from them and avoid the best of their property".[28]

Ṭalḥah ibn ʿUbaydullāh narrated: "A Bedouin with unkempt hair came to the Messenger of Allāh ﷺ and said: 'O Messenger of Allāh, inform me of what Allāh has made obligatory on me with regards to prayers'. He replied: 'Five *salāhs*, unless you do others voluntarily'. He asked the Prophet ﷺ to inform him about fasting, he ﷺ said: 'The fast of Ramaḍān, unless you do others voluntarily'. Then the Messenger of Allāh ﷺ mentioned to him zakāh. The Bedouin then asked: 'Is anything other than zakāh obligatory on me?' The Prophet ﷺ replied: 'No unless you do so voluntarily'. The Bedouin then said: 'By the One who has honoured you, I shall not add anything to it, nor shall I be deficient in what Allāh has ordered me to do'. The Messenger of Allāh ﷺ then said: 'He will enter Paradise if he is true to this'."[29]

25 *al-Aʿrāf* 156.
26 *al-Baqarah* 254.
27 *al-Baqarah* 267.
28 al-Bukhārī, *k. al-zakāh, b. wujūb al-zakāh;* Muslim, *k. al-īmān, b. al-duʿā' ilā al-shahādatayn.*
29 al-Bukhārī, *k. īmān, b. al-zakāh min al-islām;* Muslim, *k. al-īmān, b. bayān al-ṣalawāt al-lati hiya aḥad arkān al-islām.*

REJECTION OF ZAKĀH

There is scholarly consensus on its obligatory condition.[30] Anyone who denies its obligation will be considered as an unbeliever.[31] ᶜAbdullāh ibn Masᶜūd said: "The one who does not pay zakāh, he is not a Muslim".[32] Imām al-Baghawī says: "If any group of Muslims deny the obligation of zakāh, and they stop paying it, they are unbelievers. This is the consensus of all Muslims".[33]

Those who believe in its obligatory status, but do not pay it, are sinners, and it is a duty upon the rulers to take it from them with force. ᶜAlī ibn Abī Ṭālib says: "The one who stops paying zakāh is cursed".[34]

In Muslim lands if a group of people refuses to pay zakāh and if Muslims have authority they must fight them until they pay zakāh. ᶜAbdullāh ibn ᶜUmar related that the Messenger of Allāh ﷺ said: "I have been ordered to fight the people until they testify that there is no god except Allāh, and that Muḥammad is the Messenger of Allāh, and establish *salāh* and pay the zakāh. If they do this, their blood and wealth are protected from me save by the rights of Islam. Their reckoning will be with Allāh".[35]

After the death of the Prophet ﷺ Abū Bakr was appointed as his successor. A group of people refused to pay the zakāh and Abū Bakr decided to fight them for refusing to pay. It is reported that ᶜUmar said to Abū Bakr: "How do you fight the people while the Prophet ﷺ has said: 'I have been commanded to fight the people until they say: there is no god but Allāh; so whoever says: there is no god but Allāh, such a person has protected his property and life from me except with its right, and his account is with Allāh'." Abū Bakr said: "By Allāh, I will fight those who differentiate between the *ṣalāh* and zakāh, because zakāh is the right due on wealth, by Allāh if they withhold even a she-kid which they used to pay during the life-time of Allāh's Apostle, I will fight them for it". ᶜUmar said: "It was nothing but Allāh Who opened Abū Bakr's heart

30 al-Kāsānī, *Badāʾiᶜ al-ṣanāʾiᶜ, ii.* 373.

31 Ibn Ḥajar, *Fatḥ al-Bārī, iii.* 335.

32 Ibn Abī Shaybah, *al-Muṣannaf,* vi. 374.

33 al-Baghawī, *Sharḥ al-Sunnah, iii.* 317.

34 Ibn Abī Shaybah, *al-Muṣannaf, vi.* 377.

35 al-Bukhārī, *k. al-īmān, b. fa in tābū wa aqāmū al-ṣalāta wa ātaw al-zakāta fa khallū sabīlahum.*

towards the decision to fight, and I came to know that his decision was right".[36]

CONDITIONS: WHEN AND HOW ZAKĀH BECOMES OBLIGATORY

There are two types of conditions for the obligatory zakāh: 1) conditions concerning the person, 2) conditions concerning the wealth.

CONDITIONS CONCERNING THE PERSON

There are five conditions which, if fulfilled, make zakāh obligatory on a person. These conditions are explained below:

1- **Islam:** Zakāh is obligatory on Muslims only; it is not obligatory on a non-Muslim because it is an act of worship for which non-Muslims are not eligible. When a non-Muslim becomes Muslim he does not have to pay zakāh for the years prior to this. The Prophet ﷺ said: "Islam effaces whatever was before it".37

2- **Adulthood:** Zakāh is not obligatory on a child. ʿAlī ibn Abī Ṭālib related that the Messenger of Allāh ﷺ said: "The pen is raised for three, meaning that there is no obligation upon three – namely, the one who is sleeping until he wakens, the child until he becomes an adult and one who is insane until he becomes sane".[38]

That there is no zakāh obligatory on a child in his wealth is also the opinion of ʿAlī ibn Abī Ṭālib, ʿAbdullāh ibn ʿAbbās[39], Sufyān al-Thawrī and ʿAbdullāh ibn al-Mubārak.[40] Ibrāhīm al-Nakhaʿī said: "There is no zakāh on the property of an orphan unless he becomes an adult".[41] The same has been narrated from Ḥasan al-Baṣrī, Shurayḥ, ʿĀmir al-Shaʿbī and others.[42]

Nevertheless, the jurists agree that *ʿushr* (one tenth of the produce) is

36 al-Bukhārī, *k. al-zakāh, b. wujūb al-zakāh;* Muslim, *k. al-īmān, b. al-amr bi qitāl al-nās ḥattā yaqūlū lā ilāha illallāh.*

37 Muslim, *k. al-īmān, b. kawn al-islām yahdimu mā qablahū ....*

38 Abū Dāwūd, *k. al-ḥudūd, b. fī al-majnūn yasriq; al-Tirmidhī, k. al-ḥudūd, b. mā jā'a fī man lā yajibu ʿalayh al-ḥadd.*

39 al-Kāsānī, *Badā'iʿ al-ṣanā'iʿ, ii.* 378.

40 al-Baghawī, *Sharḥ al-Sunnah, iii.* 357.

41 Ibn Abī Shaybah, *al-Muṣannaf, vi.* 461.

42 ibid., *vi.* 461-2.

due on the produce of a child's land.[43] The difference between zakāh and ᶜ*ushr* is that zakāh is an act of worship which requires power of choice and a child is not qualified to choose; while ᶜ*ushr* is levied on the land, and the meaning of worship here is secondary.[44]

3-**Being of sane mind:** There is no zakāh obligatory on the wealth of an insane person. An insane person means someone who has reached the age of puberty in the state of insanity, and also those who are afflicted by temporary insanity, and this continues for a whole year. If someone loses his senses but later in the same year regains them, then zakāh is obligatory on him.[45]

4-**Freedom:** There is no zakāh to be paid by a slave, because it is a condition in zakāh that one must be an owner, and a slave is not an owner of any wealth. The slave and his properties are owned by his master.[46]

5-**Not being in debt:** Zakāh is not obligatory on someone who owes a debt to a person.[47] If the debtor's wealth is equal to or less than his debt, then zakāh is not obligatory on him, but if his wealth exceeds his debt, he pays zakāh on the excess – if that excess amounts to the *niṣāb.*

Imām Muḥammad narrated on the authority of Abū Ḥanīfah from ᶜUthmān ibn ᶜAffān that he used to say at the arrival of the month of Ramaḍān: "O people this is the month of your zakāh; if one is indebted he should pay his debt, then he should pay zakāh for the remainder". Imām Muḥammad says: "We adhere to this; zakāh is due from a person after he pays his debt".[48]

A person in debt whose debt is equal to his wealth is called a poor person, and there is no zakāh on a poor person. The Messenger of Allāh ﷺ says: "Zakāh is levied on the rich and paid to the poor".[49] People who are buying houses on mortgage[50] are considered to be indebted:

43 al-Baghawī, *Sharḥ al-Sunnah, iii.* 357

44 al-Marghīnānī, *al-Hidāyah, ii.* 5-6.

45 al-Kāsānī, *Badāʾiᶜ al-ṣanāʾiᶜ, ii.* 382-383.

46 ibid., ii. 383.

47 al-Marghīnānī, *al-Hidāyah, ii.* 7.

48 Abū Ḥanīfah, *K. al-āthār* 74.

49 al-Bukhārī, *k. al-zakāh, b. akhdh al-ṣadaqah min al-aghniyāʾ;* Muslim, *k. al-īmān, b. al-duᶜāʾ ilā al-shahadatayn wa sharaʾiᶜ al-islām.*

50 This is not the place for detail on this matter, but it is important to point out

they are obliged first to clear their debts, and before the debt has been repaid they are to be considered as poor, and they may even be eligible to receive zakāh to help them settle their debt.

Those debts which are not demanded by a human being, like *kaffārah* (expiation), or *nadhr* (vow), do not affect the payment of zakāh.[51]

CONDITIONS CONCERNING WEALTH

There are six conditions concerning the wealth, which are explained below:

1- **Ownership:** Zakāh is only compulsory on an individual in what he owns; there is no zakāh on anything which is not owned by an individual; hence there is no zakāh on endowments or any public related fund.[52] So for properties that are owned by mosques, schools, hospitals or any similar endowments belonging to this category, there is no zakāh on them.

2- **Ability to use:** If someone owns wealth but is unable to benefit from it, then there is no zakāh on that wealth. For example, lost properties or those debts which are denied by the borrower are exempted from zakāh. Similarly, if someone buried some wealth in a desert and forgot the exact place, he does not have to pay the zakāh of that wealth. Though, if someone has buried wealth in his own house and forgot the exact place, he has to pay zakāh for that, because in this case he has access to that wealth.[53]

There is no zakāh on women's dowries until they acquire full possession of them because a dowry is not a timely fixed debt and the husband has the choice to pay it later. When a woman takes possession of her dowry, if it amounts to the *niṣāb* and one year passes, then she will pay the zakāh. If she already owns other money she will add her dowry to that wealth and pay zakāh on the whole wealth.

Similarly, if someone has deposits in a bank which has been declared as bankrupt and there is no hope that one will recover the money, then there is no zakāh imposed on those deposits.

---

that the mortgage debt must be Islamically valid and incured for necessary living, not for business.

51 al-Marghīnānī, *al-Hidāyah, ii.* 7.

52 al-Kāsānī, *Badā'i' al-ṣanā'i', ii.* 389.

53 ibid., ii. 389-390.

3-**Growth:** Zakāh is only obligatory on the wealth which has real growth, like agricultural products, or are made or kept for growth, like the wealth invested in business or grazing animals, or naturally they are considered a growing wealth like gold silver, or any form of money.[54]

4-**Excess over basic needs:** In order for zakāh to be obligatory, it is a condition that the wealth is in excess of basic needs otherwise it is not deemed to be wealth upon which zakāh is due. The wealth which is needed for basic needs does not make one rich. Therefore, no zakāh is due on dwellings, clothing, household furniture, cars, and computers.[55]

5-**The passing of a year:** It is a condition in some types of wealth that a lunar year has elapsed on its ownership. The Prophet said: "There is no zakāh on wealth until a (lunar) year has passed on it".[56] It is not a condition that the *niṣāb* continues throughout the year; rather if one is owner of the *niṣāb* in the beginning and at the end of the year, then he has to pay zakāh.[57]

Whoever possesses the *niṣāb* and this is increased by the additional wealth from the same category during the year then he includes it with the rest of his wealth and pays zakāh on it too. Imām al-Zuhrī says: "Muslims liked to pay zakāh of new added wealth; when the year has passed on one's wealth, he will pay zakāh of that on which the year has not passed".[58]

If one's wealth has reached the *niṣāb* level, and before the passing of a lunar calendar year it falls below the *niṣāb,* one will not pay any zakāh. The zakāh year will start again from the time one obtains the *niṣāb* level again.[59]

If one owns *niṣāb* in the beginning of the year, and then part of the *niṣāb* was lost during the middle of the year, but regained and the wealth reached the *niṣāb* before the end of the year, he is obliged to pay zakāh.[60]

However, the lapse of a lunar year is not a condition for the zakāh on agricultural products, for their zakāh becomes obligatory on the day of harvest.

54 ibid., ii. 394.
55 ibid., ii. 394.
56 al-Dāraquṭnī, *al-sunan, k. al-zakāh, b. wujūb al-zakāh bi al-ḥawl.*
57 al-Kāsānī, *Badā'iᶜ al-ṣanā'iᶜ, ii.* 399-400.
58 ᶜAbd al-Razzāq, *al-Muṣannaf, iv.* 32.
59 al-Kāsānī, *Badā'iᶜ al-ṣanā'iᶜ, ii.* 402.
60 ibid., ii. 402.

While explaining the wisdom behind the condition of the year, Ibn al-Qayyim says: "Zakāh is payable once in a calendar year but for agricultural and fruit crops the harvesting time will mark the end of the year. No other arrangement could be more just and equitable for if zakāh was to be paid weekly or monthly it will entail a very heavy burden on the rich, and if only once in a lifetime it would be unfair on the needy. The yearly payment is, thus, most reasonable".[61]

6-**Niṣāb:** Zakāh only becomes compulsory if one owns *niṣāb* (the minimum amount which makes zakāh obligatory.) If one owns less than the *niṣāb,* then one is not considered as rich.[62] Explaining the reasoning behind *niṣāb,* Shāh Walīullah says: "*Niṣāb* on silver was estimated at five *ūqiyyahs* (five *ūqiyyahs* equal 200 *dirhams*) because that was sufficient for the smallest household to live on for one year, under reasonable prices and with average dietary habits".[63]

THE WISDOM OF *NIṢĀB*

Islam has fixed the *niṣāb* for the obligation of zakāh in a way that is fair to the rich and the poor. While discussing the wisdom of fixing the *niṣāb,* Shāh Walīullāh says: "The need was felt for fixing the rate of zakāh, for were it not done there was a danger of irregularity and confusion in its observance; everyone would have followed their own rules. It should neither be so negligible that its effect is not felt and therefore fails to serve as a corrective to miserliness nor so high as to be unbearable. The same is the case with the time of its payment and the period covered by it. It should neither be so short as to necessitate the payment of zakāh every now and then nor so long as to give a holiday to misers and, at the same time, provide no relief to the indigent. It was expedient to lay down a law for it in the same way in which the rulers fix the limit and extent of the taxes they levy on their subjects, seeing that everyone, Arabs as well as non-Arabs, were accustomed to it and paid the imposts as a matter of course".[64]

61 Ibn al-Qayyim, *Zād al-maʿād, ii.* 6.

62 al-Kāsānī, *Badāʾiʿ al-ṣanāʾiʿ*, *ii.* 404.

63 Shāh Walīullah, *Ḥujjatullāh al-bālighah, ii.* 66.

64 ibid., *ii.* 61.

Chapter 3: The Types of Wealth

Zakāh is compulsory on those four types of wealth that are the most popular sources of income among people and that constitute their fundamental needs. These are: money, trading goods, agricultural products, and animals. While explaining the wisdom behind different types of zakāh, Ibn al-Qayyim says: "The quantity of zakāh has been fixed with due regard to the diligence, industry and convenience of the *niṣāb* holders. Hence, on the wealth which falls into one's hands suddenly and all at once, such as, a mine or treasure-trove, it is not permissible to wait for the lapsing of a year but its *khums* (one fifth) will be paid immediately. On wealth which is earned by sustained labour, like agricultural produce, the *ᶜushr* is paid provided that cultivation is dependent wholly on natural rainfall and no well is dug or other irrigational devices employed. However, if recourse is taken to artificial means of irrigation only one-twentieth is paid. Again, on incomes derived from professions which require greater attention and industry than agriculture or fruit-growing, one-fortieth of the profit is handed over as zakāh. The same principle has also been followed in determining the lowest taxable limit or *niṣāb*. For savings, the *niṣāb* has been fixed at 200 *dirhams*, for gold as 20 *mithqāls* (a measure of weight equal to 87.480 grams), for silver at 612.36 grams, for agricultural produce as 5 *wasqs*, (a measurement of agricultural products which equals 60 *ṣāᶜs*) and for herds of cattle at 40 goats, 30 cows and 5 camels".[65]

In the same context, Shāh Walīullāh states: "The doors the pious rulers had opened for zakāh, without involving any trouble or inconvenience and which are also acceptable to reason, are four. First, that zakāh should be levied on goods that are capable of growth, because these goods require the greatest amount of protection and their development, moreover, is not possible without export. Such goods are of three kinds: herds of cattle, agricultural produce and articles of trade. Second, that it should be realised from the capitalists and owners of mines because

65 Ibn al-Qayyim, *Zād al-maᶜād, ii.* 6-8.

their need for security against theft and robbery is greater and the sources of their income are so vast and numerous that the addition of a new item of expenditure does not hurt them much. Third, that it should be levied on wealth which falls into one's hands without any toil or exertion like a treasure-trove found hidden in the earth. Such a wealth is in the nature of a windfall and people can spend freely from it. Fourth, that it should be realised from the ordinary traders and businessmen; if a little is taken from each of them it will add up to much and they will also not feel the pinch. Trade, agriculture and fruit-growing are the main sources of zakāh which keep on expanding. The period of assessment for them is one year because different crops are grown and various conditions prevail during it and a correct calculation of the yield can be made only at the end of the year. It is better and easier that zakāh should be paid in the form of goods on which it is levied, such as a camel from a drove of camels, a cow from a herd of cows and a goat from a herd of goats".[66]

MONEY

Money is defined as a medium of exchange. Gold and silver have been the standard forms of money from ancient times. In our time money has come to include currency notes, bank deposits and shares in companies. I will now discuss the issues of zakāh concerning all those forms of money.

Gold and silver

Allāh, Exalted is He, says of gold and silver: *"As for those who hoard up gold and silver and do not spend it in the Way of Allāh, give them news of a painful punishment on the Day it is heated up in the fire of Hell and their foreheads, sides and backs are branded with it: 'This is what you hoarded for yourselves, so taste what you were hoarding'."*[67] Hence zakāh is prescribed on gold and silver in any form, whether they are in the form of coins, ingots, or dust.

The *niṣāb* of gold

There is no zakāh payable on less than twenty *mithqāls* (i.e. 87.480 grams) of gold. If it amounts to twenty *mithqāls,* and the lunar year has

66 Shāh Walīullah, *Ḥujjatullāh al-bālighah, ii.* 61-62.

67 *al-Barā'ah* 34.

lapsed on them, then one fortieth will be payable; and any excess of twenty is reckoned proportionately. ʿAlī ibn Abī Ṭālib has narrated that the Prophet ﷺ said: "Nothing is (incumbent) upon you until you have twenty dīnār*s*. When you have twenty dīnār*s*, and the year has elapsed on it, then (what is due) on it is half a *dīnār*. Then whatever is increased it will be according to that. There is no zakāh on any wealth until a year lapses on it".[68]

The *niṣāb* of silver

As for silver, there is no zakāh payable on less than two hundred *dirhams* (i.e. 612.35 grams). If there are two hundred *dirhams* and the year has elapsed on them, then five *dirhams* are payable; and any amount more than two hundred, its zakāh is calculated at the same ratio.

Anas ibn Mālik narrated: "When Abū Bakr; sent me to (collect the zakāh from) Bahrain, he wrote the following to me: "In the name of Allāh, the Beneficent, the Merciful. These are the orders for zakāh which Allāh's Apostle ﷺ made obligatory for every Muslim, and which Allāh had ordered His Apostle to observe. Whoever amongst the Muslims is asked to pay zakāh accordingly, he should pay it (to the zakāh collector) and whoever is asked more than that (which is specified in this script) he should not pay it. For silver, the zakāh is one-fortieth of the lot (i.e. 2.5%), and if its value is less than two-hundred *dirhams*, zakāh is not required, but if the owner wants to pay he can".[69]

ʿAlī ibn Abī Ṭālib narrated that the Prophet ﷺ said: "Offer the zakāh of silver; one dirham from every forty *dirhams*. There is nothing in one hundred and ninety *dirhams*; when they reach two hundred then in them are five *dirhams*.[70] ʿAlī ibn Abī Ṭālib narrated that the Prophet ﷺ said: "When you possess two hundred (silver) *dirhams* and one year passes on them, five *dirhams* are payable. Nothing is incumbent on you, that is, on gold, till it reaches twenty (gold) *dīnārs* . When you possess twenty *dīnārs* and one year passes on them, half a *dīnār* is payable. Whatever exceeds that will be reckoned proportionally". The narrator said: I do not remember whether the words "that will be reckoned properly" were

68 Abū Dāwūd, *k. al-zakāh, b. fī zakāt al-sā'imah.*

69 al-Bukhārī, *k. sl-zakāh, b. al-farḍ fī al-zakāh.*

70 Abū Dāwūd, *k. al-zakāh, b. fī zakāt al-sā'imah*; al-Tirmidhī, *k. al-zakāh, b. mā jā'a fī zakāt al-dhahab wa al-wari.q*

uttered by ᶜAlī himself or he attributed them to the Prophet ﷺ. No zakāh is payable on property till a year passes on it".[71] Al-Tirmidhī says: "Jurists recognise that *ṣadaqah* should not be taken out of any amount less than five *ūqiyyahs* (ounces.) One *ūqiyyah* equals forty *dirhams*. Five *ūqiyyahs* equal 200 *dirhams*".[72]

Impure gold and silver

If the silver coins are mostly composed of silver, then the judgement (regarding the ratio of payment) is that of silver; if the dīnārs are mostly gold, then they are subject to the judgement (regarding the ratio of payment) of gold. However, if they are mostly adulterated, then there is no zakāh in them except if they are for trading purposes or they are used in the payment as prices then they are subject to the judgement which applies to goods for trade and their actual worth is taken into account when the *niṣāb* is reached.[73]

Ornaments

Zakāh is only payable on ornaments which are made from gold or silver. ᶜAbdullāh ibn ᶜAmr ibn al-ᶜĀṣ narrated: "Two women came to the Apostle of Allāh ﷺ who wore two heavy gold bangles on their hands. He said to them: 'Do you pay zakāh on them?' They said: 'No'. He then said: 'Are you pleased that Allāh may put two bangles of fire on your arms?' They said: 'No'. Thereupon, the Prophet ﷺ said: 'Then pay their zakāh'."[74] It is reported that Umm Salamah used to wear ornaments made of gold. She asked the Prophet ﷺ if the ornaments were regarded as *kanz* (treasure). The Prophet ﷺ replied: "Whatever reaches a quantity on which zakāh is payable is not a treasure when the zakāh is paid".[75] Asmā' bint Yazīd reported: "My aunt and I, while wearing gold bracelets, we went to the Prophet ﷺ. He asked: 'Did you pay their zakāh?' She related that they had not. The Prophet said: 'Do you not fear that Allāh will make you wear a bracelet of fire? Pay its zakāh'." ᶜUmar ibn al-Khaṭṭāb wrote to Abū Mūsā al-Ashᶜarī stating: "Command Muslim women to give zakāh on their

71 Abū Dāwūd, *k. al-zakāh, b. zakāt al-sā'imah.*

72 al-Tirmidhī, *k. al-zakāh, b. mā jā'a fī ṣadaqaht al-zarᶜ wa al-thamar wa al-ḥubūb.*

73 al-Samarqandī, *Tuḥfat al-fuqahā'* p. 125.

74 al-Tirmidhī, *k. al-zakāh, b. mā jā'a fī zakāt al-ḥuliyy.*

75 Abū Dāwūd, *k. al-zakāh, b. al-kanz mā huwa wa zakāt al-ḥuliyy.*

jewellery".[76] ʿAlqamah narrates that the wife of ʿAbdullāh ibn Masʿūd asked: "I have ornaments, should I pay its zakāh?" ʿAbdullāh ibn Masʿūd answered: "Yes, if it reaches the value of two hundred *dirhams*".[77] Among those scholars who gave *fatwā* on zakāh on jewellery are: ʿAbdullāh ibn ʿAmr ibn al-ʿĀṣ, ʿAbdullāh ibn Shaddād, Ibrāhīm al-Nakhaʿī, Saʿīd ibn Jubayr, ʿAṭā' ibn Abī Rabāḥ, Ṭāwūs, Jābir ibn Zayd, al-Zuhrī, Makḥūl, and Sufyān al-Thawrī.[78]

Precious stones and gems

There is no zakāh on precious stones like pearls, diamonds, sapphires, rubies, corals, chrysolite, or any kind of precious stones unless they are used for trading purposes. Imām Muḥammad narrates on the authority of Abū Ḥanīfah that Ibrāhīm al-Nakhaʿī said: "There is no zakāh on pearls and diamonds unless (used) for trading purpose". Imām Muḥammad says: We adhere to this and that is the opinion of Abū Ḥanīfah".[79] ʿIkrimah, Saʿīd ibn Jubayr, ʿAṭā' ibn Abī Rabāḥ, al-Zuhrī, Makḥūl, Ḥakam, and Qāsim ibn Muḥammad ibn Abī Bakr were all of the same opinion.[80]

Zakāh on loan

The loan given by a rich person is of two types:

1. if a loan is acknowledged by the borrower, then zakāh on that amount is obligatory on the lender for each year of the loan, payable when the borrower has repaid it. Imām Muḥammad narrates on the authority of Abū Ḥanīfah from ʿAlī ibn Abī Ṭālib who said: "When you have a loan over the people and you get possession of it, you have to pay zakāh of the past years". Imām Muḥammad says: "We adhere to this, and that is the opinion of Abū Ḥanīfah".[81]

2. if the borrower denies the loan and there is no legal proof of it, then the lender is not liable for zakāh on that loan. If, later on, the borrower acknowledges the debt and repays it, then the lender is not liable for

76 Ibn Abī Shaybah, *al-Muṣannaf, vi.* 470.
77 ʿAbd al-Razzāq, *al-Muṣannaf, iv.* 83.
78 Ibn Abī Shaybah, *al-Muṣannaf, vi.* 470-471.
79 Abū Ḥanīfah, *K. al-āthār* 74.
80 Ibn Abī Shaybah, *al-Muṣannaf,* vi. 447-8.
81 Abū Ḥanīfah, *K. al-āthār* 74.

zakāh of the years that have passed before the debt was admitted.[82] Nāfiᶜ narrates that ᶜAbdullāh ibn ᶜUmar said: "If there is a reliable loan then pay its zakāh, and if there is an unreliable loan, then there is no zakāh unless it is paid".[83]

Zakāh on paper money

Zakāh is obligatory on paper money, whether it is held in cash or deposited in the banks, or in the form of bonds if they reach the value of 20 *mithqāl* of gold and a year has elapsed on them; then two and half percent will be paid in zakāh.

Both gold and silver are standard money, and *niṣāb* could be calculated by either of them. Imām Mālik says: "The uncontroversial tradition that we have is that the zakāh due on twenty dīnā*rs* is like the zakāh due on two hundred *dirhams*".[84] Nevertheless, in the past both *niṣāb*s were equal, but in our time, silver has become much cheaper in relation to gold, and hence it will not be fair on people to apply the silver standard. That is why I prefer the opinion of those scholars who calculate the *niṣāb* of money and trading goods etc. in terms of gold *niṣāb.*

Shaykh Yūsuf al-Qaraḍāwī says: "It is expected that since this is a matter of human reasoning, some scholars will be inclined to consider the *niṣāb* of silver most appropriate for non-metal money because it is determined explicitly by Sunnah and *ijmāᶜ* (consensus of the scholars), and it is the smaller amount of the two in today's value, so using it as *niṣāb* will be of more benefit to the poor. This is perhaps why it is commonly used in countries like Egypt, Saudi Arabia, the Gulf States, India, and Pakistan. Other scholars tend to consider the *niṣāb* of gold more appropriate because the value of gold did not change through the centuries as much as did the value of silver. Scholars favouring gold *niṣāb* include the late Abū Zahrah, Khallāf, and Ḥasan. This view can be supported by comparing *niṣāb* on gold with *niṣāb* on camels, sheep, and crops, because one finds that under today's prices, the *niṣāb* of gold is more comparable to *niṣāb* on other items of wealth than the *niṣāb* of silver. Five camels or 40 sheep are a value that is very close to 85 grams of gold, while 595 grams of silver may not equal the price of one camel.

82 al-Samarqandī, *Tuḥfat al-fuqahā'* 139-140.

83 Ibn Abī Shaybah, *al-Muṣannaf, vi.* 485.

84 Mālik, *al-Muwaṭṭa'* 131.

Shāh Walīullāh Dihlawī in his *Ḥujjatullāh al-bālighah,* states: "*Niṣāb* on silver was estimated at five *ūqiyyahs* because that was sufficient for the smallest household to live on for one year, under reasonable prices and with average dietary habits". Can we find any country today in which the value of 595 grams of silver will be sufficient for one year's expenses for a small household? In fact, that much silver will hardly be sufficient for one month or even one week. It is much better to determine the *niṣāb* on money today at the equivalent of that on gold, i.e. the value of 85 grams of gold, because doing it otherwise will inflict great injustice on zakāh payers". [85] In the text just quoted Sh. al-Qaraḍāwī has based his estimate of the value in grams on a calculation different from mine, given above. I believe the calculation that I have used is more precise.

Zakāh on shares

Zakāh is obligatory on the shares of trading companies, based on their real value if their worth amounts to the *niṣāb* of gold; and at the end of the year zakāh has to be paid on both the capital and the profits. The payable amount will be two and half per cent.

The shares in manufacturing companies (like car makers), or in service industries (hotels, airlines etc.) are treated alike. Zakāh is not obligatory on the capital of such companies; rather, it is obligatory on their profits when the amount reaches the *niṣāb* of gold.

If the shares are invested in agriculture, then the zakāh is one-tenth or one-twentieth of the profits according to details mentioned later in the chapter on agricultural products.

THE GOODS OF TRADE

Allāh, Exalted is He, says in the Qur'ān: "*O you who believe, spend of the good things of what you have earned*"[86]. Mujāhid states: "This verse refers to trade".[87] Samurah ibn Jundub narrates: "The Prophet ﷺ used to command us to give zakāh from what we keep for trade."[88] Abū Dharr narrates that the Prophet ﷺ said: "On camels there is

85 Al-Qaraḍāwī, *Fiqh al-zakāh* i. 271-3.

86 *al-Baqarah* 267

87 al-Baghawī, *Sharḥ al-sunnah, iii.* 349.

88 Abū Dāwūd, *k. al-zakāh, b. al-ʿurūḍ idhā kānat li al-tijārah hal fīhā min zakāh.*

zakāh; on sheep there is zakāh, on cows there is zakāh, and on the clothes for trade there is zakāh".[89] Abū ᶜAmr ibn Ḥamās reported from his father that he said: "I used to sell leather and containers. Once, ᶜUmar ibn al-Khaṭṭāb passed by me and said: 'Pay the *ṣadaqah* due on your property'. I said: 'O Commander of the Faithful, it is just leather'. He replied: 'Evaluate it and then pay its due *ṣadaqah*.[90] ᶜAbdullāh ibn ᶜUmar says: "There is no zakāh in goods, except if they are kept for trade".[91] Ibn al-Mundhir has reported a consensus of jurists that zakāh on trade is obligatory.[92]

What do tradable goods include?

Tradable goods include those which are intended for trading; but as for those goods which are needed for business but not traded like buildings, its furniture, and equipment, then there is no zakāh on them. For example, if someone has a book shop, he has to pay zakāh on all cash money and the value of the books kept for selling; he has nothing to pay on the shelves, or chairs, or the shop itself, or the computer used for the business. Similarly, if one owns a restaurant, one has to pay zakāh on the savings and all the raw material for use in food. No zakāh is payable on cookers, fridges, plates, glasses, or computers being used in the business.

When zakāh is obligatory on goods of trade

Zakāh is obligatory on all goods of trade in one's possession if their worth amounts to a *niṣāb* of gold. The payable amount will be two and half per cent. Al-Baghawī affirms that most people of knowledge hold the opinion that zakāh will be obligatory on the value of tradable goods if they reach the amount of *niṣāb*, at the completion of the year; then one-fortieth (2.5%) will be payable as zakāh.[93]

If the *niṣāb* exists at the beginning and end of the year, the zakāh will be obligatory, even if the assessed worth of the goods fails to attain the *niṣāb* at any time during the year.[94]

89 al-Dāraquṭnī, *al-Sunan, k. al-zakāh, b. laysa fī al-khaḍrāwāt ṣadaqah.*

90 al-Bayhaqī, *al-sunan al-kubrā, k. al-zakāh, b. zakāt al-tijārah.*

91 ibid.

92 al-Shawkānī, *Nayl al-awtar, iv.* 154.

93 al-Baghawī, *Sharḥ al-sunnah* iii. 350.

94 al-Samarqandī, *Tuḥfat al-fuqahā'* 128.

For the calculation of the zakāh on tradable goods one has to base it on their value at the completion of the year.[95]

Zakāh on rent

The landlord, who rents out a house or a property should pay the zakāh on his earning from the rent, provided the fixed amount reaches *niṣāb* and the year has passed.

Waiting possessions

If someone has bought a piece of land, or a house, or any building, and is holding it in order to sell it for a good price, then there is no zakāh on such property, because it is not a wealth that is growing. When he sells the property, then zakāh will be due on the money received from the sale after one year has passed and the sum amounts to *niṣāb.*

Combining different types of money or trade goods

If one owns several types of wealth like silver, gold, currency notes, goods of trade, or deposits in the banks, then all of them will be added together and the zakāh will be paid if the value of all combined wealth reaches the amount of *niṣāb.*[96]

AGRICULTURAL PRODUCTS AND FRUIT

Allāh, Exalted is He, says in the Qur'ān: "*O you who believe, spend of the good things of what you have earned, and of that which We have produced from the earth for you*".[97] And, He, Exalted is He, says: "*And it is He Who produces gardens trellised and un-trellised, and date-palms, and crops of different shape and taste, and olives, and pomegranates, similar (in kind) and different (in taste). Eat of their fruit when they ripen, but pay the due thereof on the day of its harvest*".[98] ʿAbdullāh ibn ʿAbbās states: "Due (in this verse) means the obligatory zakāh". Imām Mālik says: "I heard those who say: 'It is zakāh'."[99]

95 ibid.

96 ibid.126.

97 *al-Baqarah* 267.

98 *al-Anʿām* 141.

99 Mālik, *al-Muwaṭṭa', k. al-zakāh, b. zakāt al-ḥubūb wa al-zaytūn.*

Niṣāb

According to Abū Ḥanīfah, zakāh is obligatory on what is produced from the earth irrespective of whether it is a small or large amount, excluding what is not intentionally planted and cultivated such as firewood, bamboo, grass, and those trees which bear no fruit. The Prophet ﷺ said: "In all that is watered by the rain there is one tenth".[100] The meaning is general and encompasses all types of arable produce, things which are planted and expected to grow, and therefore refers to any agricultural practices similar to the growing of grains. Simāk ibn al-Faḍl has narrated that ᶜUmar ibn ᶜAbd al-ᶜAzīz wrote (to his governors) stating that *ᶜushr* should be taken from whatever is produced in the land whether it is little or plenty.[101] Abū Ḥanīfah's opinion is supported by Mujāhid, Ibrāhīm al-Nakhaᶜī, Ḥammād ibn Abī Sulaymān, and al-Zuhrī.[102]

According to Abū Yūsuf and Muḥammad, zakāh is obligatory only if fruit remains and can be stored a year after harvest and attains five *wasqs* (198kg). Each *wasq* is sixty *ṣāᶜs* (1 *ṣāᶜ*=3.3 kg). Abū Saᶜīd al-Khudrī narrated that the Prophet ﷺ said: "There is no zakāh payable on less than five *wasqs*".[103]

Imām Abū Ḥanīfah considers the above mentioned ḥadīth of Abū Saᶜīd al-Khudrī to refer to the agricultural products used for trading, in which there is no zakāh unless they are 5 *wasqs*. What supports Abū Ḥanīfah's opinion is that the ḥadīth did not mention one-tenth. At any case, because the clarity and generality of the earlier quoted Qur'ānic verses, Abū Ḥanīfah does not regard any minimum *niṣāb* for agricultural product.[104]

Vegetables and fresh fruits

As mentioned above, zakāh is obligatory on anything that grows from the earth including vegetables and fresh fruits according to Abū Ḥanīfah. As quoted above, the Prophet ﷺ said: "In all that is watered by

100 al-Bukhārī, *k. al-zakāh, b. al-ᶜushr fīmā yusqā min mā' al-samā'.*
101 ᶜAbd al-Razzāq, *al-Muṣannaf, x. 17;* Ibn ᶜAbd al-Barr, *al-Istidhkār, ix.* 239.
102 Ibn Abī Shaybah, *al-Muṣannaf, vi.* 438-439.
103 al-Bukhārī, *k. al-zakāh, b. zakāt al-wariq;* Muslim, *k. al-zakāh.*
104 al-Kāsānī, *Badā'iᶜ al-ṣanā'iᶜ ii.* 507-508.

the rain there is one tenth".[105] The meaning is general and encompasses all types of agricultural products. This opinion is also supported by ᶜUmar ibn ᶜAbd al-ᶜAzīz, Mujāhid, Ibrāhīm al-Nakhaᶜī, Ḥammād ibn Abī Sulaymān, and al-Zuhrī.[106]

But according to Abū Yūsuf and Muḥammad, there is no zakāh on fresh green vegetables and fruits if they cannot be kept for a year. ᶜAlī ibn Abī Ṭālib narrated that the Prophet ﷺ said: "There is no *ṣadaqah* on vegetables".[107] ᶜAṭā' ibn al-Sā'ib reported that ᶜAbdullāh ibn al-Mughīrah wanted to levy *ṣadaqah* on Mūsā ibn Ṭalḥah's vegetables. The latter objected, saying: "You have no right to do that. The Messenger of Allāh used to say: 'There is no *ṣadaqah* on these [vegetables]'. Muᶜādh ibn Jabal wrote to the Prophet ﷺ asking about vegetables. The Prophet wrote back stating: "There is nothing on them".[108] After quoting this ḥadīth, al-Tirmidhī says: "The chain of this ḥadīth is not sound, and there are no sound ḥadīth in this chapter from the Prophet... The practice in this matter among the people of knowledge is that there is no *ṣadaqah* [zakāh] on vegetables". [109]

Zakāh on honey

On honey like on other products, whether it is a small quantity or large, zakāh is due according to Abū Ḥanīfah. Abū Sayyārah al-Mutaᶜī said to the Prophet: "O, Messenger of Allāh, I have honey bees". He answered: "Then pay the tenth".[110] ᶜUmar ibn al-Khaṭṭāb said: "There is one tenth in honey".[111] This is also the fatwā of al-Zuhrī.[112] Al-Tirmidhī says: "This is the practice on this matter according to most people of knowledge, and that is the opinion of Aḥmad ibn Ḥanbal and Isḥāq ibn Rāhawayh".[113]

105 al-Bukhārī, *k. al-zakāh, b. al-ᶜushr fīmā yusqā min mā' al-samā'.*
106 Ibn Abī Shaybah, *al-Muṣannaf, vi.* 438-439.
107 al-Dāraquṭnī, *al-Sunan, k. al-zakāh, b. laysa fī al-khaḍrāwāt ṣadaqah.*
108 al-Tirmidhī, *k. al-zakāh, b. mā jā'a fī al-khaḍrāwāt.*
109 ibid.
110 Ibn Mājah, *k. al-zakāh, b. zakāt al-ᶜasal.*
111 Ibn Abī Shaybah, *al-Muṣannaf, vi.* 444.
112 ibid.
113 al-Tirmidhī, *k. al-zakāh, b. mā jā'a fī zakāt al-ᶜasal.*

How much is to be paid?

The payment of one-tenth (10%) is obligatory on all agricultural products if the land is irrigated by springs, rivers or rains. Abū Hurayrah narrated that the Prophet ﷺ said: "In all that is watered by the rain is one tenth".[114]

As for anything irrigated by water skins, buckets or waterwheels, then there is one-twentieth (5%). Sālim ibn ʿAbdullāh narrated from his father that the Prophet said: "On a land irrigated by rain water or by natural water channels or if the land is watered due to a nearby water channel, one-tenth is compulsory; and on the land irrigated by the well, half of an *ʿushr* (i.e. one-twentieth) is compulsory".[115] Jābir ibn ʿAbdullāh reported Allāh's Messenger ﷺ as saying: "A tenth is payable on what is watered by rivers, or rains, and a twentieth on what is watered by camels".[116]

Lands of *kharāj*

Land of *kharāj* refers to those lands which were conquered by Muslims, and they were left in the hands of their non-Muslim owners. Those owners have to pay *kharāj* (tax) on those lands, and there is no *ʿushr* upon them, because *ʿushr* is *ʿibādah* (worship) like other forms of *ʿibādah* and it is only obligatory on Muslims. The lands of *kharāj* remain as lands of *kharāj* even if their owners, later on, embrace Islam or those lands are sold to Muslims.[117]

In our time, it is very difficult to establish whether certain lands are lands of *kharāj* or of *ʿushr*, and also in many parts of the world Muslims live under non-Islamic rule, where there cannot be any *kharāj*, because *kharāj* is a tax paid to a Muslim government. Keeping that in mind, many Ḥanafī jurists in our time hold the opinion that all lands owned by Muslims should be treated as lands of *ʿushr*. This is also the opinion of most jurists from other schools of Islamic law.

Abū Hurayrah narrated that the Messenger of Allāh ﷺ said: "There is no compensation for one killed or wounded by an animal or by falling

114 al-Bukhārī, *k. al-zakāh, b. al-ʿushr fīmā yusqā bi māʾ al-samāʾ;* Muslim, *k. al-zakāh, b. mā minhu al-ʿushr aw niṣf al-ʿushr.*

115 ibid.

116 Muslim, *k. al-zakāh, b. mā minhu al-ʿushr aw niṣf al-ʿushr.*

117 al-Samarqandī, *Tuḥfat al-fuqahāʾ* pp. 150-51.

in a well, or because of working in mines; but one fifth is compulsory on treasure".[118]

If one finds a treasure of gold or silver or any precious property in his own house or in land owned by him, then he will become the owner of the treasure and he has to pay one fifth of the value of the whole treasure.

If one finds a treasure in someone else's property, then he has to treat it as lost property and give it to the owner of that property.

If treasure is found in public land, then it should be reported to the state, and handed over to the authority.[119]

ZAKĀH ON LIVESTOCK

Zakāh is compulsory on animals when three conditions are fulfilled:

1- They amount to the *niṣāb*. The *niṣāb* of each animal is to be mentioned separately;

2- One lunar year has lapsed on them;

3- They graze on public grass for most of the year; if their owner feeds them fodder for half a year or more then there is no zakāh payable on them.

Camels

There is no zakāh on less than 5 camels; but if the number amounts to 5-9 grazing camels and a year has lapsed on their possession, then there is a sheep to pay. If the number of camels reach 10-14, then 2 sheep; if they reach to 15-19, then 3 sheep; if 20-24 camels, then 4 sheep; if they reach to 25-35, then a female camel in its second year (*bint makhādh*); if they reach 36-45, then a female camel in its third year (*bint labūn*); if they reach 46-60, then a female camel in its fourth year (*ḥiqqah*); if they reach 61-75, then a female camel in its fifth year (*jadhaᶜah*); if they reach 76-90, then two female camels in their third year (2 *bint labūns*); if they reach 91-120, then two female camels in their fourth year (2 *ḥiqqahs*) After this the ratio is repeated: so, on a further 5, a sheep together with the 2 in their fourth year, and so, on a further 10, 2 sheep; and on fifteen, 3; on twenty, 4 sheep; and on 25, a female in its second year up

118 al-Bukhārī, *k. al-zakāh, b. fī al-rikāz al-khumus;* Muslim, *k. al-ḥudūd, b. jurḥ al-ᶜajmā'.*

119 al-Samarqandī, *Tuḥfat al-fuqahā'* 154-157.

to 150, in which case there is 3 in their fourth year to pay; then the ratio is repeated: so, on a further 5, there is a sheep; on 10, 2 sheep; on 15, 3; and on 20, 4 sheep; and on 25, a female camel in its second year; on 36, a female camel in its third year. If the number amounts to 196, then 4 female camels in their fourth year up to 200; then the ratio is repeated indefinitely, just as one repeats after the 50 following the 150.[120]

Anas ibn Mālik narrated: "When Abū Bakr; sent me to (collect the zakāh from) Bahrain, he wrote the following to me: "In the name of Allāh, the Beneficent, the Merciful. These are the orders for compulsory charity (zakāh) which Allāh's Apostle ﷺ made obligatory for every Muslim, and which Allāh had ordered His Apostle ﷺ to observe. Whoever amongst the Muslims is asked to pay zakāh accordingly, he should pay it (to the zakāh collector) and whoever is asked more than that (what is specified in this script) he should not pay it; for 24 camels or less, sheep are to be paid as zakāh; for every 5 camels 1 sheep is to be paid, and if there are between 25 to 35 camels, 1 *bint makhād* (female camel in its second year)is to be paid; and if they are between 36 to 45 (camels), 1 *bint labūn* (a female camel in its third year) is to be paid; and if they are between 46 to 60 (camels), 1 *ḥiqqah* (a female camel in its fourth year) is to be paid; and if the number is between 61 to 75 (camels),1 *jadhᶜah* (a female camel in its fifth year) is to be paid; and if the number is between 76 to 90 (camels), 2 *bint labūns* are to be paid; and if they are from 91 to 120 (camels), 2 *ḥiqqahs* are to be paid; and if they are over 120 (camels), for every 40 (over 120) 1 *bint labūn* is to be paid, and for every 50 camels (over 120) 1 *ḥiqqah* is to be paid; and whoever has got only 4 camels, has to pay nothing as zakāh, but if the owner of these 4 camels wants to give something, he can. If the number of camels increases to 5, the owner has to pay 1 sheep as zakāh".[121]

ᶜAbdullāh ibn ᶜUmar narrated: "The Apostle of Allāh ﷺ wrote a letter about *ṣadaqah* (zakāh) but he died before he could send it to his governors. He had kept it by his sword. So Abū Bakr acted upon it until he died, and then ᶜUmar acted upon it until he died. It contained: "For 5 camels 1 goat is to be given; for 10 camels 2 goats are to be given; for 15 camels 3 goats are to be given; for 20 camels 4 goats are to be given; for 25 to 35 camels a she-camel in her second year is to be given. If the

120 al-Samarqandī, *Tuḥfat al-fuqahā'* 132-133.

121 al-Bukhārī, *k. al-zakāh, b. al-farḍ fī al-zakāh.*

number exceeds by 1 up to 70 camels, a she-camel in her fourth year is to be given; if they exceed by 1 up to 75 camels, a she-camel in her fifth year is to be given; if they exceed by 1 up to 90 camels, 2 she-camels in their third year are to be given; if they exceed by 1 up to one 120, 2 she-camels in their fourth year are to be given. If the camels are more than this, a she-camel in her fourth year is to be given for every 50 camels, and a she-camel in her third year is to be given for every 40 camels".[122]

Cows

No zakāh is payable on less than 30 cows. If the number amounts to 30, and a year elapses on their possession, then a male or female cow in its second year is payable; on 40, a male or female in its third year. There is nothing to pay on any more than this until the number amounts to 60 – when 2 cows either male or female in their second year are due; on 70 a female cow in its third year together with a male of 2 years; on 80, 2 females in their third year; on 90, three females of 2 years; on 100, 2 males of 2 years and a female in its third; and on this basis the amount to be paid on every further 10 varies between a male of 2 years and a female in its third year.[123]

Buffalos and cows are treated alike. Ḥasan al-Baṣrī says: "Buffalos are like cows".[124]

Muᶜādh ibn Jabal narrated: "When the Prophet ﷺ sent me to the Yemen, he ordered me to take a male or a female calf a year old for every 30 cattle and a cow in its third year for every 40".[125] Al-Ḥārith al-Aᶜwar reported from ᶜAlī ibn Abī Ṭālib, that the Prophet ﷺ said: "Regarding cattle, a yearling bull calf is payable for every 30, and a cow in her third year for 40, and nothing is payable on working animals".[126]

Sheep and goats

There is no zakāh payable on less than 40 sheep. If the number amounts

122 Abū Dāwūd, *k. al-zakāh, b. fī zakāt al-sā'imah;* al-Tirmidhī, *k. al-zakāh, b. mā jā'a fī zakāt al-ibil wa al-ghanam.*

123 al-Samarqandī, *Tuḥfat al-fuqahā'* 133-134.

124 Ibn Abī Shaybah, *al-Muṣannaf, vii.* 65.

125 Abū Dāwūd, *k. al-zakāh, b. fī zakāt al-sā'imah;* al-Tirmidhī, *k. al-zakāh, b. mā jā'a fī zakāt al-baqar.*

126 Abụ Dāwūd, ibid.

to 40 grazing livestock and a year elapses on their possession, then a sheep is payable up to 120; if the number amounts to 121, then 2 sheep are payable on them up to 200; if the number amounts to 201, then 3 sheep; if the number amounts to 400, then 4 sheep and then on for every further 100, 1 sheep is payable.[127]

The letter from Abū Bakr sent to Anas ibn Mālik mentioned earlier in the chapter also contained the following guidance: "As regards the zakāh for the (flock) of sheep; if they are between 40 and 120 sheep,1 sheep is to be paid; and if they are between 120 and 200, then 2 sheep are to be paid; and if they are between 200 and 300, then 3 sheep are to be paid; and for over 300 sheep, for every extra 100, 1 sheep is to be paid as zakāh. And if one has got less than 40 sheep, no zakāh is required, but if one wants to give, one can". [128]

Similarly, the narration mentioned earlier from ʿAbdullāh ibn ʿUmar about the letter written by the Prophet ﷺ in regards to *ṣadaqah* also stated: "For 40 to 120 goats, 1 goat is to be given; for more than 120 up to 200, 2 goats are to be given. For more than 200 up to 300, 3 goats are to be given. For every 100 goats above 300, 1 goat is to be given. Nothing is payable for less than 100 (above 300)".[129] Sheep and goats are treated alike.

Horses

If both male and female horses are set out to graze, and they are kept for growth, then, according to Abū Ḥanīfah, one has to pay one dīnār for every horse, or their owner has to assess their worth, then pay one fortieth like the zakāh of money. However, there is no zakāh to pay on only males. ʿUmar ibn al-Khaṭṭāb set the zakāh as one dīnār for every horse.[130]

Abū Yūsuf and Muḥammad said that there is no zakāh on horses. Abū Hurayrah narrated that the Prophet ﷺ said: "There is no *ṣadaqah* on the Muslim in his horse".[131] On the authority of ʿAlī, it is related

127 al-Samarqandī, *Tuḥfat al-fuqahā'* 134.

128 al-Bukhārī, *k. al-zakāh, b. al-farḍ fī al-zakāh.*

129 Abū Dāwūd, *k. al-zakāh, b. fī zakāh al-sā'imah;* al-Tirmidhī, *k. al-zakāh, b. mā jā'a fī zakāt al-ibil wa al-ghanam.*

130 ʿAbd al-Razzāq, *al-Muṣannaf,* iv. 36.

131 al-Bukhārī, *k. al-zakāh, b. laysa ʿalā al-muslim fī farasihī ṣadaqah*; Muslim, k. *al-zakāh, b. lā zakāta ʿalā al-muslim fī ʿabdihī wa farasihī.*

that the Prophet ﷺ said: "I have exempted you from paying *ṣadaqah* on horses".[132]

If the horses are kept for *jihād* or personal use, then there is no zakāh on them[133], and the above mentioned *aḥādīth* which exempted horses from zakāh refer to the horses kept for *jihād* or personal use, not for trading.

Donkeys

There is nothing to pay on mules or donkeys unless they are used for trading.[134] Abū Hurayrah related that the Messenger ﷺ was asked if there is zakāh on donkeys. He replied: "Nothing was ever mentioned [in revelation] except in the following excellent Qur'ānic verse: '*Then whosoever does good equal to an atom's weight will see it; and whosoever does evil equal to an atom's weight will see it*'."[135] Imām Muḥammad narrated on the authority of Abū Ḥanīfah from Ibrāhīm al-Nakhaʿī, who said: "There is no zakāh on grazing donkeys". Imām Muḥammad says: "We adhere to this, and this is the opinion of Abū Ḥanīfah".[136] Ḥasan al-Baṣrī says: "There is no charity (zakāh) due on donkeys".[137]

Miscellaneous points

If one is due to pay an animal in its third year as zakāh, but does not possess such an animal, then the zakāh collector takes another bigger animal and returns the excess in worth between the two, or takes a smaller animal and takes an amount in cash to make up the difference.

There is no zakāh on working animals, and on those animals used for porterage. ʿAlī ibn Abī Ṭālib says: "There is no charity (zakāh) due on working cows".[138] The same *fatwā* has been narrated from Muʿādh ibn Jabal, Ibrāhīm al-Nakhaʿī, Mujāhid, ʿUmar ibn ʿAbd al-ʿAzīz, ʿĀmir al-Shaʿbī and others.[139] Saʿīd ibn Jubayr says: "There is no charity due on a

132 Ibn Mājah, *k. al-zakāh, b. ṣadaqaht al-khayl wa al-raqīq.*

133 al-Samarqandī, *Tuḥfat al-fuqahā'* 137.

134 ibid.

135 *al-Zilzāl* 7-8.

136 Abū Ḥanīfah, *K. al-āthār* 76.

137 Ibn Abī Shaybah, *al-Muṣannaf*, vi. 468.

138 ibid., vi. 420.

139 ibid., vi. 421.

camel used for porterage, or on a working bull".[140]

There is no zakāh on those given fodder as opposed to those grazing freely. Ṭāwūs says: "There is nothing due on working cows, except those that graze freely, and the same ruling applies to camels".[141]

The zakāh collector should not take the best of someone's wealth nor the worst, but rather the average quality. Imām al-Zuhrī says: "When the zakāh collector comes, the sheep will be divided into three groups (with regard to quality): the best, the lowest and the medium. The collector will take from the medium group".[142] Ibrāhīm ibn Maysarah narrates from a man of the tribe of Thaqīf who said: "I asked Abū Hurayrah: 'In which part of the wealth is charity?' He answered: 'In the middle third'."[143] ᶜUmar ibn ᶜAbd al-ᶜAzīz wrote to his governors stating: "Sheep should be divided into three groups, the collector will take from the medium group".[144]

It is permitted for the collector to take the zakāh amount in currency.

140 ibid.
141 ibid.
142 ibid., vi. 430
143 ibid., vi. 429.
144 ibid.

Chapter 4: The Expenditures from Zakāh Funds

There are certain kinds of people who are eligible and others ineligible to receive zakāh. Both categories are explained below in detail.

THOSE TO WHOM ZAKĀH IS PAYABLE

The categories of the people who can receive zakāh are clearly mentioned in the Qur'ān. Allāh, Exalted is He, said: "*Zakàh is only for the poor and the destitute, and for those employed to collect it, and for bringing hearts together [for Islam] and for freeing captives [or slaves] and for those in debt and for the cause of Allah and for the [stranded] traveller – It is a legal obligation from Allah. And Allah is All-Knowing, All-Wise*".[145] Ziyād ibn al-Ḥārith al-Ṣudā'ī narrated a long ḥadīth at the end of which he states that: "A man came to him (the Prophet ﷺ,) and said: 'Give me some of the *ṣadaqah.* The Apostle of Allāh ﷺ replied: 'Allāh is not pleased with a Prophet's or anyone else's decision about *ṣadaqah* till He has given a decision about it Himself. He has divided those entitled to them into eight categories, so if you come within those categories, I shall give you'."[146]

CATEGORIES OF PEOPLE ELIGIBLE FOR ZAKĀH

As this verse of the Qur'ān and the ḥadīth affirm, there are eight categories of people eligible to receive zakāh, they are:

1&2: THE POOR AND THE DESTITUTE

The poor refers to those who have the minimum amount of wealth whereas the destitute are those who own nothing.[147] The Prophet ﷺ instructed Muᶜādh ibn Jabal when sending him to Yemen as a governor: "Tell them that Allāh has made zakāh obligatory upon them, which will

145 *al-Barā' ah* 60.

146 Abū Dāwūd, *k. al-zakāh, b. man yuᶜṭā min al-ṣadaqah.*

147 al-Kāsānī, *Badā'iᶜ al-ṣanā'iᶜ, ii.* 466.

be taken from the rich and given to the poor".[148]

Among the poor people, those who are relatives will be preferred, then neighbours, then others according to their needs. ᶜAmr ibn al-Ḥārith narrates: "Zaynab, the wife of ᶜAbdullāh ibn Masᶜūd said: 'I was in the mosque and heard the Prophet ﷺ saying: 'O women give alms even from your ornaments'. Zaynab used to provide for ᶜAbdullāh and orphans who were under her protection. So she said to ᶜAbdullāh: 'Will you ask the Messenger of Allāh whether it is sufficient for me to spend part of the zakāh on you and the orphans who are under my protection?' He replied: 'Will you yourself ask Allāh's Apostle?' So Zaynab said: 'So I went to the Prophet ﷺ and saw an Anṣārī woman who was standing at the door (of the Prophet) with a similar problem. Bilāl passed by and I asked him to ask the Prophet whether it is permissible for me to spend (the zakāh) on my husband and the orphans under my protection. And we requested Bilāl not to inform the Prophet about us. So Bilāl went inside and asked the Prophet regarding our problem. The Prophet ﷺ asked: 'Who are those two?' Bilāl replied that it was Zaynab. The Prophet said: 'Which Zaynab?' Bilāl said: 'The wife of ᶜAbdullāh (ibn Masᶜūd)'. The Prophet said: 'Yes, (it is sufficient for her) and she will receive a double reward (for that), one for helping relatives, and the other for giving zakāh'."[149] In another case, Zaynab, (the daughter of Umm Salamah) narrated: "My mother said: 'O Allāh's Apostle, shall I receive a reward if I spend for the sustenance of Abū Salamah's offspring, and in fact they are also my sons?' The Prophet replied: 'Spend on them and you will get a reward for what you spend on them'."[150]

After poor relatives and neighbours, one should give zakāh to the poor who are of pious and noble character and are ashamed of showing their needs. Abū Hurayrah narrated that the Prophet ﷺ said: "The poor person is not the one who asks for a morsel or two (of food) from others, but the one who has nothing and is ashamed to beg from others". In another version, Abū Hurayrah narrated that the Messenger of Allāh said: "The poor person is not the one who goes around and asks people

148 al-Bukhārī, *k. al-zakāh, b. akhdh al-ṣadaqah min al-aghniyā';* Muslim, *k. al-īmān, b. al-duᶜā' ilā al-shahādatayn wa sharā'iᶜ al-islām.*

149 al-Bukhārī, *k. al-zakāh, b. al-zakāh ᶜalā al-zawj wa al-aqārib;* Muslim, *k. al-zakāh, b. faḍl al-nafaqah wa al-ṣadaqah ᶜalā al-aqrabīn.*

150 ibid.

for a morsel or two (of food) or a date or two but a poor person is one who does not have enough (money) to satisfy his needs and whose condition is not known to others, so that others may give him something in charity, and who does not beg from people".[151]

How much the needy person should be given

What is the amount of zakāh that should be given to the poor? This differs from person to person. In most cases a poor person should be given the amount that suffices his needs. ʿUmar said: "When you give, suffice the need.[152] It is preferable to give less than the amount of the *niṣāb.* This has been narrated from Ibrāhīm al-Nakhaʿī, Ḍaḥḥāk, Muḥammad al-Bāqir and ʿĀmir al-Shaʿbī.[153] Qabīṣah ibn Mukhāriq al-Hilālī reported: "I had a debt. I went to the Messenger of Allāh ﷺ and asked for his help. He answered: 'Wait until we have funds for *ṣadaqah,* then we will give you some'. He also said: 'O Qabīṣah, *ṣadaqah* is justified only for the following three: first, a man who is in debt, for his case makes it permissible to receive [alms] until his difficulty is resolved; second, a man who is struck by calamity which destroys his holdings, which also makes it permissible for him to receive [alms] until he is in a position to earn a sustenance [or he said, '... what satisfies his needs and makes him self-sufficient']; and third, a man who has been reduced to poverty and three people of calibre from among his own testify to his desperate situation will receive until he finds for himself a means of support [or he said, '... what satisfies his needs and makes him self-sufficient']. Other than these cases, O Qabīṣah, it is not permissible. A person receiving it (*ṣadaqah*) will be consuming forbidden holdings".[154]

When begging is allowed

A person in good health and able to work is not allowed to beg. Abū Hurayrah narrated: "The Prophet ﷺ said: "No doubt, it is better for a person to take a rope and proceed in the morning to the mountains and cut wood and then sell it, and eat from this income and give alms

151 al-Bukhārī, *k. al-zakāh, b. qawlillāh taʿālā lā yas'alūna al-nāsa ilḥāfan;* Muslim, *k. al-zakāh, b. al-miskīn al-ladhī lā yajidu ghinā.*

152 Ibn Abī Shaybah, *al-Muṣannaf,* vi. 519.

153 ibid.

154 Muslim, *k. al-zakāh, b. man taḥillu lahū al-mas'alah.*

from it rather than to ask others for something".[155]

Muᶜāwiyah said: "I heard the Messenger of Allāh ﷺ saying: 'I am the treasurer. To one whom I give out of (my own) sweat, he will be blessed in that, but he whom I give yielding to his constant begging and for his covetousness is like one who would eat, but will not be satisfied'."[156]

Abū Hurayrah reported that Allāh's Messenger ﷺ said: "He who begs the riches of others to increase his own is asking only for live coals, so let him ask a little or much".[157]

ᶜAbdullāh ibn ᶜUmar reported that the Apostle of Allāh ﷺ said: "A man keeps begging from people, until he will meet Allāh (in a state) that there will be no flesh on his face".[158]

ᶜAbdullāh ibn ᶜUmar narrated: "I heard Allāh's Apostle ﷺ while he was on the pulpit speaking about charity, telling people to abstain from asking others for financial help and about begging. He said: 'The upper hand is better than the lower hand. The upper hand is that of the giver and the lower (hand) is that of the beggar'."[159]

ᶜAbdullāh ibn Masᶜūd narrated that the Prophet ﷺ said: "He who begs (from people) when he is affluent will come on the Day of Resurrection with scrapes, scratches, or lacerations on his face. He was asked: 'What constitutes affluence, Apostle of Allāh?' He replied: 'It is fifty *dirhams* or its value in gold'."[160]

ᶜAbdullāh ibn ᶜAmr ibn al-ᶜĀṣ narrates the Prophet ﷺ said: "*Ṣadaqah* may not be given to a rich man or to one who has strength and is sound in limbs".[161]

155 al-Bukhārī, *k. al-zakāh, b. al-istiᶜfāf ᶜan al-mas'alah.*

156 Muslim, *k. al-zakāh, b. karāhat al-mas'alah li al-nas.*

157 ibid.

158 al-Bukhārī, *k. al-zakāh, b. man sa'ala al-nāsa takaththuran,* Muslim, *k. al-zakāh, b. karāhat al-mas'alah li al-nās.*

159 al-Bukhārī, *k. al-zakāh, b. lā ṣadaqah illā ᶜan ẓahr ghinā,* Muslim, *k. al-zakāh, b. bayān anna al-yad al-ᶜulyā khayrun min al-yad al-suflā.*

160 Abū Dāwūd, *k. al-zakāh, b. man yuᶜṭā al-ṣadaqah,* al-Tirmidhī, *k. al-zakāh, b. mā jā'a man taḥillu lahū al-zakāh;* al-Nasā'ī, *k. al-zakāh, b. ḥadd al-ghanī;* Ibn Mājah, *k. al-zakāh, b. man sa'ala ᶜan ẓahr ghinā.*

161 Abū Dāwūd, *k. al-zakāh, b. man yuᶜṭā min al-ṣadaqah,* al-Tirmidhī, *k. al-zakāh, b. mā jā'a man lā taḥillu lahū al-ṣadaqah.*

3: THOSE WHO COLLECT ZAKĀH

They are those appointed by the ruler to collect zakāh. This also includes those who guard the zakāh money and property, those who look after zakāh animals, and those who write and calculate it. In our time, it also can include people employed in charity organisations. All these are paid an amount in proportion to their work.[162]

The wages for those people collecting or distributing zakāh can be given to them even if they are rich. Abū Saᶜīd al-Khudrī narrated: "The Prophet ﷺ said: *Ṣadaqah* may not be given to a rich man, with the exception of five cases. One of the five is "one who collects [zakāh]".[163] Ibn ᶜAbd al-Barr says: "The Scholars have a consensus that *ṣadaqah* is allowed for those who are appointed to collect it, even if they are rich".[164] Ibn al-Saᶜdī related that he came from Syria to see ᶜUmar ibn al-Khaṭṭāb, who asked him: "Is it true that you perform a certain job for the Muslims and you are given wages for that, but you do not accept them?" He answered: "Yes, indeed. I possess horses and slaves. I am well-off. I want my work to be a charity for the Muslims". Then ᶜUmar said: "I also wanted what you desired, but the Prophet ﷺ used to pay compensation to me. I would say to him: 'Give it to one who is poorer than I'. Once he gave me money and I said to him: 'Give it to a person more needy than I'. Then the Prophet ﷺ said: 'Take what Allāh, to Whom belongs might and majesty, gives you of His bounties without your having asked for it or being eager'. So take it and keep it, or give it away as charity and what is not given should not be asked for.[165]

4: THOSE WHO ARE TO BE RECONCILED

This refers to those people whose reconciliation of hearts is intended; they are given a portion of the zakāh wealth in order to reconcile their hearts.

There were three such groups in the time of the Prophet ﷺ two of

162 al-Samarqandī, *Tuḥfat al-fuqahā'* 141.

163 Abū Dāwūd, *k. al-zakāh, b. man yajūzu lahū akhdh al-ṣadaqah wa huwa ghanī,* Ibn Mājah, k. *al-zakāh, b. man taḥillu lahū al-ṣadaqah.*

164 Ibn ᶜAbd al-Barr, *al-istidhkar* ix. 203.

165 al-Bukhārī, *k. al-zakāh, b. man aᶜṭāhullāhu shay'an min ghayr mas'alah*; Muslim, *k. al-zakāh, b. ibahat al-akhdh liman aᶜta min ghayr mas'alah wa lā ishrāf;* Abū Dāwūd, *k. al-zakāh, b. fī al-istiᶜfāf.*

whom were from amongst the unbelievers, and he, on whom be peace and blessings, would give to them in order that they should become Muslims and so that their people would follow their example and become Muslims by virtue of their Islam; or he would give to the unbelievers as a protection against their evil – and this protection was instead of *jihād* at that time. There was a third group of people who were already Muslims, to whom he would give in order to strengthen them in Islam.

This category was abolished when Islam became stronger and reconciling them became unnecessary. ᶜUyaynah ibn Ḥiṣn, al-Aqraᶜ ibn Ḥābis and ᶜAbbās ibn Mirdās came, and they sought their share from Abū Bakr, which he authorised in writing. They came to ᶜUmar and showed him the writing. ᶜUmar refused to comply, tore up the letter and said: "This is something the Prophet ﷺ used to give to you to reconcile your hearts for Islam. Now Allāh has made it needless to you. If you remain in Islam this is fine, otherwise between us and you is the sword. '*And say: 'The truth is from your Lord'. Whosoever wills, let him believe and whosoever wills, let him disbelieve*'." They returned to Abū Bakr and said: "Are you the caliph or ᶜUmar? You gave us the writing and ᶜUmar tore it up". He (Abū Bakr) said: "He is, if Allāh wills". Abū Bakr did not criticise ᶜUmar on this matter. When this came to the knowledge of other Companions, they did not criticise it, which constitutes a consensus for it.[166]

ᶜUmar's practice shows that when Muslims are in a strong position, then there is no need to give zakāh for reconciliation purposes, though this category of people is eligible for zakāh when and wherever Muslims are in a weak position, as was the case during the lifetime of the Prophet. Nowadays, when Islam has again become weak and therefore zakāh can be given to this group in order to reconcile their hearts for Islam. In other words, the 'reconciling people's heart's' group only exists when Muslims are weak.[167]

Anas reported that whenever the Prophet ﷺ was asked for anything for the sake of Islam, he would give it away. A man came and asked for *ṣadaqah*. The Prophet ordered that the man be given the entire lot of sheep found between two mountains. These sheep were part of the *ṣadaqah*. The man returned to his people and said: "O my people accept Islam, for indeed Muḥammad gives in such a way as if he does

166 al-Kāsānī, *Badāʾiᶜ al-ṣanāʾiᶜ* ii. 470.

167 See: al-Kāsānī, *Badāʾiᶜ al-ṣanāʾiᶜ* ii. 470.

not fear poverty. Anas ibn Mālik says: "A man would embrace Islam not intending anything other than the world, then later Islam would become more beloved to him than the world and whatever is in it".[168]

Saʿd reports that: "The Messenger of Allāh ﷺ bestowed (some gifts) upon a group of people and I was sitting amongst them. The Messenger of Allāh ﷺ however, left out a person to whom he did not give anything and he seemed to me the most excellent among them (and thus deserved the gifts more than anyone else). So I stood up before the Messenger of Allāh ﷺ and said to him quietly: 'Messenger of Allāh, what about so and so? By Allāh, I find him a *Mu'min* (believer)'. He (the Messenger of Allāh) said: 'He may be a Muslim'. I kept quiet for a short while, and then what I knew of him urged me (to plead his case again) and I said: 'Messenger of Allāh, what about so and so? By Allāh, I find him a believer'. Upon this he (the Prophet) said: 'He may be a Muslim'. I again remained quiet for a short while, and what I knew of him again urged me (to plead his case so I) said: 'Messenger of Allāh, what about so and so? By Allāh, I find him a believer'. Upon this he (the Prophet) said: 'He may be a Muslim. I often bestow (something) upon a person, whereas someone else is dearer to me than he, because of the fear that he may fall headlong into the fire'."[169]

Anas ibn Mālik reported that when on the Day of Ḥunayn Allāh conferred upon His Apostle ﷺ the riches of Hawāzin (without armed encounter), the Messenger of Allāh ﷺ set about distributing one hundred camels, some among the Quraysh. Upon this they (the young people from the Anṣār) said: "May Allāh grant pardon to the Messenger of Allāh ﷺ that he bestowed (these camels) upon the people of Quraysh, and he ignored us, whereas our swords are still dripping blood". Anas ibn Mālik said: "Their statement was conveyed to the Messenger of Allāh ﷺ and he sent (someone) to the Anṣār and gathered them under a tent of leather. When they had assembled, the Messenger of Allāh ﷺ went there and said: 'What is this news that has reached me from you?' The wise people of the Anṣār said: 'Messenger of Allāh, so far as the sagacious amongst us are concerned they have said nothing, but we have amongst us those of immature age; they said: 'May Allāh grant pardon to the Messenger of

168 Muslim, *k. faḍā'il, b. mā su'ila rasūlullāh ....*

169 al-Bukhārī, *k. al-īmān, b. idhā lam yakun al-islām ʿalā al-ḥaqīqah;* Muslim, *k. al-īmān, b. ta'līf qalb man yukhāfu ʿalā īmānihī li ḍaʿfihī.*

Allāh ﷺ that he gave to the Quraysh and ignored us (despite the fact) that our swords are besmeared with their blood'. Upon this, the Messenger of Allāh ﷺ said: 'I give (at times material gifts) to people who were quite recently in a state of unbelief, so that I may incline them to truth. Don't you feel delighted that people should go with riches, and you should go back to your places with the Apostle of Allāh? By Allāh, that with which you return is better than that with which they return. They said: 'Yes, Messenger of Allāh, we are pleased'. The Prophet also said: 'You will find marked preference (in conferring material gifts) in future, so you should show patience till you meet Allāh and His Messenger and I will be at the *Ḥawḍ al-Kawthar* (a pool of abundant goodness in the Hereafter)'. They said: 'We will show patience'."[170]

ʿAbdullāh ibn Zayd reports that: "When the Messenger of Allāh ﷺ conquered Ḥunayn he distributed the booty, and he bestowed upon those whose hearts he intended to win. It was conveyed to him (the Prophet) that the Anṣār cherished a desire that they should be given (that very portion) which other people had got. Upon this, the Messenger of Allāh ﷺ stood up and, after having praised Allāh addressed them thus: 'O people of Anṣār, did I not find you erring and Allāh guided you through me, and in a state of destitution and Allāh made you free from want through me, and in a state of disunity and Allāh united you through me?' and they (the Anṣār) said: 'Allāh and His Messenger are most benevolent'. He (again) said: 'Why do you not answer me?' They said: 'Allāh and His Messenger are the most benevolent'. He said: 'If you wish you should say so and so, and such and such a matter'. And in this connection he made mention of so many things. Then he (the Prophet) further said: 'Don't you feel happy that (those) people should go away with goats and camels, and you go back to your place along with the Messenger of Allāh? The Anṣār are inner garments (more close to me) whereas the other people are outer garments. Had there not been migration, I would have been a man from among the Anṣār. If the people were to tread a valley or a narrow path, I would tread the valley (chosen) by the Anṣār or the narrow path (trodden) by them. And you will soon find after me preferences (over you in getting material benefits). So you should show patience until you meet me at the *Ḥawd* (*al-Kawthar*)'."[171]

170 Muslim, *k. al-zakāh, b. iʿṭā' al-mu'allafati qulūbuhum.*

171 ibid.

Shaykh Yūsuf al-Qaraḍāwī says: "If we agree that reconciliation of hearts by payment from zakāh is permissible, to whom should this share be given today? In order to answer this question, we must remember that the purpose of this share is to bring hearts closer to Islam, affirm their commitment to its cause, support the weak, and prevent harm that could be inflicted on Muslims or on their religion. These objectives could be achieved by giving aid to non-Muslim countries, persons, organisations, and tribes, to bring them closer to the cause of Islam. It could also be extended to support research and utilise the mass media that teach Islam and defend its cause against any attackers. Many people enter into the fold of this religion every year who do not find encouragement or support from their governments and communities or even from the governments of Muslim countries. The share of heart reconciliation can be expended to such people, an idea consistent with the opinions of al-Zuhrī and al-Ḥasan. Christian missionaries spend millions every year for the spread of their religion, although Christianity does not have an institution like zakāh devoted to this purpose. It is true that Islam spreads on its own merit because of its inner persuasive power, but it is equally true that most of those who embrace Islam in non-Muslim countries do not receive even nominal support or compensation for the sacrifices they endure when they embrace Islam. There are many Islamic organisations that attempt to fill this gap which are desperate for financial support, especially in areas like Africa and other poor countries".[172]

5: THE EMANCIPATION OF SLAVES

This refers to the slaves who have a contract with their masters (*mukātab*) that if they pay a certain amount then their masters will set them free. If a *mukātab* slave is experiencing difficulty in paying for his freedom, then the zakāh payment can be made in order to help him or settle the remaining instalments required to free him.[173] Al-Barā' narrates that: "A man came to the Prophet ﷺ and said to him: 'Guide me to a deed that takes me close to Heaven and far from Hell'. The Prophet ﷺ said: 'Free a person and redeem a slave'. Then I asked: 'O Messenger of Allāh, are these two not the same?' He answered: 'No. Freeing a person means

172 al-Qaraḍāwī, *Fiqh al-zakāh ii.* 616-8.
173 al-Kāsānī, *Badā'iʿ al-ṣanā'iʿ* ii. 471.

to grant him freedom [by redeeming him from his bondage], but the redeeming of the neck means buying him his freedom'."[174]

Abū Hurayrah reported that the Prophet ﷺ said: "Three people have the right to be helped by Allāh: the warrior who fights for Allāh, the contracted slave who longs to buy his freedom, and one who wishes to get married for the sake of chastity".[175]

6: FOR THOSE IN DEBT

This refers to those, on whom a debt is binding, and the debt is more than the wealth that he owns, or the debt is less than his wealth, but after paying the debt, his wealth does not reach the amount of *niṣāb*. Such indebted people are given zakāh to help pay back their debts. Anas narrated from the Prophet ﷺ saying: "Begging is not permitted except for three [kinds of people]: those living in abject poverty, those with oppressive debt and those owing a blood wit who find it very difficult to pay".[176] Abū Saʿīd al-Khudrī narrated that a man made a bad deal on fruit and then ran into heavy debt. The Prophet ﷺ said: "Give him *ṣadaqah*". Accordingly, the people gave him *ṣadaqah*..."[177]

7: FOR THOSE IN THE 'WAY OF ALLĀH'

Most scholars have interpreted the phrase *fī sabīlillāh* (in the way of Allāh) as fighting for the cause of Allāh. According to some scholars, pilgrimage (ḥajj) also falls under the zakāh designated for the cause of Allāh.[178]

In our time this category can include all interests of Muslims intended to defend their religion and lands. Religious schools and religious teachers, preachers and students can receive zakāh. Al-Kāsānī says: "In the way of Allāh, includes all pious activities: it will include all those who work in the obedience of Allāh and in the path of good if they are needy".[179]

174 al-Bayhaqī, *al-Sunan al-kubrā,* x. 273.

175 al-Tirmidhī, *k. faḍā'il al-jihād, b. mā jā'a fī al-mujāhid...*; al-Nasā'ī, *k. al-jihād, b. faḍl al-rawḥāḥ fī sabīlillāh ʿazza wa jall.*

176 Abū Dāwūd, k. *al-zakāh, b. mā tajūzu fīhi al-mas'alah*; Ibn Mājah, *k. al-tijārāt, b. bayʿ al-muzāyadah.*

177 Muslim, *k. al-musāqāh wa al-muzāraʿah, b. istiḥbāb al-waḍʿ min al-dayn.*

178 al-Kāsānī, *Badāʾiʿ al-ṣanāʾiʿ* ii. 471-72.

179 ibid.

Shaykh Yūsuf al-Qaraḍāwī says: "I believe the term 'in the way of Allah' (*fī sabīlillāh*) includes fighting and activities that achieve the same goal as fighting, which is consistent with the opinion of the majority of jurists. It must also be noted that certain activities may be included as 'in the way of Allāh' in certain periods in certain countries, which may not be included in other lands or times. Establishing an Islamic school, for example, though beneficial to Muslims, is not included in *jihād*. Yet in a country whose educational institutions are dominated by secularists, communists, or missionaries, one of the best means of *jihād* is establishing an Islamic school in order to protect Muslim children from such destructive and demoralising preaching. Likewise, an Islamic library may sometimes be only a good and beneficial project, but may at other times in other places be a *jihād*. The same thing maybe stated about an Islamic hospital that protects Muslim patients from being exploited by missionary hospitals, and other cultural projects that perform similar tasks".[180]

8: FOR TRAVELLERS

This refers to those who are stranded or far away from home: such people are given such an amount of the zakāh as to cover their needs while in a state of travelling, even if they are of means in their own country – on account of the poverty which has befallen them on their journey and their being cut off from help and friends.[181]

WHO SHOULD BE PREFERRED IN DISTRIBUTION?

The categories discussed above are the ones to whom zakāh is given. The person who possesses the *niṣāb* gives to each of these or may restrict himself to just one category.[182] This is the opinion of ᶜUmar ibn al-Khaṭṭāb, Ḥudhayfah ibn al-Yamān, ᶜAbdullāh ibn ᶜAbbās, Ibrāhīm al-Nakhaᶜī, Abū al-ᶜĀliyah, Ḥasan al-Baṣrī, and ᶜAṭā' ibn Abī Rabāḥ,[183] Sufyān al-Thawrī and Aḥmad ibn Ḥanbal.[184]

180 al-Qaraḍāwī, *Fiqh al-zakāh* ii. 665-6.
181 al-Kāsānī, *Badā'iᶜ al-ṣanā'iᶜ* ii. 473.
182 ibid.
183 Ibn Abī Shaybah, *al-Muṣannaf*, vi. 523-525.
184 al-Baghawī, *Sharḥ al-Sunnah*, iii. 378.

THOSE TO WHOM ZAKĀH IS NOT TO BE GIVEN

1- It is not permitted to give zakāh to a non-Muslim; though voluntary charity (*ṣadaqah*) can be given. As mentioned in a ḥadīth cited earlier, zakāh will be taken from the wealthy among the Muslims and returned to the poor among them. There is a consensus among jurists on this point.[185]

2- It is not permitted to use zakāh funds to build a mosque.[186]

3- It is not permitted to shroud a corpse with zakāh money.[187]

4- It is not permitted to give zakāh to a person who possesses the minimum amount on which zakāh is applicable; while it is permitted to give it to someone who possesses below this, even if he is in good health and capable of earning his living.[188]

5- It is not permitted for one to give zakāh to one's father, grandfather or further ascendants, nor to one's son or grandchildren or further descendants. One is not allowed to give zakāh to one's wife, because financial support for her is already enjoined upon the husband.[189]

However, can a wife give zakāh to her husband? According to Abū Ḥanīfah it is not valid to pay zakāh to one's husband. Abū Yūsuf and Muḥammad hold view that a wife may give zakāh to her husband because she is not financially responsible for him. Abū Saᶜīd al-Khudrī narrated that: "Zaynab, the wife of ᶜAbdullāh ibn Masᶜūd, came and asked permission to enter. It was announced: 'O Allāh's Apostle, it is Zaynab'. He asked: 'Which Zaynab?' It was replied the wife of Ibn Masᶜūd. He said: 'Yes, allow her to enter'. and she was admitted. She said: 'O Prophet of Allāh, today you ordered people to give alms and I had an ornament and intended to give it as alms, but Ibn Masᶜūd said that he and his children deserved it more than anybody else'. The Prophet replied: 'Ibn Masᶜūd had spoken the truth. Your husband and your children have more right to it than anybody else'."[190]

Imām Muḥammad says: "The wife is not paid from the zakāh (of the

185 al-Kāsānī, *Badāʾiᶜ al-ṣanāʾiᶜ* ii. 480.

186 al-Samarqandī, *Tuḥfat al-fuqahāʾ* 144.

187 Ibid

188 al-Kāsānī, *Badāʾiᶜ al-ṣanāʾiᶜ* ii. 465-7.

189 al-Kāsānī, *Badāʾiᶜ al-ṣanāʾiᶜ* ii. 483.

190 al-Bukhārī, *k. al-zakāh, b. al-zakāh ᶜalā al-zawj wa al-aqārib,* Muslim, *k. al-zakāh, b. faḍl al-nafaqah wa al-ṣadaqah ᶜalā al-aqrabīn.*

husband), and Abū Ḥanīfah says that the husband also will not be given zakāh (from the wife); but we hold that the husband can receive zakāh from the wife".[191]

6-It may not be given to the child of a rich person who owns *niṣāb* if the child is below the age of puberty.[192]

7-It may not be given to the descendants of Hāshim. Muṭṭalib ibn Rabīʿah says: "The Messenger of Allāh ﷺ said: 'These charities (zakāh) are impurities of the people; they are not allowed for Muḥammad and for his family'."[193] Abū Hurayrah narrated: "Dates used to be brought to the Messenger of Allāh ﷺ immediately after being plucked. Different people would bring their dates until a big heap was collected (in front of the Prophet). Once Ḥasan and Ḥusayn were playing with these dates, and one of them took a date and put it in his mouth. The Messenger of Allāh ﷺ looked at him and took it out of his mouth and said: 'Don't you know that Muḥammad's offspring do not eat what is given in charity?'"[194]

Descendants of Hāshim means the family of ʿAlī, the family of al-ʿAbbās, the family of Jaʿfar, the family of ʿAqīl, the family of Ḥārith ibn ʿAbd al-Muṭṭalib and their clients and freedmen.[195] Zayd ibn Arqam was once asked who are the family of the Prophet on whom zakāh is forbidden? He answered: "The family of ʿAlī, the family of ʿAqīl, the family of Jaʿfar, and the family of al-ʿAbbās".[196]

191 Abū Ḥanīfah, *k. al-āthār* 74.

192 al-Samarqandī, *Tuḥfat al-fuqahā'* 141.

193 Muslim, *k. al-zakāh, b. tark istiʿmāl al al-nabī ṣallallāhu ʿalayhi wa sallam ʿalā al-ṣadaqah.*

194 al-Bukhārī, *k. al-zakāh, b. mā yudhkaru fī al-ṣadaqah li al-nabī ṣallallāhu ʿalayhi wa sallam,* Muslim, *k. al-zakāh, b. taḥrīm al-zakāh ʿalā rasūlillāh ṣallallāhu ʿalayhi wa sallam wa ʿalā ālihī.*

195 al-Kāsānī, *Badā'iʿ al-ṣanā'iʿ* ii. 483.

196 ʿAbd al-Razzāq, *al-Muṣannaf,* iv. 52.

Chapter 5: Payment of Zakāh

This chapter deals with issues related to the payment of zakāh.

INTENTION

As stated earlier, zakāh is an act of worship; and like other acts of worship, it can only be valid when accompanied by intention. Allāh says in the Qur'ān: "*And they were not commanded, but to worship Allāh, making the religion sincerely for Him*".[197] The Prophet ﷺ said: "Every action is based upon intention. For everyone is that which he has intended. Whoever made the migration to Allāh and His Prophet, then his migration is to Allāh and His Prophet. Whoever's migration was for something of this world or for the purpose of marriage, then his migration was to what he migrated to".[198]

Payment of zakāh is not valid except if it is accompanied by an intention made immediately prior to its payment or immediately before separating the zakāh amount from one's wealth. Mullā ᶜAbd al-ᶜAlī Baḥr al-ᶜUlūm writes: "Soundness of intention is necessary at the time zakāh is paid for it is a major form of worship; and as in the case of *ṣalāh*, it should also be prompted by no other consideration than that of Divine propitiation. Thus, intention is an essential prerequisite, and just as *ṣalāh* cannot be offered without intention, zakāh also cannot be paid without it".[199]

If one forgot to make the intention before giving the zakāh to its recipient, but is able to make the intention whilst the amount is still in the hands of the recipient, then the zakāh is valid. However, if the wealth is no longer in the hands of the receiver then the zakāh is not valid.

If anyone gives away all his wealth, on which zakāh was due, as *ṣadaqah* without making the intention of giving it as zakāh, then the obligation of zakāh on it is considered to have lapsed.[200]

197 *al-Bayyinah* 5.
198 al-Bukhārī, *k. bad' al-waḥy.*
199 *Rasā'il-i arkān*, p. 163.
200 al-Kāsānī, *Badā'iᶜ al-ṣanā'iᶜ* ii. 458.

TIME OF THE PAYMENT

It is preferable to pay zakāh immediately upon it becoming obligatory. Imām Muḥammad states that delaying zakāh is not allowed.[201] ᶜUqbah ibn al-Ḥārith said: "Once I performed the *ᶜAṣr* prayer with the Prophet ﷺ. Upon concluding the prayer, he hurriedly went to his house and returned immediately. Noticing the amazed faces, he explained: 'I left a piece of gold in my house which was meant for *ṣadaqah* and I did not want to leave it for a night in my house, so I ordered it to be distributed'."[202]

Advance payment

It is allowed to pay zakāh in advance. ᶜAlī ibn Abī Ṭālib has narrated that ᶜAbbās asked the Prophet ﷺ if he could pay zakāh before the occurrence of its time. The Prophet ﷺ allowed him to do this.[203] ᶜUmar ibn Yūnus narrated that al-Zuhrī did not see any harm in paying zakāh before the end of year.[204] Ḥasan al-Baṣrī was asked if someone takes out his zakāh of three years (in advance), will it suffice. He said: "It will suffice him".[205] ᶜAṭā' ibn Abī Rabāḥ says: "There is no harm in paying zakāh in advance".[206] The same opinions have been narrated from Saᶜīd ibn Jubayr, Ibrāhīm al-Nakhaᶜī, Ḥakam and Ibn Sīrīn.[207] This can be done to help someone in an emergency. The one who pays zakāh in advance will only have an approximate idea of the amount he will earn by the actual due time of his zakāh. If he underestimated, he can make up the difference.

Payment of arrears

If someone has not paid zakāh during previous years, he must pay it, as it will remain as a debt upon him as long as he does not do so.

If someone dies without paying zakāh, and without making a will

201 ibid., ii. 374.

202 al-Bukhārī, *k. al-aḍhān, b. man ṣalla bi al-nās fa dhakara ḥājatan fatakhaṭṭāhum.*

203 Abū Dāwūd, *k. al-zakāh, b. fī taᶜjīl al-zakāh*; al-Tirmidhī, *k. al-zakāh, b. mā jā'a fī taᶜjīl al-zakāh;* Ibn Mājah, *k. al-zakāh, b. fī taᶜjīl al-zakāh qabla maḥillihā.*

204 Ibn Abī Shaybah, *al-Muṣannaf,* vi. 458.

205 ibid.

206 ibid., 457.

207 ibid., 457-8.

identifying the payment then zakāh will not be taken from the property he has left behind. But if a will was made then the zakāh will be taken from the third of the wealth.[208] Allāh says: "... *after payment of legacies and debts is what you leave* ..".[209] Zakāh is a debt payable to Allāh. A woman came to the Messenger of Allāh ﷺ and said: "My mother died while she still had to make up one month of fasting. Shall I make it up for her?" The Prophet ﷺ replied: "If there was any debt upon your mother, would you pay it off for her?" The woman answered: "Yes". The Prophet ﷺ then observed: "A debt to Allāh is more deserving to be paid off".[210]

PRAYER FOR THE ZAKĀH PAYER

It is recommended that the recipient of zakāh invokes blessings for the zakāh payer at the time of its payment. Allāh says in the Qur'ān: "*Take alms of their property that you may purify and sanctify them and pray for them. Verily, your prayers are a comfort for them*"[211]. ᶜAbdullāh ibn Abī Awfā said: "When any people brought charity to the Prophet ﷺ he would say: 'O Allāh bless the family of so and so'. Once my father brought to him his charity, and the Prophet ﷺ said: 'O Allāh, bless the family of Abū Awfā'."[212]

TRANSFERRING ZAKĀH

Transferring zakāh from one region to another is disliked; rather, the zakāh of a people should be distributed amongst them. This is substantiated by the instructions given by the Prophet ﷺ to Muᶜādh ibn Jabal in which he says: "Inform them that Allāh has enjoined on them the zakāh. And it is to be taken from the rich amongst them and given to the poor amongst them".[213] Abū Juḥayfah reported: "The

208 al-Kāsānī, *Badā'iᶜ al-ṣanā'iᶜ* ii. 492.

209 *al-Nisāᶜ* 12.

210 al-Bukhārī, *k. al-ṣawm, b. man māta wa ᶜalayhi ṣawm*; Muslim, *k. al-ṣiyām, b. qaḍā' al-ṣiyām ᶜan al-mayyit.*

211 *al-Barā' ah* 103.

212 al-Bukhārī, *k. al-zakāh, b. ṣalāt al-imām wa duᶜā'ihī li ṣāḥib al-ṣadaqah;* Muslim, *k. al-zakāh, b. al-duᶜā' liman atā bi ṣadaqah.*

213 al-Bukhārī, *k. al-zakāh, b. akhdh al-ṣadaqah min al-aghniyā',* Muslim, *k. al-īmān, b. al-duᶜā' ilā al-shahādatayn wa sharā'iᶜ al-islām.*

charity collector of the Messenger of Allāh ﷺ came to us and took zakāh from our rich and gave it to our poor. I was an orphan then, and he gave me a young she-camel".[214] ʿImrān ibn Ḥuṣayn reports that he was employed as a charity collector. When he returned from this assignment, he was asked: "Where is the collection?" He responded: "Did you send me for the collection? We took it and distributed it the way we did at the time of the Messenger of Allāh ﷺ".[215] Ibrāhīm al-Nakhaʿī and Ḥasan al-Baṣrī both disliked transferring zakāh from one town to another.[216] ʿAbd al-ʿAzīz ibn Abī Rawwād narrates that zakāh was sent from Iraq to ʿUmar ibn ʿAbd al-ʿAzīz in Syria. He returned that zakāh to Iraq.[217] Farqad al-Sabakhī says: "Zakāh was sent with me to Makkah, where I met Saʿīd ibn Jubayr. He said: 'Return it to the land from where you have taken it'."[218]

However, if the need of the people in the area where zakāh is collected is fulfilled, or one transfers the zakāh to relations or to a people who are more in need than one's own region then the transfer of zakāh is allowed. ʿAmr ibn Shuʿayb narrates that the Messenger of Allāh ﷺ appointed Muʿādh ibn Jabal to a position in Jund and during the time of ʿUmar's leadership Muʿādh sent to ʿUmar one-third of the *ṣadaqah* collected from the local people, but ʿUmar turned it down and said: "I did not appoint you to go there as a tax collector or as a tribute (*jizyah*) taker. I appointed you to collect *ṣadaqah* from their rich and to return it to their poor". Muʿādh replied: "I would not have sent you anything [from the collection] if I had found someone deserving of it [over here]". In the second year, he sent him half of the collected *ṣadaqah*, and they went into the same issue again. In the third year, he sent him all of it, and ʿUmar again argued with him. Muʿādh responded: "I could not find anyone who deserved to receive anything from me".[219] Ḍaḥḥāk says: "Keep zakāh in you locality; if there are no

214 al-Tirmidhī, *k. al-zakāh, b. mā jā'a anna al-ṣadaqah tu'khadhu min al-aghniyā' faturaddu ilā al-fuqarā'.*

215 Abū Dāwūd, *k. al-zakāh, b. fī al-zakāh tuḥmalu min balad ilā balad.*

216 Ibn Abī Shaybah, *al-Muṣannaf,* vi. 495.

217 ibid.

218 ibid.,496.

219 Abū ʿUbayd, *k. al-amwāl,* ḥadīth no. 1267.

poor people in that place, then transfer it to its neighbouring locality".[220]

ERRORS IN THE PAYMENT OF ZAKĀH

Abū Ḥanīfah and Muḥammad hold the opinion that if zakāh is given to a man believed to be poor but later it becomes clear he is a man of means, or a Hāshimī, or a non-Muslim, or paid unknowingly to a father or a son, and later this become clear, the zakāh is valid and one does not have to pay it again. Abū Yūsuf, however, held the opinion that the payment of the zakāh in all those conditions is not valid and one has to pay it again.[221]

The argument of Abū Ḥanīfah and Muḥammad is the ḥadīth of Maᶜn ibn Yazīd who narrated: "My grandfather, my father and I gave the pledge of allegiance to Allāh's Apostle ﷺ. The Prophet ﷺ had me engaged and then got me married. My father Yazīd had taken some gold coins for charity to give to the poor and kept them with a man in the mosque. But I went and took them and brought them to my father. My father said: 'By Allāh I did not intend to give them to you'. I took the case to the Messenger of Allāh ﷺ. On that, the Messenger of Allāh ﷺ said: 'O Yazīd! You will be rewarded for what you intended. O Maᶜn! Whatever you have taken is yours'."[222]

Abū Hurayrah narrated that the Messenger of Allāh ﷺ said: "A man said that he would give something in charity. He went out with his object of charity and unknowingly gave it to a thief. Next morning the people said that he had given his object of charity to a thief. On hearing this he said: 'O Allāh! All praises are for You. I will give alms again'. And so he again went out and unknowingly gave it to an adulteress. Next morning the people said that he had given his alms to an adulteress. The man said: 'O Allāh! All praises are for You. I gave my alms to an adulteress. I will give alms again'. So he went out with his alms again and unknowingly gave it to a rich person. The people next morning said that he had given his alms to a wealthy person. He said: 'O Allāh! All praises are for You. I have given alms to a thief, to an adulteress and to a wealthy man'. Then someone came and said to him: 'The alms which you gave to the thief, might make him abstain

220 Ibn Abī Shaybah, *al-Muṣannaf,* vi. 495-496.

221 al-Qudūrī, *al-Mukhtaṣar* 181.

222 al-Bukhārī, *k. al-zakāh, b. idhā taṣaddqa ᶜalā ibnihī wa huwa lā yashᶜuru.*

from stealing, and that given to the adulteress might make her abstain from adultery, and that given to the wealthy man might make him take a lesson from it and spend his wealth, which Allāh has given him, in Allāh's cause'."[223]

223 ibid., Muslim, *k. al-zakāh, b. thubūt ajr al-mutaṣaddiq wa in waqaʿat al-ṣadaqah fī yad ghayr ahlihā.*

CHAPTER 6: *ṢADAQAT AL-FIṬR*

ṢADAQAT AL-FIṬR IS a charity paid at the end of the month of Ramaḍān. It was made obligatory in *Shaᶜbān* of the second year of *hijrah* and intended as purification for the fasting person, and help for the poor and needy. ᶜAbdullāh ibn ᶜAbbās narrated: "The Apostle of Allāh ﷺ prescribed the *ṣadaqah* relating to the breaking of the fast as a purification of the fasting from empty and obscene talk and as food for the poor".[224]

Al-Ḥasan al-Baṣrī said: "Ibn ᶜAbbās preached towards the end of Ramaḍān on the pulpit (in the mosque) of Baṣrah. He said: 'Bring forth the *ṣadaqah* relating to your fast'. The people did not understand (what he meant). Then Ibn ᶜAbbās said: 'Those of you present who are from the people of Madīnah, stand with your brethren, and teach them, for they do not know. The Apostle of Allāh ﷺ prescribed this *ṣadaqah* as one *ṣāᶜ* [3.3Kg] of dried dates or barley, or half a *ṣāᶜ* [1.65Kg] of wheat payable by every freeman or slave, male or female, young or old'. When ᶜAlī came to Baṣrah, he found that the price had come down. He said: 'Allāh has given prosperity to you, so give one *ṣāᶜ* of everything as *ṣadaqah*'."[225]

ON WHOM IT IS OBLIGATORY

Ṣadaqat al-fiṭr is obligatory on every free Muslim if he possesses the minimum amount of *niṣāb* on which zakāh is applicable in addition to his home, clothing, furnishings, horse, weapon and serving-slaves.[226]

Ṣadaqat al-fiṭr is paid for oneself, ones under-age children and slaves kept for serving.[227] ᶜAbdullāh ibn ᶜUmar narrated: "The Messenger of Allāh ﷺ enjoined the payment of one *ṣāᶜ* of dates or one *ṣāᶜ* of barley as *ṣadaqat al-fiṭr* on every Muslim, slave or free, male or female, young or

224 Abū Dāwūd, *k. al-zakāh, b. zakāt al-fiṭr.*

225 Abū Dāwūd, *k. al-zakāh, b. man rawā niṣfa ṣāᶜ min qamḥ,* al-Nasā'ī, *k. al-zakāh, b. mikyalat zakāt al-fiṭr.*

226 al-Qudūrī, *al-Mukhtaṣar* 183.

227 ibid.

old, and he ordered that it be paid before the people went out to offer the *ʿĪd* prayer".[228]

One does not pay it for his wife, or his adult children even if they are still part of the family.[229] They must pay their own *ṣadaqat al-fiṭr* if they are liable.

THE AMOUNT OF *ṢADAQAT AL-FIṬR*

The *ṣadaqat al-fiṭr* is half a *ṣāᶜ* (1.65Kg) of wheat, or a ṣāᶜ (3.3Kg) of dates, or currants or barley.[230] Abū Saᶜīd al-Khudrī said: "In the lifetime of the Prophet ﷺ we used to give one *ṣāᶜ* of food or one *ṣāᶜ* of dates or one *ṣāᶜ* of barley or one *ṣāᶜ* of raisins as *ṣadaqat al-fiṭr*. And when Muᶜāwiyah became the Caliph and wheat was available in abundance he said: 'I think that one *mudd* (quarter of a *ṣāᶜ*) of wheat equals two *mudd*s (of any of the above mentioned things)'. Then the people followed it'."[231]

However, we have the narration of ᶜAbdullāh ibn ᶜAbbās who said at the end of the month of Ramaḍān: "Give the *ṣadaqah* of your fasting. The Messenger of Allāh ﷺ has prescribed this *ṣadaqah* as one *ṣāᶜ* of date or barley, and half a *ṣāᶜ* of wheat".[232] The *ṣadaqat al-fiṭr* being half a *ṣāᶜ* of wheat is also the opinion of Abū Bakr al-Ṣiddīq, ᶜUthmān ibn ᶜAffān, ᶜAlī ibn Abī Ṭālib, ᶜAbdullāh ibn Masᶜūd, Jābir ibn ᶜAbdullāh, Asmā' bint Abī Bakr, ᶜAbdullāh ibn Zubayr, ᶜUmar ibn ᶜAbd al-ᶜAzīz, Saᶜīd ibn al-Musayyab, Ṭāwūs, Mujāhid, ᶜAṭā' ibn Abī Rabāḥ, ᶜAbdullāh ibn Shaddād, Ḥasan al-Baṣrī, Ibrāhīm al-Nakhaᶜī, Shaᶜbī, Ḥakam, Ḥammād ibn Abī Sulaymān, ᶜAbd al-Raḥmān ibn al-Qāsim, and Saᶜd ibn Ibrāhīm[233], Sufyān al-Thawrī, ᶜAbdullāh ibn al-Mubārak and the people of Kūfah.[234]

228 al-Bukhārī, k. *al-zakāh, b. farḍ ṣadaqaht al-fiṭr;* Muslim, *k. al-zakāh, b. zakāt al-fiṭr ᶜalā al-muslimīn.*

229 al-Qudūrī, *al-Mukhtaṣar* 184.

230 al-Samarqandī, *Tuḥfat al-fuqahā'* 159.

231 al-Bukhārī, *k. al-zakāh, b. ṣadaqaht al-fiṭr ṣāᶜ min ṭaᶜām*; Muslim, *k. al-zakāh, b. zakāt al-fiṭr ᶜalā al-muslimīn min al-tamr wa al-shaᶜīr.*

232 Abū Dāwūd, *k. al-zakāh, b. man rawā niṣfa ṣāᶜ min qamḥ*; al-Nasā'ī, *k. al-zakāh, b. mikyalatt zakāt al-fiṭr.*

233 Ibn Abī Shaybah, *al-Muṣannaf,* vi. 500-504.

234 al-Tirmidhī, *k. al-zakāh, b. mā jā'a fī ṣadaqaht al-fiṭr.*

Can one pay its value?

It is allowed to pay the equivalent value in money. In our times, this is easier for those on whom it is compulsory, and it is more useful for the recipient. It has been narrated from Abū Yūsuf that he said: "Flour is more beloved to me than wheat, and *dirhams* (money) are more beloved to me than flour and wheat; because that is better in fulfilling the need of the needy".[235] ᶜUmar ibn ᶜAbd al-ᶜAzīz allowed *ṣadaqat al-fiṭr* to be paid in money.[236] Ḥasan al-Baṣrī says: "There is no harm in giving *ṣadaqat al-fiṭr* in money".[237] Abū Isḥāq al-Sabīᶜī says: "I have found them giving money of the value of food in the *ṣadaqah* of Ramaḍān".[238]

Since today the value of wheat is similar to that of other grains, it is preferable to calculate the value of *ṣadaqat al-fiṭr* in terms of those grains which are fixed as one *ṣāᶜ*, like dates or barley.

WHEN IT BECOMES OBLIGATORY

The *ṣadaqat al-fiṭr* becomes obligatory at the time of the *Fajr* Prayer on the day of *ᶜĪd al-fiṭr*. Whoever dies before dawn is not liable for *ṣadaqat al-fiṭr*. Whoever becomes Muslim or is born after the dawn breaks does not have to pay *ṣadaqat al-fiṭr*. But anyone who becomes Muslim before the dawn or any child born before the dawn, the *ṣadaqat al-fiṭr* becomes compulsory for them.[239]

The preferred time for payment

It is recommended for people to pay their *ṣadaqat al-fiṭr* on the day of *ᶜĪd al-fiṭr* before going out to the *ᶜĪd Prayer*. ᶜAbdullāh ibn ᶜUmar reports that the Messenger ﷺ ordered them to pay *ṣadaqat al-fiṭr* before the people went out to perform the *ᶜĪd Prayers*.[240]

If people pay it before the day of *ᶜĪd al-fiṭr* it is permitted. ᶜAlī ibn Abī Ṭālib narrated that Al-ᶜAbbās asked the Prophet ﷺ about paying the *ṣadaqah* (his zakāh) in advance before it became due, and he gave

235 al-Kāsānī, *Badāʾiᶜ al-ṣanāʾiᶜ*, ii. 541.
236 Ibn Abī Shaybah, *al-Muṣannaf*, vi. 508.
237 ibid.
238 ibid.
239 al-Samarqandī, *Tuḥfat al-fuqahā'* 160.
240 al-Bukhārī, *k. al-zakāh, b. farḍ sadqat al-fiṭr*, Muslim, *k. al-zakāh, b. zakāt al-fiṭr ᶜalā al-muslimīn.*

permission to do that".[241] Nāfiᶜ reports that ᶜAbdullāh ibn ᶜUmar used to pay it a day or two before the end of Ramaḍān. Imām Muḥammad says after narrating this practice of Ibn ᶜUmar: "We adhere to this, it is pleasing to us that one pays *ṣadaqat al-fiṭr* before going to the *musallah* (place of *ᶜĪd Prayer*), and that is the opinion of Abū Ḥanīfah".[242]

If someone delays the payment after the day of *al-fiṭr*, its payment is still not annulled – rather they are under an obligation to pay it, though it will not have the same reward.[243] ᶜAbdullāh ibn ᶜAbbās narrated: "The Apostle of Allāh ﷺ prescribed the *ṣadaqah* relating to the breaking of the fast as a purification of the fasting from empty and obscene talk and as food for the poor. If anyone pays it before the prayer, it will be accepted as zakāh. If anyone pays it after the prayer, that will be a charity like other charities".[244]

TO WHOM IT SHOULD BE PAID

Ṣadaqat al-fiṭr can be paid to all those eligible to receive zakāh, though it is preferable to pay it to poor Muslims. Abū Ḥanīfah and Muḥammad have allowed it to be given to poor non-Muslims under the protection of Muslims.[245] Allāh, Exalted is He, says: "*Allāh allows you to show kindness and deal justly with those who did not war against you on account of your religion and did not drive you out from your homes. Lo Allāh loves those who are just*".[246]

241 Abū Dāwūd, *k. al-zakāh, b. fī taᶜjīl al-zakāh;* al-Tirmidhī, *k. al-zakāh, b. mā jā'a fī taᶜjīl al-zakāh;* Ibn Mājah, *k. al-zakāh, b. fī taᶜjīl al-zakāh qabla mahillihā.*

242 Muhammad, *al-Muwaṭṭa'* 121.

243 al-Qudūrī, *al-Mukhtaṣar* 186.

244 Abū Dāwūd, *k. al-zakāh, b. zakāt al-fiṭr.*

245 al-Kāsānī, *Badā'iᶜ al-ṣanā'iᶜ*, ii. 482.

246 *al-Mumtaḥinah* 8.

Chapter 7: Voluntary Charity

As mentioned at the beginning of this volume, Islam encourages spending in the path of Allāh, and taking care of the poor and needy. Besides paying their zakāh and *ṣadaqat al-fiṭr,* people should offer voluntary charity as well. Allāh, Exalted is He, says: "*The parable of those who spend their wealth in the way of Allāh is that of a grain of corn: it grows seven ears, and each ear has a hundred grains. Allāh gives manifold increase to whom He pleases. Allāh cares for all and knows all things*"[247]. "*By no means shall you attain righteousness unless you give freely of that which you love, and whatever you give, Allāh knows it well*"[248]. "*And spend from what We have made you heir. For those of you who believe and spend, for them is a great reward*".[249]

There are many verses of the Qur'ān and *aḥadīth* (plural of ḥadīth) of the Prophet ﷺ which inform us about the rewards and virtues of charity. Some of them are mentioned below:

THE VIRTUES OF CHARITY IN THE QUR'ĀN

"*Those who spend their money in the cause of Allāh and do not follow their charity with insult or harm will receive their recompense from their Lord; they have nothing to fear, nor will they grieve*".[250] "*Allāh is fully aware of any charity you give or any charitable pledge you fulfil. As for the wicked, they will have no helpers*".[251]

"*You are not responsible for guiding anyone. Allāh is the only one who guides whoever He chooses (to be guided). Any charity you give is for your own good. Any charity you give shall be for the sake of Allāh. Any charity you give will be repaid to you, without the least injustice*".[252] "*Those who give to charity*

247 *al-Baqarah* 261
248 *Āl ʿImrān* 92.
249 *al-Ḥadīd* 7.
250 *al-Baqarah* 262.
251 *al-Baqarah* 270.
252 *al-Baqarah* 272.

night and day, secretly and publicly, receive their recompense from their Lord; they will have nothing to fear, nor will they grieve".[253] "*You cannot attain righteousness until you give to charity from the possessions you love. Whatever you give to charity, Allāh is fully aware thereof*".[254] "*Those who give in charity during good times, as well as bad times, and are suppressors of anger, and pardoners of the people. Allāh loves the charitable*".[255] "*They are those who, if we appointed them as rulers on earth, they would establish the ṣalāh and the zakāh, and would advocate righteousness and forbid evil. Allāh is the ultimate ruler*".[256] "*Believe in Allāh and His Messenger, and give from what He has bestowed upon you. Those among you who believe and give (to charity) have deserved a great recompense*".[257]

THE VIRTUES OF CHARITY IN ḤADĪTH

Closeness to Allāh

Offering charity draws one nearer to Allāh. The Messenger of Allāh ﷺ said: "Allāh, Exalted is He, shall say on the Day of Judgment: 'O son of Ādam! I was ill and you did not visit me'. He will reply: 'O my Lord! How could I visit You and You are the Lord of the Worlds?' Allāh shall say: 'Did you not know that My slave, so-and-so, was ill and you did not visit him? If you had visited him, you would have found Me with him. O son of Ādam! I asked you for food and you did not give it to me'. He will reply: 'O my Lord! How could I give You food, You are the Lord of the Worlds?' Allāh shall say: 'Did you not know that My slave, so-and-so, asked you for food and you did not give it to him? Did you not know that if you had given the food, you would have found that with Me? O son of Ādam! I asked you to quench My thirst and you did not'. He will say: 'O my Lord! How could I quench Your thirst. You are the Lord of the Worlds?' Allāh shall say: 'My slave, so-and-so, asked you to quench his thirst and you did not. If you had given him drink, you would have found that with Me'."[258]

253 *al-Baqarah* 274.
254 *Āl ʿImrān* 134.
255 *Āl ʿImrān* 92.
256 *al-Ḥajj* 41.
257 *al-Ḥadīd* 7.
258 Muslim, *k. al-birr wa al-ṣilah wa al-adab, b. faḍl ʿiyādat al-marīḍ.*

Reward in the Hereafter
Abū Saʿīd al-Khudrī narrated that the Prophet ﷺ said: "If any Muslim clothes a Muslim when he is naked, Allāh will clothe him with some green garments of Paradise; if any Muslim feeds a Muslim when he is hungry, Allāh will feed him with some of the fruits of Paradise; and if any Muslim gives a Muslim drink when he is thirsty, Allāh will give him some of the pure wine which is sealed to drink".[259]

Protection from Hellfire
Charity is very effective in protecting oneself from the fire of hell. ʿAdī ibn Ḥātim reported Allāh's Messenger ﷺ as saying: "Allāh will speak with everyone amongst you without any interpreter between them. One will look towards his right and will not find anything but the deeds which he has done before, and he will look towards the left and will not find anything but the deeds which he has done before. He will look in front of him and will find nothing but Fire just in front of his face. So protect yourselves against the Fire even if it is with the help of half a date".[260]

Compensation for spending
Those who spend their wealth for the sake of Allāh, are also compensated in this world. Abū Hurayrah narrated the Prophet ﷺ said: "Every day two angels come down from Heaven and one of them says: 'O Allāh! Compensate every person that spends in Your Cause,' and the other angel says: 'O Allāh! Destroy every miser'."[261]

Upper hand
The person who offers charity is described as having the upper hand. Ḥakīm ibn Ḥizām narrated: The Prophet ﷺ said, "The upper hand is better than the lower hand (i.e. the one who gives in charity is better than the one who receives it). One should start by first giving to one's dependents. And the best object of charity is that which is given by a

259 Abū Dāwūd, *k. al-zakāh, b. fī faḍl saqy al-mā';* al-Tirmidhī, *k. ṣifat al-qiyāmah.*

260 al-Bukhārī, *k. al-zakāh, b. al-ṣadaqah qabl al-radd;* Muslim, *k. al-zakāh, b. al-ḥathth ʿalā al-ṣadaqah wa law bi shiqqi tamrah.*

261 al-Bukhārī, *k. al-zakāh, b. qawlillāh taʿālā fa ammā man aʿṭā wattaqā*; Muslim, *k. al-zakāh, b. fī al-munfiq wa al-mumsik.*

wealthy person (from the money which is left after his expenses). And whoever abstains from asking others for financial assistance, Allāh will give him and save him from asking others; Allāh will make him self-sufficient".[262]

Encouraging spending

Mundhir ibn Jarīr reported on the authority of his father that: "While we were in the company of the Messenger of Allāh ﷺ in the early hours of the morning, some people who were barefoot, wearing torn striped woollen clothes, or cloaks, with their swords hung around their necks, came to us. Most of them, nay, all of them, belonged to the tribe of Muḍar. The colour of the face of the Messenger of Allāh ﷺ changed when he saw them in poverty. He then entered his house and came out and commanded Bilāl to pronounce *adhān*. He pronounced the *adhān* and *iqāmah*, and the Prophet ﷺ performed prayer along with his Companions and then addressed them reciting verses of the Holy Qur'ān: '*O people, fear your Lord, Who created you from a single being*" to the end of the verse, '*Allāh is ever a Watcher over you*'.[263] He then recited a verse of *Sūrah al-Ḥashr*: '*Fear Allāh. and let every soul consider that which it sends forth for tomorrow and fear Allāh*'.[264] Then the audience began to vie with one another in giving charity. Some donated a dīnār, others a *dirham*, still others clothes, some donated a *ṣāʿ* of wheat, some a *ṣāʿ* of dates; until the Prophet ﷺ said: 'Bring even if it is half a date'. Then a person from among the Anṣār came with a money bag which his hands could scarcely lift; in fact, they could not lift. (And) the people followed continuously, until I saw two heaps of eatables and clothes, and I saw the face of the Messenger ﷺ glistening, like gold on account of joy. The Messenger of Allāh ﷺ said: 'He who sets a good precedent in Islam, there is a reward for him for this act of goodness and (also gets) reward from him who followed according to it subsequently, without any deduction of his rewards; and he who sets in Islam an evil precedent, there is upon him the burden of that, and the burden of him also who acted upon it

262 al-Bukhārī, *k. al-zakāh, b. lā ṣadaqah illā ʿan ẓahr ghinā;* Muslim, *k. al-zakāh, b. bayān ann al-yad al-ʿulyā khayr...*

263 *al-Nisā'* 1.

264 *al-Ḥashr* 18.

subsequently, without any deduction from their burden.[265]

The Prophet ﷺ has taught in different *aḥadīth* that those who are generous, will find that Allāh is generous with them, and those who withhold their wealth, will find that Allāh also withholds from them. Abū Hurayrah reported Allāh's Messenger ﷺ as saying that Allāh, the Most Blessed and High, said: "O son of Ādam! Spend. I will spend on you. The right hand of Allāh is full and overflowing and nothing will diminish it, by overspending day and night".[266] Asmā' bint Abī Bakr narrated: "The Prophet ﷺ said to me: 'Do not withhold, otherwise Allāh will withhold from you'."[267]

ᶜAbdullāh ibn Masᶜūd narrated: "I heard the Prophet ﷺ say: 'There is no envy except for two: a person whom Allāh has given wealth and he spends it in the right way, and a person whom Allāh has given wisdom and he gives his decisions accordingly and teaches it to others'."[268]

Abū Hurayrah narrated that: "A man came to the Prophet ﷺ and asked: 'O Allāh's Apostle, which charity is superior in reward?' He replied: 'The charity which you do when you are in good health, fearful of poverty and wanting to hold on to what you have and to become wealthier. Do not delay it to the time of approaching death and then say: 'Give so much to so and so, and so much to so and so'. But (by then) it is already the property of so and so'."[269]

Abū Dharr reported: "I walked with the Messenger of Allāh ﷺ on the stony ground of Madīnah in the afternoon and we were looking at (Mount) Uḥud. The Messenger of Allāh ﷺ said: 'Abū Dharr'. I said: 'Messenger of Allāh, I am here at your beck and call'. He said: 'What I desire is that Uḥud be gold with me and three nights should pass and there is not left with me any dīnār but one coin which I would keep to

265 Muslim, *k. al-zakāh, b. al-ḥathth ᶜalā al-ṣadaqah wa law bi shiqq ....*

266 al-Bukhārī, *k. al-nafaqāt, b. faḍl al-nafaqah ᶜalā al-ahl;* Muslim, *k. al-zakāh, b. al-ḥathth ᶜalā al-nafaqah.*

267 al-Bukhārī, *k. al-hibah, b. hibat al-mar'ah li ghayr zawjihā;* Muslim, *k. al-zakāh, b. al-ḥathth fī al-infāq.*

268 al-Bukhārī, *k. al-ᶜilm, b. al-ightibāṭ fī al-ᶜilm wa al-ḥikmah;* Muslim, *k. ṣalāt al-musāfirīn, b. faḍl man yaqūmu bi al-qur'ān wa yuᶜallimuhū.*

269 al-Bukhārī, *k. al-zakāh, b. faḍl ṣadaqaht al-shaḥīḥ al-ṣaḥīḥ;* Muslim, *k. al-zakāh, b. bayān anna afḍal al-ṣadaqah ṣadaqaht al-ṣaḥīḥ al-shaḥīḥ.*

pay debt. I love to spend it among the slaves of Allāh like this,' and he pointed in front of him, and on his right side and on his left side. We then proceeded and he said: 'Abū Dharr,' I said: 'At your beck and call, Messenger of Allāh'. He (the Prophet) said: 'The rich would be poor on the Day of Resurrection, except he who spent like this and like this and like this,' and he pointed as he did the first time. We again went on when he said: 'Abū Dharr stay where you are until I come back to you. He (the Prophet) then moved on until he disappeared from my sight. I heard a sound and I heard a noise. I said (to myself): 'The Messenger of Allāh ﷺ might have met a mishap or an enemy'. I wished to follow him but I remembered his command for not departing until he came back. So I waited for him, and when he came I made mention of what I had heard. He said: 'It was Jibrīl, who came to me and said: 'He who dies among your *Ummah* without associating anything with Allāh will enter Paradise'. I said: 'Even if he committed fornication or theft?' The Prophet ﷺ said: 'Even if he committed fornication or theft'." [270]

Anas ibn Mālik narrated: "Abū Ṭalḥah had more date-palm gardens than any other amongst the Anṣār in Madīnah and the most beloved of them to him was *Bayruḥā'* Garden, which was in front of the Prophet's mosque. The Messenger of Allāh ﷺ used to go there to drink its clear water. When the verses: '*By no means shall you attain righteousness unless you spend (in charity) of that which you love,*' were revealed, Abū Ṭalḥah said to Allāh's Apostle: 'O Allāh's Apostle, Allāh, the Blessed, the Superior, says: '*By no means shall you attain righteousness, unless you spend (in charity) of that which you love*'. And no doubt, *Bayruḥā'* Garden is the most beloved of all my properties. So I want to give it in charity in Allāh's Cause. I expect its reward from Allāh. O Allāh's Apostle, spend it where Allāh makes you think it feasible'. On that, the Messenger of Allāh ﷺ said: 'Bravo, it is a useful property. I have heard what you have said (O Abū Ṭalḥah), and I think it would be proper if you gave it to your kith and kin'. Abū Ṭalḥah said: 'I will do so, O Allāh's Apostle'. Then Abū Ṭalḥah distributed that garden amongst his relatives and his cousins'."[271]

270 Muslim, *k. al-zakāh, b. al-targhīb fī al-ṣadaqah.*

271 al-Bukhārī, *k. al-zakāh, b. al-zakāh ʿalā al-aqārib;* Muslim, *k. al-zakāh, b. faḍl al-nafaqah wa al-ṣadaqah ʿalā al-aqrabīn.*

Earning for charity

Giving in charity was so much dearer to the hearts of the believers that they even used to work and earn in order to be able to offer charity. Abū Masʿūd al-Anṣārī narrated: "Whenever Allāh's Apostle ﷺ ordered us to give in charity, we used to go to the market and work as porters and get a *mudd* and then give it in charity. I know someone who has today one hundred thousand (dirhams) while in those days he did not have even one dirham".[272]

Competition

Realising the importance and reward of charity, the Companions of the Prophet ﷺ competed with each other in this regard; some of them would even spend all they possessed in the path of Allāh. ʿUmar ibn al-Khaṭṭāb narrated: "The Apostle of Allāh ﷺ one day commanded us to give *ṣadaqah.* At that time I had some property. I said: 'Today I shall surpass Abū Bakr if I (ever am to) surpass him'. I therefore brought half my property. The Apostle of Allāh ﷺ asked: 'What did you leave for your family?' I replied: 'The same amount'. Abū Bakr brought all that he had with him'. The Apostle of Allāh ﷺ asked him: 'What did you leave for your family?' He replied: 'I left Allāh and His Apostle for them'. I said: 'I shall never compete with you in anything'."[273]

Imām Abū ʿUmar al-Maqdisī used to say to his family: "If you do not give charity, then who will give it on your behalf? And if you do not give to the beggar, someone else will give to him".[274]

TYPES OF VOLUNTARY CHARITY

Charity is a broad concept in Islam. It is not confined to money; rather it includes all good deeds, so even poor people can share many aspects of charity. In fact, many of these charitable acts have more value than spending money. Some of the *aḥādīth* conveying this meaning are given below:

272 al-Nasāʾī, *k. al-zakāh, b. juhd al-muqill.*

273 Abū Dāwūd, *k. al-zakāh, b. fī al-rukhṣah fī dhālik*; al-Tirmidhī, *k. al-manāqib, b. fī manāqib abī bakr.*

274 al-Dhahabī, *Siyar aʿlām al-nubalāʾ* xxii. 7-8.

Every good is a charity

Jābir ibn ᶜAbdullāh and Ḥudhayfah ibn al-Yamān reported that the Messenger of Allāh ﷺ said: "Every act of goodness is a charity".[275] Abū Mūsā al-Ashᶜarī narrated that the Prophet ﷺ said: "Every Muslim has to give in charity'. The people asked: 'O Messenger of Allāh, if someone has nothing to give, what should he do?' He said: 'He should work with his hands and benefit himself and give in charity from what he earns'. The people further asked: 'If he cannot find even that?' He replied: 'He should help the needy who appeal for help'. Then the people asked: 'If he cannot do that?' He replied: 'Then he should perform good deeds and keep away from evil deeds and this will be regarded as charitable deeds'."[276]

Abū Hurayrah narrated that the Messenger of Allāh ﷺ said: "Charity is due for every joint of a person's body every day the sun rises. To administer justice between two people is charity. To assist a man upon his mount so that he may ride it is charity. To place his luggage on the animal is charity. To remove harm from the road is charity. A good word is charity. Each step taken toward prayer is charity. Removing something harmful from the road is charity".[277]

Abū Dharr al-Ghifārī said: "The Messenger of Allāh ﷺ said: '*Ṣadaqah* is (due) for every person every day the sun rises'. I said: 'O Messenger of Allāh ﷺ from what do we give *ṣadaqah* if we do not possess property?' He said: 'The doors of *ṣadaqah* are *takbīr* [to say: اللهُ أَكْبَرُ, (Allāh is Great); سُبْحَانَ اللهِ (Allāh is free from imperfection); الحَمْدُ لِلَّهِ (All praise is for Allāh); لَا إِلَهَ إِلَّا اللهُ (There is no god other than Allāh); أَسْتَغْفِرُ اللهَ (I seek forgiveness from Allāh); enjoining good; forbidding evil; removing thorns, bones, and stones from the paths of people; guiding the blind; listening to the deaf and dumb until you understand them; guiding a person to his object of need if you know where it is; hurrying with the strength of your legs to one in sorrow who is appealing for help; and supporting the weak with the strength of your arms. These are all the doors of *ṣadaqah*. (The *ṣadaqah*) from you is prescribed for you, and there is a reward for you (even) in copulation with your wife'." This is related by Aḥmad, and the

275 al-Bukhārī, *k. al-adab, b. kull maᶜrūf ṣadaqah*; Muslim, *k. al-zakāh, b. bayān anna ism al-ṣadaqah yaqaᶜu ᶜalā kull nawᶜ min al-maᶜrūf.*

276 ibid.

277 ibid.

wording is his. According to Muslim, they said: "O Messenger of Allāh ﷺ is there a reward if one satisfies his passion?" He said: "Do you know that if he satisfies it unlawfully he has taken a sin upon himself? Likewise, if he satisfies it lawfully he will be rewarded".[278]

Providing water

Saᶜd ibn ᶜUbādah asked: "Messenger of Allāh, my mother Umm Saᶜd has died. What form of *ṣadaqah* is best for her?" He replied: "Water (is best)". Then Saᶜd dug a well and said: "It is for Umm Saᶜd".[279]

Planting

Anas ibn Mālik narrated that the Messenger of Allāh ﷺ said: "A Muslim does not plant or sow anything from which a person, an animal, or anything eats but it is considered as a charity from him".[280]

Smiling

Abū Dharr narrated that the Messenger of Allāh ﷺ said: "Do not consider any good deed as minor, even if it is to meet your brother with a smiling face".[281]

CONTINUOUS CHARITY

Abū Hurayrah narrated that the Messenger of Allāh ﷺ said: "When a person dies his deeds end, except for three: a continuous charity, knowledge from which benefit is derived, or a pious child invoking Allāh for him".[282]

CHARITY ON BEHALF OF THE DEAD

ᶜĀ'ishah said that a person came to the Apostle of Allāh ﷺ and said: "My mother died suddenly without having made any will. I think she would

278 Muslim, *k. al-zakāh, b. bayān anna ism al-ṣadaqah yaqaᶜu ᶜalā kull nawᶜ min al-maᶜrūf.*

279 Abū Dāwūd, *k. al-zakāh, b. faḍl saqy al-mā';* al-Nasā'ī, *k. al-waṣāyā, b. dhikr al-ikhtilāf ᶜalā sufyān.*

280 al-Bukhārī, *k. al-adab, b. raḥmat al-nās wa al-bahā'im;* Muslim, *k. al-musāqāh, b. faḍl al-ghars wa al-zarᶜ.*

281 Muslim, *k. al-zakāh, b. istiḥbāb ṭalaqat al-wajh.*

282 Muslim, *k. al-waṣiyyah, b. mā yalḥaqu al-insāna min al-thawāb baᶜda wafātihī.*

have definitely given charity if she had been able to speak. Would she have a reward if I gave charity on her behalf?" He (the Prophet) said: Yes".[283]

GIVING ALL OF ONE'S WEALTH

It is allowed for a trader who is strong in his faith to donate all his wealth in charity. ʿUmar ibn al-Khaṭṭāb narrated: "The Apostle of Allāh ﷺ one day commanded us to give *ṣadaqah.* At that time I had some property. I said: 'Today I shall surpass Abū Bakr if I (ever am to) surpass him. I therefore brought half my property. The Apostle of Allāh ﷺ asked: 'What did you leave for your family?' I replied: 'The same amount'. Abū Bakr brought all that he had with him'. The Apostle of Allāh ﷺ asked him: 'What did you leave for your family?' He replied: 'I left Allāh and His Apostle for them'. I said: 'I shall never compete with you in anything'."[284]

However, if someone does not have a business or regular income and he is not strong in his faith, then it is disliked for him to give all his wealth in charity. Jābir narrated: "While we were with the Messenger of Allāh ﷺ a man came with what was like an egg of gold. He said: 'O Messenger of Allāh I obtained this from buried treasure, so take it. It is charity, and I do not possess anything other than it'. The Messenger of Allāh ﷺ turned away from him and the man then approached him from the direction of his left side. The Messenger of Allāh ﷺ then turned away from him again and he approached him from behind. Then the Messenger of Allāh ﷺ took it and threw it at him. If it had hit him, it would have injured him. Then he said: 'One of you comes with all his property to make *ṣadaqah,* then after [giving all he had] he sits [by the road] begging from the people. *Ṣadaqah* is given by the one who is rich'."[285]

WHO DESERVES CHARITY?

Charity should be given first to one's own children and relatives. ʿĀ'ishah narrated: A lady along with her two daughters came to me

283 al-Bukhārī, *k. al-janā'iz, b. mawt al-faj'at al-baghtah*; Muslim, *k. al-zakāh, b. wuṣūl thawāb al-ṣadaqah ʿan al-mayyit ilayh.*

284 Abū Dāwūd, *k. al-zakāh, b. fī al-rukhṣah fī dhālik*; al-Tirmidhī, *k. al-manāqib, b. fī manaqib abī bakr.*

285 Abū Dāwūd, *k. al-zakāh, b. al-rajul yukhriju min mālihī.*

asking (for some alms), but she found nothing with me except one date which I gave to her and she divided it between her two daughters, and did not eat anything herself, and then she got up and left. Then the Prophet ﷺ came in and I informed him about this story. He said: "Whoever is put on trial by these daughters and he treats them generously (with benevolence) then these daughters will act as a shield for him from Hell-Fire".[286]

Abū Hurayrah narrated that the Prophet ﷺ said: "The best charity is that which is practiced by a wealthy person. And start giving first to your dependents".[287] Abū Hurayrah also reported from Allāh's Messenger ﷺ as saying: "Of the dīnār you spend in Allāh's path, or to set free a slave, or as a *ṣadaqah* given to one in need, or to support your family, the one yielding the greatest reward is that which you spent on your family".[288] Abū Masʿūd reported from Allāh's Messenger ﷺ as saying: "When a Muslim spends on his family seeking reward for it from Allāh, it counts for him as *ṣadaqah*".[289]

Abū Qilābah narrated from Abū Asmā', who narrated from Thawbān who said Allāh's Messenger ﷺ said: "The most excellent dīnār is one that a person spends on his family, and the dīnār which he spends on his animal in Allāh's path, and the dīnār he spends on his companions in Allāh's path". Abū Qilābah said: "Who is the person with greater reward than a person who spends on young members of his family (and thus) preserves (saves them from want) (and by virtue of which) Allāh brings profit for them and makes them rich".[290]

Abū Hurayrah narrated that the Prophet ﷺ commanded to give *ṣadaqah.* A man said: "Messenger of Allāh, I have a dīnār". He said: "Spend it on yourself". He again said: "I have another". He said: "Spend it on your children". He again said: "I have another". "He said: Spend it on your wife". He again said: "I have another". He said: "Spend it on

286 al-Tirmidhī, *k. al-birr wa al-ṣilah, b. mā jā'a fī al-nafaqah ʿalā al-banāt wa al-akhawāt.*

287 al-Bukhārī, *k. al-zakāh, b. lā ṣadaqah illā ʿan ẓahr ghinā;* Muslim, *k. al-zakāh, b. bayān ann al-yad al-ʿulyā khayr.*

288 Muslim, *k. al-zakāh, b. faḍl al-nafaqah ʿalā al-ʿiyāl wa al-mamlūk.*

289 al-Bukhārī, *k. al-nafaqāt, b. faḍl al-nafaqah ʿalā al-ahl;* Muslim, *k. al-zakāh, b. faḍl al-nafaqah wa al-ṣadaqah ʿalā al-aqrabīn.*

290 Muslim, *k. al-zakāh, b. faḍl al-nafaqah ʿalā al-ʿiyāl wa al-mamlūk.*

your servant". He finally said: "I have another. He replied: "You know best (what to do with it)".[291]

Charity to non-Muslims

One can give voluntary charity to non-Muslim relatives, neighbours or those in peace with Muslims. Allāh praised a group of people (for this) when He said: "*And they feed, for His love, the indigent, orphan, and captive*"[292]. Allāh says: "*Allāh has not forbidden you with regard to those who have not made war against you on account of [your] faith and have not driven you out of your homes to deal kindly and justly with them; Allāh loves those who are just*"[293].

Asmā', the daughter of Abū Bakr, reports: "My mother came to me and she was a polytheist. I said: 'O Messenger of Allāh, (peace be upon him) my mother came to me and she is inclined (to Islam), may I make a gift to her of the kind due to a relative?' He said: 'Yes, give (in that way) to your mother".[294]

Ibrāhīm ibn Muhājir says: "I asked Ibrāhīm al-Nakhaᶜī about giving *ṣadaqah* to non-Muslims. He answered: "Do not give them from zakāh; but give them from voluntary charity".[295] Jābir ibn Zayd said: "Do not give a Jew or Christian from the zakāh; there is no harm in giving them charity".[296]

Charity on the animal

Abū Hurayrah reported that the Messenger of Allāh ﷺ said: "While a man was walking along a road, he became very thirsty and found a well. He lowered himself into the well, drank, and came out. Then he saw a dog protruding its tongue out with thirst. The man said: 'This dog has become exhausted from thirst in the same way as I'. He lowered himself into the well again and filled his shoe with water. Then he took the dog by the mouth until he had raised himself. He gave the dog some water to drink. He thanked Allāh, and [his sins were] forgiven". They asked:

291 Abū Dāwūd, *k. al-zakāh, b. fī ṣilat al-raḥim;* al-Nasā'ī, *k. al-zakāh, b. tafsīr.*

292 *al-Dahr* 6.

293 *al-Mumtaḥinah* 8.

294 Muslim, *k. al-zakāh, b. faḍl al-nafaqah wa al-ṣadaqahᶜalā al-aqrabīn* ....

295 Ibn Abī Shaybah, *al-Muṣannaf*, vi. 516.

296 ibid., vi. 517.

"O Messenger of Allāh ﷺ Is there a reward for us in our animals?" He said: "There is a reward in every living thing".[297]

Abū Hurayrah also narrated that the Messenger of Allāh ﷺ said: "While a dog was walking around a well, his thirst was near to killing him. One of the prostitutes of the *Banū* Isra'il saw him. She took off her shoe and drew water for him with it in order to quench his thirst. For that she was forgiven by Allāh".[298]

ACCEPTING WHAT COMES WITHOUT BEGGING AND WITHOUT AVARICIOUS DESIRE

It has been said earlier that begging without need is not allowed; similarly greed and looking for something to come is not encouraged. If someone receives anything without begging or desiring then he should accept it as it is from Allāh. ᶜAbdullāh ibn ᶜUmar reported that he had heard his father ᶜUmar ibn Khaṭṭāb saying: "The Messenger of Allāh ﷺ gave me a gift, but I said: 'Give it to one who needs it more than I do'. He gave me wealth for the second time but I said: 'Give it to one who needs it more than I do'. Upon this the Messenger of Allāh ﷺ said: 'Take out of this wealth which comes to you without you being avaricious and without begging, but in other circumstances do not let your heart hanker after it'." Sālim ibn ᶜAbdullāh reported on the authority of his father who said: "The Messenger of Allāh ﷺ gave to ᶜUmar ibn Khaṭṭāb some gift. ᶜUmar said to him: 'Messenger of Allāh, give it to one who needs it more than I'. Upon this the Messenger of Allāh ﷺ said: 'Take it; either keep it with you or give it as a charity, and whatever comes to you in the form of this type of wealth, without you being avaricious or begging for it, accept it, but in other circumstances do not let your heart hanker over it'. And it was on account of this that Ibn ᶜUmar never begged anything from anyone nor refused anything that was given to him'."[299]

297 al-Bukhārī, *k. al-musāqāh, b. faḍl saqy al-mā'.*

298 al-Bukhārī, *k. bad' al-khalq, b. idhā waqaᶜa al-dhubāb fī sharāb aḥadikum…*

299 al-Bukhārī, *k. al-zakāh, b. man aᶜṭāhullāhu shay'an min ghayr mas'alah;* Muslim, *k. al-zakāh, b. ibāḥat al-akhdh liman uᶜṭiya min ghayr….*

A WOMAN GIVING CHARITY FROM HER HUSBAND'S WEALTH

It is allowed for a woman to give charity from her husband's wealth if she knows that he will be pleased. ʿĀ'ishah narrated that the Messenger of Allāh ﷺ said: "When a woman gives in charity some of the foodstuff (which she has in her house) without spoiling it, she will receive the reward for what she has spent, and her husband will receive the reward because of his earning, and the storekeeper will also have a reward similar to it. The reward of one will not decrease the reward of the others".[300]

If it is a large amount or she feels that her husband does not like it if she spends without his permission, then she should ask his permission before spending any money. Abū Umāmah reports that he had heard the Messenger of Allāh ﷺ saying in his sermon during the year of the Farewell Pilgrimage: "The wife should not spend anything from the household of her husband without his permission". someone asked: "O Messenger of Allāh ﷺ not food either?" He said: "That is the most excellent of our holdings".[301]

However, a woman is allowed to give small amounts without seeking the permission of her husband. It is related from Asma', daughter of Abū Bakr, that she said to the Messenger of Allāh ﷺ: "Zubayr is a well-off man. A man in need approached me and I gave him *ṣadaqah* from my husband's household without seeking his permission". The Messenger of Allāh ﷺ said: "Give what you are in the habit of giving of what is small, and do not store property away, for Allāh shall withhold His blessings from you".[302]

WHAT INVALIDATES CHARITY

It is unlawful to show off charity or remind one of its favour. That invalidates all the reward. Allāh warns: "*O you who believe Do not invalidate your ṣadaqah by reminders of your generosity or by injury, like those who spend their property to be seen by men*".[303] Abū Dharr narrated that the Messenger of Allāh ﷺ said: "There are three [types of people]. Allāh shall not

300 al-Bukhārī, *k. al-zakāh, b. ajr al-khādim idhā taṣaddaqa;* Muslim, *k. al-zakāh, b. ajr al-khāzin al-amīn wa al-mar'ah ....*

301 al-Tirmidhī, *k. al-zakāh, b. fī nafaqat al-mar'ah min bayt zawjihā.*

302 Abū Dāwūd, *k. al-zakāh, b. fī al-shuḥḥ.*

303 *al-Baqarah* 264.

speak to them, notice them, or sanctify them; and for them is a grievous penalty". Abū Dharr inquired: "O Messenger of Allāh, who are the ones who have gone wrong and astray?" He replied: "Those who through conceit lengthen their garments to make them hang on the ground, who give nothing without reproach, and who sell their merchandise swearing untruthfully to its quality".[304]

Charity from unlawful income

Charity is not allowed from unlawful income. Abū Hurayrah reported Allāh's Messenger ﷺ as saying: O people, Allāh is Good and He therefore accepts only that which is good. And Allāh commanded the believers as He commanded the Messengers by saying: "*O Messengers, eat of the good things, and do good deeds; verily I am aware of what you do*". And He said: "*O those who believe, eat of the good things that We gave you*" He then made a mention of a person who travels widely, his hair dishevelled and covered with dust. He lifts his hand towards the sky (and thus makes the supplication): "O Lord, O Lord," whereas his diet is unlawful, his drink is unlawful, and his clothes are unlawful and his nourishment is unlawful. How then can his supplication be accepted? Abū Hurayrah narrated that the Messenger of Allāh ﷺ said: "If one gives in charity that which equals one date-fruit from pure earnings, and Allāh accepts only from pure earnings, Allāh takes it in His right (hand), then enlarges its reward for that person (who has given it), as anyone of you nurtures his pony, so much so that it becomes as large as a mountain".[305]

KEEPING CHARITY SECRET

It is allowed to give charity, especially obligatory charity, in public if it encourages others. Allāh, Exalted is He, says: "*If you publicise your almsgiving, it is alright, but if you hide it and give it to the poor, it will be better for you*"[306].

It is preferable for voluntary charity to be offered in secret. Abū Hurayra narrated: "The Prophet ﷺ said: Seven people will be shaded by

304 Abū Dāwūd, *k. al-libās, b. mā jā'a fī isbāl al-izār.*

305 al-Bukhārī, *k. al-zakāh, b. al-ṣadaqah min kasb ṭayyib;* Muslim, *k. al-zakāh, b. qabūl al-ṣadaqah min al-kasb al-ṭayyib wa tarbiyatihā.*

306 *al-Baqarah* 271.

Allāh under His shade on the day when there will be no shade except His. They are: a just ruler; a young man who has been brought up in the worship of Allāh, (i.e. worship of Allāh alone sincerely from his childhood), a man whose heart is attached to the mosque (who offers the five compulsory congregational prayers in the mosque); two who love each other only for Allāh's sake and they meet and part in Allāh's cause only; a man who refuses the call of a charming woman of noble birth for illegal sexual intercourse with her and says I am afraid of Allāh; a person that practices charity so secretly that his left hand does not know what his right hand has given (i.e. nobody knows how much he has given in charity); a person who remembers Allāh in seclusion and his eyes flood with tears".[307]

GIVING THANKS

Thanking someone who has done you some good is your reward to him. It is highly recommended that whenever anyone does good to someone the one receiving should thank him. Gratitude can be expressed by doing something similar or better, or by a prayer for the doer of good. ʿAbdullāh ibn ʿUmar reports that the Messenger of Allāh ﷺ said: "Whoever seeks the protection of Allāh, give him protection. Whoever asks you in the name of Allāh, grant him refuge. Whoever does a good deed to you, reward him and if you do not find anything, invoke Allāh on his behalf until you know that he has been rewarded".[308] Abū Hurayrah reported that the Messenger of Allāh ﷺ is reported to have said: "Whoever does not thank people, does not thank Allāh".[309] Usāmah ibn Zayd narrated that the Messenger of Allāh ﷺ said: "To whom a good deed is done and then he says to its doer: 'May Allāh reward you with goodness,' has praised him fully".[310]

Makkī ibn Ibrāhīm says: "We were in the class of Ibn Jurayj; a beggar came and asked him for some charity. Ibn Jurayj said to his secretary: 'give him a dīnār'. The secretary said: 'I do not have anything other

307 al-Bukhārī, *k. al-adhān, b. man jalasa fī al-masjid yantaẓir al-ṣalāh wa faḍl al-masājid;* Muslim, *k. al-zakāh, b. faḍl ikhfā' al-ṣadaqah.*

308 Aḥmad ibn Ḥanbal, *al-Musnad, musnad ʿabdillah ibn ʿumar.*

309 Abū Dāwūd, *k. al-adab, b. fī shukr al-maʿrūf;* al-Tirmidhī, *k. al-birr wa al-ṣilah, b. mā jā'a fī al-shukr liman aḥsana ilayk.*

310 al-Tirmidhī, *k. al-birr wa al-ṣilah, b. mā jā'a fī al-thanā' bi al-maʿrūf.*

than a dīnār, if I give it to him then you and your family will remain hungry'. Ibn Jurayj became angry and said: 'Give it to him'. Makkī ibn Ibrāhīm adds: "We still were in the class, a man brought to him a letter and a sack which was sent to him by one of his friends. The letter read: 'I have sent to you 50 dīnārs'. Ibn Jurayj untied the sack and counted the dīnār*s*, they totalled 51. Then Ibn Jurayj said to his secretary: 'You gave, and Allāh returned it back to you and added 50 dīnārs'."[311]

311 al-Tirmidhī, *k. al-birr wa al-ṣilah, b. mā jā'a fī al-thanā' bi al-maʿrūf.*

كتاب الصوم

THE BOOK OF FASTING

Chapter 1: The Importance of Fasting

The word for fasting in Arabic is *ṣawm.* Literally it means 'abstaining from'. As an Islamic term, *ṣawm* means abstaining from eating, drinking, and sexual intercourse from dawn to sunset. Fasting is an effective means for the purification of the soul, for strengthening the discipline of desire and self-control. Like *ṣalāh* and zakāh, it has been part of God's religion from the very beginning. The Qur'ān says: "*O you who have believed, decreed upon you is fasting as it was decreed upon those before you that you may become righteous*".[312] Fasting strengthens one's fear of Allāh, morality and self-control and deepens one's consciousness of Allāh.

The fact that fasting is a means to moral elevation is evident because Allāh not only imposes checks upon eating, drinking and sexual intercourse from dawn to sunset, but also exhorts His slaves to refrain from other foul acts such as backbiting, indulging in foul speech, telling lies, etc. Abū Hurayrah narrated: The Prophet ﷺ said, "Whoever does not give up forged speech and evil actions, Allāh is not in need of his leaving his food and drink".[313]

During the month of Ramaḍān the whole atmosphere is permeated with piety and devotion to Allāh. There is one extra congregational prayer, *Tarāwīḥ*, offered during the night, in which the Qur'ān is recited and Muslims are reminded of the fact that it was during the month of

312 *al-Baqarah* 183.

313 al-Bukhārī, *k. al-ṣawm, b. man lam yadaʿ qawl al-zūr.*

Ramaḍān that the revelation of the Qur'ān commenced. *Ṣadaqah* is also given with greater zeal and fervour during this month. In this way, the whole Muslim society is inspired with the love of Allāh. Abū Hurayrah reported from Allāh's Messenger ﷺ as saying: "When Ramaḍān begins, the gates of Heaven are opened, the gates of Hell are locked, and the devils are chained".[314]

THE VIRTUE OF FASTING

Since fasting is of such great importance in Islam, the Prophet ﷺ encouraged believers in many ways to observe both the obligatory and the voluntary fasting. Abū Hurayrah narrated that the Messenger of Allāh ﷺ said: "Fasting is a shield. Therefore, the person fasting should avoid talking about desire and should not behave foolishly and impudently, and if somebody fights with him or abuses him, he should tell him, 'I am fasting". The Prophet ﷺ added, "By Him in Whose Hands my soul is, the smell coming out from the mouth of a fasting person is better with Allāh than the smell of musk. Allāh says about the fasting person, 'He has left his food, drink and desires for My sake. The fast is for Me. So I will reward (the fasting person) for it and the reward of good deeds is multiplied ten times".[315]

Sahl ibn Saʿd narrated that the Prophet ﷺ said: "There is a gate in Paradise called al-Rayyān, and those who observe fasts will enter through it on the Day of Resurrection and none except them will enter through it. It will be said, 'Where are those who used to observe fasts?' They will get up, and none except them will enter through it. After their entry, the gate will be closed and nobody will enter through it".[316]

Abū Hurayrah narrates that the Messenger of Allāh ﷺ said: "Whoever gives two kinds (of things or property) in charity for Allāh's Cause, will be called from the gates of Paradise and will be addressed, 'O slaves of Allāh here is prosperity'. So, whoever was amongst the people who used to offer their prayers, will be called from the gate of the prayer; and

314 al-Bukhārī, *k. al-ṣawm, b. hal yuqālu ramaḍān;* Muslim, *k. al-ṣiyām, b. faḍl shahr ramaḍān.*

315 al-Bukhārī, *k. al-ṣawm, b. hal yaqūlu innī ṣā'im idhā shutima;* Muslim, *k. al-ṣiyām, b. faḍl al-ṣiyām.*

316 al-Bukhārī, *k. bad' al-khalq, b. ṣifat abwāb al-jannah;* Muslim, *k. al-ṣiyām, b. faḍl al-ṣiyām.*

whoever was amongst the people who used to participate in *jihād*, will be called from the gate of *jihād*; and whoever was amongst those who used to observe fasts, will be called from the gate of al-Rayyān; whoever was amongst those who used to give in charity, will be called from the gate of charity". Abū Bakr said: "Let my parents be sacrificed for you, O Allāh's Apostle. No distress or need will befall him who will be called from those gates. Will there be any one who will be called from all these gates?' The Prophet replied: 'Yes, and I hope you will be among them'."[317]

THE OBJECTIVES OF FASTING

The purpose of fasting has been described by Allāh Himself. Allāh, Exalted is He, says: "*O you who have believed, decreed upon you is fasting as it was decreed upon those before you that you may become righteous*". [318] Abū Hurayrah narrated that the Messenger of Allāh ﷺ said: "Fasting is a shield. So, the person observing fast should not use obscene language and should not behave foolishly and impudently, and if somebody fights with him or abuses him, he should tell him twice, 'I am fasting'."[319]

Imām Ghazālī remarks: "The object of fasting is that man should produce within him a semblance of the Divine Attribute of *Ṣamadiyyah* (being above lower things), that he should, as far as possible, take after the angels and cast off the beastly propensities because the angels are free from desire and the place of man too is above the animal and he has, further, been given the power of discrimination to resist the pressure of inordinate appetites. He is, of course, inferior to angels in the sense that desire often overpowers him and he has to strive hard to subdue it. When he succumbs to sensual propensities he degenerates into the lowliest of the low and joins the herds of cattle when he conquers them he attains the dizzy heights of the heavenly host and begins to dwell on the plane of the angels".[320]

Emphasising the same point Imām Ibn al-Qayyim says: "The purpose of fasting is that the spirit of man is released from the clutches of

317 al-Bukhārī, *k. al-ṣawm, b. al-rayyān li al-sā'imin*; Muslim, *k. al-zakāh, b. man jamaʿa al-ṣadaqah wa aʿmāl al-birr.*

318 *al-Baqarah* 183.

319 al-Bukhārī, *k. al-ṣawm, b. hal yaqūlu innī ṣā'im idhā shutima;* Muslim, *k. al-ṣiyām, b. faḍl al-ṣiyām.*

320 al-Ghazālī, *Iḥyā' ʿulūm al-dīn,* i. 332.

desire and moderation prevails in his carnal self, and, through it, he realises the goal of purification and everlasting felicity. It is aimed at curtailing the intensity of desire and lust by means of hunger and thirst, at inducing man to realise how many were there in the world like him who had to go even without a small quantity of food, at making it difficult for the devil to deceive him, and at restraining his organs from turning towards things in which there was the loss of both the worlds. Fasting, thus, is the bridle of the God-fearing, the shield of the crusaders and the discipline of the virtuous.... Fasting is most efficacious in the protection of the external limbs and internal organs. It guards against disorders resulting from the accumulation of effete matter. It expels the toxins that are injurious to health and cures the ailments which develop in the body due to over-indulgence. It is beneficial for health and most helpful in leading a life of piety and good-doing ... Hence, a person who wishes to marry but does not have the means to support a family is advised to observe fasting. It has been prescribed as a sovereign remedy for him, the purpose being to demonstrate that since the advantages of fasting were evident from the point of view of common sense Allāh has enjoined it as an act of mercy for the protection of His slaves".[321]

Shāh Walīullah writes: "There are two ways of reduction in diet. One is to eat sparingly and the other is to observe such a long interval between meals that the object of curtailment is gained. In the Sharīᶜah the latter course has been prescribed because it induces an adequate appreciation of the torments of hunger and thirst and strikes at the root of the carnal appetites, a definite reduction in whose force and intensity is noticed. On the contrary, in the former case, these results are not obtained owing to the continuity of meals. Besides, it is not possible to lay down a general rule for reduction as the circumstances differ from one individual to another. One person may manage on half the quantity of food that another needs. Thus, if a general limit is laid down for everyone, one will profit by it and the other will suffer.... It, again, was desirable, that the hours of fasting were not so long as to entail unbearable hardship as, for instance, three days and three nights. Apart from being opposed to the spirit of the Sharīᶜah, it would also have generally been impracticable ...It was necessary that the opportunity to

321 Ibn al-Qayyim, *Zād al-maᶜād,* ii. 28-30.

abjure food and drink occurred repeatedly and in succession in order that it could serve the purpose of an exercise in submission. To go without food only once would avail nothing".[322]

322 al-Dihlawī, *Ḥujjatullāh al-bālighah,* ii. 76.

Chapter 2: Sighting the Moon

The Islamic calendar, like many other religious calendars, is a lunar calendar. The beginning of the month is marked by sighting the crescent. As soon as the crescent is sighted the month has started and it will continue until the sighting of the next crescent. Thus, a lunar month will either be of 29 days or 30 days. ʿAbdullāh ibn ʿUmar reported from Allāh's Messenger ﷺ who said: "The month is thus, and thus, and thus, and he flapped his hands with all their fingers twice. But at the third turn, he folded his right thumb or left thumb (in order to give an idea of 29)".[323] In another version of the same ḥadīth, Allāh's Messenger ﷺ said: "The month is thus and thus (he then withdrew his thumb at the third time)". He then said: "Fast when you see it, and break your fast when you see it, and if the weather is cloudy calculate it as 30 days".[324]

People must look for the new moon on the 29th of the month of Shaʿbān and if they sight it, then they fast, but if it is hidden from their sight, then they complete the number of days for Shaʿbān, that is 30, then they start fasting. ʿĀ'ishah narrated that the Apostle of Allāh ﷺ used to count the days in Shaʿbān in a manner he did not count any other month; then he fasted when he sighted the new moon of Ramaḍān; but if the weather was cloudy he counted 30 days and then fasted".[325] ʿAbdullāh ibn ʿUmar reported that the Messenger of Allāh ﷺ mentioned Ramaḍān and said: "Do not fast unless you see the crescent (of Ramaḍān), and do not give up fasting until you see the crescent (of Shawwāl), but if the sky is overcast, then act on estimation (i.e. count Shaʿbān as 30 days)".[326] Imām Muḥammad says after narrating this ḥadīth: "We adhere to this, and this is the opinion of Abū Ḥanīfah".[327]

323 al-Bukhārī, *k. al-ṣawm, b. qawl al-nabī ṣallallāhu ʿalayhi wa sallam idhā ra'aytum al-hilāla faṣūmū;* Muslim, *k. al-ṣiyām, b. wujūb ṣawm ramaḍān li ru'yat al-hilāl.*

324 ibid.

325 Abū Dāwūd, *k. al-ṣawm, b. idhā ughmiya al-shahr.*

326 al-Bukhārī, *k. al-ṣawm, b. qawl al-nabī ṣallallāhu ʿalayhi wa sallam idhā ra'aytum al-hilāla faṣūmū*; Muslim, *k. al-ṣiyām, b. wujūb ṣawm ramaḍān li ru'yat al-hilāl.*

327 Muhammad, *al-Muwaṭṭa'*, 122.

If the horizon is clear

If the horizon is clear and there is no dust or cloud in the sky, then the testimony of one or two people is not accepted until a large group – whose report establishes certain knowledge – sights it.[328]

If the horizon is not clear

If there is some reason, for not being able to see the moon, such as clouds of dust in the sky, then the testimony of one just person's sighting of the new moon of Ramaḍān irrespective of whether it is a man or a woman will be accepted.[329] ʿAbdullāh ibn ʿUmar narrated that the people looked for the moon, so I informed the Apostle of Allāh ﷺ that I had sighted it. He fasted and commanded the people to fast".[330]

ʿAbdullāh ibn ʿAbbās narrated that a Bedouin came to the Prophet ﷺ and said: "I have sighted the moon, that is, of Ramaḍān. He (the Prophet ﷺ,) asked: 'Do you testify that there is no god but Allāh?' He replied: 'Yes'. He again asked: 'Do you testify that Muḥammad is the Apostle of Allāh?' He replied: 'Yes'. And he testified that he had sighted the moon. The Prophet ﷺ said: 'Bilāl, announce to the people that they must fast tomorrow'."[331]

As for the sighting of the crescent of Shawwāl when the horizon is not clear, the *imām* will not accept the testimony of one person; rather there should be the testimony of two just males or one male and two females.[332] ʿAlī says: "When two just men bear the testimony of sighting the crescent, then break the fast".[333]

If someone alone sees the crescent

Whoever sees the new moon of Ramaḍān when alone, should fast even

328 al-Samarqandī, *Tuḥfat al-fuqahā'* 165.

329 ibid.

330 Abū Dāwūd, *k. al-ṣawm, b. shahādat al-wāḥid ʿalā ru'yat hilāl ramaḍān*

331 al-Tirmidhī, *k. al-ṣawm, b. mā jā'a fī al-ṣawm bi al-shahādah;* Abū Dāwūd, *k. al-ṣawm, b. shahādat wāḥid ʿalā ru'yat hilāl ramaḍān;* al-Nasā'ī, *k. al-ṣiyām, b. qabūl shahādat al-rajul al-wāḥid ʿalā hilāl shahr ramaḍān;* Ibn Mājah, *k. al-ṣiyām, b. mā jā'a fī al-shahādah ʿalā ru'yat hilāl.*

332 al-Samarqandī, *Tuḥfat al-fuqahā'* 165.

333 Ibn Abī Shaybah, *al-Muṣannaf,* vi. 257.

if the *imām* does not accept his testimony.[334]

Whoever sees the new moon marking the *fiṭr,* i.e. the end of the fast when alone, he should not break his fast; rather, he should continue fasting with the community.[335]

People travelling

If one travels to a place where the month of Ramaḍān started later, one continues fasting with the people as long as the number of one's fast does not exceed 30 days. If the people of the locality continue fasting and one has completed 30 fasts, one should stop fasting, and must wait and pray *ᶜīd* with them. The reason for this is that the lunar month cannot last longer than 30 days.

If someone travels to a place where the people started their fast earlier, then one has to do *ᶜīd* with them, and does not need to do any *qaḍā'* (to perform an act of worship after one has missed its prescribed time) as long as one has fasted 29 days. If one's fast was less than 29 days then one has to do *qaḍā'* until it becomes 29 days, because there is no month lasting less than 29 days.

CONSIDERATIONS OF DIFFERENCE IN LOCATION

According to the most sound opinion, differences in location are not considered. If people of a particular place do not sight the moon, but they receive reliable information from any quarter where the sighting has been established legally, then they should follow it.[336] Ibn al-Mundhir says: "Most jurists say when it is affirmed by the report of the people that the people of any town have sighted it before them, then they have to do *qaḍā*" of the day that they did not fast; this is the opinion of Mālik, Shāfiᶜī, Aḥmad and the people of *Ra'y* (Ḥanafīs).[337]

ASTRONOMICAL CALCULATIONS

Astronomical calculations, being based on accurate computation, help in ascertaining the impossibility of sighting the crescent. The Muslim

334 al-Samarqandī, *Tuḥfat al-fuqahā'* 165.

335 See: al-Mawṣilī, *al-Ikhtiyār lit aᶜlīl al-mukhtār,* i. 168.

336 See: *Fatāwā Muṣṭafā al-Zarqā'* 170-171; al-Mawṣilī, *al-Ikhtiyār lit aᶜlīl al-mukhtār,* i. 168.

337 al-Baghawī, *Sharḥ al-sunna*h, iii. 464.

leader should reject any claim of sighting the moon while such sighting is deemed an astronomical impossibility.

THE SIZE OF THE CRESCENT

The beginning of the month is confirmed by sighting the crescent. If the crescent is not sighted on the 29th, and on the next night the crescent appears bigger than it would normally be on the first night, it is nevertheless counted as the first night of the new month. Abū al-Bakhtarī reported: "We went out to perform *ᶜumrah* and when we encamped in the valley of Nakhlah, we tried to sight the new moon. Some of the people said it was three nights old, and others said that it was two nights old. We then met ᶜAbdullāh ibn ᶜAbbās and told him we had seen the new moon, but that some of the people said it was three nights old and others that it was two nights old. He asked on which night we had seen it; and when we told him we had seen it on such and such night, he said the Prophet of Allāh ﷺ had said: 'Allāh deferred it till the time it is seen, so it is to be reckoned from the night you saw it'."[338]

THE DAY OF DOUBT

If it is cloudy or there is dust on the horizon, and people are unable to sight the crescent, then to fast the next day with the intention of Ramaḍān whilst in doubt is disliked.[339] Abū Isḥāq reported on the authority of Ṣilah ibn Zufar who said: "We were with ᶜAmmār on the day when the appearance of the moon was doubtful. (The meat of a) goat was brought to him. Some people kept aloof from (eating) it. ᶜAmmār said: 'He who keeps fast on this day disobeys Abū al-Qāsim (i.e. the Prophet) ﷺ'."[340] Ḥudhayfah narrated: "The Prophet ﷺ said: 'Do not fast (for Ramaḍān) before the coming of the month until you sight the moon or complete the number (30 days); then fast until you sight the moon or complete the number (of 30 days)."[341]

If the day of doubt is a day during which one used to do *nafl* (supererogatory)fasting, then one is allowed to fast. Abū Hurayrah

338 Muslim, *k. al-ṣiyām, b. bayān annahū lā iᶜtibār bikibar al-hilāl wa ṣigharih.*

339 al-Kāsānī, *Badāʾiᶜ al-ṣanāʾiᶜ*, ii. 562.

340 al-Bukhārī, *k. al-ṣawm, b. qawl al-nabī ṣallallāhu ᶜalayhi wa sallam idhā raʾaytum al-hilāla faṣūmū;* Abū Dāwūd, *k. al-ṣiyām, b. karāhiyat yawm al-shakk.*

341 al-Nasāʾī, *k. al-ṣiyām, dhikr al-ikhtilāf ᶜalā manṣūr.*

narrates: "The Prophet ﷺ said: 'None of you should fast a day or two before the month of Ramaḍān unless he has the habit of fasting, then he can fast that day'."[342] ʿAbdullāh ibn ʿAbbās narrates: "The Prophet ﷺ said: 'Do not fast one day or two days just before Ramaḍān except in the case of a man who has been in the habit of observing a fast (on that day); and do not fast until you sight it (the moon). Then fast until you sight it. If a cloud appears on that day (i.e. 29th of Ramaḍān) then complete the number (30 days) and then end the fasting: a month consists of 29 days."[343]

FOLLOW THE *JAMĀʿAH*

When there is confusion in any locality regarding the beginning of the month, people should follow the *jamāʿah*. *Jamāʿah* means a group of Muslims with a leader. If there is no leader, people must agree to select a leader on the basis of consultation, and then they should follow his decision. Once a decision is made by the *jamāʿah* concerning the beginning of the month, then that is the beginning of the month and people are not allowed to follow their individual opinions in these collective matters. Abū Hurayrah narrates that the Prophet ﷺ said: "The fasting is the day the people fast, and the end of Ramaḍān is on the day when they end it, and the *ʿīd* (festival) of sacrifice is on the day when they sacrifice".[344] The meaning of the ḥadīth is that the fasting and *ʿīd* are done with the *jamāʿah* and the majority of the people.[345]

342 al-Bukhārī, *k. al-ṣawm, b. lā yataqaddamanna ramaḍān bi ṣawm yawm aw yawmayn;* Muslim, *k. al-ṣiyām, b. lā taqaddamu ramaḍān bi ṣawm yawm aw yawmayn.*

343 Abū Dāwūd, *k. al-ṣiyām, b. man qāla fa in ghumma ʿalaykym faṣūmū thalāthīn.*

344 Abū Dāwūd, *k. al-ṣawm, b. idhā akhṭa'a al-qawm al-hilāl;* al-Tirmidhī, *k. al-ṣawm, b. mā jā'a al-ṣawm yawma taṣūmūn.*

345 al-Baghawī, *Sharḥ al-sunnah,* iii. 465.

Chapter 3: A description of Fasting

Fasting consists of certain *farḍs* (a definitive obligation) acts and some *Sunnahs*, which are explained below:

THE *FARḌS* IN FASTING

There are two *farḍs* in fasting:

1- Desisting from eating, drinking and sexual intercourse during the day, from daybreak to sunset.[346] Allāh, Exalted is He, says: "*So now, have relations with them and seek that which Allāh has decreed for you. And eat and drink until the white thread of dawn becomes distinct to you from the black thread [of night]. Then complete the fast until the sunset*'.[347] White thread means light of the day, and black thread means the darkness of the night.

ʿAbdullāh ibn ʿAbbās while explaining the Qur'ānic verse: "*O you who have believed, decreed upon you is fasting as it was decreed upon those before you that you may become righteous,*" said: "During the lifetime of the Prophet ﷺ when the people offered night prayer, they were asked to abstain from food and drink and (intercourse with) women, they kept fasting till the next night. A man betrayed himself and had intercourse with his wife after he had offered the night prayer, and he continued his fast. So Allāh, Exalted is He, intended to make it (fasting) easy for the living, thus providing a concession and benefit. Allāh, the Glorified, said: '*Allāh knows what you used to do secretly among yourselves*'. By this Allāh benefited the people and provided concession and ease to them'."[348]

Al-Barā' narrated: "It was the custom among the Companions of Muḥammad ﷺ when fasting and food was presented for them (for *ifṭār* – breaking of the fast), however, they fell asleep before eating, they would not eat that night and the following day until sunset. Qays ibn Ṣirmah al-Anṣārī was fasting and came to his wife at the time of *ifṭār* and asked her whether she had anything to eat. She replied: 'No, but I will go and

346 al-Samarqandī, *Tuḥfat al-fuqahā'* 162.

347 *al-Baqarah* 187.

348 Abū Dāwūd, *k. al-ṣiyām, b. mabda' farḍ al-ṣiyām.*

bring some for you'. He used to do hard work during the day and so was overwhelmed by sleep and slept. When his wife came and saw him, she said: 'Disappointment for you'. When it was midday on the following day, he fainted. The Prophet ﷺ was informed about the whole matter and the following verses were revealed: *'You are permitted to go to your wives (for sexual relations) on the night of fasting'*. So, they were overjoyed by it. And then Allāh also revealed: *'And eat and drink until the white thread of dawn appears to you distinct from the black thread, then complete your fasting till the nightfall'*."[349]

ᶜAdī ibn Ḥātim narrated: "When the verse '*Until the white thread appears to you, distinct from the black thread,*' was revealed, I took two (hair) strings, one black and the other white, and kept them under my pillow and went on looking at them throughout the night but could not make anything out of it. So, the next morning I went to the Messenger of Allāh ﷺ and told him the whole story. He said to me: 'That verse means the darkness of the night and the whiteness of the dawn'."[350]

ᶜUmar ibn al-Khaṭṭāb narrates: "The Messenger of Allāh ﷺ said: 'When night falls from this side and the day vanishes from this side and the sun sets, then the fasting person should break his fast".[351]

2- Making *niyyah* (intention) because fasting is an act of worship and all acts of worship require intention. Allāh says: "*And they were not commanded, but to worship Allāh, making the religion sincerely for Him*".[352] The Prophet ﷺ said: "Every action is based upon intention. For everyone is that which he intended. Whoever made the migration to Allāh and His Prophet, then his migration is to Allāh and His Prophet. Whoever's migration was for something of this world or for the purpose of marriage, then his migration was to what he migrated to".[353] As a result of this verse and this ḥadīth, all scholars agree that fasting, like any other act of worship, cannot be valid without intention.

Intention, as has been explained in the Book of *Ṣalāh* (*Al-Fiqh Al-Islāmī* – Volume 1), is an act of the heart; one does not need to utter anything

349 *al-Baqarah* 187.

350 Muslim, *k. al-ṣiyām, b. bayān anna al-dukhūla fī al-ṣawm yaḥṣulu ....*

351 al-Bukhārī, *k. al-ṣawm, b. matā yaḥillu fiṭr al-ṣā'im;* Muslim, *k. al-ṣiyām, b. bayān waqt inqiḍā' al-ṣawm wa khurūj al-nahār.*

352 *al-Bayyinah* 5.

353 al-Bukhārī, *k. bad' al-waḥy.*

verbally. There are two timings for making intention depending on the types of fasts:

i- In the fasting of the *qaḍā'*, *kaffārah* and vows of un-specified days, one must make intention before the dawn. All the scholars agreed on this.[354] Ḥafṣah narrated that the Prophet ﷺ said: "The fasting of those who did not make their intention before the dawn is no fasting for them".[355]

ii-In the obligatory fasting of Ramaḍān, vows of fasting on specific days, and all *Sunnah* and *nafl* fasting, one can make intention any time from the night until before the *zawāl* (midday, when the sun begins to decline).[356] ᶜĀ'ishah narrated that: "The Prophet ﷺ used to come to me in the day and ask: 'Do you have anything to eat?' I would say: 'No'. Then he would say: 'Then I am fasting'."[357] Umm al-Dardā' narrates: "Abū al-Dardā' would ask: 'Do you have food? If we said: 'No', he would reply: 'Then I am fasting'."[358] The same was the practice of Abū Ṭalḥah, Abū Hurayrah, ᶜAbdullāh ibn ᶜAbbās and Ḥudhayfah.[359]

Those places where the days or nights are very long

In these places, nevertheless, within any period of 24 hours, both sunrise and sunset are witnessed. In such places, the period of fasting will be calculated in the usual way with respect to the sunrise and sunset. However, if doing so will lead to harm – severe illness or death – for a particular person, due to the length of the fast, it is permissible for that person not to fast while the risk of harm is present. Mere conjecture is not sufficient in this regard; rather, the individual must be almost certain that serious harm will result from fasting. This can be known from certain symptoms or from experience, or from the advice of a health professional who affirms that fasting will lead to severe illness or death or that it will aggravate an illness or endanger recovery from a previous illness. Each person is different in this regard. Those people

354 al-Baghawī, *Sharḥ al-sunnah,* iii. 476.

355 Abū Dāwūd, *k. al-ṣawm, b. al-niyyah fī al-ṣiyām;* al-Tirmidhī, *k. al-ṣawm, b. mā jā'a lā ṣiyāma li man lam yaᶜzim min al-layl.*

356 al-Samarqandī, *Tuḥfat al-fuqahā'* 167.

357 Muslim, *k. al-ṣiyām, b. jawāz al-nāfilah bi niyyatin min al-nahār qab al-zawāl.*

358 al-Baghawī, *Sharḥ al-sunnah,* iii. 477.

359 ibid.

who leave fasting for such reasons should make up the missed fasts when they are able to do so.[360]

In some of these places, the nights are so short that there is either no time or very little time for *ʿIshā'* Prayer because the twilight does not disappear. In this situation the time of the *suḥūr* (the pre-dawn meal) will be based on an estimate. The people resident in such places should consider what, in other seasons, the shortest period of time is between sunset and *ʿIshā'*, and between dawn and sunrise. That shortest period should then be taken as the norm for the season when the twilight does not disappear. In the United Kingdom, for example, if the shortest period between sunset and *ʿIshā'* is one and a quarter hours, and the shortest period between dawn and sunrise is one and half hours, then people should pray *ʿIshā'* and *Tarāwīḥ* in the difficult summer months one and a quarter hours after sunset, and they should finish the *suḥūr* one and half hours before sunrise.

Those places where the days or nights cannot be distinguished

Very exceptionally, Muslims may find themselves living temporarily in or passing through places where the sun hardly appears or disappears at all in some periods of the year. In such situations, the most practicable solution is to follow the prayer and fasting times of the nearest large town where Muslims are permanently resident.[361]

THE *SUNNAHS* OF FASTING

There are certain *Sunnahs* and recommended matters which, once observed, fulfil the purpose of fasting. They are as follows:

SUḤŪR

Suḥūr is a meal which one eats before dawn when intending to fast. It is *Sunnah* to take *suḥūr* and the Prophet ﷺ has recommended it in many *aḥādīth*. Anas ibn Mālik narrated that the Prophet ﷺ said: "Take *suḥūr* as there is a blessing in it".[362] Al-ʿIrbāḍ ibn Sāriyah narrated: "The Apostle

360 See: *Fatāwā al-Shaykh Makhlūf*, i. 272, *Majallat al-buḥūth al-islāmiyyah*, issue 25, p,32.

361 See: *Qarārāt majlis al-majmaʿ al-fiqhi al-islāmī*, p. 91.

362 al-Bukhārī, *k. al-ṣawm, b. barakat al-suḥūr min ghayr ījāb;* Muslim, *k. al-ṣiyām, b. faḍl al-suḥūr.*

of Allāh ﷺ invited me to a meal shortly before dawn during the month of Ramaḍān saying: 'Come to the blessed morning meal'."[363] ʿAmr ibn al-ʿĀṣ reported Allāh's Messenger ﷺ as saying: "The difference between our fasting and that of the people of the Book is eating at the time of *suḥūr*".[364]

Its timing

The time of *suḥūr* is from midnight to the beginning of the *Fajr*. It is better to delay *suḥūr* so that one has *suḥūr* as close as possible to *Fajr*. Anas ibn Mālik narrates that Zayd ibn Thābit said: "We had *suḥūr* with the Messenger of Allāh ﷺ and then we stood up for the (*Fajr*) prayer". Anas said: "I asked him how long the gap between *suḥūr* and the prayer was?" Zayd answered: "The amount needed to read 50 verses".[365]

ʿAbdullāh ibn Masʿūd, ʿAbdullāh ibn ʿUmar and ʿĀ'ishah all narrated that Bilāl used to pronounce the *adhān* at night, so the Messenger of Allāh ﷺ said: "Carry on taking your meals (eat and drink) until Ibn Umm Maktūm pronounces the *adhān*, for he does not pronounce it till it is dawn".[366] Sahl ibn Saʿd reported: "I used to take my *suḥūr* meals with my family and then hurry up for presenting myself for the (*fajr*) prayer with Allāh's Apostle".[367] Ibrāhīm al-Nakhaʿī says: "It is *Sunnah* to delay the *suḥūr*".[368] Mujāhid says: "It is from the etiquettes of the Prophets to delay the *suḥūr*".[369]

IFṬĀR

Ifṭār means breaking the fast. It is Sunnah to break the fast as soon as the sun is set, and to delay it is disliked. Sahl ibn Saʿd narrated: "The Messenger of Allāh ﷺ said: 'People will remain on the right path as

363 Abū Dāwūd, *k. al-ṣawm, b. man sammā al-suḥūr al-ghadā';* al-Nasā'ī, *k. al-ṣiyām, b. daʿwat al-suḥūr.*

364 Muslim, *k. al-ṣiyām, b. faḍl al-suḥūr.*

365 al-Bukhārī, *k. mawāqīt al-ṣalāh, b. waqt al-fajr;* Muslim, *k. al-ṣiyām, b. faḍl al-suḥūr.*

366 Muslim, *k. al-ṣiyām, b. bayān anna al-dukhūla fī al-ṣawm yaḥṣulu....*

367 al-Bukhārī, *k. al-ṣawm, b. taʿjīl al-suḥūr.*

368 Ibn Abī Shaybah, *al-Muṣannaf,* vi. 121.

369 ibid., vi. 122.

long as they hasten the breaking of the fast'."[370] Abū Hurayrah narrated that Prophet ﷺ said: "Religion will continue to prevail as long as people hasten to break the fast, because the Jews and the Christians delay doing so".[371] ʿAbdullāh ibn Abī Awfā reported: "We were with the Messenger of Allāh ﷺ on a journey during the month of Ramaḍān. When the sun had sunk he said: 'So and so, get down (from your ride) and prepare the meal of parched barley for us'. He said: 'Messenger of Allāh, still (there is light of) day'. He (the Prophet) said: 'Get down and prepare the meal of parched barley for us'. So he got down and prepared the meal of parched barley and offered it to him, and the Apostle of Allāh ﷺ drank that (liquid meal). He then with the gesture of his hand informed us that when the sun sank from that side and the night appeared from that side, then the observer of the fast should break it".[372]

Abū ʿAṭiyyah reported: "I and Masrūq went to ʿĀ'ishah and said to her: 'Mother of all Believers, there are two people among the Companions of Muḥammad ﷺ, one among whom hastens in breaking the fast and in observing prayer, and the other delays breaking the fast and delays observing prayer'. She said: 'Who among the two hastens in breaking the fast and observing prayers?' We said: 'It is ʿAbdullāh, (i.e. ibn Masʿūd) whereupon she said: 'This is what the Messenger of Allāh ﷺ did. Abū Kurayb added: "The second one was Abū Mūsā".[373] In another version of the ḥadīth, the name of the first companion is mentioned as Ḥudhayfah rather than ʿAbdullāh. Imām Muḥammad says: "We adhere to the practice of Ḥudhayfah, and this is the opinion of Abū Ḥanīfah".[374] Ibrāhīm al-Nakhaʿī says: "It is Sunnah to hasten the *ifṭār*".[375]

With what should one break the fast?

It is Sunnah to break the fast with dates. Salmān ibn ʿĀmir reported that the Prophet ﷺ said: "When one of you is fasting, he should break his fast with dates; but if he cannot get any, then (he should break his

370 al-Bukhārī, *k. al-ṣawm, b. taʿjīl al-ifṭār;* Muslim, *k. al-ṣiyām, b. faḍl al-suḥūr.*

371 Abū Dāwūd, *k. al-ṣawm, b. mā yustaḥabbu min taʿjīl al-fiṭr;* Ibn Mājah, *k. al-ṣiyām, b. mā jā'a fī taʿjīl al-ifṭār.*

372 Muslim, *k. al-ṣiyām, b. waqt inqiḍā' al-ṣawm …*

373 Muslim, *k. al-ṣiyām, b. faḍl al-suḥūr.*

374 Abū Ḥanīfah, *K. al-āthār* 71.

375 Ibn Abī Shaybah, *al-Muṣannaf*, vi. 127.

fast) with water, for water is purifying".[376] Anas ibn Mālik narrated: "The Apostle of Allāh ﷺ used to break his fast before praying with some fresh dates; but if there were no fresh dates, he had a few dry dates, and if there were no dry dates, he took some mouthfuls of water".[377]

READING THE QUR'ĀN

It is strongly recommended that one recites the Qur'ān as much as possible while fasting and especially during the month of Ramaḍān; this is because the month of Ramaḍān bears very strong relations with the Qur'ān. ʿAbdullāh ibn ʿAbbās narrates: "The Prophet ﷺ was the most generous amongst the people, and he used to be more so during the month of Ramaḍān when Jibrīl visited him, and Jibrīl used to meet him on every night of Ramaḍān until the end of the month. The Prophet used to recite the Holy Qur'ān to Jibrīl, and when Jibrīl met him, he used to be more generous than a fast wind (which causes rain and welfare).[378]

DUʿĀ'

It is recommended that one makes *duʿā'* (supplications) while fasting and also at the time of breaking the fast. ʿAbdullāh ibn ʿAmr ibn al-ʿĀṣ narrated that the Prophet ﷺ said: "The fasting person has a supplication at the time of breaking the fast which will not be rejected".[379]

Marwān ibn Sālim al-Muqaffaʿ said: "I saw Ibn ʿUmar holding his beard with his hand and cutting what exceeded a handful of it. He (Ibn ʿUmar) said that the Prophet ﷺ when he broke his fast said:

ذَهَبَ الظَّمَأُ وَابْتَلَّتِ الْعُرُوقُ وَثَبَتَ الْأَجْرُ إِنْ شَاءَ اللهُ تَعَالَى

"Thirst has gone, the arteries are moist, and the reward is sure, if Allāh wills".[380]

376 Abū Dāwūd, *k. al-ṣawm, b. mā yufṭiru ʿalayhi;* Ibn Mājah, *k. al-ṣiyām, b. mā jā'a ʿalā mā yustaḥabbu al-fiṭr.*

377 Abū Dāwūd, *k. al-ṣawm, b. mā yufṭiru ʿalayhi;* al-Tirmidhī, *k. al-ṣawm, b. mā jā'a mā yustaḥabbu ʿalayhi al-ifṭār.*

378 al-Bukhārī, *k. al-ṣawm, b. ajwad mā kāna al-nabī ..;* Muslim, *k. al-faḍā'il, b. kān al-nabī …*

379 Ibn Mājah, *k. al-ṣiyām, b. fī al-ṣā'im lā turaddu daʿwatuhū.*

380 Abū Dāwūd, *k. al-ṣawm, b. al-qawl ʿinda al-ifṭār.*

Muᶜādh ibn Zuhrah narrates: "The Prophet of Allāh ﷺ used to say when he broke his fast:

اللَّهُمَّ لَكَ صُمْتُ وَعَلَى رِزْقِكَ أَفْطَرْتُ

'O Allāh, for You I have fasted, and with Your provision I have broken my fast'".[381]

REFRAINING FROM SINS AND VAIN PURSUITS

The fasting person should control his tongue and refrain from any sinful or useless words and actions. Abū Hurayrah narrated that the Messenger of Allāh ﷺ said: "Fasting is a shield. So, the person observing the fast should not use obscene language, and should not behave foolishly and impudently, and if somebody fights with him or abuses him, he should say to him: 'I am fasting, 'I am fasting".[382] Abū Hurayrah also narrated that the Prophet ﷺ said: "Whoever does not give up forged speech and evil actions, Allāh is not in need of him leaving his food and drink".[383] And that the Prophet ﷺ said: "When it is the day of fasting for any of you, he should neither use obscene language nor do any act of ignorance. And if anyone slanders him or quarrels with him, he should say: "I am fasting".[384]

Abū Ṣāliḥ al-Ḥanafī narrates from his brother Ṭalq ibn Qays that Abū Dharr said: "When you fast refrain as much as you can". Abū Ṣāliḥ says: "Whenever Ṭalq fasted, he would not leave his house except for a prayer".[385] Jābir says: "When you fast, then your ears, your eyes and your tongue also should fast from lying and sin, leave hurting the servant, there should be calmness and seriousness upon you on the day of your fasting, and do not make the day of not fasting and the day of fasting the same".[386] It has been narrated from ᶜUmar and ᶜAlī that: "Fasting does

381 ibid.

382 al-Bukhārī, *k. al-ṣawm, b. hal yaqūlu innī ṣā'im idhā shutima;* Muslim, *k. al-ṣiyām, b. faḍl al-ṣiyām.*

383 al-Bukhārī, *k. al-ṣawm, b. man lam yadaᶜ qawl al-zūr.*

384 Ibn Mājah, *k. al-ṣiyām, b. mā jā'a fī al-ghībati wa al-rafath li al-ṣā'im.*

385 Ibn Abī Shaybah, *al-Muṣannaf,* vi. 98-99.

386 ibid., vi. 100.

not mean abstaining from eating and drinking; rather fasting means abstaining from lying, and false and useless things".[387]

387 ibid., vi. 101.

CHAPTER 4: Types of Fasting

THERE ARE FIVE types of fasting, they are:
1- fasting during the month of Ramaḍān
2- *qaḍā'* and *kaffārah*;
3- fasting of a specific vow
4- fasting of a nonspecific vow
5- *nafl* fasting.

I will discuss the fasting of the month of Ramaḍān, then I will discuss *nafl* fasting. Other types of fasting will be explained in their relevant places.

THE FASTING OF RAMAḌĀN

Ramaḍān, the 9th month of the Islamic calendar, has been chosen by Allāh for fasting. The Qur'ān, Sunnah and *Ijma* (consensus) of the *ummah* all affirm the obligatory nature of fasting during the month of Ramaḍān.

Allāh, Exalted is He, says: "*O you who have believed, decreed upon you is fasting as it was decreed upon those before you that you may become righteous – [Fasting for] a limited number of days. So whoever among you is ill or on a journey [during them] – then an equal number of days [are to be made up]. And upon those who are able [to fast, but with hardship] – a ransom [as substitute] of feeding a poor person [each day]. And whoever volunteers excess – it is better for him. But to fast is best for you, if you only knew. The month of Ramaḍān [is that] in which was revealed the Qur'ān, a guidance for the people and clear proofs of guidance and criterion. So whoever sights [the new moon of] the month, let him fast it; and whoever is ill or on a journey – then an equal number of other days. Allāh intends for you ease and does not intend for you hardship and [wants] for you to complete the period and to glorify Allāh for that [to] which He has guided you; and perhaps you will be grateful*".[388]

ᶜAbdullāh ibn ᶜUmar reported that the Prophet ﷺ said: "Islam is built

388 *al-Baqarah* 183-185.

on five things: bearing witness that there is no god but Allāh and that Muḥammad is the Messenger of Allāh, establishing the prayer, giving the zakāh, fasting the month of Ramaḍān, and the *ḥajj* (the pilgrimage to Makkah) of the House".[389]

Ṭalḥah ibn Ubaydullāh narrated: "A Bedouin with unkempt hair came to the Messenger of Allāh ﷺ and said: 'O Messenger of Allāh, inform me of what Allāh has made obligatory on me as regards praying'. He replied: 'Five *ṣalāhs*, unless you do others voluntarily'. He asked the Prophet to inform him about fasting, and he said: 'The fast of Ramaḍān, unless you do others voluntarily'. Then he asked him about charity and the Messenger of Allāh informed him... The Bedouin then said: 'By the One who has honoured you, I shall not add anything to it, nor shall I be deficient in what Allāh has ordered me to do'. The Messenger of Allāh ﷺ then said: 'He will enter Paradise if he is true to this'."[390]

The *ummah* has consensus on the obligatory nature of the fasting during Ramaḍān. It is a pillar of Islam; no one denies it except an unbeliever.[391]

When was fasting made obligatory?

Fasting during the month of Ramaḍān was made obligatory in the month of Shaᶜbān in the 2nd year of the *hijrah*. The Prophet fasted for nine Ramaḍāns. ᶜĀ'ishah narrated that "People used to fast on *ᶜĀshūrā'* (the 10th day of the month *Muḥarram*) before the fasting of Ramaḍān was made obligatory. And on that day the *Kaᶜbah* used to be covered with a cover. When Allāh made fasting during the month of Ramaḍān compulsory, the Messenger of Allāh ﷺ said: 'Whoever wishes to fast (on the day of *ᶜĀshūrā'*) may do so; and whoever wishes to leave it can do so'."[392] ᶜAbdullāh ibn ᶜUmar reported that (the Arabs of) pre-Islamic days used to observe the fast on the day of *ᶜĀshūrā'* and the Messenger of Allāh ﷺ observed it and the Muslims too (observed it) before fasting during Ramaḍān became obligatory. But when it became obligatory, the Messenger of Allāh ﷺ said: '*ᶜĀshūrā'* is one of the days of Allāh, so he

389 al-Bukhārī, *k. al-īmān, b. duᶜā'ukum īmānukum;* Muslim, *k. al-īmān, b. bayān arkān al-islām wa daᶜā'imihī al-ᶜiẓām.*

390 al-Bukhārī, *k. īmān, b. al-zakāh min al-islām.*

391 al-Kāsānī, *Badā'iᶜ al-ṣanā'iᶜ*, ii. 550.

392 Abū Dāwūd, *k. al-ṣiyām, b. ṣawm yawm ᶜāshūrā'.*

who wishes should observe the fast and he who wishes otherwise should abandon it'."[393]

Ibn al-Qayyim says: "Since to liberate man from the clutches of sensuality is an extremely difficult task and it takes a lot of time, the command of the obligation of fasting was not revealed until such time after the migration when it had become clear that the creed of monotheism and the duty of *ṣalāh* had sunk deep into them and they had become thoroughly oriented to the injunctions of the Qur'ān. The command of fasting, was, thus, revealed in the second year of migration and the Prophet kept the fasts of Ramaḍān for nine years before he departed from the world".[394]

THE VIRTUES OF THE MONTH OF RAMAḌĀN

The month of Ramaḍān has special virtue. There are many *aḥādīth* confirming the virtues of this month, some of which includes:

Abū Hurayrah narrated that the Messenger of Allāh ﷺ said: "When Ramaḍān begins, the gates of Paradise are opened". In another version of the same ḥadīth, Allāh's Messenger ﷺ said: "When the month of Ramaḍān starts, the gates of Paradise are opened and the gates of Hell are closed and the devils are chained".[395]

One of the great virtues of this month is that after fasting the whole month, one's sins are forgiven. Abū Hurayrah narrates: "The Prophet ﷺ said: 'Whoever established prayers on the night of *Qadr* out of sincere faith and hoping for a reward from Allāh, then all his previous sins will be forgiven; and whoever fasts in the month of Ramaḍān out of sincere faith, and hoping for a reward from Allāh, then all his previous sins will be forgiven'."[396]

The Prophet ﷺ used to be more active during the month of Ramaḍān. ʿAbdullāh ibn ʿAbbās narrates: "The Prophet was the most generous amongst the people, and he used to be more so during the month of Ramaḍān when Jibrīl visited him, and Jibrīl used to meet him on every

393 Muslim, *k. al-ṣiyām, b. ṣawm yawm ʿāshūrā'.*

394 Ibn al-Qayyim, *Zād al-maʿād,* ii. 30.

395 al-Bukhārī, *k. al-ṣawm, b. hal yuqālu ramaḍān;* Muslim, *k. al-ṣiyām, b. faḍl shahr ramaḍān.*

396 al-Bukhārī, *k. al-īmān, b. ṣawm ramaḍān iḥtisāban min al-īmān;* Muslim, *k. ṣalāt al-musāfirīn, b. al-targhīb fī qiyām ramaḍān.*

night of Ramaḍān until the end of the month. The Prophet used to recite the Holy Qur'ān to Jibrīl, and when Jibrīl met him, he used to be more generous than a fast wind (which causes rain and welfare)".[397]

The following ḥadīth makes the reward of fasting unique compared to all other acts of worship. Abū Hurayrah narrated that the Prophet ﷺ said: "Allāh said: 'All the deeds of Ādam's sons (people) are for them, except fasting which is for Me, and I will give the reward for it'. Fasting is a shield or protection from the fire and from committing sins. If one of you is fasting, he should avoid obscene language and quarrelling, and if somebody should fight or quarrel with him, he should say: 'I am fasting'. By Him in Whose Hands my soul is, the unpleasant smell coming out from the mouth of a fasting person is better in the sight of Allāh than the smell of musk. There are two pleasures for the fasting person, one at the time of breaking his fast, and the other at the time when he will meet his Lord; then he will be pleased because of his fasting'."[398]

The sin of not fasting during Ramaḍān

There are many warnings for those who do not fast during the month of Ramaḍān. For example: ʿAbdullāh ibn Abbās reported that the Prophet ﷺ said: "The ties of Islam and the foundations of religion are three, and whoever leaves one of them becomes an unbeliever, and his blood becomes lawful: testifying that there is no god but Allāh, the obligatory *ṣalāh*s, and the fast of Ramaḍān".[399]

Abū Hurayrah reported that the Messenger of Allāh ﷺ said: "Whoever breaks his fast during Ramaḍān without having one of the excuses that Allāh will excuse him for, then even a perpetual fast, if he were to fast it, will not make up for that day".[400]

The wisdom behind fixing days for fasting

Shāh Walīullah writes: "If the right to exercise one's own judgement in fasting is conceded it will open the door of evasion, the path of

397 al-Bukhārī, *k. al-ṣawm, b. ajwad mā kāna al-nabī ...*; Muslim, *k. al-faḍā'il, b. kān al-nabī ...*

398 al-Bukhārī, *k. al-ṣawm, b. hal yaqūlu innī ṣā'im idhā shutima;* Muslim, *k. al-ṣiyām, b. faḍl al-ṣiyām.*

399 Abū Yaʿlā, *al-Musnad* 2349.

400 Abū Dāwūd, *k. al-ṣawm, b. al-taghlīẓ fī man afṭara ʿamdan;* Ibn Mājah, *k. al-ṣiyām, b. mā jā'a fī kaffārati man afṭara yawman min ramaḍān.*

sanctioning what is allowed and forbidding what is prohibited will be obstructed and this foremost event of obeisance in Islam will fall into negligence ... It was also necessary to determine its period and duration so that no room would be left for excess or slackness. But for it, some people would have been fruitless while others would have carried it so far as to inflict upon themselves excessive hardship. In truth, fasting is a remedy to counteract the effects of the poison of sensuality and, therefore, it is essential that it should be administered in the right quantity".[401]

ON WHOM THE FASTING IS OBLIGATORY

Fasting during the month of Ramaḍān is obligatory upon Muslims who are sane and have reached puberty. ʿAlī ibn Abī Ṭālib related that the Messenger of Allāh ﷺ said: "The pen is raised for three [meaning that there is no obligation upon three categories of individuals] namely those who are sleeping until they waken, the child until it becomes an adult and the insane until they become sane".[402]

If a child becomes of age or a *kāfir* (non-Muslim) becomes a Muslim during Ramaḍān, then that individual must abstain from eating, drinking or sexual intercourse for the rest of that day and then carry on fasting the days following this but they do not make up the days missed.[403]

If one faints during Ramaḍān then one is not required to make up the day on which one fainted, but one does have to make up the following missed days if any.[404] This is on condition that the person has not done anything to break the fast. If the person remains unconscious the next day, their intention to fast the day on which they fainted is no longer valid.

Although fasting is not obligatory on one who is insane, if such a person recovers his sanity during a Ramadan then he is obliged to fast the remaining days of the month and make up any days in that month before he recovered his senses.[405]

401 al-Dihlawī, *Ḥujjatullāh al-bālighah,* ii. 75-76.

402 Abū Dāwūd, *k. al-ḥudūd, b. fī al-majnūn yasriq;* al-Tirmidhī, *k. al-ḥudūd, b. mā jāʾa fī man lā yajibu ʿalayh al-ḥadd.*

403 al-Qudūrī, *al-Mukhtaṣar* 195.

404 ibid.

405 ibid.

The fasting of children

Fasting is not compulsory for children though their guardians are commanded to instil love for and a habit of fasting in them from an early age. Rubayyiᶜ bint Muᶜawwidh narrated: "The Prophet ﷺ sent a messenger to the village of the Anṣār in the morning of the day of ᶜĀshūrā' to announce: 'Whoever has eaten something should not eat but complete the fast, and whoever is observing the fast should complete it'." She further said: "Since then we used to fast on that day regularly and also make our children fast. We used to make toys of wool for the boys and if anyone of them cried he was given those toys until it was the time of breaking the fast".[406] Ibn Sīrīn says: "The child should be commanded to perform *ṣalāh* when he recognises his right hand from his left and fasting when he can do it".[407] The same has been narrated from al-Zuhrī, Qatādah and ᶜUrwah ibn al-Zubayr.[408]

Women in a state of menstruation

Women in a state of menstruation or postnatal bleeding are not allowed to fast. Abū Saᶜīd reported that the Prophet ﷺ said: "Isn't it true that a woman does not pray and does not fast on menstruating? And that is the defect (a loss) in her religion".[409]

Nevertheless the fasting is obligatory on those women, and they have to complete the number of days of fasting later. It is reported that Muᶜādhah al-ᶜAdawiyyah asked ᶜĀ'ishah: "Why is it that a woman in a state menstruation does the *qaḍā'* of fasting, and does not do the *qaḍā'* of *ṣalāh*?" ᶜĀ'ishah answered: "That used to happen to us, that we would be commanded to do the *qaḍā'* of fasting, not the *qaḍā'* of *ṣalāh*".[410] There is no harm if the women delay the *qaḍā'* for a reason. ᶜĀ'ishah narrated: "Sometimes I missed some days of Ramaḍān, but could not fast in lieu of them except in the month of Shaᶜbān". Yaḥyā ibn Saᶜīd, a

406 al-Bukhārī, *k. al-ṣawm, b. ṣawm al-ṣibyān;* Muslim, *k. al-ṣiyām, b. man akala fī ᶜāshūrā' falyakuffa baqiyyata yawmihī.*

407 ᶜAbd al-Razzāq, *al-Muṣannaf,* iv. 153.

408 ibid.

409 al-Bukhārī, *k. al-ḥayd, b. tark al-ḥā'iḍ al-ṣawm;* Muslim, *k. al-īmān, b. bayān nuqṣān al-īmān bi naqṣ al-ṭāᶜāt.*

410 Muslim, *k. al-ḥayḍ, b. wujūb qaḍā' al-ṣawm ᶜalā al-ḥā'iḍ.*

sub-narrator, says: "She used to be busy serving the Prophet ﷺ".[411]

If a woman begins her menstruation or has post-natal bleeding while fasting, she breaks her fast and makes it up when she becomes pure again. Similarly, if a woman becomes pure after dawn, she is not allowed to fast that day neither for Ramaḍān nor for any voluntary fast.[412]

The invalid and the traveller

As for those who are ill or travelling, it is permitted for them not to fast during the month of Ramaḍān for the duration of their illness or travel. The Qur'ān states: "*So whoever sights [the new moon of] the month, let him fast it; and whoever is ill or on a journey – then an equal number of other days. Allāh intends for you ease and does not intend for you hardship and [wants] for you to complete the period and to glorify Allāh for that [to] which He has guided you; and perhaps you will be grateful*".[413] Abū al-Dardā' narrated: "We set out with Allāh's Messenger on one of his journeys on a very hot day. It was so hot that one had to put ones hand over ones head because of the severity of the heat. None of us was fasting except the Prophet ﷺ and Ibn Rawāḥah".[414]

Nevertheless, if a sick person fasts during his illness and a traveller fasts during his journey, this is allowed. ʿĀ'ishah narrates: "Ḥamzah ibn ʿAmr al-Aslamī asked the Prophet: 'Should I fast while travelling?' The Prophet replied: 'You may fast if you wish, and you may not fast if you wish'."[415] Anas ibn Mālik narrated: "We were travelling with the Prophet ﷺ while some of us were fasting, and some of us did not fast".[416] Ṭāwūs narrated that Ibn ʿAbbās said: "The Messenger of Allāh ﷺ set out from Madīnah to Makkah and he fasted until he reached ʿUsfān, where he asked for water and raised his hand to let the people see him, and then broke the fast, and did not fast after that until he reached Makkah,

411 al-Bukhārī, *k. al-ṣawm, b. matā yaqḍī qaḍā'a ramaḍān;* Muslim, *k. al-ṣiyām, b. qaḍā' ramaḍān fī shaʿbān.*

412 al-Kāsānī, *Badā'iʿ al-ṣanā'iʿ*, ii. 596-7.

413 *al-Baqarah* 185.

414 al-Bukhārī, *k. al-ṣawm, b. idhā ṣāma ayyāman min ramaḍān.*

415 al-Bukhārī, *k. al-ṣawm, b. al-ṣawm fī al-safar wa al-ifṭār;* Muslim, *k. al-ṣiyām, b. al-takhyīr fī al-ṣawm wa al-fiṭr fī al-safar.*

416 al-Bukhārī, *k. al-jihād, b. faḍl al-khidmah fī al-al-ghazw,* Muslim, *k. al-ṣiyām, b. ajr al-mufṭir fī al-safar idhā tawallā al-ʿamal.*

and that happened during Ramaḍān".[417] Ibn ᶜAbbās used to say: "Allāh's Messenger ﷺ (sometimes) fasted and (sometimes) did not fast during journeys so whoever wished to fast could fast, and whoever wished not to fast, could do so".[418] Abū Saᶜīd al-Khudrī reported: "We went out on an expedition with Allāh's Messenger ﷺ on the 16th of Ramaḍān. Some of us fasted and some of us broke the fast. But neither the observer of the fast found fault with the one who broke it, nor the breaker of the fast found fault with the one who observed it".[419]

However, if the fasting affects them, then it is better not to fast. Ibn ᶜAbbās narrated: "The Messenger of Allāh ﷺ set out for Makkah during Ramaḍān and he fasted, and when he reached Al-Kadīd, he broke his fast and the people with him broke their fast too". Al-Bukhārī said: "Al-Kadīd is a place of water between ᶜUsfān and Qudayd".[420] Jābir ibn ᶜAbdullāh narrates an incident while the Messenger of Allāh ﷺ was on a journey and saw a crowd of people shading a man. Upon seeing this, the Prophet ﷺ asked: "What is the matter?" They said: "He (the man) is fasting". The Prophet said: "It is not righteousness that you fast on a journey".[421] Jābir ibn ᶜAbdullāh also reported that: "The Messenger of Allāh ﷺ went out to Makkah during Ramaḍān in the year of Victory, and he and the people fasted until he came to Kurāᶜ al-Ghumaym. He then called for a cup of water which he raised until the people saw it, and then he drank. He was told afterwards that some people had continued to fast, and he said: 'These people are the disobedient ones; they are the disobedient ones'."[422]

However, if the journey is comfortable and one feels no difficulty then one should fast. Salamah ibn al-Muḥabbaq al-Hudhalī narrated: "The Apostle of Allāh ﷺ said: 'If anyone has a riding beast which carries him

417 al-Bukhārī, *k. al-ṣawm, b. man afṭara fī al-safar li yarāhu al-nās;* Muslim, *k. al-ṣiyām, b. jawāz al-ṣawm wa al-fiṭr fī shahr ramaḍān li al-musāfir.*

418 al-Bukhārī, *k. al-ṣawm, b. man afṭara fī al-safar li yarāhu al-nās;* Muslim, *k. al-ṣiyām, b. jawāz al-ṣawm wa al-fiṭr fī shahr ramaḍān li al-musāfir.*

419 Muslim, *k. al-ṣiyām, b. jawāz al-ṣawm wa al-fiṭr fī shahr ramaḍān li al-musāfir.*

420 al-Bukhārī, *k. al-ṣawm, b. idhā ṣāma ayyāman fī ramaḍān thumma sāfar.*

421 al-Bukhārī, *k. al-ṣawm, b. qawl al-nabī ṣallallāhu ᶜalayhi wa sallam liman ẓullila ᶜalayh;* Muslim, *k. al-ṣiyām, b. jawāz al-ṣawm wa al-fiṭr fī shahr ramaḍān li al-musāfir.*

422 Muslim, *k. al-ṣiyām, b. jawāz al-ṣawm wa al-fiṭr fī shahr ramaḍān li al-musāfir.*

to where he can get sufficient food, he should keep the fast of Ramaḍān wherever he is when it comes'."[423]

When the sick person has been cured and the traveller has returned home, then they must fast the numbers of the day which they have missed.[424]

If the sick person or traveller dies and they die in this state of being ill or travelling, then the obligation of having to make up their fast is removed and therefore no *kaffārah* is required to be paid by their inheritors.[425]

If the sick person recovers or the traveller becomes resident, and then they die, the obligation of making up for the missed days of fasting in accordance with the number of days they were healthy or resident prior to their death remains.[426] In such cases *kaffārah* is required to be paid by their inheritors.

If a traveller arrives at his destination or the menstruating woman becomes pure at some moment during the day, then out of respect for the month, they should abstain from eating, drinking or intercourse for the rest of that day.[427]

Those physically unable to fast

As for the elderly and the sick that are unable to fast and there is no hope of their recovery, then they are excused from fasting. Instead, they should feed a poor person half a *ṣāʿ* of wheat or a *ṣāʿ* of dates or barley for each day of the fast.[428] When Anas ibn Mālik reached old age and was unable to fast, he commanded that the poor be fed; so they were fed bread and meat until they were full.[429]

If a pregnant woman or breast feeding mother fear for the wellbeing of their children or themselves, then they may break their fast and make it up, but they are not required to pay any compensation.[430] Anas ibn

423 Abū Dāwūd, *k. al-ṣawm, b. man ikhtāra al-ṣiyām.*
424 al-Qudūrī, *al-Mukhtaṣar* 192.
425 ibid.,193.
426 ibid.
427 al-Kāsānī, *Badāʾiʿ al-ṣanāʾiʿ*, ii. 596-7.
428 al-Qudūrī, *al-Mukhtaṣar* 194; ibid., ii. 616.
429 al-Bukhārī, *k. al-tafsīr, b. ayyāman maʿdūdāt…*
430 al-Kāsānī, *Badāʾiʿ al-ṣanāʾiʿ*, ii. 614-5.

Mālik, a man from the *Banu* (clan) of ᶜAbdullāh ibn Kaᶜb brethren of *Banu* Qushayr (not Anas ibn Mālik, the well-known Companion), said: "A contingent from the cavalry of the Apostle of Allah ﷺ raided us. I reached", or (he said,) "I went to the Apostle of Allah ﷺ who was taking his meals. He said: 'Sit down, and take some from this meal of ours'. I said: 'I am fasting,' he said: 'Sit down. I shall tell you about prayer and fasting. Allah has lifted (the obligation) of half the prayer for a traveller, and (that of) fasting for the traveller, and from the woman who is suckling an infant or the woman who is pregnant'. I swear by Allah, he mentioned both (i.e. suckling and pregnant women) or one of them. I deeply regretted not eating from the meal of the Apostle of Allah ﷺ'."[431] Imām al-Tirmidhī after narrating this ḥadīth said: "The people of knowledge follow this ḥadīth whereby the woman who is suckling an infant and the woman who is pregnant, when they fear for the wellbeing of their children, are allowed not to fast, but later they will do *qaḍā*".

Whoever dies while still under the obligation of making up missed fasts of Ramaḍān and he has given instructions in this regard, in his testament or before his death, then his executor on his behalf feeds a destitute person half a *ṣāᶜ* of wheat or a *ṣāᶜ* of dates or barley for each day not fasted.[432] ᶜAbdullāh ibn ᶜUmar narrated that the Prophet ﷺ said: "For the one who has died whist having the obligation of fasting a month, one poor person should be fed, on his behalf, (in compensation) for every day (of fast due.)"[433] This is also the opinion of Ibrāhīm al-Nakhaᶜī, Mālik, Sufyān al-Thawrī and Shāfiᶜī.[434]

NAFL FAST

Nafl fast include all Sunnah, recommended and voluntary fasting. Fasting is encouraged in Islam and people are advised to do voluntary fasts besides the fasting of Ramaḍān. ᶜAbdullāh ibn Shaqīq reported: "I said to ᶜĀ'ishah: 'Did the Apostle of Allāh ﷺ observe the fast for a full

431 Abū Dāwūd, *k. al-ṣawm, b. ikhtiyār al-fiṭr;* al-Tirmidhī, *k. al-ṣawm, b. mā jā'a fī al-rukhṣah fī al-ifṭār li al-ḥublā wa al-murḍiᶜ;* al-Nasā'ī, *k. al-ṣiyām, b. waḍᶜ al-ṣiyām ᶜan al-ḥublā wa al-murḍiᶜ;* Ibn Mājah, *k. al-ṣiyām, b. mā jā'a fī al-ifṭār li al-ḥāmil wa al-murḍiᶜ.*

432 al-Qudūrī, *al-Mukhtaṣar* 194.

433 al-Tirmidhī, *k. al-ṣawm, b. mā jā'a min al-kaffārah.*

434 al-Baghawī, *Sharḥ al-sunnah,* iii. 510.

month besides Ramaḍān?' She said: 'I do not know of any month in which he fasted throughout, but that of the month of Ramaḍān, and I do not know a month in which he did not fast at all, until he ran the course of his life'."[435] ʿAbdullāh ibn ʿAbbās reported: "The Messenger of Allāh ﷺ did not fast throughout any month except during Ramaḍān. And when he observed the fast, he fasted so continuously that one would say that he would not break them and when he abandoned (fasting), he abandoned so continuously that one would say: 'By Allāh, perhaps he would never fast'."[436]

There are certain voluntary fasts which are recommended by the Prophet ﷺ. These are mentioned below:

The six days of *Shawwāl*

Abū Ayyūb al-Anṣārī reported Allāh's Messenger ﷺ said: "For him who observed the fast of Ramaḍān and then followed it with six days of fasting during the month of *Shawwāl*, it is as if he fasted perpetually".[437]

It is perhaps better not to fast continuously during the few days after ʿ*īd* in order to avoid it seeming to extend Ramaḍān, and to distinguish *farḍ* from Sunnah.[438]

The Day of ʿArafah

It is recommended that one fasts on the Day of ʿArafah[439] (9th *Dhū al-ḥijjah.)* Abū Qatādah narrated that the Messenger of Allāh ﷺ said: "Fasting on the Day of ʿArafah removes the sins of two years: the previous year and the coming year".[440]

However, it is disliked for those performing *ḥajj* to fast on the Day of ʿArafah. ʿIkrimah said: "We were with Abū Hurayrah in his house

435 Muslim, *k. al-ṣiyām, b. ṣiyām al-nabī ṣallallāhu ʿalayhi wa sallam fī ghayr ramaḍān.*

436 al-Bukhārī, *k. al-ṣawm, b. mā yudhkaru min ṣawm al-nabī ṣallallāhu ʿalayhi wa sallam wa ifṭārih;* Muslim, *k. al-ṣiyām, b. ṣiyām al-nabī ṣallallāhu ʿalayhi wa sallam fī ghayr ramaḍān.*

437 Muslim, *k. al-ṣiyām, b. istiḥbāb ṣawm sittati ayyām min shawwāl.*

438 al-Samarqandī, *Tuḥfat al-fuqahā'* 163; al-Kāsānī, *Badā'iʿ al-ṣanā'iʿ*, ii. 562.

439 ʿArafah is a pilgrimage site in Makkah. Staying there on the 9th of *Dhū al-ḥijjah* is the most important pillar of the *ḥajj.*

440 Muslim, *k. al-ṣiyām, b. istiḥbāb thalāthati ayyām min kulli shahr...*

when he narrated to us: 'The Apostle of Allāh ﷺ prohibited fasting on the Day of ʿArafah at ʿArafah'."[441] Umm al-Faḍl bint al-Ḥārith narrated: "While the people were with me on the Day of ʿArafah they differed as to whether the Prophet was fasting or not; some said that he was fasting while others said that he was not fasting. So, I sent to him a bowl full of milk while he was riding over his camel and he drank it".[442] Kurayb, who was the freed slave of Ibn ʿAbbās reports from Maymūnah, the wife of the Apostle of Allāh ﷺ that: "People had doubt about the fasting of Allāh's Messenger on the day of ʿArafah. Maymūnah sent him a cup of milk and he was halting at a place and he drank it and the people saw him".[443]

ʿĀshūrā'

ʿĀshūrā' means the 10th of Muḥarram. The Prophet ﷺ used to fast that day, and he said the year he died that if he lived the next year then he would fast one day before it or one day after it. The reason being to avoid similarity with the Jews who fasted the 10th only. Since then the established Sunnah is to fast on the 9th and 10th or 10th and 11th of Muḥarram.

ʿAbdullāh ibn ʿUmar said that: "The Arabs of pre-Islamic days observed the fast on the Day of *ʿĀshūrā'* and the Messenger of Allāh ﷺ observed it and so did the Muslims. This was before fasting during Ramaḍān became obligatory. When fasting during Ramaḍān became obligatory, the Messenger of Allāh ﷺ said: 'ʿĀshūrā' is one of the Days of Allāh, so he who wishes should observe the fast and he who wishes otherwise should abandon it'."[444]

Ibn ʿAbbās said: "When the Messenger of Allāh ﷺ fasted on the Day of *ʿĀshūrā'* and commanded that it should he observed as a fast, they (his Companions) said to him: 'Messenger of Allāh, it is a day which the Jews and Christians hold in high esteem'. Thereupon, the Messenger of Allāh ﷺ said: 'When the next year comes, Allāh willing, we will observe

441 Abū Dāwūd, *k. al-ṣawm, b. fī ṣawm yawm* ʿArafah *bi* ʿArafah*;* al-Nasā'ī, *k. al-ḥajj, b. al-nahy ʿan ṣawm yawm* ʿArafah

442 al-Bukhārī, *k. al-ṣawm, b. ṣawm yawm* ʿArafah*;* Muslim, *k. al-ṣiyām, b. istiḥbāb al-fiṭr li al-ḥājj yawm* ʿArafah.

443 Muslim, *k. al-ṣiyām, b. istiḥbāb al-fiṭr li al-ḥājj yawm* ʿArafah.

444 Muslim, *k. al-ṣiyām, b. ṣawm yawm ʿāshūrā'.*

the fast on the 9th'. But the Messenger of Allāh ﷺ died before the advent of the next year'."[445]

Abū Qatādah narrated that the Messenger of Allāh ﷺ said: "Fasting on the Day of ʿĀshūrā', I expect from Allāh, the removal of the sins of the previous year".[446]

Fasting on Mondays and Thursdays

The Prophet ﷺ mostly kept fast on Mondays and Thursdays. Abū Hurayrah narrates: "The Prophet mostly fasted on Mondays and Thursdays. On being asked about this, the Prophet said: 'The deeds are presented (to Allāh) every Monday and Thursday, then Allāh forgives the sins of every Muslim except two who cut ties (with each other); it is said (about them): 'delay them'."[447] The client of Usāmah ibn Zayd said that he went along with Usāmah to Wādī al-Qurā in pursuit of his camels. Usāmah would fast on Mondays and Thursdays. His client said to him: "Why do you fast on Monday and Thursday while you are an old man?" He said: "The Prophet of Allāh ﷺ used to fast on Monday and Thursday. When he was asked about this, he said: 'The deeds of the slaves are presented on Monday and Thursday'."[448] It has been narrated from a large number of Companions and Successors that they kept fast on Mondays and Thursdays. Among them are, ʿAlī, ʿAbdullāh ibn Masʿūd, Abū Hurayrah, Usāmah ibn Zayd, ʿUmar ibn ʿAbd al-ʿAzīz and Makḥūl.[449]

Three days of every month

It is recommended that one fasts three days in every month: namely 13th, 14th and 15th. ʿAbdullāh ibn Masʿūd narrated: "The Apostle of Allāh ﷺ used to fast three days every month".[450] Qatādah ibn Milḥān al-Qaysī

445 Muslim, *k. al-ṣiyām, b. ayy yawm yuṣāmu fī ʿāshūrā'.*

446 Muslim, *k. al-ṣiyām, b. istiḥbāb thalāthati ayyām min kulli shahr…*

447 al-Tirmidhī, k. *al-ṣawm, b. mā jā'a fī ṣawm al-ithanyn wa al-khamīs;* Ibn Mājah, *k. al-ṣiyām, b. ṣiyām yawm al-ithnayn wa al-khamīs.*

448 Abū Dāwūd, *k. al-ṣiyām, b. ṣawm al-ithnayn wa al-khamīs.*

449 Ibn Abī Shaybah, *al-Muṣannaf*, vi. 190-193.

450 Abū Dāwūd, *k. al-ṣawm, b. fī ṣawm al-thalath min kull shahr*; al-Tirmidhī, *k. al-ṣawm, b. mā jā'a fī ṣawm yawm al-jumuʿah;* al-Nasā'ī, *k. al-ṣiyām, b. ṣawm al-nabī ṣallallāhu ʿalayhi wa sallam.*

narrated: "The Apostle of Allāh ﷺ used to command us to fast the days of the white nights (full moon): the 13th,14th and 15th of the month. He (the Prophet ﷺ) said: 'This is like keeping a perpetual fast'."[451]

Abū Qatādah reported that: "A person came to the Apostle of Allāh ﷺ and said: 'How do you observe the fast?' The Messenger of Allāh ﷺ felt annoyed. When ʿUmar noticed his annoyance, he said: 'We are well pleased with Allāh as our Lord, with Islam as our Code of Life, and with Muḥammad as our Prophet. We seek refuge with Allāh from the anger of Allāh and that of His Messenger'. ʿUmar kept on repeating these words until his (the Prophet's) anger calmed down. Then ʿUmar said: 'Messenger of Allāh, what is the position of one who perpetually observes the fast?' Thereupon, he said: 'He neither fasted nor broke it,' or he said: 'He did not fast and he did not break it'. He (ʿUmar) said: 'What about him who observes the fast for two days and breaks one day'. Thereupon, he said: 'Is anyone capable of doing it?' He (ʿUmar) said: 'What is the position of him who observes the fast for a day and breaks on the other day?' Thereupon, he (the Prophet) said: 'That is the fast of David (peace be upon him)'. He (ʿUmar) said: 'What about him who observes the fast one day and breaks it for two days'. Thereupon, he (the Messenger of Allāh) said: 'I wish I were given the strength to observe that'. Thereafter, he said: 'The observance of three days fast every month and that of Ramaḍān every year is perpetual fasting. I seek from Allāh that fasting on the Day of 'Arafah may atone for the sins of the preceding and coming years. and I seek from Allāh that fasting on the Day of Ashura may atone for the sins of the preceding year'."[452]

Fasting on alternate days

ʿAbdullāh ibn ʿAmr ibn al-ʿĀṣ narrates: "The Messenger of Allāh ﷺ said to me: 'O ʿAbdullāh! Have I not been informed that you fast during the day and offer prayers all the night?" ʿAbdullāh replied: 'Yes, O Messenger of Allāh'. The Prophet said: 'Don't do that, fast for a few days and then give it up for a few days, offer prayers and also sleep at night, as your body has a right on you, and your wife has a right on you, and your guest has a right on you. And it is sufficient for you to fast three days in

451 Abū Dāwūd, *k. al-ṣawm, b. fī ṣawm al-thalāth min kulli shahr;* Ibn Mājah, *k. al-ṣiyām, b. mā jā'a fī ṣiyām thalāthat ayyām min kulli shahr.*

452 Muslim, *k. al-ṣiyām, b. istiḥbāb thalāthat ayyām min kulli shahr.*

a month, as the reward of a good deed is multiplied ten times, so it will be like fasting throughout the year'. I insisted (on fasting) and so I was given a hard instruction. I said: 'O Allāh's Apostle! I have power'. The Prophet said: 'Fast like the fasting of the Prophet David and do not fast more than that'. I said: 'How was the fasting of the Prophet of Allāh, David?' He said: 'Half of the year,' (i.e. he used to fast on every alternate day)'." It is reported that when ʿAbdullāh became old, he used to say: "It would have been better for me if I had accepted the permission of the Prophet which he gave me (to fast only three days a month)".[453]

When voluntary fasting becomes compulsory

Whoever begins a voluntary fast but then invalidates it, must make up for it. Details about this will be given later in the chapter.

453 al-Bukhārī, *k. al-ṣawm, b. ḥaqq al-jism fī al-ṣawm;* Muslim, *k. al-ṣiyām, b. al-nahy ʿan ṣawm al-dahr.*

Chapter 5: Days when Fasting is Forbidden or Disliked

There are certain days when fasting is either forbidden or disliked.

FORBIDDEN DAYS

There are five days during the year when fasting is forbidden namely, the Day of ᶜĪd *al-fiṭr*, the Day of ᶜĪd *al-aḍḥā*, and the three days of *tashrīq* (11th, 12th and 13th Dhī al-ḥijjah). Abū ᶜUbayd says: "I attended ᶜ*Īd* Prayer with ᶜUmar ibn al-Khaṭṭāb; he started the prayer before the *khuṭbah* and said: 'The Messenger of Allāh ﷺ forbade fasting of these two days: the day of ᶜ*Īd al-fiṭr*, and the Day of Sacrifice (ᶜ*Īd al-aḍḥā*). As for ᶜ*Īd al-fiṭr*, that is the day for the breaking of the fast. And as for ᶜ*Īd al-aḍḥā*, that is the day when you have to eat from your sacrifice'."[454] Qazaᶜah related: "I heard from Abū Saᶜīd a ḥadīth which impressed me, and I said to him: 'Did you hear it from the Messenger of Allāh ﷺ?' Thereupon, he said: " (Is it possible) that (I should) say about the Messenger of Allāh ﷺ that which I have not heard? I heard him saying: 'It is not proper to fast on two days, Day of *fiṭr* (at the end) of Ramaḍān, and the Day of Sacrifice'."[455]

Abū Hurayrah narrated that the Messenger of Allāh said: "The days of Minā (10th, 11th, 12th and 13th) are the days of eating and drinking".[456] Nubayshah al-Hudhalī reported Allāh's Messenger ﷺ as saying: "The days of *tashrīq* are days of eating and drinking".[457] Ibn Kaᶜb ibn Mālik reported on the authority of his father that the Messenger of Allāh ﷺ sent him and Aws ibn Ḥadathān during the days of *tashrīq* to make this announcement: "None but the believer would be admitted into Paradise, and the days of Minā are the days meant for eating and drinking".[458]

454 al-Bukhārī, *k. al-ṣawm, b. ṣawm yawm al-fiṭr;* Muslim, *k. al-ṣiyām, b. al-nahy ᶜan ṣawm yawm al-fiṭr wa yawm al-aḍḥā.*

455 ibid.

456 Muslim, *k. al-ṣiyām, b. ṣawm ayyām al-tashrīq.*

457 Muslim, *k. al-ṣiyām, b. taḥrīm ṣawm ayyām al-tashrīq.*

458 ibid.

DISLIKED DAYS

There are certain days when fasting is disliked.

Day of doubt

Fasting is disliked on the day of doubt; the details of which have been mentioned earlier.

Friday

Fasting on Friday alone is disliked, but if one fasts one day before or after it as well, then there is no harm. ʿAbdullāh ibn ʿAmr reported that the Messenger of Allāh entered the room of Juwayriyah bint al-Ḥārith while she was fasting on a Friday. He asked her: "Did you fast yesterday?" She answered, "No". He said: "Do you plan to fast tomorrow?" She answered, "No". Therefore he said: "Then break your fast".[459]

Muḥammad ibn ʿAbbād ibn Jaʿfar reported: "I asked Jābir ibn ʿAbdullāh while he was circumambulating the House (Kaʿbah) whether the Messenger of Allāh ﷺ had forbidden fasting on Friday, whereupon he said: 'Yes, by the Lord of this House'."[460] Abū Hurayrah reported the Apostle of Allāh ﷺ said: "None among you should observe the fast on Friday, but only that he observes the fast before it and after it".[461]

Saturday

It is also disliked to fast on a Saturday alone. ʿAbdullāh ibn Busr related from his sister al-Ṣammā' that the Messenger of Allāh ﷺ said: "Do not fast on Saturdays unless it is an obligatory fast. [You should not fast] even if you do not find anything [to eat] save some grape peelings or a branch of a tree to chew on".[462] Umm Salamah narrates: "The Prophet used to fast more often on Saturdays and Sundays than on the other days. He would say: 'They are the *ʿīds* of the polytheists, and I love to

459 al-Bukhārī, *k. al-ṣawm, b. ṣawm yawm al-jumuʿah.*

460 al-Bukhārī, *k. al-ṣawm, b. ṣawm yawm al-jumuʿah*; Muslim, *k. al-ṣiyām, b. karāhiyat ṣawm yawm al-jumuʿah.*

461 al-Bukhārī, *k. al-ṣawm, b. ṣawm yawm al-jumuʿah*; Muslim, *k. al-ṣiyām, b. karāhiyat ṣawm yawm al-jumuʿah.*

462 Abū Dāwūd, *k. al-ṣawm, b. al-nahy an yukhaṣṣa yawm al-sabt bi ṣawm*; al-Tirmidhī, *k. al-ṣawm, b. mā jā'a fī ṣawm yawm al-sabt*; Ibn Mājah, *k. al-ṣiyām, b. mā jā'a fī ṣiyām yawm al-sabt.*

differ from them".[463] This ḥadīth makes it clear that if another day is added then there is no harm in fasting on Saturday.

Wiṣal

Wiṣāl means continuous fasting even after sunset; it can continue until the sunset of the next day, or even further. *Wiṣāl* fasting is also disliked.[464] Abū Hurayrah reported that the Messenger of Allāh ﷺ said: "Do not perform *al-wiṣāl*". He said this three times and the people said to him: "But you perform *al-wiṣāl*, O Messenger of Allāh" He said: "You are not like me in that matter. I spend the night in such a state that Allāh feeds me and gives me to drink. Devote yourselves to the deeds which you can perform".[465] Anas reported: "The Messenger of Allāh ﷺ was observing prayer during Ramaḍān. I came and stood by his side. Then another man came and he stood likewise until we became a group. When the Apostle of Allāh ﷺ noticed that we were behind him, he lightened the prayer. He then went to his abode and observed such (a long) prayer (the like of which) he never observed with us. When it was morning we said to him: 'Did you notice us during the night?' Upon this he said: 'Yes, it was this (realisation) that led me to do that which I did'. He (the narrator) said: 'The Messenger of Allāh ﷺ began to observe *wiṣāl* fasting at the end of the month (of Ramaḍān), and some among his Companions began to observe *wiṣāl* fast, whereupon the Apostle of Allāh ﷺ said: 'What about such persons who observe *wiṣāl* fasts? You are not like me. By Allāh! if the month were lengthened for me, I would have observed *wiṣāl*, so that those who act with an exaggeration would (have been obliged) to abandon their exaggeration".[466] Imām Muḥammad says after narrating the above ḥadīth of Abū Hurayrah: "We adhere to this, the *wiṣāl* is disliked, and it is that one continues fasting for two days without eating anything at night, and that is the opinion of Abū Ḥanīfah and the majority of scholars".[467]

463 Aḥmad, *al-Musnad, musnad al-nisā'*.

464 al-Samarqandī, *Tuḥfat al-fuqahā'* 163.

465 al-Bukhārī, *k. al-ṣawm, b. al-tankīl li man akthara al-wiṣāl*; Muslim, *k. al-ṣiyām, b. al-nahy ʿan al-wiṣāl fī al-ṣawm*.

466 Muslim, *k. al-ṣiyām, b. al-nahy ʿan al-wiṣāl fī al-ṣawm*.

467 Muhammad, *al-Muwaṭṭa'*, 129.

The whole year

It is also disliked to fast the whole year. ʿAbdullāh ibn ʿAmr ibn al-ʿĀṣ narrates that the Messenger of Allāh ﷺ said: "There is no fasting for the one who continually fasts".[468] Imām al-Tirmidhī says: "A group of scholars dislike fasting every day if it includes the *ʿīds* (*ʿīd al-Fiṭr, ʿīd al-aḍḥā*), and the days of *tashrīq*. If one breaks the fast on those days, one's action is no longer disliked, as one is no longer fasting the whole year".[469]

However, most scholars consider such fasting as disliked, and prefer to fast every other day like Prophet Dāwūd. ʿAbdullāh ibn ʿAmr ibn al-ʿĀṣ reported that the Messenger of Allāh ﷺ was informed that he could stand up for prayer throughout the night and observe the fast every day so long as he lived. Thereupon, the Messenger of Allāh ﷺ said: "Is it you who said this? I said to him: 'Messenger of Allāh, it is I who said that'. Thereupon, the Messenger of Allāh ﷺ said: 'You are not capable enough of doing so. Observe the fast and break it; sleep and stand for prayer, and observe the fast for three days during the month; for every good is multiplied ten times and this is like fasting for ever'. I said: 'Messenger of Allāh. I am capable of doing more than this. Thereupon he said: 'Fast one day and do not fast for the next two days'. I said: Messenger of Allāh, 'I have the strength to do more than that'. The Prophet ﷺ said: 'Fast one day and break on the other day. That is the fasting of David ﷺ and that is the best of fast'. I said: 'I am capable of doing more than this'. Thereupon, the Messenger of Allāh ﷺ said: 'There is nothing better than this'. ʿAbdullāh ibn ʿAmr said: 'Had I accepted the three days (fasting during every month) as the Messenger of Allāh ﷺ had said, it would have been dearer to me than my family and my property'."[470]

Fasting without the consent of one's husband

It is also disliked for a woman to practice *nafl* fasting while her husband is present except with his explicit consent. Abū Hurayrah reported that the Prophet ﷺ said: "A woman is not to fast [even] for one day while her husband is present except with his consent, unless it is during

468 Muslim, *k. al-ṣiyām, b. al-nahy ʿan ṣawm al-dahr.*

469 al-Tirmidhī, *k. al-ṣawm, b. mā jā'a fī ṣawm al-dahr.*

470 al-Bukhārī, *k. al-ṣawm, b. ḥaqq al-jism fī al-ṣawm*; Muslim, *k. al-ṣiyām, b. al-nahy ʿan ṣawm al-dahr.*

Ramaḍān".[471] Abū Saᶜīd al-Khudrī narrated: "The Apostle of Allāh ﷺ forbade women from fasting without the permission of their husbands".[472]

471 al-Bukhārī, *k. al-nikāḥ, b. ṣawm al-mar'ah bi idhn zawjihā;* Muslim, *k. al-zakāh, b. mā anfaqa al-ᶜabd min* māl *mawlāh;* Abū Dāwūd, *k. al-ṣawm, b. al-mar'ah taṣūm bi ghayr idhn zawjihā;* al-Tirmidhī, *k. al-ṣawm, b. mā jā'a fī karāhiyat ṣawm al-mar'ah illā bi idhn zawjihā;* Ibn Mājah, *k. al-ṣiyām, b. fī al-mar'ah taṣūm bi ghayr idhn zawjihā.*

472 Ibn Mājah, *k. al-ṣiyām, b. fī al-mar'ah taṣūm bi ghayr idhn zawjihā.*

Chapter 6: What is Allowed during Fasting

Eating and drinking forgetfully

If the fasting person eats, drinks or has sexual intercourse out of forgetfulness, he does not break his fast and does not have to make up [any fast] or pay any *kaffārah*.[473] Abū Hurayrah narrated that the Prophet ﷺ said: "If somebody eats or drinks forgetfully then he should complete his fast, for what he has eaten or drunk has been given to him by Allāh".[474]

Tasting the food

If one tastes something [introduced into one's mouth] one does not break the fast but doing so is disliked. If a woman is obliged to chew food for her child this is also disliked. If the dust of flour or from the road or smoke enters one's throat, this does not break the fast.[475]

Getting up in the morning as *junubī*

If someone had sexual relation during the night and gets up in the morning in the state of *janābah* (a state of major impurity when *ghusl* is compulsory), it does not affect one's fasting and one can bathe during the day to become ritually clean. ᶜĀ'ishah and Umm Salamah narrated: "At times the Messenger of Allāh ﷺ used to get up in the morning in the state of *janābah* after having sexual relations with his wives. He would then take a bath and fast".[476]

ᶜĀ'ishah narrates that a person once came to the Apostle of Allāh ﷺ asking him a question. The man said to the Prophet ﷺ: "Messenger of Allāh, (the time of) prayer overtakes me as I am in a state of *janābah*;

473 al-Samarqandī, *Tuḥfat al-fuqahā'* 169.

474 al-Bukhārī, *k. al-ṣawm, b. al-ṣā'im idhā akala aw shariba nāsiyan*; Muslim, *k. al-ṣiyām, b. akl al-nāsī wa shurbuh wa jimāᶜuhu lā yufṭir.*

475 al-Samarqandī, *Tuḥfat al-fuqahā'* 169; al-Kāsānī, *Badā'iᶜ al-ṣanā'iᶜ*, ii. 635.

476 al-Bukhārī, *k. al-ṣawm, b. al-ṣā'im yuṣbiḥu junuban;* Muslim, k. *al-ṣiyām, b. ṣiḥḥat ṣawm man ṭalaᶜa ᶜalayh al-fajr wa huwa junub.*

should I observe fast (in this state)?' Upon this the Messenger of Allāh ﷺ said: '(At times, the time of) prayer overtakes me while I am in a state of *janābah*, and I observe the fast (in that very state)'. Whereupon, he (the man) said: 'Messenger of Allāh, you are not like us, Allāh has pardoned all your sins, the previous ones and the later ones'. Upon this he (the Prophet) said: 'By Allāh, I hope I am the most God-fearing of you, and possess the best knowledge among you of those things against which I should guard'."[477]

Abū Bakr ibn ʿAbd al-Raḥmān ibn Ḥārith reported: "I heard Abū Hurayrah narrating that he who is overtaken by dawn in a state of *janābah* should not observe fast. I made a mention of it to ʿAbd al-Raḥmān ibn Ḥārith (i.e. his father) but he denied it. ʿAbd al-Raḥmān went and I also went along with him until we came to ʿĀ'ishah and Umm Salamah and ʿAbd al-Raḥmān asked them about it. Both of them said: 'At times it so happened that the Apostle of Allāh ﷺ woke up in the morning in a state of *janābah*, (not because of a dream), and observed fast'. We then proceeded until we came to Marwān and ʿAbd al-Raḥmān made mention of it to him. Upon this Marwān said: 'I stress upon you (with an oath) that you better go to Abū Hurayrah and refute to him what is said about it'. So we came to Abū Hurayrah and ʿAbd al-Raḥmān made mention of it to him, whereupon Abū Hurayrah said: 'Did they (the two wives of the Prophet) tell you this?' He replied: 'Yes'. Upon this Abū Hurayrah said: 'They have better knowledge'. Ibn Jurayj (one of the narrators) reported: 'I asked ʿAbd al-Malik, if they (the two wives) said the statement with regard to Ramaḍān, whereupon he said: 'It was so, and he (the Prophet) woke up in the morning in a state of *janābah* which was not due to a wet dream and then observed the fast'."[478]

Kissing

It is allowed for husbands and wives to kiss each other during the day as long as they are sure that this will not lead to sexual relations and that they will not have an emission. ʿĀ'ishah narrated: "The Prophet used to kiss and embrace (his wives) while he was fasting, and he had more

477 Muslim, k. *al-ṣiyām, b. ṣihhat ṣawm man ṭalaʿa ʿalayh al-fajr wa huwa junub.*
478 ibid.

power to control his desires than any of you".[479] ʿĀ'ishah also narrated: "The Apostle of Allāh ﷺ used to kiss during the month of Ramaḍān when he was fasting".[480] ʿUmar ibn al-Khaṭṭāb narrated: "I kissed my wife while I was fasting, I then said: 'Apostle of Allāh, I have done a big deed; I kissed while I was fasting'. He said: 'What do you think if you rinse your mouth with water while you are fasting?'[481] ʿĀ'ishah narrated that the Prophet ﷺ used to kiss her and suck her tongue when he was fasting.[482]

Aswad reported: "I and Masrūq went to ʿĀ'ishah and asked her if the Messenger of Allāh ﷺ embraced (his wives) while fasting? She said: "Yes; but he had control over his desire".[483]

ʿUmar ibn Abū Salamah reported that he asked the Messenger of Allāh ﷺ: "Can one observing the fast kiss his wife?" The Messenger of Allāh ﷺ said to him: "Ask her (Umm Salamah)". She informed him that the Messenger of Allāh ﷺ did that, where upon he said: "Messenger of Allāh, Allāh pardoned you all your sins, the previous and the later ones". Upon this, the Messenger of Allāh ﷺ said: "By Allāh, I am the most Allāh conscious among you and I fear Him most among you".[484]

Abū Hurayrah narrated: "A man asked the Prophet ﷺ whether one who was fasting could embrace (his wife) and he gave him permission; but when another man came to him, and asked him, he forbade him. The one to whom he gave permission was an old man and the one whom he forbade was a youth".[485]

Wet dream

If one sleeps during the day and has a wet dream or one looks at one's wife and thinks about sexual matters and has an emission, this does not

479 al-Bukhārī, *k. al-ṣawm, b. al-mubāsharah li al-ṣā'im;* Muslim, *k. al-ṣiyām, b. bayān anna al-qublah fī al-ṣawm laysat muḥarramah ʿalā man lam tuḥarrik shahwatah.*

480 Muslim, *k. al-ṣiyām, b. bayān anna al-qublah fī al-ṣawm laysat muḥarramah ʿalā man lam tuḥarrik shahwatah.*

481 Abū Dāwūd, *k. al-ṣiyām, b. al-qublah li al-ṣā'im.*

482 Abū Dāwūd, *k. al-ṣawm, b. al-ṣā'im yablaʿu al-rīq.*

483 al-Bukhārī, *k. al-ṣawm, b. al-mubāsharah li al-ṣā'im*; Muslim, *k. al-ṣiyām, b. bayān anna al-qublah fī al-ṣawm laysat muḥarramah ʿalā man lam tuḥarrik shahwatah.*

484 Muslim, *k. al-ṣiyām, b. bayān anna al-qublah fī al-ṣawm laysat muḥarramah ʿalā man lam tuḥarrik shahwatah.*

485 Abū Dāwūd, *k. al-ṣawm, b. al-qublah li al-ṣā'im wa karāhiyatihī li al-shābb.*

affect one's fasting.[486] Abū Saᶜīd al-Khudrī narrated that the Messenger of Allāh ﷺ said: "Three things do not cause breaking of the fast: cupping, vomiting, and wet dreams".[487]

Applying oil

It is allowed to apply oil, or drop oil or medicine in one's eyes.[488] However, if one drops medicine into the nose or ear and it reaches the throat, this will break the fast.[489]

If drops are introduced into the penis this does not break the fast according to Abū Ḥanīfah and Muḥammad, while Abū Yūsuf said that it does.[490]

Cooling with water

It is allowed for one to cool oneself in water or to put wet clothes on the body during fasting. Anas says: "I have a tub, in which I enter while I am fasting".[491] Abū Bakr ibn ᶜAbd al-Raḥmān, a Companion of the Prophet ﷺ, said: "I have seen the Apostle of Allāh ﷺ in al-ᶜArj (name of a place between Madinah and Makkah) pouring water over his head while he was fasting, either because of thirst or because of heat". [492] ᶜAbdullāh ibn ᶜUmar moistened a cloth, then it was put on him while he was fasting.[493]

Applying *kuḥl*

Kuḥl is a black powder (antimony) applied to the eyes. It is allowed to apply *kuḥl*. ᶜĀ'ishah said that: "The Messenger of Allāh ﷺ applied *kuḥl* while he was fasting".[494] Anas reported that: "A man came to the Prophet ﷺ and said: 'My eye is hurting, can I apply *kuḥl* while I am fasting?' He

486 al-Kāsānī, *Badā'iᶜ al-ṣanā'iᶜ*, ii. 602.
487 al-Tirmidhī, *k. al-ṣawm, b. mā jā'a fī al-ṣā'im yadhraᶜuhu al-qay'.*
488 al-Kāsānī, *Badā'iᶜ al-ṣanā'iᶜ, ii.* 606.
489 ibid.
490 al-Qudūrī, *al-Mukhtaṣar* 192.
491 al-Bukhārī, *k. al-ṣawm, b. ightisāl al-ṣā'im.*
492 Abū Dāwūd, *k. al-ṣiyām, b. al-ṣā'im yuṣabbu ᶜalayhi al-mā' min al-ᶜaṭash…*
493 al-Bukhārī, *k. al-ṣawm, b. ightisāl al-ṣā'im.*
494 Ibn Mājah, *k. al-ṣiyām, b. mā jā'a fī al-siwāk wa al-kuḥl li al-ṣā'im.*

answered: 'Yes'."[495] Aᶜmash says: "I did not see any of my teachers dislike *kuḥl* for the fasting person".[496]

Injection

Injections for medical reasons are allowed. Furthermore, it does not matter if what was injected reaches the stomach, as it does not reach the stomach through the customary manner (that food does).[497]

Cupping

If one is subjected to cupping this does not break one's fast. ᶜAbdullāh ibn ᶜAbbās narrated: "The Messenger of Allāh ﷺ had himself cupped when he was fasting and wearing *iḥrām*".[498] Abū Saᶜīd al-Khudrī narrated that the Messenger of Allāh ﷺ said: "Three things do not cause the breaking of the fast: cupping, vomiting, and wet dreams".[499]

Using *miswāk* or toothpaste

Using *miswāk* (a small twig for brushing teeth) is Sunnah during Ramaḍān throughout the day, as it is Sunnah during other days. ᶜĀmir ibn Rabīᶜah narrated: "I have seen the Apostle of Allāh ﷺ more often than I could count, using a *miswāk* while he was fasting".[500]

Similarly there is no harm in using toothpaste or tooth powder during fasting, as long as one makes sure they do not enter the throat.

495 al-Tirmidhī, *k. al-ṣawm, b. mā jā'a fī al-kuḥl li al-ṣā'im.*

496 Abū Dāwūd, *k. al-ṣawm, b. fī al-kuḥl ᶜinda al-nawm li al-ṣā'im.*

497 See: *Fatawa Muṣṭafā al-Zarqā'* 173.

498 al-Bukhārī, *k. al-ṣawm, b. al-ḥijāmah wa al-qay' li al-ṣā'im;* Muslim, *k. al-ḥajj, b. jawāz al-ḥijāmah li al-muḥrim.*

499 al-Tirmidhī, *k. al-ṣawm, b. mā jā'a fī al-ṣā'im yadhraᶜuhu al-qay'.*

500 Abū Dāwūd, *k. al-ṣawm, b. al-siwāk li al-ṣā'im*; al-Tirmidhī, *k. al-ṣawm, b. mā jā'a fī al-siwāk li al-ṣā'im.*

Chapter 7: What Breaks the Fast

Those things which break the fast are of two types:

1- Those which break the fast and necessitate both *qaḍā'* and *kaffārah.*

2- Those which break the fast and necessitate *qaḍā'* only.

WHAT MAKES BOTH *QAḌĀ'* AND *KAFFĀRAH* COMPULSORY?

Qaḍā' means to make up what has been missed. If what has been missed is the result of a wilful sin then, in addition, *kaffārah* (or expiation of the sin) is also required. For example, whoever deliberately has sexual intercourse or deliberately eats or drinks something - either to nourish himself or as a medicine – during the day in the fasting of Ramaḍān has committed a sin and nothing can compensate for it. Abū Hurayrah reported: "The Prophet ﷺ said: 'If anyone breaks his fast one day during Ramaḍān without a concession granted to him by Allāh, a perpetual fast will not atone for it".[501]

Such a person must repent and must do both *qaḍā'* and *kaffārah.*[502] *Qaḍā'* is on account of the invalidation of his fast, and there is no difference of opinion in this. As for *kaffārah,* Abū Hurayrah narrated: "While we were sitting with the Prophet ﷺ a man came and said: 'O Messenger of Allāh! I have been ruined'. The Messenger of Allāh ﷺ asked him what was the matter. He replied: 'I had sexual intercourse with my wife while I was fasting'. The Messenger of Allāh ﷺ said to him: 'Can you afford to manumit a slave?' He replied in the negative. The Messenger of Allāh ﷺ said to him: 'Can you fast for two successive months?' He replied in the negative. The Prophet ﷺ asked him: 'Can you afford to feed 60 poor people?' He replied in the negative. The Prophet ﷺ kept silent and while we were in that state, a big basket full of dates was brought to the Prophet ﷺ. He asked: 'Where is the questioner?' He replied: 'I (am here)'. The Prophet ﷺ said (to him): 'Take this (basket of dates) and give it in charity'. The man said: 'Should I give it to a person poorer than I?

501 Abū Dāwūd, *k. al-ṣawm, b. al-taghlīẓ fī man afṭara ʿamdan.*

502 al-Samarqandī, *Tuḥfat al-fuqahā'* 174.

By Allāh; there is no family between its (i.e. Madīnah's) two mountains who are poorer than I'. The Prophet ﷺ smiled until his premolar teeth became visible and then said: 'Feed your family with it'."[503]

Ḥumayd ibn ʿAbd al-Raḥmān reported that Abū Hurayrah had narrated to him that the Messenger of Allāh ﷺ commanded the person that broke the fast during Ramaḍān to free a slave or observe fasts for two (consecutive) months or feed 60 poor people. Imām Muḥammad says after narrating this ḥadīth: "We adhere to this, whoever breaks his fast deliberately during the month of Ramaḍān by eating or drinking or having sexual relations, has to do *qaḍā'* of one day in its place and to do *kaffārah* of *ẓihār* (i.e. compensation as mentioned above in the hadith of Abū Hurayrah).[504] *Ẓihār* is the name of a particular oath common among the Arabs before the coming of Islam. This form of oath is strongly condemned in the Qur'ān, especially when used as a form of divorce in the expression: "You are for me as the back of my mother".

Imām al-Zuhrī says that anyone who eats deliberately during Ramaḍān is the same as one who has sexual relations with his wife, (i.e. he has to do *qaḍā'* and *kaffārah* both).[505]

Smoking

Smoking tobacco (in whatever form) or chewing tobacco (in whatever form) are strongly disapproved at any time. However, if one deliberately consumes tobacco while fasting then it will break one's fast and one must offer both *qaḍā'* and *kaffārah.*[506]

WHAT NECESSITATES *QAḌĀ'* ONLY?

The following necessitates *qaḍā'*, but without any obligation to do *kaffārah.*

Breaking the fast by mistake

If one breaks one's fast by mistake one should continue the fast. There is no sin incurred but one has to do *qaḍā'*.

503 al-Bukhārī, *k. al-ṣawm, b. idhā jāmaʿa fī ramaḍān;* Muslim, *k. al-ṣiyām, b. taghlīẓ taḥrīm al-jimāʿ fī nahār ramaḍān.*

504 Muhammad, *al-Muwaṭṭa'*, 123.

505 ʿAbd al-Razzāq, *al-Muṣannaf,* iv. 197.

506 *Ḥāshiyat al-Ṭaḥṭāwī ʿalā marāqī al-falāḥ,* i. 364.

If one gets up in the morning and believes that dawn has not broken and eats or breaks his fast considering that the sun has set, (and) then realises that dawn has broken or the sun has not set, one should continue fasting, and makes up that day, but does not have to do *kaffārah.*[507] Imām Muḥammad narrates on the authority of Abū Ḥanīfah from Ibrāhīm al-Nakhaʿī that: "ʿUmar ibn al-Khaṭṭāb and his companions broke the fast on a cloudy day thinking that the sun had set. Then the sun appeared. ʿUmar said: 'We did not commit a sin, we will complete this day and will fast another day in its place. Imām Muḥammad says: "We adhere to this... and this is the opinion of Abū Ḥanīfah".[508]

Breaking the fast for medical reasons

If one has begun a fast but then has an urgent need to take medication and taking that medication (this includes the use of inhalers) breaks the fast, in such a case, one must do *qaḍā'*, but not *kaffārah.*[509]

Resorting to medical treatment that does not entail anything that may be considered as taking food or drink will not break the fast: for example, if someone needs oxygen to assist their breathing.

Sexual contact that is less than *jimāʿ*

Whoever has sexual contact but without *jimāʿ* [penetration of the private parts] and ejaculates must make it up, but does not do *kaffārah.*[510]

If one has an emission as a result of kissing or touching, then he must make it up but he does not do *kaffārah.*[511]

Vomiting deliberately

If one is overcome by vomiting it does not break one's fast but if one induces vomiting and it fills one's mouth one must then make up the fast.[512] Abū Hurayrah narrated: "The Prophet ﷺ said: 'If one has a sudden attack of vomiting while one is fasting, no *qaḍā'* is required

507 al-Qudūrī, *al-Mukhtaṣar* 196.
508 Abū Ḥanīfah, *K. al-āthār* 71.
509 al-Qudūrī, *al-Mukhtaṣar* 191.
510 al-Samarqandī, *Tuḥfat al-fuqahā'* 172.
511 ibid.
512 al-Qudūrī, *al-Mukhtaṣar* 190.

of him, but if one vomits intentionally one must do *qaḍā*'".[513] Imām Muḥammad narrates on the authority of Abū Ḥanīfah from Ibrāhīm al-Nakhaᶜī about vomiting that there is no *qaḍā'* on that person, except if one vomits deliberately, then in this case one has to complete the fasting and do the *qaḍā'* later. Imām Muḥammad says: "We adhere to this, and this is the opinion of Abū Ḥanīfah".[514] ᶜAlī says: "If vomiting happens to someone, then there is no *qaḍā'* on him, but if he vomits deliberately then there is *qaḍā'* on him".[515] This is also the opinion of ᶜAbdullāh ibn ᶜUmar, ᶜAlqamah, Ḥasan al-Baṣrī, Muḥammad ibn Sīrīn, ᶜAṭā' ibn Abī Rabāḥ, Qāsim ibn Muḥammad, ᶜĀmir al-Shaᶜbī, Mujāhid. [516]

Eating something which is not food

Whoever swallows a stone, or piece of iron or date stone breaks his fast and must make up the fast.[517]

Breaking a fast other than during the month of Ramaḍān

If one breaks his fast deliberately outside the month of Ramaḍān, whether it is obligatory fasting or voluntary then there is no *kaffārah* to pay, but one has to do *qaḍā'*.[518] ᶜĀ'ishah narrated: "Some food was presented to me and Ḥafṣah. We were fasting, but broke our fast. Then the Apostle of Allāh ﷺ entered upon us. We said to him: 'A gift was presented to us; we coveted it and we broke our fast'. The Apostle of Allāh ﷺ said: 'There is no harm to you; keep a fast another day in lieu of it'."[519] Imām Muḥammad says after narrating this ḥadīth: "We adhere to this, whoever fasts voluntarily, and breaks it then he has to do *qaḍā'*, and this is the opinion of Abū Ḥanīfah".[520] ᶜUthmān al-Battī narrates that: "Anas ibn Sīrīn fasted on the day of ᶜArafah, and became very thirsty, so

513 Abū Dāwūd, *k. al-ṣawm, b. al-ṣā'im yastaqī'u ᶜāmidan*; al-Dārimī, *k. al-ṣawm, b. al-qay' li al-ṣā'im.*

514 Abū Ḥanīfah, *K. al-āthār* 72.

515 Ibn Abī Shaybah, *al-Muṣannaf*, vi. 180.

516 ibid., vi. 180-184.

517 al-Samarqandī, *Tuḥfat al-fuqahā'* 170.

518 al-Kāsānī, *Badā'iᶜ al-ṣanā'iᶜ*, ii. 625-6.

519 Abū Dāwūd, *k. al-ṣawm, b. man ra'ā ᶜalayh al-qaḍā';* al-Tirmidhī, *k. al-ṣawm, b. mā jā'a fī ījāb al-qaḍā' ᶜalayh.*

520 Muhammad, *al-Muwaṭṭa'* 127.

he broke the fast. Then he asked a number of the Companions of the Prophet ﷺ. They commanded him to fast another day in its place".[521] ʿAṭā' ibn Abī Rabāḥ narrates from Ibn ʿAbbās that one has to fast another day in its place.[522]

Delaying the *qaḍā'*

One should do the *qaḍā'* of fasting as soon as one is able to do so; but if one delays the *qaḍā'* for a reason, then there is no sin for delaying. Abū Salamah reported: "I heard ʿĀ'ishah as saying: 'I had to complete some of the fasts of Ramaḍān, but I could not do it but during the month of Shaʿbān due to my duties to the Messenger of Allāh ﷺ or with the Messenger of Allāh ﷺ".[523]

If one delays this until the next Ramaḍān begins, one fasts this second Ramaḍān and makes up the first afterwards and does not have to pay compensation. This is the opinion of Ḥasan al-Baṣrī and Ibrāhīm al-Nakhaʿī.[524]

Separation between *qaḍā'* fasts

In doing the *qaḍā'* of Ramaḍān, a person may fast separate or consecutive days. Al-Ḥakam says: "Saʿīd ibn Jubayr and Mujāhid used to say: 'There is no harm in doing the *qaḍā'* of Ramaḍān separately'."[525] Ḥasan al-Baṣrī says: "There is no harm in doing the *qaḍā'* of Ramaḍān separately as long as one counts the number of missed days". [526]

521 Ibn Abī Shaybah, *al-Muṣannaf,* vi. 161.

522 ibid.

523 al-Bukhārī, *k. al-ṣawm, b. matā yaqḍī qaḍā'a ramaḍān*; Muslim, k. *al-ṣiyām, b. qaḍā' ramaḍān fī shaʿbān.*

524 al-Baghawī, *Sharḥ al-sunnah,* iii. 507.

525 ibid., iii. 508.

526 ibid.

Chapter 8: The Night of *al-Qadr*

The Night of *al-Qadr* (Night of Decree) is the best and most auspicious night in the whole year. Allāh, Exalted is He, says: "*Indeed, We sent the Qur'ān down during the Night of Decree. And what can make you know what the Night of Decree is? The Night of Decree is better than a thousand months. The angels and the Spirit descend therein by permission of their Lord for every matter. Peace it is until the emergence of dawn*".[527]

Imām Mālik narrates: "The Messenger of Allāh ﷺ was shown the lifespans of people who had gone before him. The Prophet looked at the shorter lifespan of his *ummah* and that they will not reach in deeds what others have reached due to the length of their lifespan. So Allāh granted him the Night of *Qadr*, which is better than a thousand months".[528]

SEEKING THE NIGHT OF *AL-QADR*

It is recommended that one seeks for the Night of *Qadr*, especially during the month of Ramaḍān. ʿĀ'ishah has narrated that the Messenger of Allāh ﷺ said: "Search for the Night of *Qadr* in the odd nights of the last ten days of Ramaḍān".[529] The Companions of the Prophet ﷺ the pious people of the later generations and Muslims all over the world have always made an effort to seek this night. The revelation of a whole *surah* (chapter) in the Qur'ān about this night and the concern of the Prophet ﷺ the Companions and people of the later generations leaves no doubt that this is the most important night of the whole year.

527 *al-Qadr.*

528 Mālik, *al-Muwaṭṭa', k. al-iʿtikāf, b. mā jā'a fī laylat al-qadr.* Ibn ʿAbd al-Barr says: "I do not know of this been narrated anywhere other than *al-Muwaṭṭa'*; and this is one of those four *aḥādīth* which do not exist except in *al-Muwaṭṭa'*. (*al-Istidhkār*, x. 342.)

529 al-Bukhārī, *k. faḍl laylat al-qadr, b. taḥarri laylat al-qadr fī al-witr min al-ʿashr al-awākhir.*

WHICH NIGHT IS IT?

There is a difference of the opinion among scholars as to which night is the Night of *Qadr.* In what follows, I shall give the most important opinions in this regard:

1- Some people say that this night moves throughout the years; though mostly it is during Ramaḍān, nevertheless, it keeps changing every year. When the Qur'ān was revealed, it was during Ramaḍān. That is the opinion of ʿAbdullāh ibn Masʿūd, Abū Ḥanīfah, Abū Yūsuf and Muḥammad.[530]

2- Some say it is any night of the last ten nights of Ramaḍān. ʿĀ'ishah narrated: "The Messenger of Allāh ﷺ used to do *iʿtikāf* in the last ten nights of Ramaḍān and used to say: 'Look for the Night of *Qadr* in the last ten nights of the month of Ramaḍān'." [531] Abū Qilābah says: "The Night of *Qadr* moves across all ten nights".[532] That is the opinion of Mālik, Sufyān al-Thawrī, Shāfiʿī, Aḥmad ibn Ḥanbal, Isḥāq ibn Rāhawayh and Abū Thawr.[533]

3- Some people say it is definitely the 27th night of Ramaḍān. Zirr ibn Ḥubaysh narrates: "I asked Ubayy ibn Kaʿb: 'Your brother (in faith) Ibn Masʿūd says: 'He who stands for the night prayer throughout the year will find the Night of *Qadr,*' whereupon, he said: 'May Allāh have mercy upon him; he said these words with the intention that people might not rely only on one night, whereas he knew that it is during the month of Ramaḍān and it is the 27th night'. He then took an oath (without making any exception, i.e. without saying inshā'Allāh) that it was the 27th night. I said to him: 'Abū Mundhir, on what grounds do you say this?' Thereupon, he said: 'By the indication or by the sign which the Messenger of Allāh ﷺ gave us, and that is that on that day (the sun) will rise without having any ray in it'."[534] Most people say it is any odd night during the last ten nights of Ramaḍān. ʿAbdullāh ibn ʿAbbās narrates that the Prophet ﷺ said: "Look for the Night of *Qadr* during the last ten nights of Ramaḍān, on the night when nine or seven or

530 Ibn ʿAbd al-Barr, *al-Istidhkār,* x. 337.

531 al-Bukhārī, *k. faḍl laylat al-qadr, b. taḥarrī laylat al-qadr fī al-witr min al-ʿashr al-awākhir.*

532 Ibn Abī Shaybah, *al-Muṣannaf,* vi. 271.

533 Ibn ʿAbd al-Barr, *al-Istidhkār,* x. 338.

534 Muslim, *k. al-ṣiyām, b. faḍl laylat al-qadr.*

five nights remain out of the last ten nights of Ramaḍān (i.e. 21, 23, and 25, respectively)".[535] ʿUbādah ibn al-Ṣāmit narrated: "The Prophet came out to inform us about the Night of *Qadr* but two Muslims were quarrelling with each other. So, the Prophet said: 'I came out to inform you about the Night of *Qadr* but so-and-so were quarrelling, so the news about it has been taken away; yet that might be for your own good, so search for it on the 29th, 27th and 25th (of Ramaḍān)".[536] Abū Saʿīd al-Khudrī narrated: "We did *iʿtikāf* with the Messenger of Allāh ﷺ in the middle ten days of Ramaḍān and in the morning of the 20th he came out and (then) said: 'Whoever was in *iʿtikāf* with me should remain in *iʿtikāf* for the last ten days, for I was informed (of the date) of the Night (of *Qadr*) but I have been caused to forget it. (In the dream) I saw myself prostrating in mud and water in the morning of the night (of *Qadr*). So, look for it in the last ten nights and in the odd ones of them'. It rained that night and the roof of the mosque dribbled as it was made from the leaf stalks of date-palms. I saw with my own eyes the mark of mud and water on the forehead of the Prophet (i.e. in the morning of the 21st)".[537] Abū Qilābah says: "The Night of *Qadr* moves in the odd nights of the last ten days of Ramaḍān".[538]

Shāh Walīullah writes: "Know that the Night of *Qadr* is of two kinds: one is in which the Qur'ān, the whole of it, was sent down to the firmament of the world, and, thereafter, was revealed little by little. This night comes only once in a year and it is also not necessary that it should be during the month of Ramaḍān. But, most probably, it is so. On the occasion of the revelation of the Qur'ān, the night was during Ramaḍān. The other Night of *Qadr* is that in which a kind of spirituality is felt and the angels descend upon earth. The Muslims devote themselves to prayer during this night and they are benefited by each other's spiritual exaltation and blissfulness. The angels come close to them, the devils run away, and their devotions are accepted. The night occurs every year in the odd nights of the last ten days of Ramaḍān. It can occur a little sooner

535 al-Bukhārī, *k. faḍl laylat al-qadr, b. taḥarrī laylat al-qadr fī al-witr min al-ʿashr al-awākhir.*

536 al-Bukhārī, *k. faḍl laylat al-qadr, b. rafʿ maʿrifat laylat al-qadr...*

537 al-Bukhārī, *k. faḍl laylat al-qadr, b. iltimās laylat al-qadr fī al-sabʿ al-awākhir;* Muslim, *k. al-ṣiyām, b. faḍl laylat al-qadr.*

538 ʿAbd al-Razzāq, *al-Muṣannaf,* iv. 252.

or later, but it is always during the month of Ramaḍān. Thus, when a person speaks of the former Night of *Qadr* he says that it rotates in the year and when he speaks of the latter he says that it is found during the last ten days of Ramaḍān".[539]

WORSHIP DURING THIS NIGHT

ʿĀ'ishah narrated that: "With the start of the last ten days of Ramaḍān, the Prophet ﷺ used to tighten his waist belt (i.e. work hard) and used to pray all the night, and used to keep his family awake for the prayers".[540]

ʿĀ'ishah also said: "I asked the Messenger of Allāh ﷺ if I know which night is the Night of *Qadr*, then what should I say in it? He answered: 'Say:

اَللَّهُمَّ إِنَّكَ عَفُوٌّ تُحِبُّ الْعَفْوَ فَاعْفُ عَنِّي

'O Allāh! Verily You are all-forgiving, You love forgiveness, so forgive me'."[541]

539 al-Dihlawī, *Ḥujjatullāh al-bālighah,* ii. 85.

540 al-Bukhārī, *k. faḍl laylat al-qadr, b. al-ʿamal fī al-ʿashr al-awākhir min ramaḍān;* Muslim, *k. al-iʿtikāf, b. al-ijtihād fī al-ʿashr al-awākhir min ramaḍān.*

541 al-Tirmidhī, *k. al-daʿawāt;* Ibn Mājah, *k. al-duʿā', b. al-duʿā' bi al-ʿafw wa al-ʿāfiyah.*

Chapter 9: *Iʿtikāf*

Iʿtikāf means to associate oneself with something, or to retire to devote oneself to it – be it good or bad. Allāh, Exalted is He, says: "*What are these statues to which you are devoted?*"[542] – that which you are standing at and worshipping.

Here *iʿtikāf* refers to staying in the mosque with the intention of attaining closeness to Allāh, Exalted is He, while fasting.

Iʿtikāf is a completion of the benefits of the fasting. Ibn al-Qayyim writes: "The basic purpose of *iʿtikāf* is that the heart gets attached to God, and with it, one attains inner composure and equanimity and pre-occupation with the mundane things of life ceases and absorption in the Eternal Reality takes its place, and the state is reached in which all fears, hopes and apprehensions are superseded by the love and remembrance of God, every anxiety is transformed into anxiety for Him, and every thought and feeling is blended with the eagerness to gain His nearness and earn His good favour, and devotion to the Almighty is generated instead of devotion to the world and it becomes the provision for the grave where there will be neither a friend nor a helper. This is the high aim and purpose of *iʿtikāf* which is the speciality of the most sublime part of Ramaḍān, i.e. the last ten days".[543]

Shāh Walīullah remarks: "Since *iʿtikāf* in the mosque is a means to the attainment of peace of the mind and purification of the heart, and it affords an excellent opportunity for forging an identity with the angels and having a share in the blissfulness of the Night of Power (*Qadr*) and for devoting oneself to prayer and meditation, Allāh has set apart the last ten days of the month of Ramaḍān for it and made it a Sunnah for His pious and virtuous slaves".[544]

542 *al-Anbiyā'* 52.

543 Ibn al-Qayyim, *Zād al-maʿād*, ii. 87.

544 al-Dihlawī, *Ḥujjatullāh al-bālighah*, ii. 86.

TYPES OF *Iᶜ TIKĀF*

There are three types of *iᶜtikāf*:

Wājib iᶜtikāf

If one commits oneself to a certain number of days for *iᶜtikāf*, then it becomes *wājib (compulsory)* for one to make *iᶜtikāf* during the corresponding nights, while fasting. *Wājib iᶜtikāf* is not allowed without fasting.[545] ᶜAbdullāh ibn ᶜUmar narrated: "ᶜUmar took a vow in the pre-Islamic days to spend a night or a day in devotion near the Kaᶜbah (in the sacred mosque). He asked the Prophet ﷺ about it. He said: 'Observe *iᶜtikāf* (i.e. spend a night or a day near the Kaᶜbah) and fast'."[546]

Similarly if someone starts *iᶜtikāf* then it becomes *wājib* on him to complete it.[547]

Sunnah *iᶜtikāf*

Iᶜtikāf in the last ten days and nights of Ramaḍān is Sunnah. Ubayy ibn Kaᶜb narrated: "The Prophet ﷺ used to observe *iᶜtikāf* during the last ten days of Ramaḍān. One year he did not observe *iᶜtikāf*. When the next year came, he observed *iᶜtikāf* for twenty nights (i.e. days)".[548] ᶜAbdullāh ibn ᶜUmar reported that: "The Apostle of Allāh ﷺ used to observe *iᶜtikāf* during the last ten days of Ramaḍān".[549] ᶜĀ'ishah narrated: "The Prophet ﷺ used to do *iᶜtikāf* during the last ten nights of Ramaḍān until he passed away. Then after him his wives did *iᶜtikāf*".[550]

Mustaḥabb iᶜtikāf

Mustaḥabb iᶜtikāf can be done any time during the year.

545 al-Kāsānī, *Badā'iᶜ al-ṣanā'iᶜ*, iii. 6-7.

546 al-Bukhārī, *k. al-iᶜtikāf, b. al-iᶜtikāf laylan;* Muslim, *k. al-aymān, b. nadhr al-kāfir wa mā yafᶜalu fihi idhā aslama.*

547 al-Kāsānī, *Badā'iᶜ al-ṣanā'iᶜ*, iii. 4.

548 Abū Dāwūd, *k. al-ṣawm, b. al-iᶜtikāf;* al-Tirmidhī, *k. al-ṣawm, b. mā jā'a fī al-iᶜtikāf idhā kharāja minh.*

549 al-Bukhārī, *k. al-iᶜtikāf, b. al-iᶜtikāf fī al-ᶜashr al-awākhir;* Muslim, *k. al-iᶜtikāf, b. iᶜtikaf al-ᶜashr al-awākhir min ramaḍān.*

550 al-Bukhārī, *k. al-iᶜtikāf, b. al-iᶜtikāf fī al-ᶜashr al-awākhir;* Muslim, *k. al-iᶜtikāf, b. iᶜtikaf al-ᶜashr al-awākhir min ramaḍān.*

CONDITIONS FOR THE VALIDITY OF *IʿTIKĀF*

Apart from the condition of Islam (i.e. being a Muslim) and sanity there are certain other conditions for *iʿtikāf* to be valid. These are:

1- The person doing *iʿtikāf* must be pure from *janābah, ḥayḍ* (menstruation) or *nifās* (postnatal bleeding) The reason that *iʿtikāf* is not valid from an impure person is that *iʿtikāf* is done in the mosque and an impure person is not allowed to enter into the mosque.[551] While being in *iʿtikāf*, if one has a wet dream, then one must leave the mosque immediately, have a bath and return.

If a woman starts her period during *iʿtikāf* she should cancel her *iʿtikāf*, and do *qaḍā'* later. Imām al-Zuhrī says: "When a woman has her period during *iʿtikāf*, then she should leave for her house, and when she becomes pure, she should do *qaḍā*".[552] The same has been narrated from Ibrāhīm al-Nakhaʿī, and ʿAṭā' ibn Abī Rabāḥ.[553]

2- Intention is compulsory; because it is an act of worship, and an act of worship is not valid without the intention.[554]

3-Fasting. ʿĀ'ishah has narrated the Prophet ﷺ said: "There is no *iʿtikāf* without fasting".[555] ʿAbdullāh ibn ʿUmar and ʿAbdullāh ibn ʿAbbās said: "There is no *iʿtikāf* without fasting".[556] ʿĀ'ishah said: "Whoever does *iʿtikāf*, he should fast".[557] This is the opinion of al-Zuhrī and ʿUrwah ibn al-Zubayr.[558]

In *nafl iʿtikāf*, some people have allowed it to be for less than a day, in which case fasting will not be compulsory.[559]

4-It must be done in the *masjid* (mosque). Allāh says: "*But touch them not [that is, your wives] while you are in retreat (iʿtikāf) in the mosques*".[560] According to Abū Ḥanīfah, *iʿtikāf* is not allowed except in a *masjid*

551 al-Kāsānī, *Badā'iʿ al-ṣanā'iʿ*, iii. 5.

552 ʿAbd al-Razzāq, *al-Muṣannaf*, iv. 368.

553 ibid., iv. 368-369.

554 al-Kāsānī, *Badā'iʿ al-ṣanā'iʿ*, iii. 6.

555 al-Ḥākim, *al-Mustadrak, k. al-ṣawm, b. al-iʿtikāf;* al-Dāraquṭnī, *al-sunan, k. al-ṣiyām, b. al-iʿtikāf;* al-Bayhaqī, *al-sunan al-kubrā, k. al-ṣiyām, b. al-muʿtakif yaṣūm.*

556 ʿAbd al-Razzāq, *al-Muṣannaf*, iv. 353.

557 ibid., iv. 354.

558 ibid., iv. 354-355.

559 al-Kāsānī, *Badā'iʿ al-ṣanā'iʿ*, iii. 10.

560 *al-Baqarah* 187.

in which the five daily prayers are performed.[561] Ḥudhayfah narrated that the Prophet ﷺ said: "Every mosque that has a caller to prayer and an *imām* is acceptable for *iʿtikāf*".[562] Most people of knowledge, like Abū Ḥanīfah, hold that *iʿtikāf* is allowed in any (normally functioning) mosque. That is the opinion of ʿĀ'ishah, Saʿīd ibn Jubayr, Ibrāhīm al-Nakhaʿī, Abū Qilābah, al-Zuhrī, al-Ḥakam, Ḥammād ibn Abī Sulaymān, Mālik and Shāfiʿī.[563] It is also the opinion of Abū Qilābah, Hammām ibn al-Ḥārith, Abū Salamah ibn ʿAbd al-Raḥmān, Abū al-Aḥwaṣ, al-Shaʿbī, Sufyān al-Thawrī, Ibn ʿUlayyah, Dāwūd al-Ẓāhirī and Abū Jaʿfar al-Ṭabarī.[564]

Women can do *iʿtikāf* in the *masjid* of congregation if they want, or in the *masjids* of their house if they want.[565] Al-Athram says: "Aḥmad ibn Ḥanbal was asked: 'Should women do *iʿtikāf*? He said: 'Yes'."[566] The wives of the Prophet ﷺ did *iʿtikāf* in the masjid, and they did not enter their homes except for human needs. ʿĀ'ishah says: "I would enter into the house for human need, and if there was an ill person in the house, I would not ask about him except while I was passing".[567]

TIME

Wajib iʿtikāf is for the days that one has committed oneself. It cannot be for less than a day.

Sunnah *iʿtikāf* is for the last ten days of Ramaḍān. One will enter into the mosque before the sunset of 20th of Ramaḍān, and will stay until the moon of *Shawwāl* has been sighted.

Mustaḥabb iʿtikāf can be undertaken at any time.

When one should go for the Sunnah *iʿtikāf*

ʿĀ'ishah reported that when the Messenger of Allāh ﷺ decided to

561 ibid., iii. 18.
562 al-Dāraquṭnī, *al-sunan, k. al-ṣawm, b. al-iʿtikāf.*
563 al-Baghawī, *Sharḥ al-sunnah,* iii. 551.
564 Ibn ʿAbd al-Barr, *al-Istidhkār,* x. 274.
565 al-Kāsānī, *Badā'iʿ al-ṣanā'iʿ,* iii. 25.
566 Ibn ʿAbd al-Barr, *al-Istidhkār,* x. 306.
567 al-Bukhārī, *k. al-iʿtikāf, b. lā yadkhulu al-bayta illā li ḥājah;* Muslim, *k. al-ḥayḍ, b. al-iḍṭijāʿ maʿa al-ḥā'iḍ fī liḥāf wāḥid.*

observe *iʿtikāf*, he prayed in the morning and then went to the place of his *iʿtikāf*".[568]

SPECIFYING A PLACE FOR THE *MUʿTAKIF*

It is allowed for a *muʿtakif* (one making *iʿtikāf*) to make a specific place in the mosque for his *iʿtikāf* as long as it does not harm or cause a major obstruction to the people coming for the congregational prayer. Abū Saʿīd reported that the Prophet ﷺ performed *iʿtikāf* under a Turkish tent which had something over its openings.[569] ʿAbdullāh ibn ʿUmar narrated that when the Prophet made *iʿtikāf*, his bed would be placed behind the Pillar of Repentance (a pillar in the Prophet's mosque to which a Companion had tied himself until Allāh accepted his repentance)".[570]

Nevertheless, if the *imām* fears that people specifying their places do not have good intention, or that it is going to harm the congregation, then he can stop people from doing so. ʿĀ'ishah reported that when the Messenger of Allāh ﷺ decided to observe *iʿtikāf*, he prayed in the morning and then went to the place of his *iʿtikāf*, and he commanded that a tent should be pitched for him, and it was pitched. He (once) decided to observe *iʿtikāf* during the last ten days of Ramaḍān. Zaynab (the wife of the Prophet) commanded that a tent should be pitched for her. It was pitched accordingly. And some other wives of Allāh's Apostle ﷺ commanded that tents should be pitched for them too. And they were pitched. When the Messenger of Allāh ﷺ offered the morning prayer, he looked and found (so many) tents. Thereupon, he said: "What is this virtue that these (ladies) have decided to acquire?" He commanded his tent to be struck and abandoned *iʿtikāf* during the month of Ramaḍān and postponed it to the first ten days of *Shawwāl*".[571]

WHAT ONE SHOULD DO DURING *IʿTIKĀF*

The person doing *iʿtikāf* should engage in acts of worship, like prayer, reading the Qur'ān, remembrance of Allāh, and reading useful books.

568 al-Bukhārī, *k. al-iʿtikāf, b. al-akhbiyah fī al-masjid;* Muslim, *k. al-iʿtikāf, b. matā yadkhulu man arāda al-iʿtikāf fī muʿtakafihi.*

569 Ibn Mājah, *k. al-ṣiyām, b. al-iʿtikāf fī khaymat al-masjid.*

570 Ibn Mājah, *k. al-ṣiyām, b. fī al-muʿtakif yalzamu makānan fī al-masjid.*

571 al-Bukhārī, *k. al-iʿtikāf, b. al-akhbiyah fī al-masjid;* Muslim, *k. al-iʿtikāf, b. matā yadkhulu man arāda al-iʿtikāf fī muʿtakafihi.*

One should only speak words of good and it is disliked for one to remain silent.[572]

ᶜĀ'ishah reported that when the last ten nights began Allāh's Messenger ﷺ kept awake at night (for prayer and devotion), awakened his family, and prepared himself to observe prayer (with more vigour).[573]

WHAT IS ALLOWED FOR THE *MUᶜTAKIF*

1- Leaving the mosque for human needs and Friday Prayer.[574] ᶜĀ'ishah reported: "When the Prophet ﷺ performed *iᶜtikāf*, he brought his head close to me so I could comb his hair, and he would not enter the house except to fulfil the needs a person has".[575]

2- Eating and drinking in the mosque.[576]

3- Combing one's hair. As quoted above: ᶜĀ'ishah reported: "When the Prophet ﷺ performed *iᶜtikāf*, he brought his head close to me so I could comb his hair, and he would not enter the house except to fulfil the needs a person has".[577]

4- There is no harm in one selling or buying in the mosque but without bringing the goods with one.[578]

WHAT INVALIDATES THE *IᶜTIKĀF*

1- It is forbidden for the one in *iᶜtikāf* to have sexual intercourse, touch a woman, kiss and if one has an emission as a result of kissing or touching then one's *iᶜtikāf* is invalidated and must be made up.[579] Allāh, Exalted is He, says: "*But touch them not [that is, your wives] while you are in retreat (iᶜtikāf) in the mosques*".[580]

Touching one's wife without there being any desire is allowed. For

572 al-Qudūrī, *al-Mukhtaṣar* 198.

573 Muslim, *k. al-iᶜtikāf, b. al-ijtihād fī al-ᶜashr al-awākhir min shahr ramaḍān.*

574 al-Samarqandī, *Tuḥfat al-fuqahā'* 181.

575 al-Bukhārī, *k. al-iᶜtikāf, b. lā yadkhulu al-bayta illā li ḥājah;* Muslim, *k. al-ḥayḍ, b. jawāz ghasl al-ḥā'id raᶜsa zawjihā wa tarjīlih…*

576 al-Samarqandī, *Tuḥfat al-fuqahā' 181.*

577 al-Bukhārī, *k. al-iᶜtikāf, b. lā yadkhulu al-bayta illā li ḥājah;* Muslim, *k. al-ḥayḍ, b. jawāz ghasl al-ḥā'id raᶜsa zawjihā wa tarjīlih…*

578 al-Qudūrī, *al-Mukhtaṣar* 198.

579 al-Kāsānī, *Badā'iᶜ al-ṣanā'iᶜ*, iii. 31.

580 *al-Baqarah* 187.

example, the statement of ʿĀ'ishah cited earlier whereby she would comb the Prophet's hair while he was performing *iʿtikāf.*

2- Loss of reason from intoxicants or becoming insane.

3-The start of menstruation or post-childbirth bleeding.[581]

4-If one goes out of the mosque for a while without an excuse, then one's *iʿtikāf* is invalidated, according to Abū Ḥanīfah, while Abū Yūsuf and Muḥammad both said that it is not invalidated unless he is away for more than half a day.[582]

ʿĀ'ishah says: "It is Sunnah on the *muʿtakif* that he does not visit an ill person, does not attend funeral prayers, does not touch a woman, does not embrace her, and does not go out except for absolute necessity. There is no *iʿtikāf* without fasting, and there is no *iʿtikāf* but in a congregational mosque".[583] The same has been narrated from al-Zuhrī, ʿAṭā' ibn Abī Rabāḥ, and ʿUrwah ibn al-Zubayr.[584] It is reported by ʿAmrah that ʿĀ'ishah, while in *iʿtikāf* would go to her house for human need and she would pass by an ill person, and would ask about him while passing but without stopping.[585] Abū Salamah ibn ʿAbd al-Raḥmān says: "The *muʿtakif* when entering into the house (for human need) would say *salam,* and can visit the ill without sitting". [586]

QAḌĀ' OF *IʿTIKĀF*

It is obligatory for a person to do the *qaḍā'* of a Sunnah or *mustahab iʿtikāf* if they do not complete it after having made the intention.[587]

As stated in ʿĀ'ishah's earlier ḥadīth that the Messenger of Allāh ﷺ once abandoned his *iʿtikāf* during the month of Ramaḍān and postponed it to the first ten days of *Shawwāl*".[588]

Imām al-Tirmidhī says: "There is a difference of opinion about a person who ends his *iʿtikāf* before his intended time has expired. Some

581 ibid., iii. 5.

582 al-Qudūrī, *al-Mukhtaṣar* 199.

583 Abū Dāwūd, *k. al-ṣawm, b. al-muʿtakif yaʿūd al-marīḍ.*

584 ʿAbd al-Razzāq, *al-Muṣannaf,* iv. 357-360.

585 ibid., iv. 358.

586 ibid.

587 al-Kāsānī, *Badā'iʿ al-ṣanā'iʿ*, iii. 4-5.

588 al-Bukhārī, *k. al-iʿtikāf, b. al-akhbiyah fī al-masjid*; Muslim, *k. al-iʿtikāf, b. matā yadkhulu man arāda al-iʿtikāf fī muʿtakafihi.*

people of knowledge say: 'If he ends his *iʿtikāf* [early], it is obligatory upon him to make it up'. They use as proof the ḥadīth which states that when the Prophet abandoned his *iʿtikāf*, he made it up during the following month of *Shawwāl*. This is the opinion of Mālik".[589]

589 al-Tirmidhī, *k. al-ṣawm, b. mā jā'a fī al-iʿtikāf idhā kharāja minhu.*

كتاب الحج

THE BOOK OF *ḤAJJ*

CHAPTER 1: *ḤAJJ*: BACKGROUND AND IMPORTANCE

THE WORD *ḤAJJ* means intending and going to visit a specific place. As a term of *fiqh*, it means intending and going to the House of Allāh in Makkah to fulfil the specified rites of pilgrimage at the appointed time. Allāh, Exalted is He, says: "*Verily, the first House appointed for mankind was that at Bakkah (Makkah), full of blessing, and a guidance for the people. In it are manifest signs, the maqām (place) of Ibrāhīm; whosoever enters it, he attains security. And ḥajj to the House is a duty that mankind owes to Allāh, those who can afford a way to it; and whoever disbelieves, then Allāh stands not in need of any of the people.*"[590]

Shāh Walīullah al-Dihlawī writes while explaining the need for *ḥajj*: "Sometimes when a man is overcome with the desire for his Lord and love surges powerfully in his chest and he looks around for the satisfaction of his inner urge it appears to him that *ḥajj* alone is the means to it".[591] Imām Ghazālī adds much more detail: "Know that there is no access to Allāh, Exalted is He, except through disdain of bestial passions, avoidance of idle pleasures, and contentment with the bare necessities of life and devotion wholly to Allāh, Exalted is He, on every (occasion), whether one is active or at rest. It is for the sake of

590 *Āl-ʿImrān* 96-97.

591 al-Dihlawī, *Ḥujjatullāh al-bālighah*, i. 142.

this that the monks of the previous religions isolated themselves from other people and lived on mountain-tops, preferring wilderness to human society in order to keep company with Allāh Most High. They abandoned present enjoyments for the sake of Allāh, Exalted is He, and took upon themselves strenuous tasks out of craving for the world beyond. Allāh, Exalted is He, has praised them in His Book saying: '*That is because amongst them are savants and monks and because they are not proud*'. When all this passed away and the people began to follow their lusts and forsook [the path of] devotion to the service of Allāh Most High, turning (rather) away from Him, He the Most High sent His Prophet Muḥammad ﷺ to restore the heavenly way (of life) and to set the Law of (previous) Apostles once again on its course. People of the [previous] religions asked him about monasticism and itinerancy in his religion. He ﷺ said: 'For us Allāh has replaced these (things) with *jihād* and with the magnification of Allāh on every high place', that is, with the Pilgrimage. Once, upon being questioned about itinerants, he ﷺ said: 'They are the ones who fast'. So, Allāh, Exalted is He, has blessed this community by making pilgrimage a monasticism for them. Accordingly, he has exalted the Ancient House by joining it to His lofty Self, and by establishing it as a destination for His slaves, making its surroundings a sacred enclosure (*ḥaram*) for His House, thus exalting it. He has made ʿArafah as a water-chute to the courts around its pool, has heightened the inviolability of the place by forbidding its game and trees, and has made it on the pattern of the castles of kings. (Therefore) visitors from all directions go to it dishevelled, dusty, humble before the Lord of the House, submitting themselves in obedience to His Majesty and in passivity to His Glory, confessing that He is above being confined by a house or encompassed by a town; for this demonstrates most eloquently their bondage and slavery and most perfectly their submission and obedience. Accordingly, He assigned to them in (the House) some acts which involve no fraternising among people and whose meaning no intellect can find out, such as casting pebbles at stones and running to and fro repeatedly between Ṣafā and Marwah for example. It is through such acts that perfect bondage and slavery is manifest. Zakāh is kindness; its meaning is understood and intellect has an inclination to it. Fasting is a break with bestial passion, which is the tool of the enemy of God, and involves concentration on worship by abstaining from (normal) occupations. Bowing (*rukūʿ*) and prostration (*sujūd*) in prayer (express) submission to Allāh, Exalted is He, through acts which represent the [outward] forms of submission; and souls have fellowship through (common) glorification of Allāh Most High, but the running to and fro (between Ṣafā and Marwah), and the casting of stones and similar acts afford no (obvious), benefit to souls nor any natural sociability; nor is the intellect able to discover their meaning. Therefore, there is no impetus to perform them other than the mere command (of God) and the intention to comply with that command, it being a command which requires obedience pure and simple. In such obedience the intellect desists from its (normal) operations and the soul and the [innate] disposition are distracted from their (proper) social course. For whatever the intellect understands, to that is nature inclined; this inclination thus cooperates with the command and together with it incites to action. Thus perfect bondage and slavery are hardly manifest. For this reason, he ﷺ said with special reference to pilgrimage: 'Here I am in pilgrimage, truly in devotion and slavery'. He did not say this of prayer or anything else'."[592]

BACKGROUND

Ḥajj is as old as the Kaᶜbah itself – the first House of Divine Worship appointed for men as cited by the verse of the Qur'ān above (*Āl ᶜImrān* 96-97). This verse corroborates the ḥadīth which tells us that the Kaᶜbah was first built by Ādam, the first man. It was later rebuilt by Ibrāhīm and his son Ismāᶜīl ﷺ. And when Ibrāhīm and Ismāᶜīl ﷺ raised the foundations of the House, they said: "*Our Lord accept from us...*".[593] An earlier revelation makes it clear that the Kaᶜbah was already there when Ibrāhīm left Ismāᶜīl ﷺ in the wilderness of Arabia: "*Our Lord I have settled a part of my offspring in a valley unproductive of fruit near Your Sacred House*".[594]

The ritual of *ḥajj* commemorates Prophet Ibrāhīm ﷺ and his family's acts of surrender and devotion to Allāh. The Prophet Muḥammad ﷺ did not innovate this institution but purged it of all evil practices and made it an obligatory act of piety by which one can develop intense consciousness of God. Mirbaᶜ al-Anṣārī reported that the Prophet ﷺ

592 al-Ghazālī, *Iḥyā' ᶜulūm al-dīn*, i. 372-373.

593 *al-Baqarah* 127.

594 *Ibrāhīm* 37.

said: "You must adhere to the traditions and rituals (of *ḥajj*), for these have come down to you from your forefather Ibrāhīm ﷺ as a legacy".[595]

ᶜAbdullāh ibn ᶜAbbās narrated: "The first lady to use a girdle was the mother of Ismāᶜīl ﷺ. She used a girdle so that she might hide her tracks from Sārah. Ibrāhīm ﷺ brought her and her son Ismāᶜīl ﷺ while she was suckling him to a place near the Kaᶜbah under a tree on the spot of Zamzam, at the highest place in the mosque. During those days there was nobody in Makkah, nor was there any water. So he made them sit there and placed near them a leather bag containing some dates and a small water-skin containing water, and set out homeward. Ismāᶜīl's mother followed him saying: 'O Ibrāhīm. Where are you going leaving us in this valley where there is no person whose company we may enjoy, nor is there anything (to enjoy)?' She repeated this to him many times, but he did not look back at her. Then she asked him: 'Has Allāh ordered you to do so?' He said: 'Yes'. She said: 'Then He will not neglect us,' and returned while Ibrāhīm ﷺ proceeded onwards, and on reaching a corner such that she could not see him, he faced the Kaᶜbah, and raising both hands, invoked Allāh saying the following prayers: '*O our Lord I have made some of my offspring dwell in a valley without cultivation, by Your Sacred House in order, O our Lord, that they may offer prayer perfectly. So fill some hearts among men with love towards them, and provide them with fruits, so that they may give thanks*'. Ismāᶜīl's mother went on suckling Ismāᶜīl ﷺ and drinking from the water (she had).

"When the water in the water-skin had all been used up, she became thirsty and her child too became thirsty. She started looking at him (i.e. Ismāᶜīl ﷺ) tossing in agony, then left him as she could not endure looking at him and found that the Mountain of Ṣafā was the nearest mountain to her on that land. She stood on it and started looking keenly at the valley so that she might see somebody, but she could not see anybody. Then she descended from Ṣafā and when she reached the valley, she tucked up her robe and ran through the valley like a person in distress and trouble, until she crossed the valley and reached the Mountain of Marwah where she stood and started looking, expecting to see somebody, but she could not see anybody. She repeated this (running between Ṣafā and Marwah) seven times'.

"The Prophet said: 'This is the source of the tradition of the walking

595 al-Nasā'ī, *k. al-manāsik, b. rafᶜ al-yadayn fī al-duᶜā' bi ᶜArafah.*

of people between them (i.e. Ṣafā and Marwah). When she reached Marwah (for the last time) she heard a voice and she asked herself to be quiet and listened attentively. She heard the voice again and said: 'O, (whoever you may be) you have made me hear your voice; have you got something to help me?' And behold she saw an angel at the place of Zamzam, digging the earth with his heel (or his wing) until water flowed from that place. She started to make something like a basin around it, using her hand – in this way – and started filling her water-skin with water with her hands, and the water was flowing out after she had scooped some of it'.

"The Prophet ﷺ added: 'May Allāh bestow mercy on Ismāʿīl's mother, had she let Zamzam flow without trying to control it (or had she not scooped from that water to fill her water-skin), Zamzam would have been a stream flowing on the surface of the earth'. The Prophet further added: 'Then she drank (water) and suckled her child. The angel said to her: 'Don't be afraid of being neglected, for this is the House of Allāh which will be built by this boy and his father, and Allāh never neglects His people'. The House at that time was on a high place resembling a hillock, and when torrents came, they flowed to its right and left. She lived in this way until some people from the tribe of Jurhum or a family from Jurhum passed by her and her child, as they (i.e. the Jurhum people) were coming through the way of Kadā'. They landed in the lower part of Makkah where they saw a bird that had the habit of flying around water and not leaving it. They said: 'This bird must be flying around water, though we know that there is no water in this valley'. They sent one or two messengers who discovered the source of the water, and returned to inform them. So, they all came (towards the water). The Prophet ﷺ added: 'Ismāʿīl's mother was sitting near the water. They asked her: 'Will you allow us to stay with you?' She replied: 'Yes, but you will have no right to possess the water'. They agreed to this. The Prophet ﷺ further said: 'Ismāʿīl's mother was pleased with the whole situation as she used to love to enjoy the company of people. So, they settled there, and later on they sent for their families who came and settled with them so that some families became permanent residents there. The child (i.e. Ismāʿīl ﷺ) grew up and learnt Arabic from them and (his virtues) caused them to love and admire him as he grew up, and when he reached the age of puberty they had him marry a woman from amongst them.

"After Ismāʿīl's mother died, Ibrāhīm عليه السلام came after Ismāʿīl's marriage in order to see his family that he had left before, but he did not find Ismāʿīl عليه السلام there. When he asked Ismāʿīl's wife about him, she replied: 'He has gone in search of our livelihood'. Then he asked her about their way of living and their condition, and she replied: 'We are living in misery; we are living in hardship and destitution', complaining to him. He said: 'When your husband returns, convey my salutations to him and tell him to change the threshold of the gate (of his house)'. When Ismāʿīl عليه السلام came, he seemed to have felt something unusual, so he asked his wife: 'Has anyone visited you?' She replied: 'Yes, an old man of so-and-so description came and asked me about you and I informed him, and he asked about our state of living, and I told him that we were living in hardship and poverty'. On hearing this Ismāʿīl عليه السلام said: 'Did he leave any advice?' She replied: 'Yes, he told me to convey his salutation to you and to tell you to change the threshold of your gate'. Ismāʿīl عليه السلام said: 'It was my father, and he has ordered me to divorce you. Go back to your family'. So, Ismāʿīl عليه السلام divorced her and married another woman from amongst them (i.e. the Jurhum).

"Then Ibrāhīm عليه السلام stayed away from them for as long a period as Allāh wished and called on them again but did not find Ismāʿīl عليه السلام. So he came to Ismāʿīl's wife and asked her about Ismāʿīl. She said: 'He has gone in search of our livelihood'. Ibrāhīm عليه السلام asked her: 'How are you getting on?', asking her about their sustenance and living. She replied: 'We are prosperous and well-off (i.e. we have everything in abundance)'. Then she thanked Allāh. Ibrāhīm عليه السلام said: 'What kind of food do you eat?' She said. 'Meat'. He said: 'What do you drink?' She said: 'Water'. He said: 'O Allāh! bless their meat and water'. The Prophet ﷺ added: 'At that time they did not have grain, and if they had grain, he would also have invoked Allāh to bless it'. The Prophet ﷺ added: 'If somebody has only these two things as his sustenance, his health and disposition will be badly affected, unless he lives in Makkah'. The Prophet ﷺ added: 'Then Ibrāhīm عليه السلام said to Ismāʿīl's wife: 'When your husband comes, give my regards to him and tell him that he should keep firm the threshold of his gate'. When Ismāʿīl عليه السلام came back, he asked his wife: 'Did anyone call on you?' She replied: 'Yes, a good-looking old man came to me', so she praised him and added. 'He asked about you, and I informed him, and he asked about our livelihood and I told him that we were in a good condition'. Ismāʿīl عليه السلام asked her: 'Did he leave you any advice?' She said: 'Yes, he told me to give his regards to you and ordered that you should keep firm the threshold of your gate'. On this Ismāʿīl عليه السلام said: 'It was my father, and you are the threshold (of the gate). He has ordered me to keep you with me'.

"Then Ibrāhīm عليه السلام stayed away from them for as long a period as Allāh wished, and called on them afterwards. He saw Ismāʿīl عليه السلام under a tree near Zamzam, sharpening his arrows. When he saw Ibrāhīm عليه السلام, he rose up to welcome him (and they greeted each other as a father does his son or a son his father). Ibrāhīm عليه السلام said: 'O Ismāʿīl, Allāh has given me an order'. Ismāʿīl عليه السلام said: 'Do what your Lord has ordered you to do'. Ibrāhīm عليه السلام asked: 'Will you help me?' Ismāʿīl عليه السلام said: 'I will help you'. Ibrāhīm عليه السلام said: 'Allāh has ordered me to build a house here,' pointing to a hillock higher than the land surrounding it. The Prophet ﷺ added: 'Then they raised the foundations of the House (i.e. the Kaʿbah). Ismāʿīl عليه السلام brought the stones and Ibrāhīm عليه السلام was building, and when the walls became high, Ismāʿīl عليه السلام brought this stone and put it for Ibrāhīm عليه السلام who stood over it and carried on building, while Ismāʿīl عليه السلام was handing him the stones, and both of them were saying: '*O our Lord, accept (this service) from us, You are the All-Hearing, the All-Knowing*'.[596] The Prophet said: 'Then both of them went on building and going round the Kaʿbah saying: '*O our Lord, accept (this service) from us, You are the All-Hearing, the All-Knowing*'."[597]

ʿAbdullāh ibn ʿAbbās also narrated: "When Ibrāhīm عليه السلام had differences with his wife, (because of her jealousy of Hājar, Ismāʿīl's mother) he took Ismāʿīl عليه السلام and his mother and went away. They had a water-skin with them containing some water, Ismāʿīl's mother used to drink water from the water-skin so that her milk would increase for her child. When Ibrāhīm عليه السلام reached Makkah, he made her sit under a tree and afterwards returned home. Ismāʿīl's mother followed him, and when they reached Kadā', she called him from behind: 'O Ibrāhīm, to whom are you leaving us?' He replied: '(I am leaving you) to Allāh's (care)'. She said: 'I am satisfied to be with Allāh'. She returned to her place and started drinking water from the water-skin, and her milk increased for her child. When the water had all been

596 *al-Baqarah* 127

597 al-Bukhārī, *k. aḥadīth al-anbiyā'.*

used up, she said to herself: 'I'd better go and look so that I may see somebody'. She ascended the mountain of Ṣafā and looked, hoping to see somebody, but in vain. When she came down to the valley, she ran until she reached the Mountain of Marwah. She ran to and fro between the two mountains many times. Then she said to herself: 'I'd better go and see the state of the child,' she went and found it in a state of one on the point of dying. She could not endure to watch it dying and said (to herself): 'If I go and look, I may find somebody'. She went and ascended the Mountain of Ṣafā and looked for a long while but could not find anybody. Thus, she completed seven rounds (of running) between Ṣafā and Marwah. Again she said (to herself): 'I'd better go back and see the state of the child'. But suddenly she heard a voice, and she said to that strange voice: 'Help us if you can offer any help'. Lo! It was Jibrīl ﷺ (who made the noise). Jibrīl ﷺ hit the earth with his heel like this (Ibn ᶜAbbās hit the earth with his heel to illustrate it), and so water gushed out. Ismāᶜīl's mother was astonished and started digging. Abū Al-Qāsim (i.e. the Prophet ﷺ) said: 'If she had left the water, (flow naturally without her intervention), it would have been flowing on the surface of the earth'. Ismāᶜīl's mother started drinking from the water and her milk increased for her child. Afterwards some people of the tribe of Jurhum, while passing through the bottom of the valley, saw some birds, and that astonished them, they said: 'Birds can only be found at a place where there is water'. They sent a messenger who searched the place and found the water, and returned to inform them about it. Then they all went to her and said: 'O Ismāᶜīl's mother! Will you allow us to be with you (or dwell with you)?' (And thus they stayed there.) Later on her boy reached the age of puberty and married a lady from them. Then an idea occurred to Ibrāhīm ﷺ which he disclosed to his wife (Sārah): 'I want to call on my dependents I left (at Makkah)'. When he went there, he greeted (Ismāᶜīl's wife) and said: 'Where is Ismāᶜīl?' She replied: 'He has gone out hunting'. Ibrāhīm ﷺ said (to her): 'When he comes, tell him to change the threshold of his gate'. When he came, she told him the same whereupon Ismāᶜīl ﷺ said to her: 'You are the threshold, so go to your family (i.e. you are divorced)'. Again Ibrāhīm ﷺ thought of visiting his dependents whom he had left (at Makkah), and he told his wife (Sārah) of his intentions. Ibrāhīm ﷺ came to Ismāᶜīl's house and asked: 'Where is Ismāᶜīl?' Ismāᶜīl's wife replied: 'He has gone out hunting,' and added: 'Will you stay (for some time) and have something to eat and drink?' Ibrāhīm ﷺ asked: 'What is your food and what is your drink?' She replied: 'Our food is meat and our drink is water'. He said: 'O Allāh bless their meals and their drink'. Abū Al-Qāsim said: 'Because of Ibrāhīm's invocation there are blessings (in Makkah)'. Once more Ibrāhīm ﷺ thought of visiting his family he had left (at Makkah), so he told his wife (Sārah) of his decision. He went and found Ismāʿīl ﷺ behind the Zamzam well, mending his arows. He said: 'O Ismāʿīl, Your Lord has ordered me to build a house for Him'. Ismāʿīl ﷺ said: 'Obey (the order of) your Lord'. Ibrāhīm ﷺ said: 'Allāh has also ordered me that you should help me therein'. Ismāʿīl ﷺ said: 'Then I will do so'. Both of them rose and Ibrāhīm ﷺ started building (the Kaʿbah) while Ismāʿīl ﷺ went on handing him the stones, and both of them were saying, '*O our Lord, accept (this service) from us, Verily, You are the All-Hearing, the All-Knowing*'. When the building became high and the old man (i.e. Ibrāhīm ﷺ) could no longer lift the stones (to such a high position), he stood over the stone of *Al-Maqām* and Ismāʿīl ﷺ carried on handing him the stones, and both of them were saying: '*O our Lord, accept (this service) from us, Verily, You are All-Hearing, All-Knowing*'."[598]

Reconstruction of the Kaʿbah

ʿĀ'ishah reported: "Allāh's Messenger ﷺ said to me: 'Had your people not quite recently accepted Islam, I would have demolished the Kaʿbah and would have rebuilt it on the foundation laid by Ibrāhīm ﷺ; for when the Quraysh built the Kaʿbah, they reduced its (area), and I would also have built (a door) in the rear'."[599] ʿĀ'ishah also narrated that Allāh's Messenger ﷺ said: "Didn't you see that when your people built the Kaʿbah, they reduced (its area with the result that it no longer remains) on the foundations laid by Ibrāhīm ﷺ. I said: 'Messenger of Allāh, why don't you rebuild it on the foundations laid by Ibrāhīm ﷺ?' Thereupon, Allāh's Messenger ﷺ said: 'Had your people not been new converts to Islam, I would have done so'."[600] ʿAbdullāh ibn ʿUmar said: "If ʿĀ'ishah had heard it from Allāh's Messenger ﷺ I would not have

598 al-Bukhārī, *k. aḥādīth al-anbiyā'*.

599 al-Bukhārī, *k. al-ḥajj, b. faḍl makkah*; Muslim, *k. al-ḥajj, b. naqḍ al-kaʿbah*.

600 Muslim, *k. al-ḥajj, b. naqḍ al-kaʿbah*.

seen Allāh's Messenger ﷺ abandoning the touching of the two corners situated near al-Ḥijr, but (for the fact) that it was not completed on the foundations laid by Ibrāhīm".[601]

ʿAṭā' ibn Abī Rabāḥ narrates: "The House was burnt during the time of Yazīd ibn Muʿāwiyah when the people of Syria had fought (in Makkah) and that which (was meant to) occur (with respect to the Kaʿbah) occurred. ʿAbdullāh ibn Zubayr left it (in the same state) until the people came in the season (of *Hajj*). (The idea behind it was) that he wanted to exhort them or incite them (to war) against the people of Syria. When the people had arrived he said to them: 'O people, advise me about the Kaʿbah. Should I demolish it and then build it from its very foundation, or should I repair whatever has been damaged of it?' Ibn ʿAbbās said: 'A suggestion has come to mind, according to which I think you should only repair (the portion which has been) damaged, leaving the House as it was when people embraced Islam, leaving the stones as they were when people embraced Islam and as it was when Allah's Apostle's ﷺ prophetic mission began'. Thereupon, Ibn Zubayr said: 'If the house of any one of you was burnt down, he would not be satisfied until he had reconstructed it, so what about the House of your Lord? I will seek guidance from my Lord for three (nights) and then I will decide about this affair'. After three nights he decided on demolishing it. The people turned away fearing that a calamity might fall from the heavens on the first person to climb on top (of the Kaʿbah to demolishing it), until a man ascended (the roof), and threw down one of its stones. When the people saw no calamity befalling him, they followed him, and demolished it until it was levelled to the ground. Then Ibn Zubayr erected pillars and covered them with curtains until (the walls) were raised again. Ibn Zubayr said: 'I heard ʿĀ'ishah say that the Messenger of Allah ﷺ had said: 'If the people had not only recently (abandoned) unbelief and if I had sufficient means to reconstruct it, which I had not, I would have definitely included in it (the Kaʿbah) five cubits of area from the Ḥijr and I would also have constructed a door for the people to enter, and a door for their exit'. Today I have (the means to spend) and I have nothing to fear from the people (that they would protest against this change)'. So he added five cubits of area from the side of Ḥijr to it so that there appeared (the old) foundation (upon

601 ibid.

which Ibrāhīm had built the Kaʿbah) and the people saw that and it was upon this foundation that the wall was raised. The height of the Kaʿbah was eighteen cubits; after the addition was made to it (which was in its breadth) it appeared to have decreased (in height). Therefore, an addition of ten cubits was (also) made to its height. He also made two doors, one to enter by and the other to exit from. When Ibn Zubayr was killed, al-Ḥajjāj wrote to 'Abd al-Malik ibn Marwān informing him about (his death), and telling him that Ibn Zubayr had re-built (the Kaʿbah) on those very foundations (which were laid by Ibrāhīm) and which reliable persons among the Makkans had witnessed. 'Abd al-Malik wrote to him stating: 'We are not concerned with the censuring of Ibn Zubayr in anything. Keep intact the addition made by him in its height, and whatever he has added from the side of Ḥijr revert it to (its previous) foundation, and wall up the door which he had opened'. Thus, he (al-Ḥajjāj) demolished it (that portion) and rebuilt it on (its previous) foundations'."[602]

ʿAbdullāh ibn ʿUbayd reported that: "Ḥārith ibn ʿAbdullāh led a deputation to ʿAbd al-Malik ibn Marwān during his caliphate. ʿAbd al-Malik said to them: 'I do not think that Abū Khubayb (i.e. ʿAbdullāh ibn Zubayr) had heard from ʿĀ'ishah what he said he heard (about the intended wish of the Prophet ﷺ in regard to the alteration of the Kaʿbah)'. Ḥārith said: 'Yes, I myself did hear from her'. He (ʿAbd al-Malik) said: 'Well, tell me what you heard from her'. He stated that she (ʿĀ'ishah) had said that Allāh's Messenger ﷺ remarked: 'Verily your people have reduced (the area) of the House from its (original) foundations, and if they had not recently abandoned polytheism (and embraced Islam) I would have reversed it to (those foundations) which they had left out of it. And if your people would take initiative after me in rebuilding it, then come along with me so that I can show you what they have left out of it'. He showed her about 15 cubits of area from the side of Ḥaṭīm (that they had separated). Allāh's Apostle ﷺ further said: 'I would have made two doors on the level of the ground facing the east and the west. Do you know why your people raised the level of its door (i.e. the door of the Kaʿbah)?' She said: 'No'. He said: '(They did it) out of vanity so that they (are in a position to) grant admittance only to whom they wished. When a person intended to get into it, they let him climb (the

602 ibid.

stairs), and as he was about to enter, they pushed him and he fell down'. ʿAbd al-Malik said to Ḥārith; 'Did you yourself hear her saying this?' He said: 'Yes'. Ḥārith said that ʿAbd al-Malik scratched the ground with his staff for some time and then said: 'I wish I had left his (ʿAbdullāh ibn Zubayr's) work there'."[603]

The *Ḥaram* and its boundaries

Since the Prophet Ibrāhīm ﷺ built the Kaʿbah in Makkah and made his descendants live there, he appointed, with the will of Allāh, Makkah and the lands around it as *Ḥaram*, i.e. Sacred land. ʿAbdullāh ibn ʿAbbās reported Allāh's Messenger ﷺ as saying on the Day of the Conquest of Makkah: "Allāh made this town sacred on the day He created the earth and the heavens; so it is sacred by the sacredness conferred on it by Allāh until the Day of Resurrection and fighting in it was not lawful to anyone before me, and it was made lawful for me only during an hour on one day, for it is sacred by the sacredness conferred on it by Allāh until the Day of Resurrection. Its thorns are not to be cut, its game is not to be molested, and the things dropped are to be picked up only by one who makes a public announcement of it, and its fresh herbage is not to be cut". Al-ʿAbbās said: "Messenger of Allāh, exception may be made in case of rush, for it is useful for their blacksmiths and for their houses". He (the Prophet), conceding the suggestion of al-ʿAbbās, said: "Except rush".[604]

Abū Shurayḥ al-ʿAdawī reported that he said to ʿAmr ibn Saʿīd when he was sending troops to Makkah: "Let me tell you something O Commander, which Allāh's Messenger ﷺ said on the day following the Conquest which my ears heard and my heart has retained, and my eyes saw as he spoke it. He praised Allāh and extolled Him and then said: 'Allāh, not men, has made Makkah sacred; so it is not permissible for any person believing in Allāh and the Last Day to shed blood in it, or lop a tree in it. If anyone seeks a concession on the basis of the fighting of Allāh's Messenger ﷺ tell him that Allāh permitted His Messenger, but not you, and He gave him permission only for an hour on one day, and its sacredness was restored on the very day like that of yesterday. Let

603 ibid.

604 al-Bukhārī, *k. jazā' al-ṣayd, b. lā yaḥillu al-qitāl bimakkah*; Muslim, *k. al-ḥajj, b. taḥrīm makkah wa ṣaydihā*.

him who is present convey the information to him who is absent'." It was said to Abū Shurayḥ: "What did ʿAmr say to you? He said: 'I am better informed of that than you, Abū Shurayḥ, but the sacred territory does not grant protection to one who is disobedient, or one who runs away after shedding blood, or one who runs away after some act of mischief".[605]

Abū Hurayrah said: "When Allāh, Exalted is He, granted Allāh's Messenger ﷺ victory over Makkah, he stood before people and praised and extolled Allāh and then said: 'Verily Allāh held back the elephants from Makkah and gave the domination of it to His Messenger and believers, and it (this territory) was not violable to anyone before me and it was made violable to me for an hour of a day, and it shall not be violable to anyone after me. So neither molest the game, nor weed out thorns from it. And it is not lawful for anyone to pick up a thing dropped except by making a public announcement of it. And if a relative of anyone is killed he is entitled to opt for one of two things. Either he should be paid blood-money or he can take life as (a just retribution)'. ʿAbbās said: 'Allāh's Messenger, except for *idhkhir* (a kind of herbage), for we use it for our graves and for our houses'. Whereupon, Allāh's Messenger ﷺ said: 'With the exception of *idhkhir*'. A person known as Abū Shāh, one of the people of Yemen, stood up and said: 'Messenger of Allāh, (kindly) write it for me'. Thereupon, Allāh's Messenger ﷺ said: 'Write it for Abū Shāh'. Walīd said: "I asked al-Awzāʿī what did his saying: 'Write it for me, Messenger of Allāh?' mean. He said: 'This very address that he had heard from Allāh's Messenger ﷺ'."[606]

Abū Hurayrah also reported: "The people from the tribe of Khuzāʿah killed a man from the tribe of Layth in the Year of Victory in retaliation for one whom they (the tribe of Layth) had killed. It was reported to Allāh's Messenger ﷺ. He mounted his camel and delivered this address: 'Verily Allāh, Exalted is He, held back the elephants from Makkah, and gave its domination to His Messenger and believers. Behold, it was not violable for anyone before me and it will not be violable for anyone after me. Behold, it was made violable for me for an hour of a day; and at this very hour it has again been made inviolable (for me as well as for others). So its thorns are not to be cut, its trees are not to be lopped, and (no one is allowed to) pick up a thing dropped, but the one who

605 al-Bukhārī, *k. al-maghāzī, b.* 52; Muslim, *k. al-ḥajj, b. taḥrīm makkah.*

606 Muslim, *k. al-ḥajj, b. taḥrīm makkah.*

makes an announcement of it. And one whose fellow is killed is allowed to opt between two alternatives: either he should receive blood-money or get the life of the (murderer) in return'. He (the narrator said): 'A person from the Yemen, who was called Abū Shāh, came to him and said: 'Messenger of Allāh, write it 'down for me'. Whereupon he (Allāh's Messenger) said: 'Write it down for Abū Shāh'. One of the people from among the Quraysh also said: 'Except *idhkhir*, for we use it in our houses and our graves'. Thereupon, Allāh's Messenger ﷺ said: 'Except *idhkhir*'."[607]

The boundaries of the *Ḥaram* of Makkah include the area around Makkah, marked on all roads leading to, or from Makkah. Nowadays, there are checkpoints at the entrance of the *Ḥaram* on every road leading to Makkah. On the northern side, the *Ḥaram* extends to Tanᶜīm, 6 kilometres from *al-Masjid al-Ḥarām*, and on the southern side to Aḍāh, 12 kilometres from the Masjid. On its eastern side, 16 kilometres away, lies al-Jiᶜirrānah, while on its north-eastern border lies the valley of Nakhlah, which is 14 kilometres from the Masjid. On the western border, lies al-Ḥudaybiyyah, which is 15 kilometres from the Masjid.

THE IMPORTANCE OF *ḤAJJ*

The importance of *ḥajj* is well explained in the sources of Islam. Imām Ghazālī, states in this regards: "Know then, the *ḥajj* is one of the Pillars and foundations of Islam, the act of worship of a lifetime, the seal of all that is commanded, the perfection of Islam and the completion of religion. Concerning it Allāh the Most High has revealed His statement: "*This day have I perfected your religion for you and completed My favour upon you and have chosen for you Islam as your religion*". And concerning it the Prophet ﷺ said: "Whoever dies without, having performed the *ḥajj* let him die, if he wish, either a Jew or a Christian".[608]

Principal virtues of *ḥajj*

Allāh, Exalted is He, says: "*And remember when We showed Ibrāhīm the site of the House: Associate not anything with Me, and sanctify My House for those who circumambulate it, and those who stand up for prayer, and those who bow and make prostration. And proclaim to mankind the ḥajj. They will come to you on feet and on every lean camel, they will come from every deep and distant*

607 ibid.

608 al-Ghazālī, *Iḥyā' ᶜulūm al-dīn*, i. 336.

mountain highway. That they may witness things that are of benefit to them, and mention the name of Allāh on appointed days over the beast of cattle that He has provided for them. Then eat thereof and feed therewith the poor who have a very hard time. Then let them complete the prescribed duties for them, and perform their vows, and circumambulate the Ancient House".[609]

Abū Hurayrah narrated that the Prophet was asked: "Which is the best deed?" He said: "To believe in Allāh and His Apostle'. He was then asked which is the next (in goodness)? He said: "To participate in *jihād* in Allāh's Cause." He was then asked, which is the next? He said: "To perform *Ḥajj Mabrūr* (a *ḥajj* that is accepted by Allāh)'."[610]

Abū Hurayrah also narrated that Prophet ﷺ said: "*ᶜUmrah* (minor *ḥajj*) is expiation for the sins committed (between it and the previous one). And the reward of *Ḥajj Mabrūr* is nothing except Paradise".[611]

In another narration Abū Hurayrah states that the Prophet ﷺ said: "Whoever performs the *ḥajj* for Allāh's pleasure and does not do shameful acts, and does not do evil or sins then he will return (after *ḥajj* free from all sins) as if he were born anew".[612]

Imām Ghazālī says: "As for longing [to perform the pilgrimage]: this results from understanding and from the realisation that the House belongs to Allāh Most High, that it was established on the analogy of a royal palace such that whoever visits it is [in reality] visiting Allāh, Exalted is He, and whoever betakes himself to the House [while] in this life is worthy not to have his visit wasted, for the object of the visit, which is the vision of Allāh Most High, will be granted to him in its fixed time in the Eternal Residence. For the finite and perishable eye is not prepared, while still in this life, to receive light with which to see the Face of Allāh Most High; it is not able to bear that Light, nor is it fit, because of its finiteness, to be adorned [with that Light]. But when it is granted immortality in the life to come and freed from the cause of change and mortality, it becomes ready for the vision and

609 *al-Ḥajj* 26-29.

610 al-Bukhārī, *k. al-īmān, b. man qāla inna al-īmāna huwa al-ᶜamal;* Muslim, *k. al-īmān, b. bayān kawn al-īmān billah taᶜālā afḍal al-aᶜmāl.*

611 al-Bukhārī, *k. al-ᶜumrah, b. al-ᶜumrah;* Muslim, *k. al-ḥajj, b. fī faḍl al-ḥajj wa al-ᶜumrah.*

612 al-Bukhārī, *k. al-ḥajj, b. faḍl al-ḥajj al-mabrūr;* Muslim, *k. al-ḥajj, b. fī faḍl al-ḥajj wa al-ᶜumrah.*

the sight. And because of [its intention] to visit the House and to look at it, it deserves to meet the Lord of the House by virtue of Gracious Promise. The longing to meet Allāh, Exalted is He, most surely makes one long for the means of that meeting. Besides, every lover is longing for everything that has any connection with his love. The House is connected to Allāh Most High; therefore, it is proper for [the pilgrim] to have a keen desire for it just because of this connection, quite apart from any desire to receive the great reward which has been promised to him".[613]

The virtue of spending in *ḥajj*

As indicated earlier the reward for an accepted *ḥajj* is immense. However, the preparation, effort and expenditure associated with *ḥajj* are also rewarded. In this regard, Muḥammad ibn ʿAbbād narrated that the Messenger of Allāh ﷺ said: "Spending on *ḥajj* is like spending in the path of Allāh; a *dirham* is multiplied in reward by 700 times".[614]

The purpose of *ḥajj*

Shaykh Abū al-Ḥasan ʿAlī Nadwī in explaining the purpose of *ḥajj* states: "It stands for unqualified obedience and earnest yielding to a demand. Sometimes the pilgrim is seen in Makkah and sometimes in Minā, ʿArafah and Muzdalifah. Sometimes he makes a halt and sometimes he travels. At one time he pitches his tent and at another he knocks it down. He is the slave of every nod and gesture and does simply what he is called upon to do. He has no choice of his own. He has hardly halted at Minā before he is required to move on to ʿArafah but without breaking the journey at Muzdalifah. On reaching ʿArafah he engages himself in prayer throughout the day and when the sun has set he finds himself tired and wanting to spend the night there but is commanded to proceed to Muzdalifah. He has been regular in prayer all his life, there he is told to forgo the *Maghrib Ṣalāh* for he is the bondman of Allāh, not of the *ṣalāh* or habit. The *ṣalāh* he offers at Muzdalifah jointly with that of *ʿIshā'*. His stay at Muzdalifah is very pleasant and he wishes to prolong it but it is not allowed for him and he is bidden to leave for Minā. The same was the practice of

613 al-Ghazālī, *Iḥyā' ʿulūm al-dīn, i.* 374.

614 Ibn Abī Shaybah, *al-Muṣannaf,* viii. 31

Ibrāhīm and of all the Divine apostles and men of faith and virtue, now travelling, now staying, now meeting, now parting, neither servile to desire nor yielding to caprice".[615]

Shaykh Abū al-Ḥasan Nadwī, further says: "One of the chief purposes of the *ḥajj* is the renewal of bond or contact with the Prophet Ibrāhīm, the founder of *al-millah al-ḥanīfiyyah* (the way that is pure from any trace of polytheism). It affords a splendid opportunity to safeguard his legacy, to compare one's own way of living with the way he had shown and to take stock of the condition of Muslims with a view to improving it. The *ḥajj* is a kind of annual concourse through which the Muslims can look into themselves, discover their faults and chalk out plans for their regeneration and for ridding themselves of the influences they may have accepted from peoples and communities among which they live".[616]

THE OBLIGATION OF *ḤAJJ*

The obligation of *ḥajj* was revealed in the ninth year of *hijrah* with the revelation of the verse: "*Verily, the first House appointed for mankind was that at Bakkah (Makkah), full of blessing, and a guidance for the people. In it are manifest signs, the maqām (place) of Ibrāhīm; whosoever enters it, he attains security. And ḥajj to the House is a duty that mankind owes to Allāh, those who can afford a way to it; and whoever disbelieves, then Allāh stands not in need of any of the people*".[617]

ᶜAbdullāh ibn ᶜUmar reported that the Prophet ﷺ said: "Islam is built on five things: bearing witness that there is no God but Allāh and that Muḥammad is the Messenger of Allāh, establishing the prayer, giving the *zakāh*, fasting the month of Ramaḍān, and the *ḥajj* of the House".[618]

Abū Hurayrah narrated that the Messenger of Allāh ﷺ said: "O people, the *ḥajj* has been made obligatory upon you, so do *ḥajj*".[619]

There is a consensus among the Companions and all scholars after

615 Abū al-Ḥasan ᶜAlī Nadwi, *The Four Pillars of Islam*, p. 229.

616 ibid., p. 231.

617 *Āl ᶜImrān* 96-97.

618 al-Bukhārī, *k. al-īmān, b. duᶜāʼukum īmānukum*; Muslim, *k. al-īmān, b. bayān arkān al-islām wa daᶜāʼimihī al-ᶜiẓām.*

619 Muslim, *k. al-ḥajj, b. farḍ al-ḥajj marratan fī al-ᶜumur.*

them on its obligatory nature.[620] Al-Aswad said to a rich person: "Had you died without doing *ḥajj* I would not have attended your funeral prayer".[621] Similar narrations are recorded from ʿUmar ibn al-Khaṭṭāb and Saʿīd ibn Jubayr.[622]

It is obligatory once in a life time

There is scholarly consensus that *ḥajj* is obligatory only once in a lifetime.[623] Abū Hurayrah reported that: "Allāh's Messenger ﷺ addressed us and said: 'O people, Allāh has made *ḥajj* obligatory for you; so perform *ḥajj*'. Thereupon, a person said: 'Messenger of Allāh, is it to be performed every year?' He (the Prophet) kept quiet, the person repeated [these words] thrice, whereupon Allāh's Messenger ﷺ said: 'If I were to say 'Yes', it would become obligatory for you to perform it every year and you would not be able to do so'. Then he said: 'Leave me with what I have left to you, for those who were before you were destroyed because of excessive questioning, and for their opposition to their apostles. So when I command you to do anything, do it as much as what lies in your power and when I forbid you to do anything, then abandon it'."[624] ʿAbdullāh ibn ʿAbbās said: "Aqraʿ ibn Ḥābis said to the Prophet ﷺ: 'Apostle of Allāh, *ḥajj* is to be performed annually or only once?' He replied: 'Only once, and if anyone performs it more often, he performs a supererogatory act'."[625]

One should not delay it

As soon as the *ḥajj* becomes obligatory, one should not delay it and should perform it immediately. ʿAbdullāh ibn ʿAbbās narrates that the Messenger of Allāh said: "Whoever intends *ḥajj* he should hasten, for one can fall ill, or can miss the mount, or some other need can come".[626]

620 al-Kāsānī, *Badāʾiʿ al-ṣanāʾiʿ*, iii. 40.
621 Ibn Abī Shaybah, *al-Muṣannaf*, viii. 458.
622 ibid., viii. 459.
623 al-Kāsānī, *Badāʾiʿ al-ṣanāʾiʿ*, iii. 41.
624 Muslim, *k. al-ḥajj, b. farḍ al-ḥajj marratan fī al-ʿumur.*
625 Abū Dāwūd, *k. al-manāsik, b. farḍ al-ḥajj.*
626 Ibn Mājah, *k. al-manāsik, b. al-khurūj ilā al-ḥajj.*

When it becomes obligatory

Ḥajj is obligatory when the following conditions are fulfilled:

1- Being a Muslim
2- Adulthood
3- Being sane
4- Freedom
5- Ability

The first three conditions are required for all obligatory acts of worship. ᶜAlī ibn Abī Ṭālib related that the Messenger of Allāh ﷺ said: "The pen is raised from three (meaning that there is no obligation), on the one who is sleeping until he awakens, the child until he becomes an adult and the one who is insane until he becomes sane".[627]

Freedom is a condition for *ḥajj*, because it requires time and ability. The slave is busy in serving his master, and does not have the ability or the freedom to perform *ḥajj*.[628]

The condition of being able to perform *ḥajj*

One of the conditions for *ḥajj* to become obligatory is to have ability. Allāh, Exalted is He, says: "*And ḥajj to the House is a duty that mankind owes to Allāh, those who can afford a way to it*".[629] The ability is acquired if one has:

1- Good health. There is no *ḥajj* upon the one who is ill, paralysed, the elderly who are unable to travel on a mount and the one in prison,[630]

2- That the journey is safe,[631]

3- That one owns the provisions and mount. Provision not only means having the funds for the journey and stay during *ḥajj* itself. It also means leaving provisions for the daily necessities of one's family until one returns.[632] What is considered in the mount is that it facilitates the journey to *ḥajj* and back, whether it is by land, sea, or by air. As for those who live near Makkah and can walk there, then a mount is not relevant for them.[633]

627 Abū Dāwūd, *k. al-ḥudūd, b. fī al-majnūn yasriq;* al-Tirmidhī, *k. al-ḥudūd, b. mā jā'a fī man lā yajibu ᶜalayh al-ḥadd.*
628 al-Kāsānī, *Badā'iᶜ al-ṣanā'iᶜ*, iii. 45.
629 *Āl ᶜImrān* 96-97
630 al-Kāsānī, *Badā'iᶜ al-ṣanā'iᶜ*, iii. 47.
631 al-Samarqandī, *Tuḥfat al-fuqahā'* 189.
632 al-Kāsānī, *Badā'iᶜ al-ṣanā'iᶜ*, iii. 51-3.
633 al-Samarqandī, *Tuḥfat al-fuqahā'* 188.

ᶜAbdullāh ibn ᶜAbbās narrated that the people of Yemen would come for *ḥajj* and not bring enough provisions with them. They would say that they depend on Allāh. On their arrival in Madīnah they used to beg of the people, and so Allāh revealed: "*And take a provision (with you) for the journey, but the best provision is the fear of Allāh*".[634] A man asked Imām Aḥmad ibn Ḥanbal: "I want to go to Makkah relying on Allāh, without taking any provision?' Imām Aḥmad said: 'Then go without the company of people'. The man said: 'I must go with the people'. Imām Aḥmad said: 'Then your reliance is on the sacks (provisions) of the people'."[635]

Ḥajj of a child

Ḥajj is not obligatory on a child; nevertheless if undertaken it will be valid, but will not suffice for the obligatory *ḥajj*. When he reaches adulthood, he has to do *ḥajj* again if he has the ability.[636]

Al-Sā'ib ibn Yazīd narrated: "While in the company of my parents I was made to perform *ḥajj* with the Messenger of Allāh ﷺ and I was a seven-year-old boy then".[637] ᶜAbdullāh ibn ᶜAbbās narrates that a woman raised aloft a child to the Messenger of Allāh ﷺ and said: "Is *ḥajj* of such a little child valid as a *ḥajj*?" He said: "Yes, and you will have the reward".[638] ᶜAbdullāh ibn ᶜAbbās narrates that the Prophet ﷺ said: "Any child who does *ḥajj*, and then he reaches adulthood has to do another *ḥajj*".[639]

Ḥajj of a woman

Ḥajj is obligatory on the woman as it is obligatory on the man. However, there are some additional conditions which must be fulfilled.

If the distance between the woman and Makkah requires three days travel or 48 miles (77 kilometres) or more she must be accompanied by her husband or a *maḥram* (a man with whom she cannot marry at all).[640] ᶜAbdullāh ibn ᶜAbbās narrated: "The Prophet ﷺ said: 'A woman should not travel except with a *maḥram*, and no man may visit her except in

634 al-Bukhārī, *k. al-ḥajj, b. qawlillāh taᶜālā wa tazawwadū.*
635 Ibn al-Jawzi, *Talbīs iblīs* 168.
636 al-Samarqandī, *Tuḥfat al-fuqahā'* 186.
637 al-Bukhārī, *k. jazā' al-ṣayd, b. ḥajj al-ṣibyān.*
638 Muslim, *k. al-ḥajj, b. ṣiḥḥat ḥajj al-ṣabī.*
639 al-Ṭabarānī, *musnad ᶜabdillāh ibn ᶜabbās.*
640 al-Samarqandī, *Tuḥfat al-fuqahā'* 189.

the presence of a *maḥram.* A man got up and said: 'O Allāh's Apostle, I intend to go to join such and such army and my wife wants to perform *ḥajj*'. The Prophet said (to him): 'Go along with her (to *ḥajj*)'."[641] Abū Saʿīd al-Khudrī narrated that the Messenger of Allāh ﷺ said: "No woman is allowed to go on a journey of three days except with her son, or her father, or her brother, or her husband, or a *maḥram*".[642]

If the woman is travelling for her *farḍ ḥajj,* then her husband should not forbid her; though it is recommended that she should get his permission.[643] Yaḥyā ibn Abī Kathīr says: "A man should facilitate for his wife to do the *ḥajj* if she has not done one". [644] Makḥūl said: "You should make you wives do *ḥajj*". [645] Ibrāhīm al-Nakhaʿī said: "If a woman is doing her *farḍ ḥajj* and she has a *maḥram,* then she does not need her husband's permission".[646] Ḥasan al-Baṣrī was asked about a woman who has not done her *ḥajj*? He answered: "She should seek the permission of her husband, if he allows her then that is more beloved to me, but if he does not allow her then she should go with a *maḥram,* because it is a *farḍ* of Allāh in which she does not have to obey her husband". [647]

Undertaking *ḥajj* on behalf of someone else

If someone on whom *ḥajj* was compulsory passes away, then his relative can appoint someone to do *ḥajj* on his behalf. ʿAbdullāh ibn ʿAbbās said: "A woman came to the Prophet and said: 'My mother had vowed to perform *ḥajj* but she died before performing it. May I perform *ḥajj* on my mother's behalf?' The Prophet replied, 'Perform *ḥajj* on her behalf. Had there been a debt on your mother, would you have paid it or not? So, pay Allāh's debt as He has more right to be paid'."[648] ʿAṭā' ibn Abī Rabāḥ said: "The *ḥajj* can be done on behalf of the dead person even if he did not make a will for this". [649]

641 al-Bukhārī, *k. al-jihād, b. man uktutiba fī jaysh fakharajat imr'atuhu ḥajjatan;* Muslim, *k. al-ḥajj, b. safar al-mar'ah maʿa maḥram.*

642 Muslim, *k. al-ḥajj, b. safar al-mar'ah maʿa maḥram.*

643 al-Samarqandī, *Tuḥfat al-fuqahā'* 189.

644 Ibn Abī Shaybah, *al-Muṣannaf,* viii. 231.

645 ibid.

646 ibid., viii. 532.

647 ibid.

648 Muslim, *k. al-ṣiyām, b. qaḍā' al-ṣiyām ʿan al-mayyit.*

649 Ibn Abī Shaybah, *al-Muṣannaf,* viii. 535.

If someone can afford the *ḥajj*, and later becomes unable to do *ḥajj* because of illness or old age, then it is compulsory on him to appoint someone who can perform *ḥajj* on his behalf. ᶜAbdullāh ibn ᶜAbbās said: "Al-Faḍl was riding behind the Prophet and a woman from the tribe of Khathᶜam came up to him. Al-Faḍl started looking at her and she looked at him. The Prophet turned al-Faḍl's face to the other side. She said: 'My father has come under Allāh's obligation of performing *ḥajj* but he is a very old man and cannot sit properly on his mount. Shall I perform *ḥajj* on his behalf?' The Prophet replied in the affirmative. This happened during *ḥajjat al-wadāᶜ* (the Farewell Pilgrimage) of the Prophet'."[650]

It is not a condition to have done one's own *ḥajj* before doing *ḥajj* on behalf of someone else.[651] This is also the opinion of ᶜAlī ibn Abī Ṭālib, Mujāhid, Saᶜīd ibn al-Musayyab,[652] Ḥasan al-Baṣrī, ᶜAṭā', Mālik and Sufyān al-Thawrī.[653]

It is allowed for a man to appoint a man or a woman to do *ḥajj* on his behalf; just as it is allowed for a woman to appoint a man or a woman to do *ḥajj* on her behalf.[654] This is substantiated by the ḥadīth of ᶜAbdullāh ibn ᶜAbbās of a woman from Khathᶜam who came to the Prophet ﷺ and said: "My father is an old and aged person; Allāh's obligation on His slaves, the *ḥajj* has got him, and he is not able to do *ḥajj*. Will it suffice if I do *ḥajj* on his behalf? The Messenger of Allāh ﷺ said: 'Yes'."[655]

Departing for *ḥajj*

Imām Ghazālī in explaining how a pilgrim should begin his journey states: "He ought to begin with repentance, redress grievances, pay debts, arrange for provisions [for those whom he must provide for until his return], return the trusts entrusted to him, take in hand a lawful and fair [sum of] money that will be sufficient for him [on his way] to

650 al-Bukhārī, *k. al-ḥajj, b. al-ḥajj ᶜan man yuḥajju ᶜanhu*; Muslim, *k. al-ḥajj, b. al-ḥajj ᶜan al-ᶜājiz.*

651 al-Kāsānī, *Badāʾiᶜ al-ṣanāʾiᶜ*, iii. 273.

652 Ibn Abī Shaybah, *al-Muṣannaf,* viii. 189.

653 al-Baghawī, *Sharḥ al-Sunnah,* iv. 19.

654 al-Kāsānī, *Badāʾiᶜ al-ṣanāʾiᶜ*, iii. 274.

655 Abū Dāwūd, *k. al-manāsik, b. al-rajul yaḥujju ᶜan ghayrihī*; al-Tirmidhī, *k. al-ḥajj, b. mā jāʾa fī al-ḥajj ᶜan al-shaykh al-kabīr wa al-mayyit;* Ibn Mājah, *k. al-manāsik, b. al-ḥajj ᶜan al-ḥayy idhā lam yastaṭiᶜ*.

and fro without parsimony [on his part], and [will enable him] to be liberal with his provisions and benevolent toward the weak and destitute. Furthermore, he should, before setting out, give away something as alms, as well as buy for himself or hire a strong beast of burden that will not weaken [under the strain of the journey]. If he hires [the beast], he must inform the hirer what he intends to load on it, no matter how little or great, and obtain [the hirer's] consent in the matter".[656]

As for the decision to proceed with the pilgrimage Imām Ghazālī says: "Let one know that this decision means separation from his family and country as well as the abandonment of bestial desires and pleasures as one directs one's attention to visiting the House of Allāh Most High. Let him realise the importance of the House and the grandeur of the Lord of the House. Let him [also] know that he has intended to do something of an extremely lofty and serious nature, and that whoever seeks after an important thing jeopardises another thing. Let him [further] be sure that his decision is sincere in the Face of Allāh, Exalted is He, and far from the contaminations of hypocrisy and fame. And let him realise that [God] does not accept anyone who goes to Him or [accept] his deed unless he is sincere, and that it is a most despicable thing to go to the palace of a king and his family while in reality one's aim is something else. Therefore, let [the pilgrim] rectify his intention in his mind; such rectification is through sincerity which is the avoidance of everything that has in it hypocrisy, ostentation and desire for celebrity; let him beware the danger of exchanging what is higher for what is lower".[657]

Imām Ghazālī further says: "As for the severance of relations this means restitution for all injustices and sincere repentance before Allāh, Exalted is He, for all sins. Every injustice is a relation and every relation is like a creditor present [before the pilgrim] clinging to his neck, crying out [to those around him], saying: "Where are you headed? Are you going to the palace of the King of kings while you are neglecting His affairs in your house, despising and neglecting Him? Are you not ashamed to go to Him as a disobedient servant would go to Him, lest He rejects and not accept you? If you desire to have your visit accepted, let His orders be executed, denounce all injustice, return to Him [by rejecting] all sins, severe your heart from all, turning back to

656 al-Ghazālī, *Iḥyā' ʿulūm al-dīn, i.* 346.
657 ibid., i. 374.

what is behind you, so that you will be facing Him with the face of your heart as you are facing His House with the face of your exterior. If you do not do that, you gain nothing from your journey except, firstly, toil and unhappiness, and then ultimately expulsion and rejection". Let [the pilgrim] severe all relations, with his country in the same manner as one who departs from his country assuming that he will not return. And let him write his will to his children and family, for the traveller and his wealth are in danger except for that which is safeguarded by Allāh Most High. When severing relations for the pilgrimage journey, let him reflect on the severance of relations for the journey to the Last Abode, for [that journey] is before him and the journey he is undertaking is an expectation that the [last] journey will be made easier, for that journey is to an [everlasting] abiding place to which all things return. Therefore, it is not proper to ignore that journey while preparing for this one".[658]

Duʿā' on setting out for *ḥajj*

When one sets out for *ḥajj* one should do so by reciting the *duʿā'* prescribed by the Prophet ﷺ for all journeys. It is reported by ʿAbdullāh ibn ʿUmar that whenever the Messenger of Allāh ﷺ mounted his camel when setting out on a journey, he glorified Allāh, saying: الله أكبر ، الله أكبر ، الله أكبر (God is Great) thrice, and then said:

اَلْحَمْدُ لِلَّهِ الَّذِيْ سَخَّرَ لَنَا هَذَا وَمَا كُنَّا لَهُ مُقْرِنِيْنَ وَإِنَّا إِلَى رَبِّنَا لَمُنْقَلِبُوْن ، اَللَّهُمَّ إِنَّا نَسْأَلُكَ فِيْ سَفَرِنَا هَذَا الْبِرَّ وَالتَّقْوَى وَمِنَ الْعَمَلِ مَا تُحِبُّ وَتَرْضَى ، اَللَّهُمَّ هَوِّنْ عَلَيْنَا سَفَرَنَا هَذَا ، وَاطْوِ لَنَا بُعْدَه ، اَللَّهُمَّ أَنْتَ الصَّاحِبُ فِي السَّفَر ، وَالْخَلِيْفَةُ فِيْ الْأَهْلِ وَالْمَالِ ، اَللَّهُمَّ إِنِّيْ أَعُوْذُ بِكَ مِنْ وَعْثَاءِ السَّفَرِ ، وَكَآبَةِ الْمَنْظَرِ ، وَسُوْءِ الْمُنْقَلَبِ فِي الْمَالِ وَالْأَهْلِ

("All praise and thanks are for Allāh, Who subdued for us this (ride) when we were not ourselves powerful enough to use it as a ride, and we are going to return to our Lord. O Allāh, we seek virtue and piety from You in this journey of ours and the act which pleases You. O Allāh, lighten this journey of ours, and make its distance easy for us. O

658 ibid.

Allāh, You are our companion during the journey, and the guardian of our family. O Allāh, I seek refuge with You from the hardships of the journey, the gloominess of the sights, and the finding of evil changes in property and family upon return".[659]

Earning money during *ḥajj*

It is allowed for the one undertaking *ḥajj* to do business or to be involved in earnings while performing the rituals of *ḥajj*. ᶜAbdullāh ibn ᶜAbbās narrated that: "Dhū al-Majāz and ᶜUkāẓ were the markets of the people during the pre-Islamic period of ignorance. When the people embraced Islam, they disliked to do bargaining there till the following verses were revealed: '*There is no harm for you if you seek of the bounty of your Lord (during ḥajj by trading)*'.[660] Ibn ᶜAbbās recited this verse: "*There is no harm for you that you seek the bounty of your Lord*", and said: "The people would not trade in Minā (during the *ḥajj*), so they were allowed to trade when they proceeded from ᶜArafah".[661] Abū Umāmah at-Taymī said: "I was a man who used to give (riding-beasts) on hire for this purpose (for travelling during the pilgrimage) and the people would tell (me) 'Your *ḥajj* is not valid'. So I met Ibn ᶜUmar and said to him: 'Abū ᶜAbd al-Raḥmān, I am a man who gives (riding-beast) on hire for this purpose (i.e. for *ḥajj*), and the people say to me: 'Your *ḥajj* is not valid'. Ibn ᶜUmar replied: 'Do you not put on *iḥrām* (the pilgrim dress), call the *talbiyah* (the pronouncement pilgrims make during *ḥajj* and ᶜ*umrah*), circumambulate the Kaᶜbah, return from ᶜArafah and lapidate the *jamrahs*, (three pillars built of stone at Minā. One of the rites of *ḥajj* is to throw pebbles at these stone pillars)?' I said: 'Why not?' Then he said: 'Your *ḥajj* is valid. A man came to the Prophet ﷺ and asked him the same question you have asked me. The Apostle of Allāh ﷺ kept silent and did not answer him until this verse came down: '*There is no harm for you to seek the bounty of your Lord*'. The Apostle of Allāh ﷺ sent for the man and recited the verse to him and said: 'Your *ḥajj* is valid'."'[662]

659 Muslim, *k. al-ḥajj, b. istiḥbāb al-dhikr idhā rakiba dābbatahu....*

660 *al-Baqarah* 198, al-Bukhārī, *k. al-ḥajj, b. al-tijārah ayyām al-mawsim.*

661 Abū Dāwūd, *k. al-manāsik, b. al-tijārah fī al-ḥajj.*

662 Abū Dāwūd, *k. al-manāsik, b. al-kary.*

Chapter 2: *Farḍs* of the *Ḥajj*

There are three *farḍs* concerning the *ḥajj*: *iḥrām, wuqūf* in ʿArafah, and *ṭawāf al-ifāḍah.*

1. *IḤRĀM*

Iḥrām refers to the condition of being bound, of defining a boundary. It is a condition of sanctity. It is activated by two things: intention to do *ḥajj* or ʿ*umrah*, and saying the *talbiyah.*

Mawāqīt of *iḥrām*

Mawāqīt is the plural of *mīqāt. Mīqāt* means a specific time or specific place. Both are explained below.

Specific times

Ḥajj must take place at the time specified for *ḥajj*. Allāh, the Exalted says in the Qur'ān: "*They ask you about the crescents. Say they are (mawāqīt) signs to mark fixed periods of time for the people and for the ḥajj*". [663] In another verse, Allāh, Exalted is He, says: "*The ḥajj is in known months*".[664] These known months are *Shawwāl, Dhū al-qaʿdah* and the ten days of *Dhū al-ḥijjah* as narrated from ʿAbdullāh ibn ʿUmar.[665]

The *ḥajj* contains a number of different rites and ceremonies, a few of which are fixed as to date such as the stay at ʿArafah can only be done on the 9th *Dhū al-ḥijjah,* and others rituals which can be done at some time during 'the known months', for example *ṭawāf.*

Entering into *iḥrām* before the due time

It is disliked for one to enter into the *iḥrām* of *ḥajj* before the above mentioned known months.[666]

663 *al-Baqarah* 189.

664 *al-Baqarah* 197.

665 al-Bukhārī, *k. al-ḥajj, b. qawlillāh taʿālā al-ḥajj ashhurun maʿlūmāt.*

666 al-Samarqandī, *Tuḥfat al-fuqahā'* 191; al-Mawṣilī, *al-Ikhtiyar li taʿlīl al-mukhtār,* i. 182.

Specific places

As for the specific places, they are those from where the pilgrim puts on the *iḥrām* of *ḥajj* or *ᶜumrah.* There are five *mīqāts*:

Dhū al-Ḥulayfah: i.e. Abyar ᶜAlī, a place at the distance of 450 kilometres from Makkah to the north. This is the *mīqāt* point for the people of Madīnah,

Dhāt ᶜIrq: A place 94 kilometres from Makkah to the northeast. This is the *mīqāt* point for the people of Iraq,

al-Juḥfah: A place 187 kilometres northwest from Makkah. This is the *mīqāt* point for the people of Shām (Greater Syria: present Syria, Lebanon, Jordan and Palestine).

Qarn al-Manāzil: 94 kilometres east of Makkah. This is the *mīqāt* point for the people of Najd (the highlands of Arabia.)

Yalamlam: A mountain 54 kilometres south of Makkah. This is the *mīqāt* point for the people of Yemen.

These are the *mīqāts* for all those who are coming from those directions. Nāfiᶜ narrated that ᶜAbdullāh ibn ᶜUmar said: "The Messenger of Allāh ﷺ said: 'The people of Madīnah should assume *iḥrām* from Dhū al-Ḥulayfah; the people of Sham from al-Juḥfah; and the people of Najd from Qarn". And ᶜAbdullāh added: "I was informed that the Messenger of Allāh ﷺ had said: 'The people of Yemen should assume *iḥrām* from Yalamlam".[667] Imām Muḥammad says after narrating this ḥadīth: "We adhere to it; these are the *mīqāts* appointed by the Messenger of Allāh ﷺ; no one intending to do *ḥajj* or *ᶜumrah* should exceed them except in a state of *iḥrām*".[668]

ᶜAbdullāh ibn ᶜAbbās narrated: "Allāh's Apostle ﷺ made Dhū al-Ḥulayfah as the *mīqāt* for the people of Madīnah; Al-Juḥfah for the people of Shām; Qarn-al-Manāzil for the people of Najd; and Yalamlam for the people of Yemen; and these *mawāqīt* are for the people at those very places, and besides them for those who come through those places with the intention of performing either *ḥajj* and *ᶜumrah*; and whoever is living within these boundaries can assume *iḥrām* from the place he sets out on the pilgrimage, and the people

667 al-Bukhārī, *k. al-ḥajj, b. mawāqīt al-ihlāl*; Muslim, *k. al-ḥajj, b. mawāqīt al-ḥajj wa al-ᶜumrah.*

668 Muhammad, *al-Muwaṭṭa'* 133.

of Makkah can assume *iḥrām* from Makkah.[669]

Abū Zubayr heard Jābir ibn ᶜAbdullāh say when he was asked about (the place for entering upon the) state of *iḥrām*: "I heard (and I think he attributed it directly to the Apostle of Allāh) him say: 'For the people of Madīnah Dhū al-Ḥulayfah is the place for entering upon the state of *iḥrām*, and for (the people coming from the other direction, i.e. Syria) it is Juḥfah; for the people of Iraq it is Dhāt al-ᶜIrq; for the people of Najd it is Qarn al-Manāzil and for the people of Yemen it is Yalamlam."[670]

Shāh Walīullah writes: "The real idea behind the determination of *mawāqīt* is that while, on the one hand, it is enjoined upon the pilgrims to present themselves in Makkah with their hair dishevelled and in a distressed condition, on the other there is an open difficulty for them in setting forth from their homes with the *iḥrām* wrapped round their bodies – some of whom have to do a month or two of travelling, or even more – some special places have been marked on all sides of Makkah and before crossing these places it is necessary to put on *iḥrām*. Care has been taken that these places are well known as points of transit. The *mīqāt* for people coming from Madīnah is at the farthest distance. This is because Madīnah is the centre of Divine revelation, the citadel of faith, the home of migration and the first city to embrace Islam at the call of Allāh and the Apostle. The people of Madīnah, as such, have a greater claim to be in the vanguard of those who strive in the path of Allāh and ahead of everyone in worship. As against Jawāth, Ṭā'if and Yamāmah, Madīnah is counted among the earliest towns to have entered into the fold of Islam and given proof of single-minded devotion to faith. There is, therefore, no harm if the *mīqāt* for it has been fixed so far away".[671]

The *mīqāts* of people arriving by air

Today, most people arrive to Makkah by air. They are required to put on their *iḥrām* garments as soon as they are opposite to any *mīqāt* from the direction they are coming. Since putting on *iḥrām* in the aeroplane causes difficulty many people put on their *iḥrām* at the airport of their country of origin.

669 al-Bukhārī, *k. al-ḥajj, b. mīqāt ahl al-madīnah;* Muslim, *k. al-ḥajj, b. mawāqīt al-ḥajj wa al-ᶜumrah.*

670 Muslim, *k. al-ḥajj, b. mawāqīt al-ḥajj wa al-ᶜumrah.*

671 al-Dihlawī, *Ḥujjatullāh al-bālighah,* ii. 92.

After a detailed discussion, Shaykh Muṣṭafā al-Zarqā' reached the conclusion that the *mīqāt* of the people coming by air and landing in Jeddah should be Jeddah itself.[672]

Passing *mīqāt* without putting on *iḥrām*

It is not allowed for anyone entering into Makkah to pass the *mīqāt* without *iḥrām*. ᶜAbdullāh ibn ᶜAbbās has narrated that the Prophet ﷺ said: "Do not pass the *mīqāt*s without *iḥrām*". And in another ḥadīth the Prophet ﷺ asserted: "Do not enter into Makkah except in a state of *iḥrām*".[673]

The entrance of the Prophet into Makkah without *iḥrām* at the time of its conquest was a concession for him. Ṭāwūs says: "The Prophet ﷺ never entered Makkah without *iḥrām* except on the day of the Conquest of Makkah".[674] ᶜAlī said: "Do not enter Makkah without *iḥrām*".[675]

Similar narration has been reported from ᶜAbdullāh ibn ᶜAbbās as well.[676] Ḥasan al-Baṣrī did not like anyone entering Makkah without *iḥrām*.[677] Ibrāhīm al-Nakhaᶜī says: "They loved not to enter into Makkah without *iḥrām*".[678] ᶜAṭā' ibn Abī Rabāḥ said: "It is not for anyone to enter into Makkah without *iḥrām*".[679] Ṭāwūs, Ḥakam, Mujāhid and Qāsim have narrated similar statements.[680]

Iḥrām* before *mīqāt

It is permitted to enter a state of *iḥrām* before the above mentioned *mīqāt*s, though it is against the Sunnah. ᶜUmar ibn al-Khaṭṭāb and ᶜUthmān ibn ᶜAffān did not like anyone entering into *iḥrām* before the *mīqāt*.[681] However, ᶜAlī, Ibn ᶜĀmir, ᶜImrān ibn Ḥuṣayn, Ibn ᶜUmar, Ibn ᶜAbbās, al-Aswad, Qāsim, and Ibrāhīm have allowed this practice.[682] Zubayr ibn

672 *Fatāwā Muṣṭafā al-Zarqā'* 177-190.
673 al-Bayhaqī 9940.
674 Ibn Abī Shaybah, *al-Muṣannaf*, viii. 228.
675 ibid., viii. 227.
676 Ibn Abī Shaybah, *al-Muṣannaf*, viii. 227.
677 ibid.
678 ibid.
679 ibid.
680 ibid., viii. 228.
681 ibid., viii. 41.
682 ibid., viii. 34-40.

Bakkār narrates that: "A man came to Imām Mālik and asked him from where he should put on *iḥrām*? Imām Mālik answered: 'From Dhū al-Ḥulayfah, where the Prophet ﷺ put on *iḥrām*'. The man said: 'I want to put on *iḥrām* from the Mosque of the Prophet'. Imām Mālik said: 'Do not do that'. The man said: 'I want to put on *iḥrām* from the grave of the Prophet'. Imām Mālik said: 'Do not do that, I fear a *fitnah* (calamity) will befall you'. The man said: 'What *fitnah* is here; it is only a few miles which I am adding'. Imām Mālik said: 'Is there any *fitnah* greater than you thinking that you have preceded with a virtue which the Messenger of Allāh did not have. I have heard Allāh say (in the Qur'ān): "*Let those who disobey his orders beware, lest some trial befall them or a painful punishment be inflicted on them*'."[683]

The *Mīqāt* of the people of *al-Ḥill*

If one's home is located after the *mīqāts*, then his *mīqāt* is *al-Ḥill*.[684] *Al-Ḥill* refers to the area between *mīqāt* and the boundaries of the *Ḥaram* of Makkah.

Whoever lives in Makkah, then his *mīqāt* on *ḥajj* is the *Ḥaram*, and for *ᶜumrah*, *al-Ḥill*.[685] ᶜAbdullāh ibn ᶜAbbās narrated: "The Prophet ﷺ fixed Dhū al-Ḥulayfah as the *mīqāt* for the people of Madīnah, Al-Juḥfah for the people of Shām, Qarn al-Manāzil for the people of Najd, and Yalamlam for the people of Yemen; and these *mawāqīt* are for those living at those very places, and besides them for those whom come through them with the intention of performing *ḥajj* and *ᶜumrah*; and whoever is living within these *mawāqīt* should assume *iḥrām* from where he starts, and the people of Makkah can assume *iḥrām* from Makkah". [686]

ᶜĀ'ishah narrated: "We set out with the Prophet with the intention of performing *ḥajj* only. The Prophet reached Makkah and performed *ṭawāf* of the Kaᶜbah and (ran) between Ṣafā and Marwah and did not finish the *iḥrām*, because he had the *hady* (sacrificial animal) with him. His Companions and his wives performed *ṭawāf* (of the Kaᶜbah and ran between Ṣafā and Marwah), and those who had no *hady* with them

683 al-Shāṭibī, *al-Iᶜtiṣām* 97. The verse quoted in the ḥadīth is from *surah al-Nūr* verse 63.

684 al-Samarqandī, *Tuḥfat al-fuqahā'* 193.

685 ibid.

686 Muslim, *k. al-ḥajj, b. mawāqīt al-ḥajj wa al-ᶜumrah.*

finished their *iḥrām.* I got the menses and performed all the ceremonies of *ḥajj.* So, when the night of *ḥaṣbā'* (Night of Departure) came, I said, 'O Allāh's Apostle, all your Companions are returning with *ḥajj* and *ᶜumrah* except me'. He asked me: 'Didn't you perform *ṭawāf* of the Kaᶜbah (*ᶜumrah*) when you reached Makkah?' I said, 'No'. He said: 'Go to Tanᶜīm with your brother ᶜAbd al-Raḥmān, and assume *iḥrām* for *ᶜumrah* and I will wait for you at such and such a place'. So I went with ᶜAbd al-Raḥmān to Tanᶜīm and assumed *iḥrām* for *ᶜumrah*'."[687]

THE REQUIREMENTS OF *IḤRĀM*

There are eight requirements of *iḥrām:*

1- It is a Sunnah to do *ghusl* (bath) before *iḥrām.* It is allowed to do *wuḍū'* (ablution) only; though *ghusl* is better. ᶜAbdullāh ibn ᶜUmar says that it is Sunnah to do *ghusl* when one intends *iḥrām.*[688] ᶜĀ'ishah narrated the Prophet ﷺ when he left for Makkah would have *ghusl* while intending *iḥrām.*[689]

This *ghusl* is for cleaning oneself and not for the ritual purification; that's why it is also required from women in menstruation or postnatal bleeding. ᶜĀ'ishah reported that Asmā' bint ᶜUmays gave birth to Muḥammad ibn Abī Bakr near Dhū al-Ḥulayfah. The Messenger of Allāh ﷺ commanded Abū Bakr to convey to her that she should take a bath and then enter into the state of *iḥrām.*[690]

If there is no water, then this requirement is dropped and *tayammum* will not be done, because *tayammum* does not clean.

2- Before the *ghusl of iḥrām* one should cut ones nails, trim ones moustache, and shave the under arms and one's pubic hair.[691]

3- Intimate relations with one's spouse. If one is married, it is recommended that one have relations with one's wife before putting on *iḥrām.*[692]

687 al-Bukhārī, *k. al-ḥajj, b. Kayfa tuhillu al-ḥā'iḍ wa al-nufasā'*; Muslim, *k. al-ḥajj, b. bayān wajūh al-iḥrām.*

688 al-Ḥākim, *al-Mustadrak,* i. 615; al-Dāraquṭnī, *al-Sunan,* ii. 220; al-Bayhaqī, *al-Sunan al-kubrā,* v. 33.

689 al-Ṭabarānī, *al-Muᶜjam al-awsaṭ,* v. 138.

690 Muslim, *k. al-ḥajj, b. iḥrām al-nufasā' wa istiḥbāb ightisālihā li al-iḥrām.*

691 *al-Fatāwā al-hindiyyah, i. 222;* Al-Mawsili, *al-Ikhtiyar lit aᶜlil al-mukhtar,* i. 184.

692 *al-Fatāwā al-hindiyyah, i. 222.*

4-Men will wear the un-sewn garments of *iḥrām* known as *izār* and *rida. Izār* is a cloth that covers the body from the naval to the knees, and *ridā'* is a piece of cloth wrapped over the back, chest and shoulders. It is recommended that both, *izār* and *ridā'* be new or washed and that they are white.[693] ᶜAbdullāh ibn ᶜUmar reported that a person asked the Messenger of Allāh ﷺ what a *muḥrim* (one in a state of *iḥrām*) should put on as a dress. Thereupon, the Messenger of Allāh ﷺ said: "Do not put on a shirt or a turban, or trousers or a cap, or leather socks except one who does not find sandals; he may put on socks but should trim them below the ankles. And do not wear clothes to which saffron or *warse* (a sweet smelling plant that was used to dye clothes yellow) has been applied".[694]

Women will wear their normal clothes covering their heads and not covering their faces; because their *iḥrām* is declared by their faces being uncovered, just as for men their *iḥrām* is declared by their heads being uncovered.[695] ᶜAbdullāh ibn ᶜUmar says: the *iḥrām* of the man is in his head, and the *iḥrām* of the woman is in her face.[696] ᶜAbdullāh ibn ᶜUmar narrated that the Messenger of Allāh ﷺ said: "The woman in a state of *iḥrām* will not put on the *niqāb* (covering the face) and gloves". [697] Ibn ᶜUmar also narrated that he heard the Messenger of Allāh ﷺ forbid women in a state of *iḥrām* from wearing gloves and *niqāb*.[698]

5-It is recommended that one applies perfume on one's body and clothes before getting into a state of *iḥrām*.[699] ᶜĀ'ishah narrated: "I used to scent the Messenger of Allāh ﷺ when he wanted to assume *iḥrām* and also on finishing *iḥrām* before the *ṭawāf* round the Kaᶜbah *(ṭawāf-al-ifāḍ ah)*".[700] Saᶜīd ibn Jubayr narrated: "Ibn ᶜUmar used to oil his hair. I told this to Ibrāhīm (al-Nakhaᶜī) who said: 'What do you think about this statement Aswad narrated from ᶜĀ'ishah: 'As if I were now observing

693 al-Kāsānī, *Badā'iᶜ al-ṣanā'iᶜ*, iii. 109.

694 al-Bukhārī, k. al-*ṣalāh, b. al-ṣalāh fī al-qamīṣ wa al-sarāwīl;* Muslim, *k. al-ḥajj, b. mā yalbasu al-muḥrim.*

695 al-Qudūrī, *al-Mukhtaṣar* 223; al-Samarqandī, *Tuḥfat al-fuqahā'* 205.

696 al-Dāraquṭnī, al-Sunan, ii. 294; al-Bayhaqī, *al-Sunan al-kubrā,* v. 47.

697 al-Bukhārī, *k. al-ḥajj, b. mā lā yalbasu al-muḥrim min al-thiyāb.*

698 Abū Dāwūd, *k. al-manāsik, b. mā yalbasu al-muḥrim.*

699 al-Kāsānī, *Badā'iᶜ al-ṣanā'iᶜ*, iii. 109-110.

700 al-Bukhārī, *k. al-ḥajj, b. al-ṭīb ᶜinda al-iḥrām;* Muslim, *k. al-ḥajj, b. al-ṭīb li al-muḥrim ᶜinda al-iḥrām.*

the glitter of the scent in the parting of the hair of the Prophet while he was *muḥrim*?"[701] ᶜUrwah ibn al-Zubayr said: "I asked ᶜĀ'ishah with what substance she perfumed the Messenger of Allāh ﷺ at the time of entering upon the state of *iḥrām*. She said: 'With the best of perfume'."[702]

Muḥammad ibn al-Muntashir reported on the authority of his father: "I asked ᶜAbdullāh ibn ᶜUmar about a person who applied perfume and then (on the following) morning entered upon a state of *iḥrām*. Thereupon, he said: 'I do not like to enter upon the state of *iḥrām* shaking off the perfume. Rubbing of tar (upon my body) is dearer to me than doing this (i.e. the applying of perfume)'. I went to ᶜĀ'ishah and told her that Ibn ᶜUmar stated: 'I do not like to enter upon the state of *iḥrām* shaking off the perfume. Rubbing of tar (upon my body) is dearer to me than doing it (the applying of perfume)'. Thereupon, ᶜĀ'ishah said: 'I applied perfume to the Messenger of Allāh ﷺ at the time of his entering upon a state of *iḥrām*. He then went round his wives and in the morning got in a state of *iḥrām* while the perfume spread from him'."[703]

6-It is Sunnah to pray two *rakᶜahs* (unit of prayer) after all this, if it is not at a disliked time. *Farḍ* Prayer can suffice if one does *iḥrām* after it.[704] Nāfiᶜ narrated: ᶜAbdullāh ibn ᶜUmar said: "The Messenger of Allāh ﷺ made his camel sit (i.e. he dismounted) at al-Baṭḥā' in Dhū al-Ḥulayfah and offered the prayer". ᶜAbdullāh ibn ᶜUmar used to do the same.[705] ᶜAbdullāh ibn ᶜAbbās narrated that the Prophet ﷺ said the *talbiyah* loudly (started *iḥrām*) after the prayer.[706]

7-After the prayer one should say: اَللّٰهُمَّ إِنِّي أُرِيدُ الْحَجَّ فَيَسِّرْهُ لِي وَتَقَبَّلْهُ مِنِّي (O Allāh, I am intending to do *ḥajj*, so make it easy for me and accept it from me).[707]

8-After this one should pronounce the *talbiyah*.[708]

701 al-Bukhārī, *k. al-ḥajj, b. al-ṭīb ᶜinda al-iḥrām;* Muslim, *k. al-ḥajj, b. al-ṭīb lilmuḥrim ᶜinda al-iḥrām;* al-Nasā'ī, *k. al-ḥajj, b. mawḍiᶜ al-ṭīb.*

702 al-Nasā'ī, *k. al-manāsik, b. ibāḥat al-ṭīb ᶜinda al-iḥrām.*

703 al-Nasā'ī, *k. al-manāsik, b. mawḍiᶜ al-ṭīb.*

704 al-Kāsānī, *Badā'iᶜ al-ṣanā'iᶜ*, iii. 111.

705 al-Bukhārī, *k. al-ḥajj, b. al-ihlāl mustaqbil al-qiblah;* Muslim, *k. al-ḥajj, b. al-talbiyah wa ṣifatihā wa waqtihā.*

706 al-Tirmidhī, *k. al-ḥajj, b. mā jā'a matā aḥram …*

707 al-Samarqandī, *Tuḥfat al-fuqahā'* 195.

708 al-Kāsānī, *Badā'iᶜ al-ṣanā'iᶜ*, iii. 111.

TALBIYAH

Talbiyah means a prayer which praises and glorifies Allāh. This is a requisite condition for the validity of *iḥrām*. If someone intends *ḥajj* or ᶜ*umrah* but does not do the *talbiyah*, the *iḥrām* is not valid, because *iḥrām* is a combination of intention and the specific rites of *ḥajj*.[709] Umm Salamah reported: "I heard Allāh's Messenger ﷺ saying: 'O family of Muḥammad, who so among you intends to do *ḥajj* must raise his voice uttering the *talbiyah*'."[710]

The wording of the *talbiyah*

As regards the wording of the *talbiyah* during *ḥajj* ᶜAbdullāh ibn ᶜUmar said: "The *talbiyah* of the Messenger of Allāh ﷺ was:

لَبَّيْكَ اللَّهُمَّ لَبَّيْكَ، لَبَّيْكَ لَا شَرِيكَ لَكَ لَبَّيْكَ، إِنَّ الْحَمْدَ وَالنِّعْمَةَ لَكَ وَالْمُلْكَ لَا شَرِيكَ لَكَ.

(I respond to Your call O Allāh, I respond to Your call, and I am obedient to Your orders, You have no partner, I respond to Your call. All the praises and blessings are for You. All sovereignty is for You, And You have no partners)".[711] ᶜĀ'ishah narrated: "I know how the Prophet used to say the *talbiyah* and it was:

لَبَّيْكَ اللَّهُمَّ لَبَّيْكَ، لَبَّيْكَ لَا شَرِيكَ لَكَ لَبَّيْكَ، إِنَّ الْحَمْدَ وَالنِّعْمَةَ لَكَ وَالْمُلْكَ لَا شَرِيكَ لَكَ.

(I respond to Your call O Allāh, I respond to Your call, and I am obedient to Your orders, You have no partner, I respond to Your call. All the praises and blessings are for You, All the sovereignty is for You, And You have no partners)".[712] ᶜAbdullāh ibn ᶜUmar said: "The Messenger of Allāh ﷺ used to offer two *rak*ᶜ*ahs* of prayer at Dhū al-Ḥulayfah and then when his camel stood up with him on its back near the mosque at Dhū al-Ḥulayfah, he pronounced these words [of *Talbiyah*]:

لَبَّيْكَ اللَّهُمَّ لَبَّيْكَ، لَبَّيْكَ وَسَعْدَيْكَ، وَالْخَيْرُ فِي يَدَيْكَ، لَبَّيْكَ وَالرَّغْبَاءُ إِلَيْكَ وَالْعَمَلُ

709 al-Samarqandī, *Tuḥfat al-fuqahā'* 195.

710 Aḥmad ibn Ḥanbal, *al-Musnad, musnad al-nisā'*.

711 al-Bukhārī, *k. al-ḥajj, b. al-talbiyah*; Muslim, *k. al-ḥajj, b. al-talbiyah wa ṣifatihā*.

712 al-Bukhārī, *k. al-ḥajj, b. al-talbiyah.*

(I respond to Your call O Allāh, I respond to Your call, and I am obedient to Your orders, and good is in Your Hands. I respond to Your call. Unto You is the yearning and the doing (is also for You).[713]

Imām Muḥammad says after narrating this ḥadīth: "We adhere to it; the *talbiyah* is the first *talbiyah* which has been narrated from the Prophet ﷺ whatever you add that is fine. This is the opinion of Abū Ḥanīfah and most of our jurists".[714]

Ṣalāh on the Prophet ﷺ and supplication

After the *talbiyah* one should say in a subdued voice a *ṣalāh* (prayer) on the Prophet ﷺ. Al-Qāsim ibn Muḥammad ibn Abī Bakr said: "It is commendable for a pilgrim to send greetings and blessings on the Prophet ﷺ after saying the *talbiyah*".[715] Khuzaymah ibn Thābit narrated: "The Prophet ﷺ used to seek Allāh's pleasure and Paradise, and used to seek protection and His Mercy from the fire after having said his *talbiyah*."[716]

The virtue of the *talbiyah*

There is much virtue and reward in the utterance of the *talbiyah.* Sahl ibn Saᶜd al-Sāᶜidī reported that the Prophet ﷺ said: "When any Muslim says the *talbiyah*, everything [including] every rock, every tree and every pebble on his right and his left side responds with a similar *talbiyah*, until the whole earth resounds with it".[717]

The places where the *talbiyah* should be said

One should say the *talbiyah* as much as one can after every *farḍ* prayer, whenever one meets people, or mounts to a high place, or goes down in a lower place, and at dawn, and when one wakes up from sleep; because it has been narrated that the Companions of the Messenger of Allāh ﷺ used to do this.[718]

713 al-Bukhārī, *k. al-ḥajj, b. al-ihlāl mustaqbil al-qiblah;* Muslim, *k. al-ḥajj, b. al-talbiyah wa ṣifatihā wa waqtihā.*

714 Muhammad, *al-Muwaṭṭa'* 135.

715 al-Dāraquṭnī, *al-Sunan*, ii. 238; al-Bayhaqī, *al-Sunan al-kubrā*, v. 46.

716 ibid.

717 al-Tirmidhī, *k. al-ḥajj, b. mā jā'a fī faḍl al-talbiyah wa al-naḥr;* Ibn Mājah, *k. al-manāsik, b. al-talbiyah.*

718 al-Kāsānī, *Badā'iᶜ al-ṣanā'iᶜ*, iii. 112.

Times for the *talbiyah*

One should begin pronouncing the *talbiyah* from the time one enters the state of *iḥrām* and continue until the first pebble is thrown at the *Jamrah al-ᶜaqabah* on the 10th of *Dhū al-ḥijjah.*[719] ᶜAbdullāh ibn ᶜAbbās narrated that the Prophet ﷺ said the *talbiyah* until he threw pebbles at *Jamrah al-ᶜaqabah.*[720] ᶜAbdullāh ibn ᶜAbbās also narrated from his brother al-Faḍl ibn ᶜAbbās that Allāh's Messenger ﷺ continued pronouncing the *talbiyah* until he reached *Jamrah al-ᶜaqabah.*[721]

Imām Muḥammad narrates on the authority of Abū Ḥanīfah that Ibrāhīm al-Nakhaᶜī said: "The *muḥrim* ends the *talbiyah* of *ᶜumrah* as soon as he does the *istilām* (kiss) of the Black Stone, and ends the *talbiyah* of *ḥajj* as he throws the first pebble at the *Jamrah al-ᶜaqabah*". Imām Muḥammad says: "We adhere to this, and that is the opinion of Abū Ḥanīfah".[722]

One is allowed to interchange between the *talbiyah* and the *takbīr.* ᶜAbdullāh ibn ᶜUmar reported on the authority of his father, who said: "As we proceeded in the morning along with the Messenger ﷺ from Minā to 'ᶜArafah, some of us pronounced the *talbiyah,* and some pronounced the *takbīr*".[723]

Muḥammad ibn Abū Bakr al-Thaqafī asked Anas ibn Mālik while on their way from Minā to ᶜArafah in the morning: "What did you do on this day in the company of Allāh's Messenger ﷺ?" Thereupon he said: "Some of us pronounced the *tahlīl* (to say لا إله إلا الله, 'There is no god but Allāh') and we met with no disapproval (from the Prophet), and some of us pronounced the *takbīr,* and also met with no disapproval".[724]

Uttering *talbiyah* aloud

It is recommended that one says the *talbiyah* aloud.[725] ᶜAbdullāh ibn ᶜUmar reported that the Prophet ﷺ was asked: "Which *ḥajj* is the best?"

719 al-Qudūrī, *al-Mukhtaṣar* 217.
720 Ibn Mājah, *k. al-manāsik, b. matā yaqṭaᶜu al-ḥājj al-talbiyah.*
721 al-Bukhārī, *k. al-ḥajj, b. al-talbiyah wa al-takbīr ghadāt al-naḥr…*; Muslim, *k. al-ḥajj, b. bayān anna al-saᶜya lā yukarrar.*
722 Abū Ḥanīfah, *K. al-āthār* 83.
723 Muslim, *k. al-ḥajj, b. istiḥbāb idāmat al-ḥājj al-talbiyah…*
724 al-Bukhārī, *k. al-ḥajj, b. al-talbiyah wa al-takbīr idhā ghadā min minā ilā ᶜArafah;* Muslim, *k. al-ḥajj, b. istiḥbāb idāmat al-ḥājj al-talbiyah…*
725 al-Kāsānī, *Bada'i al-sana'iᶜ*, iii. 112.

He replied: "One in which voices are raised when saying the *talbiyah* and a sacrifice is offered".[726] Al-Sā'ib ibn Khallād reported that the Prophet ﷺ said: "Jibrīl ﷺ came to me and told me: 'Command your Companions to raise their voices when saying the *talbiyah*, because it is one of the rituals of *ḥajj*".[727] Imām Muḥammad says after narrating this ḥadīth: "We adhere to it; raising the voice in the *talbiyah* is better, and that is the opinion of Abū Ḥanīfah and most of our jurists".[728] Ḥasan ibn Furāt says: "Ibn Abī Mulaykah asked us: 'Are you in the state of *iḥrām*?' We said: 'Yes,' He said: 'Then say the *talbiyah*".[729] Bakr (al-Muzanī) says: "I was with Ibn ᶜUmar, and he said the *talbiyah* in a voice that could be heard between the two mountains". [730]

As for women, they may raise their voices when reciting *talbiyah* so that the voices are audible to themselves. To raise their voices above this is disliked. ᶜAbdullāh ibn ᶜAbbās says: "The woman will not raise her voice during the *talbiyah*".[731] Similar narration has come from ᶜAbdullāh ibn ᶜUmar.[732] It has also been narrated from Ibrāhīm and ᶜAṭā', both of them said: "Women will not raise their voice during the *talbiyah*".[733]

The inner meaning of the *talbiyah*

Imām Ghazālī says: "As for the state of sanctification (*iḥrām*) and the *talbiyah* from the *mīqāt*, let the pilgrim know that this has the sense of answering the call of Allāh, Exalted is He. Therefore, have the hope that you will be accepted, as well as the fear that you will be told: 'You are neither accepted nor blessed', so that you will waver between hope and fear, and be stripped of your might and power, (thereby) becoming (completely) dependent on the Grace and Generosity of Allāh, Exalted is He. For the time of *talbiyah* is the (real) beginning

726 al-Tirmidhī, *k. al-ḥajj, b. mā jā'a fī faḍl al-talbiyah wa al-naḥr;* Ibn Mājah, *k. al-manāsik, b. mā yūjib al-ḥajj.*

727 Abū Dāwūd, *k. al-manāsik, b. kayfiyyat al-talbiyah*; al-Tirmidhī, *k. al-ḥajj, b. mā jā'a fī rafᶜ al-ṣawt bi al-talbiyah.*

728 Muhammad, *al-Muwaṭṭa'* 136.

729 Ibn Abī Shaybah, *al-Muṣannaf,* viii. 609.

730 ibid.

731 ibid., viii. 507.

732 ibid., viii. 508.

733 ibid., viii. 507.

of the matter and the place of the danger. Sufyān ibn ʿUyaynah said: "ʿAlī ibn al-Ḥusayn once performed the *ḥajj*. When he had entered the state of sanctification and was well mounted on his camel, he suddenly turned pale; then he trembled and a shiver befell him to the extent that he could not recite the *talbiyah*. When it was said to him: 'Why are you not reciting the *talbiyah*?' He said: 'I fear that it will be said to me: 'You are neither accepted nor blessed'. And when he (later) recited the *talbiyah* he fainted and fell off his camel. This continued to happen to him until he completed his pilgrimage'. Aḥmad ibn al-Ḥawārī said: 'I was with Abū Sulaymān al-Dārānī when he declared his intention to enter the state of sanctification, but he did not recite the *talbiyah* until we had walked for about one mile. Then a swoon came over him, and when he recovered consciousness he said: 'O Aḥmad, Allāh, Exalted is He, has revealed to Mūsā: 'Bid the oppressors among the Children of Israel to decrease their remembrance of me for I remember, with a curse those among them who remember Me'. May Allāh have mercy on you, O Aḥmad – (a tradition]) has reached me that he who performs pilgrimage unlawfully and chants the *talbiyah*, Allāh, Exalted is He, says to him: 'You are neither accepted nor blessed until you return that which is in your possession'. There is no assurance that the same will not be said to us'. Let him who recites the *talbiyah* remember when he raises his voice with the *talbiyah* in the *mīqāt* his response is to the call of Allāh, Exalted is He, when He said: '*And proclaim unto mankind the pilgrimage*', and (let him reflect on) the calling forth of the creatures by the blowing of the trumpet, and their resurrection from graves, and their thronging together in the courtyard of the resurrection in response to the call of Allāh Most High, being divided into two groups: those who have achieved nearness to Allāh and those who are the detested ones, those who are accepted and those who are rejected. (For these resurrected ones too will) waver at first between fear and hope, as does the pilgrim in the *mīqāt*, not knowing whether it will be possible for him to complete the Pilgrimage and whether it will be accepted or not".[734]

WHAT IS FORBIDDEN IN A STATE OF *IḤRĀM*

The following acts are forbidden in a state of *iḥrām*:

734 al-Ghazālī, *Iḥyā' ʿulūm al-dīn*, i. 376.

1- **Sexual relation or touching and kissing with desire**.[735]

2- **Committing any sin**. Abū Hurayrah narrates that the Prophet ﷺ said: "Whoever performs *ḥajj* for Allāh's pleasure and is free of any shameful act and does not do evil or sin will return (after *ḥajj* free from all sins) as if he were born anew".[736]

3- **Quarrelling with companions or anyone else.** Allāh says in the Qur'ān: "*The ḥajj is in the known months. So whoever intends to perform the ḥajj therein should not use obscene language, nor commit any sin, nor engage in any dispute during the ḥajj*[737]". Abū Hurayrah narrates that the Prophet ﷺ said: "Whoever performs the *ḥajj* for Allāh's pleasure and does not use obscene language, and does not do evil or sins then he will return (after *ḥajj* free from all sins) as if he were born anew".[738]

4- **Wearing sewn cloth for men**. ʿAbdullāh ibn ʿUmar narrated: "A man asked, 'O Messenger of Allāh, what kind of clothes should a *muḥrim* wear?' The Messenger of Allāh ﷺ replied: 'He should not wear a shirt, a turban, trousers, a head cloak or leather socks except if he can find no slippers, he then may wear leather socks after cutting off what might cover the ankles. And he should not wear clothes which are scented with saffron or *warse* (a sweet smelling plant that was used to dye clothes yellow) ".[739]

5- **Covering the head, face, hands and feet for men**. Footwear should not cover the rising bones of the feet. As mentioned earlier, covering the face and palms for women is also not allowed.

ʿAbdullāh ibn ʿUmar said: "Allāh's Messenger ﷺ forbade female pilgrims from wearing gloves, veils, and clothes dyed with saffron or *warse*. Besides these, they may wear anything else, any colour, silk clothes, ornaments, trousers, a shirt or shoes".[740] Ibrāhīm al-Nakhaʿī says: "*Muḥrim* woman can

735 al-Qudūrī, *al-Mukhtaṣar* 205.

736 al-Bukhārī, *k. al-ḥajj, b. faḍl al-ḥajj al-mabrūr;* Muslim, *k. al-ḥajj, b. fī faḍl al-ḥajj wa al-ʿumrah.*

737 *al-Baqarah* 197.

738 al-Bukhārī, *k. al-ḥajj, b. faḍl al-ḥajj al-mabrūr;* Muslim, *k. al-ḥajj, b. fī faḍl al-ḥajj wa al-ʿumrah.*

739 al-Bukhārī, *k. al-ḥajj, b. mā lā yalbasu al-muḥrim min al-thiyāb;* Muslim, *k. al-ḥajj, b. mā yubāḥu li al-muḥrim bi ḥajj aw ʿumrah wa mā lā yubāḥ.*

740 Abū Dāwūd, *k. al-manāsik, b. mā yalbasu al-muḥrim.*

wear any clothes that she likes except the *burqaʿ* and gloves".[741] The same has been narrated from ʿAṭā' ibn Abī Rabāḥ.[742]

However, there is no harm if a woman covers her face with something other than a veil. She may also use an umbrella or similar item as a screen between men and herself. ʿĀ'ishah said: "Men on camels used to pass by us while we were with the Prophet ﷺ and in a state of *iḥrām*. We would cover our faces with our gowns when they passed by us, and then uncover them again".[743] Jābir ibn Zayd and Ṭāwūs did not like a woman to put on a veil while doing *ṭawāf*.[744]

6-**Applying perfume or henna on the body or the clothes**. Once in a state of *iḥrām* putting on any cloth that has been coloured with saffron or similar thing is not allowed except if it has been washed and the smell has gone. It is not allowed to use soap containing perfume, or eat or drink anything which has been mixed with perfume if it has not been cooked after mixing and the perfume is dominant. Ṣafwān ibn Yaʿlā narrated that his father Yaʿlā ibn Umayyah asked ʿUmar to let him witness when the Prophet receives revelation. Yaʿlā says: "A person came to the Apostle of Allāh ﷺ as he was with a group of his Companions at Jiʿirrānah and he (the person) had been putting on a cloak which was perfumed. That person said (to the Prophet): 'What do you command me to do during my *ʿumrah*?' (It was at this juncture) that the revelation came to the Apostle of Allāh ﷺ and he was covered with a cloth, and ʿUmar said to Yaʿlā: 'Would it please you to see the Apostle of Allāh ﷺ receiving the revelations?' ʿUmar lifted a corner of the cloth and Yaʿlā looked at him and he was emitting a sound of snorting. When he was relieved of this he (the Prophet) said: 'Where is he who asked about *ʿumrah*?' When the person came, the Prophet ﷺ said: 'Wash out the perfume and take off the cloak and do in your *ʿumrah* what you do in your *ḥajj*.'"[745]

The Kaʿbah often times may have perfume on its walls in which case there is no harm if one gets perfumed from touching the Kaʿbah. Ṣāliḥ

741 Ibn Abī Shaybah, *al-Muṣannaf*, viii. 410.
742 ibid.
743 Abū Dāwūd, *k. al-manāsik, b. fī al-muḥrimah tughaṭṭī wajhahā*.
744 ʿAbd al-Razzāq, *al-Muṣannaf*, v. 25.
745 al-Bukhārī, *k. al-ḥajj, b. ghasl al-khalūq thalātha marrāt min al-thiyāb*; Muslim, *k. al-ḥajj, b. mā yubāḥu li al-muḥrim bi ḥajj aw ʿumrah wa mā lā yubāḥ*.

ibn Ḥayyān said: "I have seen Anas ibn Mālik in the state of *iḥrām*, while some perfume from the Kaᶜbah rubbed on his *ḥajj* garb, but he did not wash it off".[746] ᶜAṭā' was asked what someone who becomes perfumed from the Kaᶜbah should do. ᶜAṭā answered: "It does not harm him". [747]

7- **Cutting the hair or nails.**[748] Allāh says: "*And do not shave your heads until the offering reaches the place of sacrifice*".[749] There is consensus among the scholars that a person in the state of *iḥrām* is forbidden to clip his fingernails without any genuine excuse. However, if a nail is broken, one may remove it without incurring any penalty. Removing hair is permitted, only if it becomes bothersome. In such a case one must pay atonement, except for the removal of eyelash if it bothers one. Allāh, Exalted is He, says: "*And if any of you is ill, or has an ailment in his scalp [necessitating shaving], he should in compensation either fast, or feed the poor, or offer sacrifice*".[750]

Kaᶜb ibn ᶜUjrah reported: "The Messenger of Allāh ﷺ came to me on the occasion of Ḥudaybiyyah and I was kindling fire under my cooking pot and lice were creeping on my face. Thereupon, he (the Prophet) said: 'Do the vermin harm your head?' I said: 'Yes'. He said: 'Get your head shaved and (in lieu of it) observe fasts for three days or feed six needy people, or offer the sacrifice (of an animal)'."[751]

8- **Hunting wild animals or assisting in their hunting**. Al-Ṣaᶜb ibn Jaththāmah al-Laythī narrates that he presented a wild ass to Allāh's Messenger ﷺ when he was at al-Abwā', or Waddān, and he refused to accept it. He (the narrator) said: "When the Messenger of Allāh ﷺ looked into my face (which had the mark of dejection as my present had been rejected by him) he (in order to console me) said: 'We have refused it only because we are in a state of *iḥrām*'."[752]

However, if the pilgrims have not helped in the hunting, then they

746 Ibn Abī Shaybah, *al-Muṣannaf*, viii. 226.

747 ibid.

748 al-Qudūrī, *al-Mukhtaṣar* 206.

749 *al-Baqarah* 196.

750 ibid.

751 al-Bukhārī, *k. al-muḥṣar, b. al-iṭᶜām fī al-fidyah niṣf ṣāᶜ*; Muslim, *k. al-ḥajj, b. jawāz ḥalq al-ra's li al-muḥrim...*

752 al-Bukhārī, *k. jazā' al-ṣayd, b. idhā ahdā li al-muḥrim ḥimāran waḥshiyyan ḥayyan lam yaqbal;* Muslim, *k. al-ḥajj, b. taḥrīm al-ṣayd li al-muḥrim.*

are allowed to eat from it. ʿAbdullāh ibn Abū Qatādah reported: "My father (Abū Qatādah) went with the Messenger of Allāh ﷺ in the year of Ḥudaybiyyah. His Companions entered into a state of *iḥrām* whereas he (Abū Qatādah) did not, for it was conveyed to the Messenger of Allāh ﷺ that the enemy was hiding at Ghayqah. The Messenger of Allāh ﷺ went forth. He (Abū Qatādah) said: 'Meanwhile I went to his Companions, some of whom smiled at me. I saw a wild ass and attacked it with a spear and caught it, and begged for their assistance, but they refused to help me. Then (later) we ate its meat. We became afraid lest we should be separated (from the Messenger of Allāh). So I proceeded on (with a view to) seeking (out) the Messenger of Allāh ﷺ. Sometimes I dashed my horse and sometimes I made it run at a leisurely pace (keeping pace with others). In the meanwhile, I met a person from Banū Ghifār in the middle of the night. I said to him: 'Where did you meet the Messenger of Allāh ﷺ,?' He replied: 'I left him at Taʿhin and he intended to halt at Suqyā to spend the afternoon'. I met (up with) him (the Prophet) and said: 'Messenger of Allāh, your Companions convey salutations and the benedictions of Allāh to you and they fear that they may be separated from you (and the enemy may harm you), so wait for them', and he (the Prophet) waited for them. I said: 'Messenger of Allāh, I killed game and there is left with me (some of the meat)'. The Apostle of Allāh ﷺ said to the people: 'Eat it'. And they were in a state of *iḥrām*'."[753]

9-**Cutting the grass or trees of the *Ḥaram*.** ʿAbdullāh ibn ʿAbbās narrated: "The Prophet ﷺ said: 'Allāh has made Makkah a sanctuary, as it was a sanctuary before me and will continue to be a sanctuary after me. It was made legal for me (i.e. I was allowed to fight in it) for a few hours of a day. It is not allowed to uproot its shrubs or to cut its trees, or to chase (or disturb) its game, or to pick up its *luqaṭah* (fallen things) except by a person who announces (what he has found) publicly'. Al-ʿAbbās said: 'O Allāh's Apostle. Except *idhkhir* for it is used by our goldsmiths and for our graves'. The Prophet then said: 'Except *idhkhir*'." ʿIkrimah said: 'Do you know what "chasing or disturbing" the game means? It means driving [the animal] out of the shade in order to take its place [in the shade]". [754]

753 al-Bukhārī, *k. al-jihād, b. ism al-faras wa al-ḥimār;* Muslim, *k. al-ḥajj, b. taḥrīm al-ṣayd li al-muḥrim.*

754 al-Bukhārī, *k. jazā' al-ṣayd, b. lā yaḥill al-qitāl bi makkah*; Muslim, *k. al-ḥajj, b.*

WHAT IS ALLOWED IN A STATE OF *IḤRĀM*

It is allowed for a *muḥrim* to do the following:

1- **Have a bath** with the condition that one does not use any soap that has perfume or can kill lice.[755] ʿAbdullāh ibn ʿUmar said: "We used to be in the gulf of the sea in Juḥfah, we used to dip in the water, while ʿUmar saw us, and did not criticise us, and we were in a state of *iḥrām*".[756] Ibrāhīm al-Nakhaʿī said: "There is no harm if a *muḥrim* has a bath, even without major impurity".[757] ʿAbdullāh ibn ʿAbbās entered a public bath at al-Juḥfah (to take a bath), while he was in a state of *iḥrām*. He was asked: "How can you do so while in a state of *iḥrām*?" He replied: "Allāh is not impressed by our being dirty".[758]

Ibrāhīm ibn ʿAbdullāh ibn Ḥunayn narrated on the authority of his father that: "There cropped up a difference of opinion between ʿAbdullāh ibn ʿAbbās and al-Miswar ibn Makhramah at a place called Abwā'. ʿAbdullāh ibn ʿAbbās contended that a *muḥrim* (is permitted) to wash his head, whereas Miswar contended that a *muḥrim* is not (permitted) to wash his head. So Ibn ʿAbbās sent me (the father of Ibrāhīm) to Abū Ayyūb al-Anṣārī to ask him about it. (So I went to him) and found him taking a bath behind two poles covered by a cloth. I gave him salutation, whereupon he asked: 'Who is this?' I said: 'I am ʿAbdullāh ibn Ḥunayn. ʿAbdullāh ibn ʿAbbās has sent me to you to find out how the Messenger of Allāh ﷺ washed his head in a state of *iḥrām*'. Abū Ayyūb placed his hand on the cloth and lowered it a little until his head became visible to me; and he said to the man who was pouring water upon him to pour water. He poured water on his head. He (Abū Ayyūb) then moved his head with the help of his hands and moved the hands forward and backward and then said: 'This is how I saw him (the Messenger of Allāh) doing (it)'."[759]

Ḥammād ibn Abī Sulaymān said: "I asked Ibrāhīm al-Nakhaʿī how can a *muḥrim* have a bath? He answered: 'What will Allāh do with his dirt?'

---

taḥrīm makkah wa ṣaydihā.

755 al-Qudūrī, *al-Mukhtaṣar* 206.

756 Ibn Abī Shaybah, *al-Muṣannaf*, viii. 71.

757 ibid.

758 al-Bayhaqī, *al-sunan al-kubrā, k. al-ḥajj, b. al-ightisāl baʿd al-iḥrām.*

759 al-Bukhārī, *k. jaza' al-ṣayd, b. al-ightisāl li al-muḥrim;* Muslim, *k. al-ḥajj, b. jawāz ghasl al-muḥrim badanahū wa ra'sahū.*

Imām Muḥammad says: "We adhere to this and do not consider any harm in having a bath, and this is the opinion of Abū Ḥanīfah".[760]

2- **To benefit from the shadow of anything** with the condition that it is not directly placed on one's head or face. ʿAbdullāh ibn ʿĀmir reported: "ʿUmar used to throw a piece of leather on a tree and sit under its shade while he was in a state of *iḥrām*".[761] Umm al-Ḥusayn reported: "I performed the Farewell *Ḥajj* with the Prophet ﷺ. I saw Usāmah ibn Zayd and Bilāl. One of them was holding the noseband of the Prophet's she-camel, and the other was shading him with a cloth from the sun until he threw the pebbles at ʿAqabah".[762] Ṭāwūs did not see any harm if a *muḥrim* shades himself from the sun.[763] Ibrāhīm al-Nakhaʿī was asked what a *muḥrim* should do when it rains. He answered: "He should hold his covering above his head, but should not put it on the head".[764]

3- **Cleaning one's teeth**. Ibrāhīm al-Nakhaʿī says: "The *muḥrim*, whether man or woman, will clean their teeth. Imām Muḥammad says: "We adhere to this, and this is the opinion of Abū Ḥanīfah".[765] Using *miswāk* has also been allowed by ʿAbdullāh ibn ʿUmar, ʿAṭā', Ṭāwūs, Mujāhid, Ḥasan, Muḥammad ibn ʿAlī, ʿĀmir al-Shaʿbī, Sālim, Qāsim and ʿAbd al-Raḥmān ibn al-Aswad.[766] ʿIkrimah was asked: "Can a *muḥrim* use a *miswāk*?" He answered: "Yes, *miswāk* is cleaning". [767] Toothpaste is also permissible as long as it is not artificially perfumed.

4- **Looking into the mirror**. ʿAbdullāh ibn ʿUmar did not see any harm for the *muḥrim* to look into a mirror.[768] ʿAbdullāh ibn ʿAbbās says: "There is no harm for a *muḥrim* to look in a mirror".[769] ʿUmar ibn ʿAbd al-ʿAzīz used to look in the mirror and used a tooth-stick (*miswāk*) while in a state of *iḥrām*. ʿAṭā' ibn Abī Rabāḥ did not see any harm in looking into

760 Abū Ḥanīfah, *K. al-āthār* 87.
761 Ibn Abī Shaybah, *al-Muṣannaf*, viii. 416.
762 Abū Dāwūd, *k. al-manāsik, b. fī al-muḥrim yuẓallal.*
763 Ibn Abī Shaybah, *al-Muṣannaf*, viii. 417.
764 ibid., viii. 418.
765 Abū Ḥanīfah, *K. al-āthār* 87.
766 Ibn Abī Shaybah, *al-Muṣannaf*, viii. 55-56.
767 ibid., viii. 55.
768 ibid., viii. 68.
769 ibid.

a mirror.[770] The same *fatwā* is also narrated from Ṭāwūs and ʿIkrimah.[771]

5-**Wearing a belt to keep money and any precious belongings**.[772] Ibn ʿAbbās said: "There is no harm if a *muḥrim* wears a belt-pocket to keep his money".[773] The same has been narrated from ʿAbdullāh ibn Zubayr, Abū Jaʿfar, ʿAṭā' ibn Abī Rabāḥ, Ṭāwūs, Sālim, Ibrāhīm al-Nakhaʿī, Qāsim, Saʿīd ibn Jubayr, Mujāhid, and ʿUrwah.[774] Khārijah ibn ʿAbdullāh said: "I asked Saʿīd ibn al-Musayyab about a *muḥrim* wearing a belt. He answered: 'There is no harm in it'. Imām Muḥammad says: 'We adhere to this, and this is the opinion of Abū Ḥanīfah".[775]

6-**Killing harmful animals**. ʿĀ'ishah narrated that the Messenger of Allāh ﷺ said: "Five kinds of animals are harmful and could be killed in the *Ḥaram*. These are the crow, the kite, the scorpion, the mouse and the rabid dog". In another version ʿĀ'ishah said: "I heard Allāh's Messenger ﷺ say: 'Four are the vicious (birds, beasts and reptiles) which should be killed in a state of *iḥrām* or otherwise: the kite (and vulture), crow, rat, and the voracious dog'." ʿUbaydullāh ibn Miqsam who is one of the narrators of this ḥadīth said to Qāsim who heard the narration from ʿĀ'ishah: "What about the snake?" He said: "Let it be killed with disgrace".[776] Sālim reported on the authority of his father that the Apostle of Allāh ﷺ said: "Five [beasts] which if one kills them in the precincts of the Kaʿbah or in a state of *iḥrām* entail no sin: the rat, scorpion, crow, kite and voracious dog".[777] Imām Muḥammad says: "We adhere to this, and this is the opinion of Abū Ḥanīfah, and any beast that attacks you, and you kill it, there is nothing upon you".[778]

7-**To get married.** It is allowed for one in a state of *iḥrām* to marry but it is not allowed to kiss or touch one's spouse with desire until

770 ibid.

771 ibid.

772 al-Qudūrī, *al-Mukhtaṣar* 207.

773 Ibn Abī Shaybah, *al-Muṣannaf*, viii. 701.

774 ibid.

775 Abū Ḥanīfah, *K. al-āthār* 89.

776 Muslim, *k. al-ḥajj, b. mā yundabu li al-muḥrim wa ghayrihi qatluhu min al-dawābb fī al-ḥill wa al-ḥaram.*

777 Muslim, *k. al-ḥajj, b. mā yundabu li al-muḥrim wa ghayrihi qatluhu min al-dawābb fī al-ḥill wa al-ḥaram.*

778 Abū Ḥanīfah, *K. al-āthār* 90.

one is out of *iḥrām*. ᶜAbdullāh ibn ᶜAbbās narrated that the Prophet ﷺ married Maymūnah bint al-Ḥārith at ᶜUsfān in a state of *iḥrām*.[779] Imām Muḥammad says: "We adhere to this, we do not consider any harm in it, but it is not allowed to kiss or touch until one becomes ḥalāl (out of *iḥrām*), and this is the opinion of Abū Ḥanīfah".[780]

The inner meaning of being in a state of *iḥrām*

Ghazālī says: "As for the purchase of the two *iḥrām* garments: let (the pilgrim) at this (point) reflect upon the winding sheet and his being wrapped in it, for he will wear and put on the *iḥrām* garments when he is near to the House of Allāh, Exalted is He, and it may be that his journey to it will not be completed; [on the other hand] he will most assuredly meet Allāh, Exalted is He, when he is wrapped in the winding sheet (shroud). As he does not come to the House of Allāh, Exalted is He, except when he has broken with his usual mode of dress and form, so he will not meet Allāh, Exalted is He, after death except in a style of dress different from the style of dress of this life; and the [*iḥrām*] garment is very much like that one [i.e. the shroud] as it is not sewn, just as is the case with the winding sheet".[781]

Shāh Walīullah writes: "*Iḥrām* which is worn during *ḥajj* and ᶜ*umrah* is like the *takbīr* of *ṣalāh*. It is a symbol of the believer's faith, sincerity and endeavour. Its purpose is to make the self lowly before Allāh, to make it bow down before Him in submission and to serve as an expression of anguish, distress and suffering for His sake".[782]

WHAT IS REQUIRED BEFORE AND UPON ENTERING MAKKAH

1- To be in a state of *iḥrām*. It is not allowed to enter into Makkah without *iḥrām*.[783] ᶜAbdullāh ibn ᶜAbbās narrated that the Prophet ﷺ said: "Entering into Makkah without *iḥrām* is not allowed".[784] ᶜAlī said: "Do

779 al-Bukhārī, *k. jazā' al-ṣayd, b. tazwīj al-muḥrim;* Muslim, *k. al-nikāḥ, b. taḥrīm nikāḥ al-muḥrim.*

780 Abū Ḥanīfah, *K. al-āthār* 90.

781 al-Ghazālī, *Iḥyā' ᶜulūm al-dīn*, i. 375.

782 al-Dihlawī, *Ḥujjatullāh al-bālighah,* ii. 91.

783 al-Kāsānī, *Badā'iᶜ al-ṣanā'iᶜ*, iii. 160-161.

784 al-Bayhaqī, *al-Sunan al-kubrā, k. al-ḥajj, man marra bi al-mīqāt yurīdu ḥajjan aw ᶜumratan...*

not enter into Makkah without *iḥrām*".[785] Ḥasan al-Baṣrī did not like anyone entering into Makkah without *iḥrām.*[786] Ibrāhīm al-Nakhaʿī says: "[People] loved not to enter into Makkah without *iḥrām*".[787] ʿAṭā' ibn Abī Rabāḥ said: "It is not allowed for anyone to enter into Makkah without *iḥrām*".[788]

2- To clean oneself and have a bath. Nāfiʿ said that Ibn ʿUmar would take a bath before entering Makkah and used to say that the Prophet ﷺ did the same.[789] Imām Muḥammad says: "*Ghusl* before entering Makkah is good, but is not *wājib*".[790]

3-After storing one's luggage in one's accommodation or any secure place, one should begin by going to *al-Masjid al-Ḥarām,* and say the *takbīr* and *tahlīl* as soon as one sees the Kaʿbah.[791]

4-If one is coming from outside Makkah and has enough time, one should do *ṭawāf al-qudūm.*[792] However, if one sets out directly for ʿArafah without entering Makkah and stands there in the manner that has been explained earlier then the Sunnah of the *ṭawāf* of arrival is removed and one does not have to pay anything in compensation.

Imām Ghazālī says: "As for the entrance into Makkah, let [the pilgrim] remember then that he has arrived at the shrine of Allāh safely and let him hope [at that place] to be saved from the chastisement of Allāh, Exalted is He, by virtue of his entrance, [therein]. Let him fear that he may not deserve being near [to God], such that he will be by virtue of his entrance into the sacred place, ineffectual and deserving of chastisement. Let his hope be at all times predominant, for God's generosity is All-encompassing, the Lord is Merciful, the honour of the House is great, the right of the visitor is honoured, and the security of the one who seeks protection and refuge is not neglected".[793]

785 Ibn Abī Shaybah, *al-Muṣannaf,* viii. 227.

786 ibid.

787 ibid.

788 ibid.

789 al-Bukhārī, *k. al-ḥajj, b. al-ightisāl ʿinda dukhūl makkah;* Muslim, *k. al-ḥajj, b. istiḥbāb al-mabīt bi dhī ṭuwa.*

790 Muhammad, *al-Muwaṭṭa'* 159.

791 al-Marghīnānī, *al-Hidāyah,* ii. 176.

792 al-Qudūrī, *al-Mukhtaṣar* 209; al-Samarqandī, *Tuḥfat al-fuqahā'* 197.

793 al-Ghazālī, *Iḥyā' ʿulūm al-dīn,* i. 376.

IN THE EVENT OF A *MUḤRIM*'S DEATH

ᶜAbdullāh ibn ᶜAbbās reported that a person fell down from his camel (in a state of *iḥrām*) and his neck was broken and died. Thereupon, Allāh's Apostle ﷺ said: "Bathe him with water mixed with the leaves of the lote tree and shroud him in his two (pieces of) cloth (*iḥrām*), and do not cover his head for Allāh will raise him on the Day of Resurrection pronouncing the *talbiyah*".[794] On the basis of this ḥadīth most jurists hold the opinion that if someone dies in the state of *iḥrām*, then his head should not be covered and no perfume should be applied.

However, according to the *hanafi* opinion, once someone has died, his *iḥrām* has finished. Nāfiᶜ narrated that when ᶜAbdullāh ibn ᶜUmar's son Wāqid ibn ᶜAbdullāh died in a state of *iḥrām* at Juḥfah, ᶜAbdullāh ibn ᶜUmar enshrouded him and covered his head.[795] Imām Muḥammad says after narrating this practice of Ibn ᶜUmar: "We adhere to this, and this is the opinion of Abū Ḥanīfah. When someone dies, his *iḥrām* has ended". [796] Ṭāwūs said: "A *muḥrim's* head should be covered when he dies".[797] Ḥasan al-Baṣrī says: "When a *muḥrim* dies he comes out of *iḥrām*". [798] The same has been narrated from ᶜĀ'ishah, ᶜĀmir al-Shaᶜbī, ᶜIkrimah, ᶜAṭā' ibn Abī Rabāḥ and Muḥammad al-Bāqir. [799]

WHEN ONE COMES OUT OF *IḤRĀM*

The *muḥrim* of ᶜ*umrah* 'becomes ḥalāl' (i.e. comes out of a state of *iḥrām*) after completing the ᶜ*umrah* and shaving or shortening his hair.[800]

The *Muḥrim* of *ḥajj* comes out of a state of *iḥrām* after shaving or shortening the hair and everything becomes lawful for him except relations with his wife which is only allowed after the *ṭawāf* of *ifāḍah*.[801]

794 al-Bukhārī, *k. jazā' al-ṣayd, b. al-muḥrim yamūtu bi ᶜArafah;* Muslim, *k. al-ḥajj, b. mā yufᶜalu bi al-muḥrim idhā māt.*

795 Muhammad, *al-Muwaṭṭa'*, 171.

796 ibid.

797 Ibn Abī Shaybah, *al-Muṣannaf*, viii. 453.

798 ibid.

799 ibid., viii. 453-5.

800 al-Samarqandī, *Tuḥfat al-fuqahā'* 192.

801 ibid., 201.

2. *WUQŪF* IN ᶜARAFAH

The second *farḍ* of *ḥajj* is the *wuqūf* (staying) in ᶜArafah.

The virtue of the Day of ᶜArafah

The Day of ᶜArafah is one of the most significant days of the year. Jābir reported that the Prophet ﷺ said: "The ten days of the month of *Dhū al-ḥijjah* are the best days in the sight of Allāh". A man asked, "Are these days better than an equivalent number of days that are spent fighting for the cause of Allāh?" The Prophet ﷺ answered: "They are better than an equivalent number of days spent fighting in the cause of Allāh. And there is no day better in the sight of Allāh than the Day of ᶜArafah. On this day Allāh, the Almighty and the Exalted One, descends to the nearest heaven, and He is proud of His slaves on the earth, and says to those in heaven: 'Look at My servants. They have come from far and near, with hair dishevelled and faces covered with dust, to seek My Mercy, even though they have not seen my chastisement'. Far more people are freed from the Hellfire on the Day of ᶜArafah than on any other day'."[802]

ᶜĀ'ishah reported that the Prophet ﷺ said: "Allāh frees far more people from Hellfire on the Day of ᶜArafah than on any other day, and that Allāh comes closer this day and proudly says to the angels, 'What do these people want and seek?'"[803] Ṭalḥah ibn ᶜUbaydullāh ibn Kurayz narrated that the Prophet ﷺ said: "On no other day does the Satan feel so belittled, humiliated, and angry as he does on the Day of ᶜArafah".[804]

The legal position of *Wuqūf* in ᶜArafah

Staying in ᶜArafah is the most important *farḍ* of the *ḥajj*. ᶜAbd al-Raḥmān ibn Yaᶜmur reported that the Prophet ﷺ ordered an announcer to proclaim: " The *ḥajj* is ᶜArafah".[805]

802 al-Baghawī, *Sharḥ al-sunnah, k. al-ḥajj, b. faḍl yawm ᶜArafah.*

803 Muslim, *k. al-ḥajj, b. fī faḍl al-ḥajj wa al-ᶜumrah wa yawm ᶜArafah.*

804 Mālik, *al-Muwaṭṭa', k. al-ḥajj, b. jāmiᶜ al-ḥajj;* al-Baghawī, *Sharḥ al-sunnah, k. al-ḥajj, b. faḍl yawm ᶜArafah.*

805 Abū Dāwūd, *k. al-manāsik, b. man lam yudrik ᶜArafah*; al-Tirmidhī, *k. al-ḥajj, b. mā jā'a fīman adraka al-imām bijamᶜ faqad adraka al-ḥajj*; al-Nasā'ī, *k. al-ḥajj, b. farḍ al-wuqūf biᶜArafah;* Ibn Mājah, *k. al-manāsik, b. man atā ᶜArafah qabl al-fajr laylata jamᶜ.*

ʿĀ'ishah said: "The Quraysh (of the pre-Islamic days) and those who followed their religious practices stayed at Muzdalifah, and they named themselves as Ḥums, whereas all other Arabs stayed at ʿArafah. With the advent of Islam, Allāh, Exalted is He, commanded His Apostle ﷺ to come to ʿArafah and stay there, and then move on from there, and this is the significance of the words of Allāh: "*Then move on from where the people move on*".[806]

Hishām ibn ʿUrwah narrated on the authority of his father, that the Arabs with the exception of Ḥums who were Quraysh, and their descendants, circumambulated the House naked. They kept circumambulating in this state of nudity until the Ḥums provided them with clothes. The male provided (clothes) to the male and the female provided clothes to the female. And the Ḥums did not move out of Muzdalifah, whereas the people (other than the Quraysh) went to ʿArafah. Hishām said on the authority of his father who related from ʿĀ'ishah who said: "Ḥums are those about whom Allāh, Exalted is He, revealed this verse: '*Then move on from where the people moved*'." She (further) said: "The people moved on from ʿArafah, whereas Ḥums moved on from Muzdalifah", and said: 'We do not move on except from *Ḥaram*.' But when this (verse) was revealed: "*Move on from where the people move on*," they (the Quraysh) then went to ʿArafah."[807]

Which part of ʿArafah is recommended?

A pilgrim may spend the Day of ʿArafah anywhere within the boundary of ʿArafah which is clearly signposted. The only exception is the bottom of the valley called 'Urnah which is to the west of ʿArafah.[808] There is consensus that staying at ʿUrnah does not fulfil the condition of staying at ʿArafah. Jābir narrated that the Prophet ﷺ said: "The whole of ʿArafah can be stayed in except for the valley of ʿUrnah".[809]

It is commendable to spend the time near the *Jabal al-Raḥmah* (Mountain of Mercy) or as close to it as possible. However, this may not be possible due to the immense numbers of people attending the *ḥajj*. This is the place where the Prophet ﷺ stopped and said: "I have

806 Muslim, *k. al-ḥajj, b. fī al-wuqūf.*

807 al-Bukhārī, *k. al-tafsīr, sūrat al-baqarah*; Muslim, *k. al-ḥajj, b. fī al-wuqūf.*

808 al-Kāsānī, *Badā'iʿ al-ṣanā'iʿ*, iii. 60.

809 Muslim, *k. al-ḥajj, b. ḥajjat al-nabī salallahu ʿalayhi wa sallam.*

stopped here, but the whole of ᶜArafah is a stopping place (for the Day of ᶜArafah)".[810]

Climbing the Mountain of Mercy or any other mountain there with the belief that standing on it is better than standing in any other place is wrong. This is not substantiated by any Sunnah of the Prophet ﷺ or the early generations.

THERE IS ONE CONDITION (*FARḌ*), ONE *WĀJIB* AND A NUMBER OF SUNNAHS FOR STAYING AT ᶜARAFAH

Its condition

The condition is that it must be at ᶜArafah during the legally set time frame. The legal time frame is from the decline of the sun (*zawāl*) on the 9th day of *Dhū al-ḥijjah* till the dawn of the 10th.[811] If one is present at ᶜArafah in this time, his *ḥajj* is valid, whether one intends so or not, whether one knows that one is in ᶜArafah or not, or one is unconscious or sleeping.[812] It is reported from Saᶜīd ibn Hassan that: "When al-Ḥajjāj killed ᶜAbdullāh ibn Zubayr, he sent a message to ᶜAbdullāh ibn ᶜUmar to ask him at which moment the Apostle of Allāh ﷺ used to proceed to ᶜArafah this day? He replied: 'When it happens so, we shall proceed'. When Ibn ᶜUmar intended to proceed, the people said: 'The sun did not decline'. He (Ibn ᶜUmar) asked: 'Did it (not) decline?' They replied: 'It did not decline'. When they said that the sun had declined, he proceeded'."[813] ᶜAbd al-Raḥmān ibn Yaᶜmur al-Daylī narrates: "I came to the Prophet ﷺ when he was in ᶜArafah. Some people or a group of people came from the Najd. They commanded someone (to ask the Prophet about *ḥajj*). So he called the Apostle of Allāh ﷺ saying: 'How is the *ḥajj* done?' He (the Prophet) ordered a man (to reply) loudly: 'The *ḥajj*, the *ḥajj* is on the day of ᶜArafah. If anyone arrives there before the dawn prayer on the night of al-Muzdalifah, his *ḥajj* will be complete. The period of halting at Minā is three days. Whoever hastens (his

810 Abū Dāwūd, *k. al-manāsik, b. al-ṣalāh bi jamᶜ;* al-Tirmidhī, *k. al-ḥajj b. mā jā'a anna ᶜArafah kullahā mawqif.*

811 al-Kāsānī, *Badā'iᶜ al-ṣanā'iᶜ*, iii. 62.

812 al-Samarqandī, *Tuḥfat al-fuqahā'* 200.

813 Abū Dāwūd, *k. al-manāsik, b. al-rawāḥ ilā ᶜArafah;* Ibn Mājah, *k. al-manāsik, b. al-manzil bi ᶜArafah.*

departure) by two days, it is no sin for him, and whoever delays it there is no sin for him'." The narrator said that the Prophet then put a man behind him on the camel so that he could proclaim this loudly.[814]

Its *wājib*

If the pilgrim is at ʿArafah during the daytime then it is *wājib* that he continue his stay there until sunset. This does not apply if the pilgrim does not reach ʿArafah until after sunset.[815]

SUNNAHS OF STAYING AT ʿARAFĀH

1- Having a bath for the stay in ʿArafah. ʿAbdullāh ibn Masʿūd and ʿAbdullāh ibn ʿUmar used to take a bath on the eve of the Day of ʿArafah.[816] Similarly ʿUmar used to take a bath in ʿArafah while he was saying *talbiyah.*[817] The same has been narrated from al-Aswad, Mujāhid, Ibrāhīm al-Nakhaʿī and ʿAbd al-Raḥmān ibn Abī Laylā.[818]

2- On the occasion of combining the *Ẓuhr* and *ʿAṣr* prayers, the *Imām* gives a *khuṭbah* (sermon) in two parts, while standing, separating them with a brief interval when he sits down, on the same pattern as for the *khuṭbah* of *Jumuʿah.*[819] Sālim ibn ʿAbdullāh ibn ʿUmar (the son of ʿAbdullāh ibn ʿUmar) narrates that: "ʿAbd al-Malik ibn Marwān wrote to al-Ḥajjāj that he should follow ʿAbdullāh ibn ʿUmar in all the ceremonies of *ḥajj.* So when it was the Day of ʿArafah, and after the sun had deviated or declined from the middle of the sky, I and (ʿAbdullāh) Ibn ʿUmar came and he shouted near the cotton (cloth) tent of al-Ḥajjāj, 'Where is he?' Al-Ḥajjāj came out. Ibn ʿUmar said: 'Let us proceed (to ʿArafah)'. Al-Ḥajjāj asked: 'Just now?' Ibn ʿUmar replied: 'Yes'. Al-Ḥajjāj said: 'Wait for me until I pour water on me (i.e. take a bath)'. So, Ibn ʿUmar dismounted (and waited) until al-Ḥajjāj came out. He was walking between me and my father. I said to al-Ḥajjāj: 'If you want to follow the Sunnah today, then you should shorten the sermon

814 Abū Dāwūd, *k. al-manāsik, b. man lam yudrk ʿArafah*; Ibn Mājah, *k. al-manāsik, b. man atā ʿArafah qabl al-jamʿ laylata jamʿ.*

815 al-Kāsānī, *Badāʾiʿ al-ṣanāʾiʿ*, iii. 65.

816 Ibn Abī Shaybah, *al-Muṣannaf*, viii. 723-4.

817 ibid., 723.

818 ibid., 724.

819 al-Samarqandī, *Tuḥfat al-fuqahā'* 199.

and then hurry up for the stay (at ʿArafah)'. Ibn ʿUmar said: 'He (Sālim) has spoken the truth'."[820]

3-Combining *Ẓuhr* and *ʿAṣr Ṣalāh* at the time of *Ẓuhr*. After the *adhān* the *iqāmah* will be made for *Ẓuhr* and after completing the *Ẓuhr Ṣalāh* another *iqāmah* will be made for the *ʿAṣr Ṣalāh*.[821] As narrated by Jābir, in which he described the *ḥajj* of the Prophet ﷺ the Prophet combined in ʿArafah *Ẓuhr* and *ʿAṣr*. This is a matter agreed upon among jurists.

Ibrāhīm al-Nakhaʿī says: "When you pray on the Day of ʿArafah at your place (i.e. you do not go to pray behind the *imām* at the mosque), then pray each prayer at its due time (i.e. not combining *Ẓuhr* and *ʿAṣr*), and do not depart until you finish the prayer. Imām Muḥammad says: "Abū Ḥanīfah adhered to this, but in our opinion one prays in his place as one prays with the *imām*, combining them with one *adhān* and two *iqāmahs*, because *ʿAṣr* has been brought forward for the reason of *wuqūf* (the stopping over at ʿArafah). This is what has come to our knowledge from ʿĀ'ishah, the Mother of the Believers, from ʿAbdullāh ibn ʿUmar, ʿAṭā' ibn Abī Rabāḥ and Mujāhid".[822]

4-Refrain from fasting. Umm al-Faḍl narrates: "The people doubted whether the Prophet was observing the fast on the Day of ʿArafah, so I sent something for him to drink and he drank it".[823] Yaḥyā ibn Abī Isḥāq says: "I asked Saʿīd ibn al-Musayyab about fasting on the Day of ʿArafah? He answered: 'ʿAbdullāh ibn ʿUmar did not fast'."[824] Saʿīd ibn Jubayr did not fast on the day of ʿArafah and said: "I want to have strength for the supplication".[825]

5-To make *talbiyah, tasbīḥ* (to glorify Allāh by saying *subḥān'allāh*), *ṣalāh* (salutations) on the Prophet ﷺ and *duʿā'* at all time.[826] Usāmah ibn Zayd reported: "I was riding behind the Prophet ﷺ in ʿArafah, while he raised his hands in supplications to Allāh".[827]

820 al-Bukhārī, *k. al-ḥajj, b. al-jamʿ bayn al-ṣalātayn bi ʿArafah.*

821 al-Samarqandī, *Tuḥfat al-fuqahā'* 199.

822 Abū Ḥanīfah, *K. al-āthār* 84-85.

823 al-Bukhārī, *k. al-ṣawm, b. ṣawm yawma ʿArafah*; Muslim, *k. al-ṣiyām, b. istiḥbāb al-fiṭr li al-ḥājj yawma ʿArafah.*

824 Ibn Abī Shaybah, *al-Muṣannaf*, viii. 194.

825 ibid.

826 al-Samarqandī, *Tuḥfat al-fuqahā'* 199.

827 al-Nasā'ī, *k. al-manāsik, b. rafʿ al-yadayn fī al-duʿā' bi ʿArafah.*

ᶜAmr ibn Shuᶜayb reported from his father, who reports from his grandfather, that the Prophet ﷺ said: "The best supplication is the supplication of the Day of ᶜArafah. The best thing that I and the prophets before me said is:

لَا إِلَهَ إِلَّا اللَّهُ وَحْدَهُ لَا شَرِيكَ لَهُ، لَهُ الْمُلْكُ وَلَهُ الْحَمْدُ، وَهُوَ عَلَى كُلِّ شَيْءٍ قَدِيرٌ

('There is no deity worthy of worship but Allāh Alone. He has no partners. To Him alone belongs the Kingdom, and all praise, and He has power over all things'.)"[828]

Imām Ghazālī says: "As for the standing on [Mount] ᶜArafah keep in memory what you see [there] of the crowding together of people, the raised voices, the variety of languages, the adherence of [different] groups to [the ways of] their leaders: in their visitation of shrines, imitating them and following their practices – [remember when you see all this] the open field of the Day of Resurrection, the gathering of [the different] nations with their prophets and leaders, [and] each nation's imitation of its prophet, and [their] craving his intercession, and the trembling in that place between rejection and acceptance [of their pleas for intercession]. When you remember all this, let your heart cleave to submission and humility to Allāh Most High, so that you will be resurrected among the group of the ones who are successful and forgiven."[829]

MOVING FROM ᶜARAFAH

Pilgrims should leave ᶜArafah after sunset quietly and calmly.[830] ᶜAbdullāh ibn ᶜAbbās narrated that he was accompanying the Prophet ﷺ on the Day of ᶜArafah. Then the Prophet heard behind him [people] spurring their camels violently. So he pointed at them with his riding whip and said: "O people, calm down; obedience (does not consist in) rushing".[831] It is also reported that the Prophet ﷺ let his she camel go at a normal pace, but when he found ample space in front of him he urged it to go faster. He did this out of compassion and consideration for the people.[832] Mujāhid

828 al-Tirmidhī, *k. al-daᶜawāt, b. fī duᶜā' yawm ᶜArafah.*

829 al-Ghazālī, *Iḥyā' ᶜulūm al-dīn*, i. 378.

830 al-Qudūrī, *al-Mukhtaṣar* 214.

831 al-Bukhārī, *k. al-ḥajj, b. amr al-nabī ṣallallāhu ᶜalayhi wa sallam bi al-sakīnah….*

832 al-Bukhārī, *k. al-ḥajj, b. al-sayr idhā dafaᶜa min ᶜArafah, k. al-jihād, b. al-surᶜah fī*

says: "They thought that forgiveness descends at the time of moving from ʿArafah".[833]

Pilgrims should say the *talbiyah* and make remembrance of Allāh as much as possible. The Prophet ﷺ repeated the *talbiyah* right until he threw pebbles at *Jamrah al-ʿaqabah*.[834] Ashʿath ibn Sulaym reported that his father said: "I went with Ibn ʿUmar from ʿArafah to Muzdalifah. He did not stop *takbīr* and *tahlīl* until we reached Muzdalifah".[835]

3. *ṬAWĀF*

The third *farḍ* of *ḥajj* is the *Ṭawāf* (circumambulation) of the Kaʿbah. The *ṭawāf* is done seven times keeping the Kaʿbah on one's left side.

Seeing the Kaʿbah

ʿAbd al-Raḥmān ibn Ṭāriq ibn ʿAlqamah narrates from his mother, who said that when the Prophet ﷺ came to a place in the house of Yaʿlā (from where he could see the Kaʿbah) he faced the *qiblah* (the direction of the Kaʿbah) and made *duʿā'*.[836] Imām Ghazālī says: "As for the first glimpse of the Kaʿbah, it is recommended that [the pilgrim] recall at that time and place the majesty of the House in his [heart], and that he be deemed by virtue of the intensity of his magnification of the House, to be beholding the Lord of the House [Himself]. You should hope that Allāh, Exalted is He, will bless you with the Vision of His noble Face as He blessed you with the vision of His majestic House. Thank Allāh, Exalted is He, for bringing you to this position and for joining you to the groups that came to Him. And remember [again] at that place the surging forth of people on the Day of Resurrection in the direction of Paradise, hoping that they all will enter it. [And reflect on] their division into those who are permitted to enter [it] and those who are driven away, [resembling] the division of pilgrims into those who are accepted and those who are rejected".[837]

---

al-sayr, k. al-maghāzī, b. ḥajjat al-wadāʿ; Muslim, *k. al-ḥajj, b. al-ifāḍah min ʿarafat.*

833 Ibn Abī Shaybah, *al-Muṣannaf*, viii. 235.

834 al-Bukhārī, *k. al-ḥajj, b. al-talbiyah wa al-takbīr ghadāt al-naḥr;* Muslim, *k. al-ḥajj, b, istiḥbāb idāmat al-ḥājj al-talbiyah....*

835 Abū Dāwūd, *k. al-manāsik, b. al-ṣalāh bi jamʿ.*

836 al-Nasā'ī, *k. al-manāsik, b. al-duʿā' ʿinda ru'yat al-bayt.*

837 al-Ghazālī, *Iḥyā' ʿulūm al-dīn*, i. 376.

The virtue of *ṭawāf*

ᶜAbdullāh ibn ᶜUmar narrates: "I heard the Messenger of Allāh ﷺ say: 'Whoever does *ṭawāf* of the house and prays two *rakᶜahs*, it will be like freeing a slave".[838]

Imām Ghazālī says: As for the circumambulation of the House, know that it is [akin to] prayer. Therefore, recall at that stage that which we have already mentioned in detail in the chapter on prayer such as reverence, fear, hope and affection. Know that through circumambulation you resemble the angels who have attained nearness to Allāh and surround the Throne, circumambulating it. Do not think that the purpose behind circumambulation lies in your bodily circumambulation of the House; the purpose is rather circumambulation with your heart through recollecting Allāh the Lord of the House ...Know too that the noble circumambulation is the heart's circumambulation of the Presence of Lordship, and the House is a phenomenal representation in the realm of earthly power of that Presence, which the eyes cannot see: that is the Realm of Spiritual Power (*malakūt*)... This parallel (between the seen and the unseen realms) is borne out by the fact that the House inhabited in the heavens is a counterpart to the Kaᶜbah, and the cirumambulation of angels around the former is similar to the circumambulation of people around this House. Since the level of the great majority of people falls short of the [heavenly] circumambulation, they are enjoined to simulate it as far as possible, and are promised that: "He who imitates a people is one of them". [839]

TYPES OF *ṬAWĀF*

The *farḍ ṭawāf* is *ṭawāf al-ifāḍah.* It is also named as *ṭawāf al-ziyārah.* Its time is from the dawn on the 10th of *Dhū al-ḥijjah* until the end of the month of *ḥajj*, if one has already stayed in ᶜArafah.[840]

Besides *farḍ ṭawāf*, there are three other types of *ṭawāf*:

1- *ṭawāf al-qudūm* (arrival circumambulation).
2- *ṭawāf al-ṣadr* (farewell circumambulation).
3- *ṭawāf al-taṭawwuᶜ* (supererogatory circumambulation).

838 Ibn Mājah, *k. al-manāsik, b. faḍl al-ṭawāf.*
839 al-Ghazālī, *Iḥyā' ᶜulūm al-dīn*, i. 377.
840 al-Kāsānī, *Badā'iᶜ al-ṣanā'iᶜ*, iii. 78.

Pilgrims coming from outside Makkah should do as many *ṭawāf*s as they can, because for them *nafl ṭawāf* is better than the *nafl ṣalāh.*[841]

CONDITIONS OF *ṬAWĀF*

For the validity of any *ṭawāf* the following conditions must be met:

1- It should be inside *Masjid al-Ḥarām*, even if it is beyond *Zamzam.* If someone does *ṭawāf* outside the *Masjid al-Ḥarām*, then his *ṭawāf* is not valid.[842]

2- If it is *ṭawāf al-ifāḍah*, then its timing begins from the rising of dawn on the 10th *Dhū al-ḥijjah*; and it is not valid before then.[843]

WĀJIBS OF *ṬAWĀF*

Ṭawāf has the following *wājibs*:

1- **Purification**: It is *wājib* to be pure from any minor and major impurity while performing *ṭawāf.*[844] ʿUrwah narrated that ʿĀ'ishah said: "The first thing the Prophet did on reaching Makkah was the ablution and then he performed *ṭawāf* of the Kaʿbah.[845] ʿAbdullāh ibn ʿAbbās reported that the Prophet ﷺ said: "*Ṭawāf* is prayer, but [unlike the prayer] Allāh, the Almighty, has made talking permissible (in *ṭawāf*). Then, whoever speaks (during *ṭawāf*) should speak only good things".[846] ʿĀ'ishah also reported that the Prophet ﷺ entered her apartment and found her crying. He asked her: "Has your monthly course begun?" She replied: "Yes". Upon this the Prophet ﷺ said: "This is a matter decreed by Allāh, the Almighty, for all daughters of Ādam. You should do all the rites of *ḥajj*, except *ṭawāf* - which you should do after the *ghusl* (after the end of your period)".[847]

841 See: Ibn ʿĀbidīn, *Radd al-muḥtār ʿalā al-durr al-mukhtār*, vii. 81.

842 al-Kāsānī, *Badā'iʿ al-ṣanā'iʿ*, iii. 76.

843 ibid., iii. 78.

844 ibid., iii. 69.

845 al-Bukhārī, *k. al-ḥajj, b. al-ṭawāf ʿalā wuḍū'*; Muslim, *k. al-ḥajj, b. mā yalzamu man ṭāfa bi al-bayt wa saʿā.*

846 al-Tirmidhī, *k. al-ḥajj, b. mā jā'a fī al-kalām fī al-ṭawāf;* al-Dārimī, *k. al-manāsik, b. al-kalām fī al-ṭawāf.*

847 al-Bukhārī, *k. al-ḥayḍ, b. al-amr bi al-nufasā' idhā nufisna;* Muslim, *k. al-ḥajj, b. bayān wujūh al-iḥrām.*

2- **Covering the *ᶜawrah*:** [848] Abū Hurayrah said: "In the year prior to the farewell *ḥajj* when the Messenger of Allāh ﷺ made Abū Bakr the leader of the pilgrims, the latter (Abū Bakr) sent me in the company of a group of people to make a public announcement (that): 'No pagan is allowed to perform *ḥajj* after this year, and no naked person is allowed to perform *ṭawāf* of the Kaᶜbah".[849]

3- **Performing *ṭawāf* from beyond the *ḥaṭīm*:** The *ḥaṭīm* is part of Kaᶜbah[850] and *ṭawāf* is not to be made from inside of the House. Allāh, Exalted is He, says: "...*And circumambulate the Ancient House*".[851] It has been narrated that ᶜAṭā' ibn Abī Rabāḥ, Sālim and Ḥasan al-Baṣrī forbade people from doing *ṭawāf* from inside the *ḥaṭīm.*[852]

4- **To start the *ṭawāf* from the Black Stone**: If one does not start the *ṭawāf* from the Black Stone it must be redone while one is in Makkah. If one realises the mistake after leaving Makkah, one must offer a sacrifice as expiation. It is best to begin the *ṭawāf* from before the Stone so that one passes by the whole of the Stone during the *ṭawāf.*

5- **Performing *ṭawāf* from the right side while keeping the Kaᶜbah on the left**. The Kaᶜbah is like the *imām*, and a single follower stands on the right of the *imām.* Jābir reported: "When Allāh's Messenger arrived in Makkah, he went to the Black Stone, kissed it, and then walked on its right side. He ran three rounds and walked the remaining four".[853]

6- **To complete seven *shawṭs* (rounds)**: One *shawṭ* starts from the Black Stone and ends at the Black Stone.[854] The *aḥādīth* which describes the *ṭawāf* of the Prophet ﷺ all state that he did seven rounds.

7- **To pray two *rakᶜahs* after the completion of the *ṭawāf*.** This can be done anywhere though it is recommended to do it behind the *Maqām* of Ibrāhīm.[855] The Qur'ān says: "*And take the Station of Ibrāhīm as a place*

848 al-Kāsānī, *Badā'iᶜ al-ṣanā'iᶜ*, iii. 72.
849 al-Bukhārī, *k. al-ḥajj, b. lā yaṭūfu bi al-bayt ᶜuryān*; Muslim, *k. al-ḥajj, b. lā yaḥujju bi al-bayt mushrik.*
850 al-Kāsānī, *Badā'iᶜ al-ṣanā'iᶜ*, iii. 76.
851 *al-Ḥajj* 29.
852 Ibn Abī Shaybah, *al-Muṣannaf,* viii. 331-2.
853 Muslim, *k. al-ḥajj, b. mā jā'a anna ᶜarafah kullahā mawqif.*
854 al-Kāsānī, *Badā'iᶜ al-ṣanā'iᶜ*, iii. 80.
855 ibid., iii. 123.

of prayer".[856] ᶜAmr ibn Dīnār narrated from Ibn ᶜUmar who said: "The Messenger of Allāh ﷺ arrived (in Makkah) and circumambulated the Kaᶜbah seven times, then offered two *rakᶜahs* behind the *Maqām* of Ibrāhīm (the Station of Ibrāhīm)".[857] Ibrāhīm al-Nakhaᶜī says: "ᶜAlqamah read the Qur'ān during the night, then did the *ṭawāf* seven times, then came to the *Maqām* and prayed next to it".[858] Ḥasan al-Baṣrī liked one to pray the two *rakᶜahs* of the *ṭawāf* behind the *Maqām*, and he did not see any harm if one did not pray behind the *Maqām*.[859] The same narrations have come from ᶜUmar, Anas ibn Mālik, ᶜAbdullāh ibn ᶜUmar and ᶜAbdullāh ibn Masᶜūd.[860] ᶜAṭā' said: "Pray two *rakᶜahs* of the *ṭawāf* in your house if you want".[861]

It is not permitted to do these two *rakᶜahs* in disliked times, that is while the sun is rising, nor at midday, nor at sunset. 'Uqbah ibn ᶜĀmir al-Juhanī said: "There are three times during which the Prophet prohibited us from praying or burying our deceased: sunrise until the sun had risen some distance, when the sun was at its meridian, and when the sun was setting until it had completely set".[862]

Similarly these two *rakᶜahs* should not be done after the *Fajr Ṣalāh* until the sun has risen, or after the *ᶜAṣr Ṣalāh* until after the sun has set. Abū Saᶜīd reported that the Prophet ﷺ said: "There is no *ṣalāh* after the *Fajr Ṣalāh* until the sun rises".[863] ᶜAmr ibn ᶜAbasah related that he asked the following: "O Prophet of Allāh, inform me about the *ṣalāhs*. He said: 'Pray the *Fajr Ṣalāh* and then abstain from *ṣalāh* until sunrise and the sun has completely risen, for it rises between the horns of *Satan*. That is when the unbelievers prostrate to it. Then pray, as your *ṣalāh* will be witnessed and attended to, until the shadow of a spear becomes less than its length. At that time stop praying, for at that time Hell-Fire is fed with fuel. When the shade comes, you may pray, for your *ṣalāh* will be

856 *al-Baqarah125.*

857 al-Bukhārī, *k. al-ḥajj, b. ṣallā al-nabī ṣallallāhu ᶜalayhi wa sallam lisubuᶜihi rakᶜatayn;* Muslim, *k. al-ḥajj, b. mā yalzamu man aḥrama bi al-ḥajj...*

858 Ibn Abī Shaybah, *al-Muṣannaf*, viii. 605.

859 ibid., 605.

860 ibid., viii. 605-6.

861 ibid., viii. 606.

862 Muslim, *k. ṣalāt al-musāfirīn wa qaṣrihā, b. al-awqāt allatī nuhiya ᶜan al-ṣalāh fīhā.*

863 al-Bukhārī, *k. mawāqīt al-ṣalāh, b. lā yataḥarrā al-ṣalāh qabla ghurūb al-shams.*

witnessed and attended to by angels until you pray the ᶜ*Aṣr Ṣalāh.* Then abstain from praying until the sun sets, for it sets between the horns of *Satan,* and that is when the unbelievers make *sajdahs* to it'."[864] ᶜAṭā' ibn Abī Rabāḥ narrated that ᶜĀ'ishah said: "When you intend to do *ṭawāf* of the House after the prayer of *Fajr* or after the prayer of ᶜ*Aṣr,* then do *ṭawāf,* but delay the prayer until the sun sets or rises, then pray for every seven rounds two *rak*ᶜ*ahs*".[865]

SUNNAHS OF *ṬAWĀF*

The Sunnahs of *ṭawāf* are as follows:

1- **To do *iḍṭibā*ᶜ before starting the *ṭawāf* for men only**: *Iḍṭibā*ᶜ means to wrap the right side of the *ridā'* underneath the right arm and over the left shoulder leaving the right shoulder uncovered. This is done in any *ṭawāf* which is followed by *sa*ᶜ*y* (walking seven times between the hills of Ṣafā and Marwah).[866] Yaᶜlā narrated: "The Apostle of Allāh ﷺ went round the House wearing a green Yamanī mantle under his right armpit with the end over his left shoulder".[867] ᶜAbdullāh ibn ᶜAbbās narrated: "The Apostle of Allāh ﷺ and his Companions performed ᶜ*umrah* from al-Jiᶜirrānah. They did *ramal* three times round the House. They put their upper garments under their armpits and threw the ends over their left shoulders".[868]

2- **To do *ramal***: *Ramal* means to walk speedily taking short steps whilst moving the shoulders as if one was trotting. This is a Sunnah for men only in the first three rounds whilst in the condition of *iḍṭibā*ᶜ.[869] ᶜAbdullāh ibn ᶜUmar said: "When the Messenger of Allāh ﷺ performed *ṭawāf* of the Kaᶜbah for *ḥajj* or ᶜ*umrah,* he used to do *ramal* during the first three rounds, and in the last four rounds he used to walk; then after the *ṭawāf* he used to offer two *rakahs* and then performed *ṭawāf*

864 Muslim, *k. ṣalāt al-musāfirīn wa qaṣrihā, b. islām* ᶜ*mr ibn* ᶜ*abasah.*

865 Ibn Abī Shaybah, *al-Muṣannaf,* viii. 160.

866 al-Kāsānī, *Badā'i*ᶜ *al-ṣanā'i*ᶜ, iii. 122.

867 Abū Dāwūd, *k. al-manāsik, b. al-iḍṭibā*ᶜ *fī al-ṭawāf;* al-Tirmidhī, *k. al-ḥajj, b. mā jā'a anna al-nabī ṣallallāhu* ᶜ*alayhi wa sallam ṭāfa muḍṭabi*ᶜ*an*; Ibn Mājah, *k. al-manāsik, b. al-iḍṭibā*ᶜ.

868 Abū Dāwūd, *k. al-manāsik, b. al-iḍṭibā*ᶜ *fī al-ṭawāf.*

869 al-Kāsānī, *Badā'i*ᶜ *al-ṣanā'i*ᶜ, iii. 120.

between Ṣafā and Marwah".[870] Aslam said: "I heard ᶜUmar ibn al-Khaṭṭāb say: 'What is the need of *ramal*? Allāh has now strengthened Islam and obliterated disbelief and the infidels. In spite of this we shall not forsake anything that we used to do during the time of the Apostle of Allāh ﷺ'."[871] ᶜAbdullāh ibn ᶜAbbās narrated that when the Prophet ﷺ and his Companions came to Makkah, they were weakened by fever in Yathrib. Thereupon, the idolaters said: ''A people weakened with fever have come to you and they are afflicted with evil'. Allāh, the Almighty, informed His Prophet ﷺ about their saying. So he commanded them to jog through the first three rounds of *ṭawāf* around the Kaᶜbah, and to walk between its two corners. When the idolaters saw the Muslims jogging, they said: 'Are those the people you said are weak because of the fever? They are stronger and sturdier than us'." Ibn ᶜAbbās added: "The Prophet ﷺ did not command them to jog all through the seven rounds in order not to overexert themselves".[872]

Nāfiᶜ reported on the authority of ᶜAbdullāh ibn ᶜUmar that:"When Allāh's Messenger ﷺ circumambulated the House, while observing the first circomambulation, he walked swiftly in three (circuits), and walked in four circuits, and ran in the bottom of the valley as he moved between al-Ṣafā and al-Marwah. Ibn ᶜUmar also used to do this.[873] Jābir ibn ᶜAbdullāh reported: "I saw Allāh's Messenger ﷺ walking swiftly from the Black Stone till he completed three circuits up to it".[874]

There is no *ramal* on women. ᶜĀ'ishah was asked if women had to do *ramal*. She said to the women: "Don't you have an example in us? There is no *ramal* during *ṭawāf* and during *saᶜy* between Ṣafā and Marwah".[875] ᶜAbdullāh ibn ᶜUmar said: "There is no *ramal* on women around the Kaᶜbah nor while making *saᶜy* between Ṣafā and Marwah".[876] The same

870 al-Bukhārī, *k. al-ḥajj, b. man ṭāfa bi al-bayt;* Muslim, *k. al-ḥajj, b. istiḥbāb al-ramal fī al-ṭawāf wa al-ᶜumrah.*

871 Abū Dāwūd, *k. al-manāsik, b. fī al-ramal*; al-Nasā'ī, *k. al-manāsik, b. al-ramal fī al-ḥajj wa al-ᶜumrah;* al-Dārimī, *k. al-manāsik, b. man ramala thalāthan.*

872 Abū Dāwūd, *k. al-ḥajj, b. fī al-ramal.*

873 al-Bukhārī, *k. al-ḥajj, b. man ṭāfa bi al-bayt;* Muslim, *k. al-ḥajj, b. istiḥbāb al-ramal fī al-ṭawāf wa al-ᶜumrah.*

874 Muslim, *k. al-ḥajj, b. istiḥbāb al-ramal fī al-ṭawāf wa al-ᶜumrah.*

875 Ibn Abī Shaybah, *al-Muṣannaf*, viii. 89.

876 ibid.

has been narrated from ʿAbdullāh ibn ʿAbbās, ʿAṭā' ibn Abī Rabāḥ, Ḥasan al-Baṣrī and Ibrāhīm al-Nakhaʿī.[877]

3-**To touch and kiss the Black Stone at the beginning of the *ṭawāf* and at the end of every *shawṭ*:** If one is unable to do this, then one should face the Black Stone and raise one's hands with the palms facing the Black Stone, and then pronounce the *takbīr, tahlīl* and the *ṣalāh* on the Prophet ﷺ.[878] Ibn ʿAbbās narrated: "The Messenger of Allāh ﷺ performed *ṭawāf* (of the Kaʿbah) riding a camel. Whenever he came to the corner (of the Black Stone) he would point out towards it with something (he had) in his hand and say: '*Allāhu-Akbar*'."[879]

ʿĀbis ibn Rabīʿah narrated: "ʿUmar came near the Black Stone and kissed it and said 'No doubt, I know that you are a stone and can neither benefit anyone nor harm anyone. Had I not seen the Messenger of Allāh ﷺ kissing you I would not have kissed you'."[880] Nāfiʿ narrated that Ibn ʿUmar said: "I have never missed the touching of these two stones of the Kaʿbah (the Black Stone and the Yemenī Corner) both in the presence and the absence of crowds, since I saw the Prophet touching them".[881]

Imām Ghazālī says: "As for touching [the Black Stone], believe when you are performing this act that you are making an oath with Allāh, Exalted is He, to obey Him; then resolve to fulfil your oath, for whoever breaks an oath deserves chastisement. Ibn al-ʿAbbās, may Allāh be pleased with him, reported from the Apostle of Allāh ﷺ said, "The Black Stone is the right hand of Allāh, Exalted is He, on earth; with it Allāh shakes hands with His creatures as a man shakes hands with his brother".[882]

4-**To touch the Yemenī Corner**: [883] Ibn ʿUmar said: "I never saw the Prophet ﷺ touching any other parts of the Kaʿbah except the two – the Black Stone and the Yemenī Corner". And he added: "No matter how hard and difficult the circumstances, I have not failed to touch these two

877 Ibn Abī Shaybah, *al-Muṣannaf*, viii. 90.
878 al-Kāsānī, *Badā'iʿ al-ṣanā'iʿ*, iii. 117.
879 al-Bukhārī, *k. al-ḥajj, b. al-marīḍ yaṭūfu rākiban.*
880 al-Bukhārī, *k. al-ḥajj, b. mā dhukira fī al-ḥajar al-aswad*; Muslim, *k. al-ḥajj, b. istiḥbāb taqbīl al-ḥajar.*
881 Muslim, *k. al-ḥajj, b. istiḥbāb istilām al-ruknayn al-yamāniyyayn…*
882 al-Ghazālī, *Iḥyā' ʿulūm al-dīn*, i. 377.
883 al-Kāsānī, *Badā'iʿ al-ṣanā'iʿ*, iii. 122.

corners ever since I saw the Prophet ﷺ doing so".[884] Ibn ʿUmar reported from ʿĀ'ishah that the Prophet had explained to her that the Quraysh did not rebuild the whole of the House on its original foundations. Then Ibn ʿUmar connected this with the Prophet's practice of only touching the two corners that were still on the foundations established by Ibrāhīm.[885] Imām Muḥammad says: "One should not touch except the Yemenī Corner and the Black Stone; and these two are the ones ʿAbdullāh ibn ʿUmar touched. This is the opinion of Abū Ḥanīfah and most of our jurists".[886]

5- It is recommended that one does *duʿā'* at *al-Multazam* after the *ṭawāf*. *Al-Multazam* is the part of the Kaʿbah between its door and the Black Stone. ʿAbdullāh ibn ʿAbbās said: "The space between the Black Stone and the door of the Kaʿbah is called *al-Multazam*".[887] ʿAmr ibn Shuʿayb reported from his father, that his father said: "I have seen the Prophet ﷺ placing his face and chest against *al-Multazam*".[888] Al-Shaybānī says: "I saw ʿAmr ibn Maymūn embracing the part of the House between the Corner (i.e. the Corner of the Black Stone) and the Door".[889] Mujāhid says: "They used to cling to what is between the Corner and the Door and make *duʿā'*."[890] ʿIkrimah ibn Khālid, Abū Jaʿfar, ʿIkrimah the slave of Ibn ʿAbbās, Sālim, ʿAṭā' ibn Abī Rabāḥ and Ṭāwūs all used to cling to what is between the Corner and the Door and make *duʿā'*.[891]

Imām Ghazālī says: "As for the clinging to the curtains of the Kaʿbah and cleaving to *al-Multazam*: let your intention in cleaving be to seek nearness to God, [to show] affection and longing for the House and for the Lord of House, and also to obtain blessing by touching [the House], hoping to be fortified against Fire in every part of your body, for the sake of the House. Let your intention in clinging to the curtains of the

884 al-Bukhārī, *k. al-ḥajj, b. man lam yastalim illā al-ruknayn al-yamāniyyayn*; Muslim, *k. al-ḥajj, b. istiḥbab istilām al-ruknayn al-yamāniyyayn.*

885 al-Bukhārī, *k. al-ḥajj, b. faḍl makkah*; Muslim, *k. al-ḥajj, b. naqḍ al-kaʿbah.*

886 Muhammad, *al-Muwaṭṭa'* 161.

887 Ibn Abī Shaybah, *al-Muṣannaf*, viii. 293.

888 Abū Dāwūd, *k. al-manāsik, b. al-multazam*; Ibn Mājah, *k. al-manāsik, b. al-multazam.*

889 Ibn Abī Shaybah, *al-Muṣannaf*, viii. 293.

890 ibid.

891 ibid.

Kaᶜbah be persistence in seeking forgiveness and asking for peace, just as a sinner clings to the clothes of the one against whom he committed the sin, humbly beseeching his forgiveness and declaring to him that he has no refuge from him but in him and no shelter but in his generosity and forgiveness, and that he will not let go of the hem [of his garment] until he has been forgiven and assured of peace in the future".[892]

6-**Entering the Ḥaṭīm:** Only dignitaries ever get a chance to enter the Kaᶜbah today, therefore, one should not miss the opportunity of entering into the Ḥaṭīm (known also as Ḥijr, it is the half-walled area attached to the Kaᶜbah), which is part of the Kaᶜbah. Ibn ᶜUmar reported that: "The Prophet ﷺ entered the Kaᶜbah along with Usāmah ibn Zayd, and ᶜUthmān ibn Ṭalḥah and closed its door behind them. When they came out, Bilāl informed me that the Prophet ﷺ offered a prayer inside the Kaᶜbah between the two Yemenī Corners".[893]

ᶜĀ'ishah said: "O Prophet of Allāh, I (would) love to enter inside the Kaᶜbah and pray inside. The Prophet ﷺ held my hand and made me enter the *Ḥijr*, (and said) 'If you want to enter the House (and pray) (then) pray inside the *Ḥijr*. It is part of the Kaᶜbah, but your people left it out while rebuilding the Kaᶜbah and did not include it in its structure'."[894] However, if one is unable to enter the Ḥaṭīm, there is no harm. ᶜAbdullāh ibn ᶜAbbās said: "O people, your entering into the House is not a part of the *ḥajj*".[895] Khaythamah was asked about entering into the Kaᶜbah. He answered: "By Allāh it does not harm you if you do not enter into it".[896]

7-**After the two *rakᶜahs* of *ṭawāf* one makes *duᶜā'*, then drinks the water of Zamzam before heading to Ṣafā.** Abū Dharr narrated that the Prophet ﷺ said about the water of Zamzam: "It is blessed (water); it is food for the hungry and a healing for the sick".[897] Jābir narrated that the Prophet ﷺ said: "The water of Zamzam is good for whatever one

892 al-Ghazālī, *Iḥyā' ᶜulūm al-dīn*, i. 377.

893 al-Bukhārī, *k. al-ṣalāh, b. al-abwāb wa al-ghalaq lilkaᶜbah wa al-masajid, b. al-ṣalāh bayna al-sawārī fī ghayr jamāᶜah, k. al-tahajjud, b. mā jā'a fī al-taṭawwuᶜ mathnā mathnā;* Muslim, *k. al-ḥajj, b. istiḥbāb dukhūl al-kaᶜbah li al-ḥājj …*

894 al-Tirmidhī, *k. al-ḥajj, b. mā jā'a fī al-ṣalāh fī al-ḥijr.*

895 ibid., viii. 138.

896 ibid.

897 ibid., viii. 390.

intends".[898] Mujāhid says: "They used to like to come to Zamzam and drink from it before leaving the House".[899] Bakr al-Muzanī says: "I love for the man to drink from Zamzam if he can".[900]

The manner of drinking Zamzam is explained in the following practice of Ibn ᶜAbbās. Ibn Abī Mulaykah reported: "A man came to Ibn ᶜAbbās. He asked the man, 'Where are you coming from?' The man replied: 'I am coming from the well of Zamzam'. Ibn ᶜAbbās asked him: 'Did you drink of it as you are supposed to?' The man asked: 'O Ibn ᶜAbbās, how am I supposed to drink it?' Ibn ᶜAbbās replied: 'When you drink its water you should face the direction of the *qiblah*, remember Allāh, drink it in three breaths, drink as much as you can, and praise and thank Allāh when you finish drinking'. The Prophet ﷺ said: 'A major difference between us and the hypocrites is that they do not drink their fill of the Zamzam water'."[901]

It is recommended that one takes some Zamzam water to one's people after the *ḥajj* or *ᶜumrah*. ᶜUrwah ibn al-Zubayr narrates that ᶜĀ'ishah used to take water from Zamzam and used to say that the Messenger of Allāh ﷺ used to take from it. [902]

THE TIMING OF *ṬAWĀF AL-IFĀḌAH*

The beginning time of *ṭawāf al-ifāḍah* is from the dawn of the 10th *Dhū al-ḥijjah*, and it is *wājib* to do it by the end of the 12th *Dhū al-ḥijjah.* If someone delays it further, he has done the *farḍ* obligation, but he has to offer a sacrifice because of missing the *wājib.*[903] Ibn ᶜUmar reported that Allāh's Messenger ﷺ observed the circumambulation of *ifāḍah* on the Day of *Naḥr* (10th of *Dhū al-ḥijjah*), and then came back and observed the noon prayer at Minā. Nāfiᶜ said that Ibn ᶜUmar used to observe the circumambulation of *ifāḍah* on the Day of *Naḥr,* and then returned and observed the noon prayer at Minā, and mentioned that Allāh's Apostle ﷺ did thus.[904]

898 ibid., viii. 392-3.
899 ibid., viii. 175.
900 ibid., viii. 175.
901 Ibn Mājah, *k. al-manāsik, b. al-shurb min zamzam*; ᶜAbd al-Razzāq, *al-Muṣannaf*, v. 112-113.
902 al-Tirmidhī, *k. al-ḥajj, b. mā jā'a fī ḥaml mā'a zamzam.*
903 al-Kāsānī, *Badā'iᶜ al-ṣanā'iᶜ*, iii. 78.
904 Muslim, *k. al-ḥajj, b. istiḥbāb ṭawāf al-ifāḍah yawm al-naḥr.*

THE PRAYER WHILE PEOPLE ARE PASSING

In the Sacred Mosque, because of the vast numbers of people and the performance of *ṭawāf*, it is allowed to offer prayer while people are passing in front of the one praying.[905] Al-Muṭṭalib ibn Abī Wadāᶜah narrated: "I saw the Prophet ﷺ offering prayer in the Sacred Mosque in the area adjacent to the gate of *Banī* Sahm while people passed in front of him but he did not place any *sutrah* (barrier) in front of him".[906] There is also the statement of Ibn Abī ᶜAmmār who said: "I saw ᶜAbdullāh ibn al-Zubayr do *ṭawāf*, and then come to do prayer, while *ṭawāf* was being done between him and the Kaᶜbah".[907]

WOMEN DOING *ṬAWĀF*

It is permissible for women to perform *ṭawāf* alongside men though it is preferable for them to perform *ṭawāf* in those hours when there is less of a crowd and to keep themselves apart from the men's crowd, and not to mingle with the men while kissing the Black Stone.[908] Ibn Jurayj reported: "ᶜAṭā' told me that when Hishām forbade women from performing *ṭawāf* along with men he was asked: 'How dare you prevent them while the wives of the Prophet ﷺ performed *ṭawāf* along with other men?'" Ibn Jurayj added: "I asked ᶜAṭā': 'Did they do so before or after the commandment to observe veil?' He (ᶜAṭā') said: 'They did so after the revelation of the commandment to veil'. I said: 'How could they intermingle with men?' He (ᶜAṭā') said: 'They did not intermingle with men. ᶜĀ'ishah used to perform *ṭawāf* keeping apart from men and without intermingling with them'."[909]

Women may touch and kiss the Black Stone when there is an opportunity to do so and no men are around. A woman asked ᶜĀ'ishah: "O Mother of Believers, shall we touch the Black Stone and kiss it? ᶜĀ'ishah said: 'Get away from here', and she refused to go with her (to the Black Stone because there were men there)'."[910]

905 See: Ibn ᶜĀbidīn, *Radd al-nuḥtār ᶜalā al-durr al-mukhtār*, vii. 79.

906 Ibn Abī Shaybah, *al-Muṣannaf*, viii. 607. The Gate of *Banī Sahm* is now known as the Gate of ᶜ*Umrah*.

907 ibid., viii. 606.

908 al-Kāsānī, *Badā'iᶜ al-ṣanā'iᶜ*, iii. 72.

909 al-Bukhārī, *k. al-ḥajj, b. ṭawāf al-nisāᶜ maᶜa al-rijāl.*

910 ibid.

ṬAWĀF WHILE RIDING

It is permissible for one to perform *ṭawāf* while riding, provided there is a valid reason for doing so.[911] Ibn ᶜAbbās reported that during the Farewell Pilgrimage the Prophet ﷺ performed *ṭawāf* while riding his camel, and touched the Black Stone with a stick (that he carried).[912] Jābir said: "During the Farewell Pilgrimage of the Prophet ﷺ he performed *ṭawāf* and made *saᶜy* between Ṣafā and Marwah while riding on his mount, so as to show people, to draw their attention, and (to give them an opportunity) to ask him any questions (they had), and the people were crowding around him".[913] Al-Kāsānī says: "It has come in a narration that the Prophet ﷺ did this when he became old, or as Jābir reported, the Prophet ﷺ did it for teaching purpose, and that is an excuse". [914]

Of course, no one rides around the House in modern times. We cite the *aḥādīth* as evidence for the permissibility for those unable to walk to be carried or to go round the House in a wheelchair.

TALKING DURING *ṬAWĀF*

Talking during *ṭawāf* is allowed though it is recommended to keep oneself busy in remembrance of Allāh and *duᶜā'*, and not talk except when there is a need.[915] Ibn ᶜAbbās said: "*Ṭawāf* of the House is *ṣalāh*, but Allāh has allowed speaking in it, so whoever speaks, he should only speak what is good".[916] ᶜAṭā' ibn Abī Rabāḥ says: "I did *ṭawāf* behind ᶜAbdullāh ibn ᶜUmar, and ᶜAbdullāh ibn ᶜAbbās, and I did not hear any of them talking during *ṭawāf*".[917] Ibrāhīm ibn Nāfiᶜ says: "I did *ṭawāf* with Ṭāwūs; I did not hear him starting a conversation with anybody, except if anyone talked with him, then he would reply".[918]

911 al-Kāsānī, *Badā'iᶜ al-ṣanā'iᶜ*, iii. 73.

912 al-Bukhārī, *k. al-ḥajj, b. istilām al-rukn bi al-miḥjan*; Muslim, *k. al-ḥajj, b. jawāz al-ṭawāf ᶜalā baᶜīr wa ghayrihī.*

913 Muslim, *k. al-ḥajj, b. jawāz al-ṭawāf ᶜalā baᶜīr wa ghayrihī.*

914 al-Kāsānī, *Badā'iᶜ al-ṣanā'iᶜ*, iii. 73.

915 ibid., iii. 75.

916 al-Tirmidhī, *k. al-ḥajj, b. mā jā'a fī al-kalām fī al-ṭawāf;* al-Dārimī, *k. al-manāsik, b. al-kalām fī al-ṭawāf;* Ibn Abī Shaybah, *al-Muṣannaf*, viii. 62.

917 ibid., viii. 63.

918 ibid.

LOOKING AT THE KAᶜBAH

Looking at the Kaᶜbah is also an act of worship. It is recommended that women, during their impurity, should sit somewhere in the area of Ṣafā and Marwah and look at the Kaᶜbah, for since they cannot perform the *ṭawāf* then at least they are able to do this. Ṭāwūs says: "Looking at the House is an act of worship".[919] Similarly, it has been narrated from Mujāhid, ᶜAṭā' ibn Abī Rabāḥ and ᶜAbd al-Raḥmān ibn al-Aswad that they said: "Looking at the House is an act of worship". [920] Ibn al-Munkadir says: "It has come to my knowledge that for every gaze that you take at the House there is a good deed".[921]

919 ibid., viii. 544.

920 Ibn Abī Shaybah, *al-Muṣannaf,* viii. 544-545.

921 ᶜAbd al-Razzāq, *al-Muṣannaf,* v. 136.

Chapter 3: *Wājibs* of the *Ḥajj*

There are seven *wājibs* in the *ḥajj*: *saʿy*, *wuqūf* in Muzdalifah, *ramy*, *hady*, shaving the head, *ṭawāf al-ṣadr*, and the sequence.

1. *SAʿY* BETWEEN ṢAFĀ AND MARWAH.

Saʿy is when a pilgrim walks seven times between the hills of Ṣafā and Marwah. This ritual act is a *wājib* of the *ḥajj*.[922] Al-Zuhrī narrated from ʿUrwah ibn al-Zubayr who said: "I asked ʿĀ'ishah how do you interpret the statement of Allāh? '*Verily, (the mountains) al-Ṣafā and al-Marwah are among the symbols of Allāh, and whoever performs the ḥajj to the Kaʿbah or performs ʿumrah, it is not harmful for him to perform ṭawāf between them (Ṣafā and Marwah)*' [923]. By Allāh (it is evident from this revelation) that there is no harm if one does not perform *ṭawāf* between Ṣafā and Marwah. ʿĀ'ishah replied: 'O, my nephew, your interpretation is not true. Had this interpretation of yours been correct, the statement of Allāh should have been: 'It is not harmful for him if he does not perform *ṭawāf* between them'. But in fact, this divine inspiration was revealed concerning the *Anṣār* who used to assume *iḥrām* for worshipping an idol called '*Manat*' which they used to worship at a place called al-Mushallal before they embraced Islam, and whoever assumed *iḥrām* (for the idol) would consider it not right to perform *ṭawāf* between Ṣafā and Marwah. When they embraced Islam, they asked Allāh's Apostle ﷺ regarding it, saying: 'O Allāh's Apostle, we used to refrain from *ṭawāf* between Ṣafā and Marwah'. So Allāh revealed: '*Verily; (the mountains) al-Ṣafā and al-Marwah are among the symbols of Allāh..*'. ʿĀ'ishah added: 'Surely, the Messenger of Allāh ﷺ set the tradition of *ṭawāf* between Ṣafā and Marwah, so nobody is allowed to omit the *ṭawāf* between them'." Al-Zuhrī says: "Later on I informed Abū Bakr ibn ʿAbd al-Raḥmān (of ʿĀ'ishah's narration) and he said: 'I have not heard of such information, but I heard learned men saying that all the people, except those whom ʿĀ'ishah mentioned,

922 al-Kāsānī, *Badā'iʿ al-ṣanā'iʿ*, iii. 81.
923 *al-Baqarah* 158.

who used to assume *iḥrām* for the sake of *Manat*, used to perform *ṭawāf* between Ṣafā and Marwah. When Allāh referred to the *ṭawāf* of the Kaᶜbah and did not mention Ṣafā and Marwah in the Qur'ān, the people asked: 'O Allāh's Apostle, we used to perform *ṭawāf* between Ṣafā and Marwah and Allāh has revealed (the verses concerning) *ṭawāf* of the Kaᶜbah and has not mentioned Ṣafā and Marwah. Is there any harm if we perform *ṭawāf* between Ṣafā and Marwah?' So Allāh revealed: *'Verily; (the mountains) al-Ṣafā and al-Marwah are among the symbols of Allāh'.* Abū Bakr ibn ᶜAbd al-Raḥmān said: 'It seems that this verse was revealed concerning the two groups'."[924]

Anas reports that the *Anṣār* were reluctant to undertake circumambulation between al-Ṣafā and al-Marwah until revelation of the verse: "*Verily, (the mountains) al-Ṣafā and al-Marwah are among the symbols of Allāh, and whoever performs the ḥajj to the Kaᶜbah or performs ᶜumrah, it is not harmful for him to perform ṭawāf between them (Ṣafā and Marwah)*'."[925]

Saᶜy has one condition, three *wājibs* and seven Sunnahs.

The conditions of the *saᶜy*

Its condition is that it must be done after the *ṭawāf*. If someone does *saᶜy* first then does *ṭawāf*, his *saᶜy* will not be considered valid and he has to repeat it.[926]

The *wājibs* of *saᶜy*

1- This consists of seven *shawṭs*, all of which are *wājib.*[927]

2- *Saᶜy* must start from Ṣafā and end at Marwah.[928]

3- *Saᶜy* is done in the *masᶜā*, the path between Ṣafā and Marwah because the Prophet ﷺ did so, and moreover he explicitly said: "Take your *ḥajj* rites from me".[929]

924 Muslim, *k. al-ḥajj, b. bayān anna al-saᶜya bayna al-ṣafā wa al-marwah..*; Abū Dāwūd, *k. al-manāsik, b. amr al-ṣafā wa al-marwah;* al-Tirmidhī, *k. al-tafsīr, b. wa min sūrat al-baqarah.*

925 Muslim, *k. al-ḥajj, b. bayān anna al-saᶜya bayna al-ṣafā wa al-marwah...*

926 al-Kāsānī, *Badāʾiᶜ al-ṣanāʾiᶜ*, iii. 85.

927 ibid., iii. 84.

928 ibid., iii. 85.

929 Muslim, *k. al-ḥajj, b. istiḥbāb ramy jamrat al-ᶜaqabah yawm al-naḥr*, Abū Dāwūd,

The Sunnahs of *saᶜy*

1- It is recommended that there not be a long time gap between *ṭawāf* and *saᶜy* .

2- It is Sunnah that one performs *saᶜy* in a state of purification. However, women during the period of impurity, can perform *saᶜy*. The Prophet ﷺ said to ᶜĀ'ishah once when she menstruated: "You may perform all rites (of *ḥajj*) as other pilgrims' do, except performing *ṭawāf* around the Kaᶜbah which you may do after you are clean and no longer menstruating".[930] ᶜĀ'ishah and Umm Salamah said: "A woman who performs the *ṭawāf*, offers the two *rakᶜah* prayer (by the Station of Ibrāhīm), and then finds that her period has started, may perform *saᶜy* between Ṣafā and Marwah'.'[931] The same has been narrated from ᶜAbdullāh ibn ᶜUmar, ᶜAṭā' ibn Abī Rabāḥ, Ḥasan al-Baṣrī, Ibrāhīm al-Nakhaᶜī, Al-Ḥakam, Ḥammād ibn Abī Sulaymān.[932]

3- It is Sunnah to climb on Ṣafā and Marwah during the *saᶜy* . Jābir has narrated in his long ḥadīth about the *ḥajj* of the Prophet ﷺ that he went through the Ṣafā gate, and on approaching Ṣafā he recited the Qur'ānic verse: "*Verily; (the mountains) al-Ṣafā and al-Marwah are among the symbols of Allāh*", and then said: 'I begin with what Allāh Himself began', (and) he climbed Ṣafā until he could see the Kaᶜbah from where he stood. He faced the Kaᶜbah, thrice proclaimed Allāh's Oneness, glorified Him, praised Him, and then said,

لَا إِلَهَ إِلَّا اللَّهُ وَحْدَهُ لَا شَرِيكَ لَهُ، لَهُ الْمُلْكُ وَلَهُ الْحَمْدُ، وَهُوَ عَلَى كُلِّ شَيْءٍ قَدِيرٌ، لَا إِلَهَ إِلَّا اللَّهُ وَحْدَهُ، أَنْجَزَ وَعْدَهُ، وَنَصَرَ عَبْدَهُ، وَهَزَمَ الْأَحْزَابَ وَحْدَهُ

('There is no deity worthy of worship except Allāh. He has no partners. To Him belongs the kingdom and all praise. He alone grants life and causes death, He has power over all things. There is no god but He. He has fulfilled His promise, given victory to His servant, and He alone defeated the confederates'.) Thrice he made similar supplications.

k. al-manāsik, b. fī ramy al-jimār.

930 al-Bukhārī, *k. al-ḥayḍ, b. kayfa kāna bad' al-ḥayḍ*; Muslim, *k. al-ḥajj, b. bayān wujūh al-iḥrām.*

931 Ibn Abī Shaybah, *al-Muṣannaf*, viii. 441.

932 ibid.

Then he walked towards Marwah and climbed it, until he could see the Kaʿbah. There he made supplications as he had at Ṣafā'.[933]

4-It is Sunnah for men to jog between the green markers at either side (indicted by green lights). Walking between Ṣafā and Marwah is commended, except between the two markers where jogging is encouraged.[934] The ḥadīth of Jābir mentions that when the Prophet ﷺ was in the main part of the valley during the *saʿy*, he speeded up.[935]

This is not required of women; rather women will walk at a normal speed. ʿAṭā' ibn Abī Rabāḥ was asked by Ibn Jurayj if women can walk fast? ʿAṭā' disapproved of this severely.[936] Mujāhid reported that: "Once ʿĀ'ishah saw some women walking fast whereupon she said to them: 'You should follow our example. You are not obligated to jog (while performing *saʿy*)'."[937]

5-It is Sunnah to engage in *dhikr* (remembrance) and *ṣalāh* (salutations) on the Prophet during the *saʿy* . Umm Salamah reported while making *saʿy* the Prophet ﷺ used to supplicate, رَبِّ اغْفِرْ وَارْحَمْ وَاهْدِنِي السَّبِيلَ الأَقْوَم('O my Lord, forgive me, have mercy upon me, and guide me to the straight path'.)[938] It has been narrated that ʿUmar ibn al-Khaṭṭāb, ʿAbdullāh ibn Masʿūd, and ʿAbdullāh ibn ʿUmar while doing *saʿy* used to supplicate, رَبِّ اغْفِرْ وَارْحَمْ وَأَنْتَ الأَعَزُّ الأَكْرَم ('O my Lord, forgive me, and have mercy upon me. You are the most Honourable, most Dignified'.)[939]

6-It is Sunnah to face the House while climbing Ṣafā and Marwah.[940] This has come from Jābir's detailed ḥadīth.[941]

7- To perform the *istilam* of the Black Stone before going for the *saʿy* .[942] This is also mentioned in Jābir's detailed ḥadīth.[943]

933 Muslim, *k. al-ḥajj, b. ḥajjat al-nabī sallallahu ʿalayhu wa sallam.*
934 al-Kāsānī, *Badā'iʿ al-ṣanā'iʿ*, iii. 125.
935 Muslim, *k. al-ḥajj, b. ḥajjat al-nabī sallallahu ʿalayhu wa sallam.*
936 al-Shāfiʿī, *k. al-umm, k. al-ḥajj, b. layasa ʿalā al-nisā' saʿy.*
937 ibid.
938 Aḥmad ibn Ḥanbal, *al-musnad, musnad al-nisā'.*
939 Ibn Abī Shaybah, *al-Muṣannaf,* xv. 323-4.
940 al-Kāsānī, *Badā'iʿ al-ṣanā'iʿ*, iii. 125.
941 Muslim, *k. al-ḥajj, b. ḥajjat al-nabī sallallahu ʿalayhu wa sallam.*
942 al-Kāsānī, *Badā'iʿ al-ṣanā'iʿ*, iii. 124.
943 Muslim, *k. al-ḥajj, b. ḥajjat al-nabī sallallahu ʿalayhu wa sallam.*

THE INNER MEANING OF *SAᶜY*

Imām Ghazālī says: "As for the running between Ṣafā and Marwah in the courtyard of the House, this resembles the movements to and fro of a slave in the courtyard of a king, coming and going time after time, [thus] showing his loyalty in service, hoping for a look of favour, in the manner of one who enters [the presence of] a king and goes out without knowing what the king has ordered with respect to his case, acceptance or repulsion, so that he keeps coming back to the courtyard time after time, hoping to be forgiven on the second [time] if not on the first. Let him ponder, while running between Ṣafā and Marwah, his fluctuation between the two pans of the Balance in the courtyard of Resurrection, let him compare Ṣafā with the pan of good deeds and Marwah with the pan of bad deeds. Let him reflect on his uncertainty before the two pans of the Balance, as he watches them increase in weight, fluctuating between chastisement and forgiveness".[944]

2. STAYING IN MUZDALIFAH

Staying in Muzdalifah for a while between the dawn of the 10th *Dhū al-ḥijjah* and the rise of the sun is *wājib.*[945]

Jābir says: "When the Prophet ﷺ reached Muzdalifah he offered both *Maghrib* and *'Ishā* Prayers, then he lay down to sleep. He slept until dawn, then got up and offered *Fajr* Prayer, and mounted his she camel, al-Qaṣwā'. When he reached al-Mashᶜar al-ḥarām (a mountain in Muzdalifah) he stopped there until there was light all around, then before sunrise, he left the place".[946]

Kurayb, the freed slave of Ibn ᶜAbbās, narrated from Usāmah ibn Zayd that: "Allāh's Messenger ﷺ proceeded from ᶜArafah, and as he approached the creek of a hill, he got down (from his camel) and urinated, and then performed a light ablution. I said to him: 'Prayer', whereupon he said: 'The prayer awaits you (at Muzdalifah)'. So he rode again, and as he came to Muzdalifah, he got down and performed ablution well. Then the *iqāmah* was pronounced for prayer, and he observed the sunset prayer. Then every person made his camel kneel down there, and the *iqāmah* was pronounced for *ᶜIshā'* Prayer and he

944 al-Ghazālī, *Iḥyā' ᶜulūm al-dīn,* i. 377-378.

945 al-Kāsānī, *Badā'iᶜ al-ṣanā'iᶜ*, iii. 89.

946 Muslim, *k. al-ḥajj, b. ḥajjat al-nabī sallallahu ᶜalayhu wa sallam.*

observed it, and he (the Prophet) did not observe any prayer in between them'."[947]

Spending the night in Muzdalifah is not *wājib*; rather it is a Sunnah.[948] If one is present in Muzdalifah at this time, one's *ḥajj* is valid, whether one intends it or not, whether one knows that one is in Muzdalifah or not, or one is insane, or unconscious or sleeping.[949]

Combining *Maghrib* and *ᶜIshā'* Prayers

In Muzdalifah, the *imām* will combine *Maghrib* and *ᶜIshā'* at the time of *ᶜIshā'* with one *adhān* and one *iqāmah.*[950] ᶜAbdullāh ibn Yazīd al-Khaṭmī reported on the authority of Abū Ayyūb that he prayed the *Maghrib* and *ᶜIshā'* prayers (together) at Muzdalifah in the company of Allāh's Messenger ﷺ on the occasion of the Farewell Pilgrimage.[951]

Saᶜīd ibn Jubayr reported that he observed the *Maghrib* and *ᶜIshā'* prayers at Muzdalifah with one *iqāmah.* He narrated on the authority of Ibn ᶜUmar that he observed prayers like this, and Ibn ᶜUmar narrated that Allāh's Apostle ﷺ did like this. Shuᶜbah reported this ḥadīth with the same chain of transmitters and said: "He (the Prophet) observed the two prayers (together) with one *iqāmah*".[952] Ibrāhīm al-Nakhaᶜī says regarding the prayer in Muzdalifah: "When you pray them in Muzdalifah you pray them with one *iqāmah*; and if you do *nafl* prayer between both of them, then make *iqāmah* for each of them". Imām Muḥammad says: "We adhere to this, and this is the opinion of Abū Ḥanīfah; and it is not pleasing to us to do any *nafl* between them".[953] Imām Muḥammad also says: "We adhere to this, one should not pray *Maghrib* until one comes to Muzdalifah, even though half of the night has passed. When one arrives in Muzdalifah then one says the *adhān* and *iqāmah*, and prays *Maghrib*

947 al-Bukhārī, *k. al-ḥajj, b. al-jamᶜ bayn al-ṣalātayn bi al-muzdalifah;* Muslim, *k. al-ḥajj, b. al-ifāḍah min ᶜarafāt ilā al-muzdalifah;* Abū Dāwūd, *k. al-manāsik, b. al-dafᶜah min ᶜArafah*; al-Nasā'ī, *k. al-manāsik, b. al-jamᶜ bayna ṣalātayn;* Ibn Mājah, *k. al-manāsik, b. al-nuzūl bayna ᶜarafat wa jamᶜ liman lahū ḥājah…*

948 al-Kāsānī, *Badā'iᶜ al-ṣanā'iᶜ*, iii. 89.

949 ibid., iii. 88.

950 ibid.,iii. 138.

951 Muslim, *k. al-ḥajj, b. al-ifāḍah min ᶜarafāt ilā al-muzdalifah.*

952 ibid.

953 Abū Ḥanīfah, *K. al-āthār* 85.

and ʿ*Ishā'* with one *adhān* and one *iqāmah*. This is the opinion of Abū Ḥanīfah and most of our jurists".[954]

According to the opinion of Zufar, the *imām* will combine *Maghrib* and ʿ*Ishā'* at the time of ʿ*Ishā'* with one *adhān* and two *iqāmahs*.[955] Usāmah ibn Zayd reported: "Allāh's Messenger ﷺ proceeded from ʿArafah, and as he approached the creek of a hill, he got down (from his camel) and urinated, and then performed a light ablution. I said to him: 'Prayer,' whereupon he said: 'The prayer awaits you (at Muzdalifah)'. So he rode again, and as he came to Muzdalifah, he got down and performed ablution well. Then the *iqāmah* was pronounced for prayer, and he observed the sunset prayer. Then every person made his camel kneel down there, and then *iqāmah* was pronounced for ʿ*Ishā'* prayer and he observed it, and he (the Prophet) did not observe any prayer in between them'."[956]

Where to stay in Muzdalifah

One may stay anywhere in Muzdalifah except in the valley called Muḥassar (between Muzdalifah and Minā).[957] Jābir ibn ʿAbdullāh narrated that the Messenger of Allāh ﷺ said: "The entire area of Muzdalifah is a place to stay, but avoid the valley of Muḥassar".[958] Jubayr ibn Muṭʿim reported that the Prophet ﷺ said: "The entire area of Muzdalifah is a place to stay, but avoid the valley called Muḥassar".[959] However, spending time at a place called Quzaḥ in Muzdalifah is better.[960] ʿAlī ibn Abī Ṭālib narrated that the Prophet ﷺ got up in the morning and stood at Quzaḥ and said: "This is Quzaḥ, the place to stop; and the entire *Jam*ʿ (Muzdalifah) is a stopping place".[961]

954 Muhammad, *al-Muwaṭṭa'*, 165.

955 al-Kāsānī, *Badā'iʿ al-ṣanā'iʿ*, iii. 138.

956 al-Bukhārī, *k. al-ḥajj, b. al-jamʿ bayn al-ṣalātayn bi al-muzdalifah*; Muslim, *k. al-ḥajj, b. al-ifāḍah min ʿarafāt ilā al-muzdalifah;* Abū Dāwūd, *k. al-manāsik, b. al-dafʿah min ʿarafah*; al-Nasā'ī, *k. al-manāsik, b. al-jamʿ bayna ṣalātayn*; Ibn Mājah, *k. al-manāsik, b. al-nuzūl bayna ʿarafāt wa jamʿ liman lahū ḥājah...*

957 al-Kāsānī, *Badā'iʿ al-ṣanā'iʿ, iii. 88.*

958 Ibn Mājah, *k. al-manāsik, b. al-mawqif bi ʿarafāt.*

959 al-Bayhaqī, *al-Sunan al-kubrā, k. al-ḥajj, b. mā jā'a fī al-wuqūf bi ʿarafah wa al-muzdalifah.*

960 al-Kāsānī, *Badā'iʿ al-ṣanā'iʿ*, iii. 89.

961 Abū Dāwūd, *k. al-manāsik, b. al-ṣalāh bi jamʿ.*

Fajr Prayer in Muzdalifah

The *imām* will lead the *Fajr* Prayer at Muzdalifah in the beginning of the time while still dark.[962] ᶜAbdullāh ibn Masᶜūd reported: "I have never seen Allāh's Messenger ﷺ but observing the prayers at their appointed times except two prayers, *Maghrib* and *ᶜIshā'* at Muzdalifah (where he deferred the sunset prayer to combine it with *ᶜIshā'*) and he observed the dawn prayer before its time in darkness (meaning before its preferred time)".[963]

EXEMPTION FOR WOMEN AND THE ELDERLY

It is allowed for women, the elderly and those who have an excuse to leave Muzdalifah before dawn.[964] ᶜĀ'ishah narrates: "Sawdah (the wife of the Prophet), who was bulky, sought permission of Allāh's Messenger ﷺ on the night of Muzdalifah to move from (that place) ahead of him and before the multitude. He gave her permission. So she set forth before his departure. We stayed there until it was dawn and departed with the Prophet. If I had sought the permission of Allāh's Messenger ﷺ as Sawdah did, I also could have gone with his permission and that would have been more beloved to me than anything else that could give (me) ease".[965]

ᶜAbdullāh, the freed slave of Asmā', reported: "Asmā', when she was in residence at Muzdalifah, asked me whether the moon had set. I said: 'No'. She prayed for some time, and again said: 'My son, has the moon set ?' I said: 'Yes'. And she said: 'Set forth along with me'. And so we set forth until (we reached Minā) and she stoned at *al-Jamrah*. She then prayed in her place [of residence]. I said to her: 'Respected lady, we set forth (in the very early part of dawn) when it was dark', whereupon she said: 'My son, there is no harm in it; Allāh's Apostle ﷺ granted this concession to women'."[966]

There is also a report by Ibn Shawwāl who was the freed slave of Umm

962 al-Kāsānī, *Badā'iᶜ al-ṣanā'iᶜ*, iii. 141.

963 al-Bukhārī, *k. al-ḥajj, b. man yuṣallī al-fajr bi jamᶜ*; Muslim, *k. al-ḥajj, b. istiḥbāb ziyādat al-taghlīs bi ṣalāt al-ṣubḥ yawm al-naḥr bi al-muzdalifah...*

964 al-Kāsānī, *Badā'iᶜ al-ṣanā'iᶜ*, iii. 89.

965 al-Bukhārī, *k. al-ḥajj, b. man qaddama daᶜafata ahlihī bi layl*; Muslim, *k. al-ḥajj, b. istiḥbāb taqdīm dafᶜ al-daᶜafah min al-nisā'...*

966 Muslim, *k. al-ḥajj, b. istiḥbāb taqdīm dafᶜ al-daᶜafah min al-nisā'...*

Ḥabībah (the wife of Allāh's Apostle) that Allāh's Apostle ﷺ sent her from Muzdalifah during the night.[967]

Ibn ᶜAbbās reported: "Allāh's Messenger ﷺ sent me from Muzdalifah ahead (of the caravan) along with the weak ones on the night of Muzdalifah".[968]

Sālim ibn ᶜAbdullāh reported that: "ᶜAbdullāh ibn ᶜUmar used to send the weak among his family early to Minā. So they used to depart from al–Mash'ar al–Haram (that is Muzdalifah) at night (when the moon had set) and invoke Allāh as much as they could, and then they would return (to Mina) before the *Imām* had started from Muzdalifah to Minā. So some of them would reach Minā at the time of the *Fajr* Prayer and some of them would come later. When they reached Minā they would throw pebbles on the *Jamrah* (*Jamrah al–ᶜaqabah*). Ibn ᶜUmar used to say: 'Allāh's Apostle gave permission to them (weak people) to do so'." [969] Imām Muḥammad says after narrating this practice of Ibn ᶜUmar: "There is no harm that one sends the weak people ahead while telling them not to do *ramy* (stoning) of the *Jamrah* before sunrise. This is the opinion of Abū Ḥanīfah and most of our jurists".[970]

3. *RAMY*

Ramy refers to the stoning of the *jamarāt* (pl. of *Jamrah* meaning pillars) at Minā with pebbles. There are three pillars in Minā: *Jamrah al-ᶜAqabah* (*al-Jamrah al-Kubrā*: the largest pillar), which is on the left side inside Minā; the *Jamrah al-Wusṭā* (the middle *jamrah*) which is at about 11,677 meters from the first one, while *Jamrah al-Ṣughrā* (the smallest *jamrah*) is 1,564 meters further from the middle one. Sālim ibn Abī al-Jaᶜd reported that Ibn ᶜAbbās said that the Prophet ﷺ said: "When Ibrāhīm ﷺ wanted to perform the *ḥajj* rites, Satan blocked his way near ᶜAqabah, Ibrāhīm threw seven pebbles at him whereupon Satan sunk into the ground. Again Satan appeared to him near the second *jamrah*. Ibrāhīm threw seven pebbles at him and he again sunk into the ground. Once again

967 ibid.

968 al-Bukhārī, *k. al-ḥajj, b. man qaddama daᶜafata ahlihī bi layl;* Muslim, *k. al-ḥajj, b. istiḥbāb taqdīm dafᶜ al-daᶜafah min al-nisā'.*

969 al-Bukhārī, *k. al-ḥajj, b. man qaddama daᶜafata ahlihī bi layl*; Muslim, *k. al-ḥajj, b. istiḥbāb taqdīm dafᶜ al-daᶜafah min al-nisā'.*

970 Muhammad, *al-Muwaṭṭa'*, 169.

Satan approached him near the third *jamrah*, and again Ibrāhīm threw seven pebbles at him and once again Satan sunk into the ground". Ibn ᶜAbbās added: "You throw pebbles at Satan, and (in doing so) you follow the path of your forefather Ibrāhīm ﷺ".[971]

The wisdom behind *ramy*

Imām Ghazālī says: "As for the throwing of pebbles, let your intention be to submit to the command of God, showing servitude and bondage, and arising only to obey without any concern for benefit either to mind or soul. Then make it your intention to imitate Ibrāhīm ﷺ to whom the devil, Allāh curse him, appeared at that place in order to cast doubt on his pilgrimage or tempt him to [commit] transgression, whereupon Allāh, Exalted is He, ordered him to throw pebbles at him to keep him away and to exterminate his hope. If the thought comes to you that the Devil [really] presented himself to him [Ibrāhīm] and he saw him and therefore threw pebbles at him, but you [are different], and the Devil does not present himself to you, know that this thought is from the Devil and he is the one who put it in your mind to weaken your determination in throwing, and to make you imagine that it is a useless deed that resembles [mere] play, so why should you bother yourself with it. Therefore, drive [this thought] away from yourself by diligence and by bracing yourself to throw (pebbles) at Satan in spite of Satan's (snares). Know that you are throwing only outwardly at *al-ᶜaqabah* while in reality you are throwing at the face of the Devil and breaking his back with it, for the Devil will only be overcome by your compliance with the commandment of Allāh Most High, and by you magnifying Him because of His commandment alone and not because of any benefit to mind or soul".[972]

The ruling related to *ramy*

Ramy of the *jamarāt* with pebbles is *wājib.*[973] Jābir said: "I saw the Prophet ﷺ riding his mount and throwing pebbles on the Day of *Naḥr* (10th of *Dhū al-ḥijjah*), and saying, 'Take your rituals from me. I do not know

971 Al-Hakim, *al-Mustadrak*, i. 638.

972 al-Ghazālī, *Iḥyā' ᶜulūm al-dīn*, i. 378.

973 al-Kāsānī, *Badā'iᶜ al-ṣanā'iᶜ*, iii. 90-91.

whether I will be able to perform another *ḥajj* after this one'."[974] There is a consensus on this being *wājib*.[975]

The size of the pebbles

Jābir narrates that the Prophet ﷺ said: "Do *ramy* with small pebbles".[976] Sulaymān ibn ᶜAmr ibn al-Aḥwaṣ al-Azdī reported from his mother that she said: "The Prophet ﷺ was at the bottom of the valley, and he was saying: 'O People! Do not kill each other when you stone the pillar, [when you stone] stone with pebbles'."[977] Ibn ᶜAbbās reported: "The Prophet said to me: 'Come, pick some pebbles for me'. I picked small pebbles like peas. When I gave these pebbles to him, he said: 'Use pebbles similar to these (in throwing), and beware against exaggerating in your religion, for those before you were destroyed because of their exaggeration in religion'."[978] Jābir ibn ᶜAbdullāh reported: "I saw Allāh's Apostle ﷺ throwing stones (*at Jamrah al-ᶜAqabah*) like pelting small pebbles".[979]

Where the pebbles should be collected from

The pebble can be collected from Muzdalifah or anywhere else.[980] It is not a condition that the pebbles be stones, rather they can be anything from earth stones, to clay, bricks, soil, or ceramics etc. [981], because the ḥadīth mentions throwing only and does not specify as to what should be used.

Mujāhid says: "The pebbles were picked from Muzdalifah to stone the pillars".[982] Muḥammad ibn Sīrīn said: "The one who does *ramy* should collects pebbles from Muzdalifah". [983] Makḥūl said: "Take the pebbles

974 Muslim, *k. al-ḥajj, b. istiḥbāb ramy jamrat al-ᶜaqabah...*

975 al-Kāsānī, *Badāʾiᶜ al-ṣanāʾiᶜ*, iii. 90.

976 Ibn Abī Shaybah, *al-Muṣannaf*, viii. 323.

977 Abū Dāwūd, *k. al-manāsik, b. fī ramy al-jimār*; Ibn Mājah, *k. al-manāsik, b. qadr ḥaṣā al-ramy.*

978 al-Nasā'ī, *k. al-manāsik, b. iltiqāṭ al-ḥaṣā;* Ibn Mājah, *k. al-manāsik, b. qadr ḥaṣā al-ramy.*

979 Muslim, *k. al-ḥajj, b. istiḥbāb kawn ḥaṣā al-jimār bi qadr ḥaṣā al-khadhf.*

980 al-Kāsānī, *Badāʾiᶜ al-ṣanāʾiᶜ*, iii. 142.

981 al-Kāsānī, *Badāʾiᶜ al-ṣanāʾiᶜ*, iii. 146.

982 Ibn Abī Shaybah, *al-Muṣannaf*, viii. 207.

983 ibid.

from Muzdalifah".[984] Qāsim ibn Muḥammad ibn Abī Bakr and Bakr al-Muzanī used to pick the pebbles from Muzdalifah.[985] It is narrated that Saᶜīd ibn Jubayr, ᶜAṭā' ibn Abī Rabāḥ and ᶜĀmir al-Shaᶜbī said pebbles can be picked from wherever one likes.[986]

It is disliked to do *ramy* with pebbles collected from the *jamrah*.[987] Al-Aswad did not like to do *ramy* with the pebbles already used for *ramy*.[988] Qatādah said: "It is disliked to do *ramy* with the pebbles used for *ramy*".[989]

The number of the pebbles

The number of pebbles that one will throw is either 70 or 49 dependent on the number of days one stays in Minā. One will throw 7 pebbles at the *Jamrah al-ᶜAqabah* on the 10th of *Dhū al-ḥijjah*; 21 on the 11th day, 7 at each of the three *jamrahs*; and similarly 21 on the 12th day, again 7 at each of the three *jamrahs*. The last 21 pebbles, 7 at each of the *jamrahs*, are thrown on the 13th day of *Dhū al-ḥijjah* taking the total number of pebbles to 70.

If a pilgrim throws pebbles for only three days (the 10th, 11th and 12th of *Dhū al-ḥijjah*) and does not throw them on the 13th day, he may do so without any harm if he leaves Minā before sunset on the 12th. In such a case the total number will be 49 pebbles.

ᶜAbdullāh ibn Masᶜūd narrated that the Prophet ﷺ came to *Jamrah al-ᶜAqabah*, and threw seven pebbles on it.[990] Jābir reported Allāh's Messenger ﷺ as saying: "An odd number of stones are to be used for cleaning (the private parts after answering the call of nature), and the casting of pebbles at the *jamrahs* is to be done by odd numbers (seven), and (the number) of circuits between al-Ṣafā and al-Marwah is also odd (seven), and the number of circuits (around the Kaᶜbah) is also odd (seven). Whenever any one of you is required to use stones (for cleaning

984 ibid., viii. 208.
985 ibid.
986 ibid., viii. 207-8.
987 al-Kāsānī, *Badā'iᶜ al-ṣanā'iᶜ*, iii. 142.
988 Ibn Abī Shaybah, *al-Muṣannaf*, viii. 205.
989 ibid., viii. 205-6.
990 al-Bukhārī, k. *al-ḥajj, b. ramy al-jimār min baṭn al-wādī, b. ramy al-jimār bi sabᶜ ḥaṣayāt*; Muslim, *k. al-ḥajj, b. ramy jamrat al-ᶜaqabah min baṭn al-wādī*.

one's private parts) one should use an odd number of stones (three, five or seven)".[991]

Where the pebbles should fall

The pebbles should fall on the pillars, or near them and one should throw them one at a time. If they fall beyond the pillars the throw will not be valid and must be repeated.[992]

DAYS OF *RAMY*

The days designated for *ramy* can be either three or four from; the 10th, to the 12th of *Dhū al-ḥijjah* and up to the 13th. [993] Allāh says in the Qur'ān: "*Make remembrance of Allāh on the appointed days. But if any one hastens to leave in two days there is no sin on him, and if anyone stays on there is no sin on him, for the one who is wary of Allāh*".[994]

On the 10th one does the *ramy* of *Jamrah al-ᶜAqabah* with seven pebbles. One should say بِسْمِ اللهِ، اللهُ أكبر (In the name of Allāh; Allāh is the Greatest) with the *ramy* of every pebble. *Talbiyah* should end as soon as one starts *ramy*. The time of the *ramy* of *Jamrah al-ᶜAqabah* is the dawn of the 10th *Dhū al-ḥijjah* to the dawn of the next day. If someone does the *ramy* before this, it will be invalid, and if one does it after this then a sacrifice will be compulsory on him. The best time for the *ramy* is after sunrise until the decline of the sun; then it is allowed until the sunset; other times are disliked. [995] Jābir reported: "I saw Allāh's Apostle ﷺ flinging pebbles while riding his camel on the Day of *Naḥr*, and he was saying: 'Take your rituals from me. I do not know whether I will be able to perform another *ḥajj* after this one."[996] Ibn ᶜAbbās said that the Prophet ﷺ permitted the old and weak people of his family to throw first. Then he said: "Do not throw pebbles at the first *Jamrah al-ᶜAqabah* before sunrise". [997] ᶜAbd al-Raḥmān ibn Yazīd reported that ᶜAbdullāh

991 Muslim, *k. al-ḥajj, b. bayān anna ḥaṣā al-jimār sabᶜun.*

992 al-Kāsānī, *Badā'iᶜ al-ṣanā'iᶜ*, iii. 95.

993 ibid., iii. 91.

994 *al-Baqarah* 203.

995 al-Kāsānī, *Badā'iᶜ al-ṣanā'iᶜ*, iii. 91-3.

996 Muslim, *k. al-ḥajj, b. istiḥbāb ramy jamrat al-ᶜaqabah yawm al-naḥr rākiban.*

997 Abū Dāwūd, *k. al-ḥajj, b. al-taᶜjīl;* al-Nasā'ī, *k. al-manāsik, b. al-nahy ᶜan ramy jamrat al-ᶜaqabah qabla ṭulūᶜ al-shams;* Ibn Mājah, *k. al-manāsik, b. man taqaddama min jamᶜ ilā minā liramy al-jimār.*

ibn Masʿūd threw seven pebbles at *Jamrah al-ʿAqabah* from the heart of the valley. He pronounced *takbīr* with every pebble. It was said to him that people fling stones from the upper side (of the valley), whereupon ʿAbdullāh ibn Masʿūd said: 'By him, besides Whom there is no other god, this is the place (of flinging stones) of the one upon whom *Sūrah al-Baqarah* was revealed (the Prophet)'.[998]

On the 11th *Dhū al-ḥijjah* one does *ramy* of all three *jamrahs*. It is Sunnah to start with the *ramy* of the first *jamrah*, that is near *Masjid al-Khayf*; then the *ramy* of the middle *jamrah*, and finally the *ramy* of *Jamrah al-ʿAqabah*. In the *ramy* of each *jamrah* one will use seven pebbles.[999] If one changes the order and for example does the *ramy* of the middle *jamrah* before the first one, then one has to repeat the *ramy*. It is Sunnah that one makes a pause of 15-20 minutes before starting the *ramy* of the next *jamrah*.

The time of the *ramy* on the 11th and 12th *Dhū al-ḥijjah* is from the decline of the sun until the sunset. It is disliked to do *ramy* after sunset until the dawn. The *ramy* will not suffice before the *zawāl*.[1000] Jābir reported that Allāh's Messenger ﷺ flung pebbles at *jamrah* on the Day of *Naḥr* after sunrise, and after that (i.e. on the 11th, 12th and 13th of *Dhū al-ḥijjah*) when the sun had declined.[1001]

Takbīr* and *duʿā'* at every *ramy

It is Sunnah to remember Allāh with every *ramy*.[1002] ʿAbdullāh ibn Masʿūd and Ibn ʿUmar at the time of throwing pebbles used to say: اللَّهُمَّ اجْعَلْهُ حَجًّا مَبْرُورًا ، وَذَنْبًا مَغْفُورًا ('O Allāh! Accept this *ḥajj* of ours and pardon our sins'.)[1003] Mughīrah says: "I asked Ibrāhīm al-Nakhaʿī what should I say when I throw the pebbles? He said: 'Say: اللَّهُمَّ اجْعَلْهُ حَجًّا مَبْرُورًا ، وَذَنْبًا مَغْفُورًا ('O Allāh! Accept this *ḥajj* of ours and pardon our sins'.) I asked him should I say it with every pebble. He said: 'Yes if you want'."[1004]

Aʿmash narrated from Ibrāhīm al-Nakhaʿī who said: "There is no

998 Muslim, *k. al-ḥajj, b. ramy jamrat al-ʿaqabah…*

999 al-Kāsānī, *Badāʾiʿ al-ṣanāʾiʿ*, iii. 149.

1000 ibid.

1001 al-Bukhārī, *k. al-ḥajj, b. ramy al-jimār*; Muslim, *k. al-ḥajj, b. bayān waqt istiḥbāb al-ramy.*

1002 al-Kāsānī, *Badāʾiʿ al-ṣanāʾiʿ*, iii. 145.

1003 Ibn Abī Shaybah, *al-Muṣannaf*, viii. 353.

1004 ibid., viii. 354.

specific supplication while standing next to the pillars. So supplicate with whatever you like".[1005] The same has been narrated from Ḥasan al-Baṣrī and ʿAṭāʾ ibn Abī Rabāḥ.[1006]

Duʿāʾ* after *ramy

After *ramy* it is recommended to stand facing the *Qiblah* to praise Allāh, while supplicating to Him. However, the *duʿāʾ* is not Sunnah after the *ramy* of *Jamrah al-ʿAqabah.* ʿAbdullāh ibn ʿUmar reports: "When the Prophet ﷺ threw pebbles at the first *jamrah,* which is near the mosque, he said, '*Allāhu Akbar*'. Thus, he threw seven pebbles and each time he repeated: '*Allāhu Akbar*'. He then turned left towards the bottom of the valley. There he stood for quite a long time facing the direction of the *Qiblah,* and raising his hands supplicated to Allāh. Then he went and threw seven pebbles at the second *jamrah* saying '*Allāhu Akbar*' with each throw. Thereafter, he went to the left of the bottom of the valley, stood there facing the *Qiblah* and supplicated to Allāh with raised hands. Then he went to the *jamrah* near ʿAqabah, threw seven pebbles at it, uttering a *takbīr* with each throw. After this he left and did not pause".[1007]

Ibn ʿAbbās has reported that after throwing pebbles at the *Jamrah al-ʿAqabah,* the Prophet ﷺ used to leave, and not stop (for supplications).[1008]

THROWING PEBBLES ON BEHALF OF OTHERS

Those who for a valid reason, illness, etc., cannot themselves throw the pebbles may ask someone else to throw on their behalf.[1009] Jābir said: "We performed *ḥajj* with the Prophet ﷺ and we had some women and children with us. We (adults) uttered the *talbiyah* and threw pebbles on behalf of the children".[1010]

4. *HADY*

Hady is the sacrificial animals pilgrims' offers for the sake of Allah. Allāh says in the Qurʾān: "*We have made the sacrifice of camels and cows*

1005 ibid., viii. 354.
1006 ibid.
1007 al-Bukhārī, *k. al-ḥajj, b. al-duʿa ʿind al-jamratayn.*
1008 Ibn Mājah, *k. al-manāsik, b. idhā ramā jamrat al-ʿaqabah lam yaqif ʿindahā.*
1009 al-Kāsānī, *Badāʾiʿ al-ṣanāʾiʿ*, iii. 91.
1010 al-Tirmidhī, *k. al-ḥajj;* Ibn Mājah, *k. al-manāsik, b. al-ramy ʿan al-ṣibyān.*

for you as among the symbols from Allāh: in them is (much) good for you: then pronounce the name of Allāh over them as they line up (for sacrifice) when they are down on their sides (after slaughter), eat you thereof, and feed the contented and the beggars: thus have We made animals subject to you, that you may be grateful. It is not their meat nor their blood that reaches Allāh: it is your piety that reaches Him".[1011]

ʿAlī ibn Abī Ṭālib narrated that the Prophet ﷺ offered a hundred camels for sacrifice.[1012]

The types of animal offered for a *hady*

There are three types of *hady*: camels, cows and sheep or goats. One may sacrifice any animal one chooses. As mentioned above, the Prophet ﷺ offered a hundred camels.[1013] The smallest animal considered to be a *hady* is a sheep.

Up to seven people can share the sacrifice of a camel or a cow as long as all those sharing in the sacrifice intend an act of *qurbah* (an act of worship that brings one closer to Allāh) by it. If one of them does not have that intention and wants his portion only for the meat, then the whole of it is not permissible for the others as a *qurbah.*[1014] Jābir said: "We slaughtered with the Prophet ﷺ in the year of Ḥudaybiyyah, a camel for seven people, and a cow for seven people".[1015] Jābir also reported: "We set out in a state of *iḥrām* for *ḥajj* along with Allāh's Messenger ﷺ. He commanded that seven people should join (together) in offering a camel or a cow for sacrifice.[1016]

A sheep is permitted for everything except in two situations: in the case of someone who makes the *ṭawāf al-ifāḍah* in the state of major impurity, or the one who has intercourse after the standing at ʿArafah – the sacrifice of a camel is required in these two cases.

1011 *al-Ḥajj* 36.

1012 al-Bukhārī, *k. al-ḥajj, b. yataṣaddaqu bi jilāl al-budn;* Muslim, *k. al-ḥajj, b. fī al-ṣadaqah bi luḥūm al-hady.*

1013 ibid.

1014 al-Samarqandī, *Tuḥfat al-fuqahā'* 426.

1015 Muslim, *k. al-ḥajj, b. al-ishtirāk fī al-hady.*

1016 ibid.

TYPES OF *HADY*

Hady is divided into two categories, one that is recommended, and the other that is *wājib* (obligatory).

The recommended *hady* is for the one who performs *ḥajj ifrād.* This is when one intends to do *ḥajj* only without performing *ᶜumrah,* or when one performs *ᶜumrah* only.

The *wājib hady* may be one of the following categories:

1- For those performing *ḥajj qirān* or *tamattuᶜ*.[1017] ᶜAbdullāh ibn ᶜUmar reported: "Allāh's Messenger ﷺ observed *tamattuᶜ* in *ḥajjat al-wadāᶜ*. He first put on *iḥrām* for *ᶜumrah* and then for *ḥajj,* and then offered animal sacrifice. So he drove the sacrificial animals with him from Dhū al-Ḥulayfah. Allāh's Messenger ﷺ commenced *iḥrām* of *ᶜumrah* and pronounced the *talbiyah* for *ᶜumrah* and then (put on *iḥrām* for *ḥajj*) and pronounced *talbiyah* for *ḥajj.* And the people performed *tamattuᶜ* in the company of Allāh's Messenger ﷺ. They put on *iḥrām* for *ᶜumrah* (first) and then for *ḥajj.* Some of them had sacrificial animals which they had brought with them, whereas some had none to sacrifice. So, when Allāh's Messenger ﷺ came to Makkah, he said to the people: 'He who amongst you has brought sacrificial animals along with him must not treat as lawful anything which has become unlawful for him until he has completed the *ḥajj*; and he, who amongst you has not brought the sacrificial animals should circumambulate the House, and run between al-Ṣafā and al-Marwah and clip (his hair) and take off the *iḥrām,* and then again put on the *iḥrām* for *ḥajj* and offer sacrifice of the animals. But he, who does not find a sacrificial animal, should observe fast for three days during the *ḥajj* and for seven days when he returns to his family'. Allāh's Messenger ﷺ circumambulated (the House) when he came to Makkah. He first kissed the corner (of the Kaᶜbah containing the Black Stone), then ran in three circuits out of seven and walked in four circuits. And then when he had finished the circumambulation of the House he observed two *rakᶜahs* of prayer at the Station (of Ibrāhīm), pronounced *Salam* (for concluding the prayer), and came to al-Ṣafā and ran seven times between al-Ṣafā and al-Marwah. After that he did not treat anything as lawful which had become unlawful until he had completed his *ḥajj* and sacrificed his animal on the day of sacrifice (10th

1017 al-Kāsānī, *Badāʾiᶜ al-ṣanāʾiᶜ*, iii. 180.

of *Dhū al-ḥijjah*), and then went back quickly (to Makkah) and performed circumambulation of the House (known as *ṭawāf ifāḍah*) after which all that was unlawful for him became lawful; and those who had brought the sacrificial animals along with them did as Allāh's Messenger ﷺ had done'."[1018]

2- For the omission of a *wājib* act of *ḥajj*. *Hady* is *wājib* as expiation for a pilgrim who misses out a *wājib* of *ḥajj*, such as, staying at ʿArafah until the sunset, or spending the night at Muzdalifah or Minā, or throwing the pebbles at the pillars, or departing Makkah without performing *ṭawāf al-wadāʿ*.

3- For committing a forbidden act in a state of *iḥrām*. The *hady* is *wājib* as expiation for a pilgrim who commits a forbidden act, other than sexual intercourse, in a state of *iḥrām*, for example, wearing perfume or shaving or cutting the hair.

4- For committing a forbidden act in the sacred precincts of the *Ḥaram* like hunting or cutting down trees.

CONDITIONS OF THE *HADY*

1- The age of a *hady* if a camel must be a minimum of five years, two years for a cow, and one year for a goat or sheep. The only exception is that if a six month old lamb is big for its age, then it can be offered.[1019]

2- One is not permitted to use an animal for sacrificial purpose if, for example, its ear, tail, foot or leg is severed; or whose eye sight is gone, emaciated or incapable of walking to the place of slaughter.[1020] It has been narrated by ʿAlī and al-Barā' ibn ʿĀzib that the Prophet ﷺ forbade those animals which have the above mentioned defects.[1021] The Prophet ﷺ said, on being asked about the slaughtering of a lame animal: "It is permitted if it can reach the place of slaughter".[1022]

1018 al-Bukhārī, *k. al-ḥajj, b. man sāqa al-budna maʿahu*; Muslim, *k. al-ḥajj, b. wujūb al-dam ʿalā al-mutamattiʿ*.

1019 al-Samaraqandī, *Tuḥfat al-fuqahā'* 426.

1020 ibid. 426-7.

1021 Abū Dāwūd, *k. al-aḍāḥī, b. mā yukrahu min al-ḍaḥāyā*; al-Tirmidhī, *k. al-aḍāḥī, b. mā yukrahu min al-aḍāḥī;* al-Nasā'ī, *k. al-aḍāḥī, b. al-kharqā'...*; Ibn Mājah, *k. al-aḍāḥī, b. mā yukrahu an yuḍaḥḥā bihī*.

1022 al-Tirmidhī, *k. al-aḍāḥī, b...*

Riding the *hady*

Whoever brings a camel with him and the need arises to ride it is allowed to do so, but if he does not need to ride it then he should not.[1023] Abū Hurayrah reported that the Prophet ﷺ saw a man driving a she-camel for *hady*. The Prophet ﷺ said to the man: "Mount it". The man replied: "It is a sacrificial animal." The Prophet ﷺ said to him twice or thrice: "Woe be to you! Mount it."[1024] It is narrated from ᶜAlī, ᶜAbdullāh ibn ᶜAbbās, Ḥasan al-Baṣrī, ᶜIkrimah, Mujāhid, ᶜAṭā' ibn Abī Rabāḥ ᶜUrwah ibn al-Zubayr that it is allowed to ride the *hady* when there is a need to do so.[1025]

One should not milk the *hady*

If the animal intended for the *hady* has milk one should not milk it but should rather sprinkle its udders with cold water until the milk stops.[1026]

If the *hady* perishes or is afflicted

If one is bringing along a sacrificial animal and it perishes, then, one does not have to sacrifice another if it was being offered as a voluntary (including recommended) sacrifice; but if it was for an obligatory sacrifice, then one must provide replacement.[1027]

If it is afflicted with a major defect, then one must replace it with another, and may do whatever one wishes with the defective animal.[1028] If a camel cannot complete the journey and the camel was intended as a voluntary offering, then one slaughters it by piercing its throat, smears its garlands with its blood and strikes one of its flanks with them but neither he nor others who are of means should eat of it; and if it was an obligatory sacrificial animal, then one should find another in its place and do whatever one wants with it (i.e. the afflicted animal).[1029]

Mūsā ibn Salamah al-Hudhalī narrates: "I and Sinān ibn Salamah proceeded to Makkah to perform ᶜ*umrah*. Sinān had a sacrificial camel

1023 al-Qudūrī, *al-Mukhtaṣar* 254.

1024 al-Bukhārī, *k. al-ḥajj, b. rukūb al-budn*; Muslim, *k. al-ḥajj, b. jawāz rukūb al-badanat al-muhdāh li man iḥtāja ilayhā*.

1025 Ibn Abī Shaybah, *al-Muṣannaf*, viii. 577-581.

1026 al-Qudūrī, *al-Mukhtaṣar* 254.

1027 ibid., 254-5.

1028 ibid., 255.

1029 Abū Ḥanīfah, *K. al-āthār* 89; al-Qudūrī, *al-Mukhtaṣar* 255.

with him which he was driving. The camel stopped on the way being completely exhausted and this made Sinān helpless. He thought if it is unable to proceeding further how he will be able to take it along with him. He said: 'I will definitely find out (the religious verdict) about it'. We moved on in the morning and as we encamped at al-Baṭḥā', Sinān said: 'Come (along with me) to Ibn ᶜAbbās so that we narrate to him (this incident)'and he (Sinān) reported the incident of the sacrificial camel. He (Ibn ᶜAbbās) said: 'You have referred the matter to a well informed person. Now listen. Allāh's Messenger ﷺ sent 16 sacrificial camels with a man whom he put in charge of them. The man set out and came back and said: 'Messenger of Allāh, what should I do with those who are completely exhausted and become powerless to move on?' Whereupon, the Prophet said: 'Slaughter them, and dye their hoofs in their blood and put them on the sides of their humps, but neither you nor anyone among those who are with you must eat any part of it'."[1030]

The time of slaughtering

It is not permitted to slaughter the sacrificial animal of the voluntary, the *tamattuᶜ* or the *qirān* except on the Day of Sacrifice while it is permitted to slaughter the rest of the sacrificial animals (for example *hady* for an expiation) at any time one wishes.[1031] Nāfiᶜ narrates: "Ibn ᶜUmar intended to perform *ḥajj* in the year when Ḥajjāj attacked Ibn al-Zubayr. Somebody said to Ibn ᶜUmar: 'There is a danger of an impending war between them'. Ibn ᶜUmar said: 'Verily, in the Messenger of Allāh you have a good example. (And if it happens as you say) then I will do the same as the Messenger of Allāh ﷺ had done. I make you witness that I have decided to perform *ᶜumrah*'. Then he set out and when he reached al-Baida', he said: 'The ceremonies of both *ḥajj* and *ᶜumrah* are similar. I make you witness that I have made *ḥajj* compulsory for me along with *ᶜumrah*'. He drove (to Makkah) a *hady* which he had bought from (a place called) Qudayd and did not do more than that. He did not slaughter the *hady* or finish his *iḥrām*, or shave or cut short his hair until the day of slaughtering the sacrifices (10th *Dhū al-ḥijjah*). Then he slaughtered his *hady* and shaved his head'."[1032]

1030 Muslim, *k. al-ḥajj, b. mā yafᶜalu bi al-hady idhā ᶜaṭiba fī al-ṭarīq.*

1031 al-Qudūrī, *al-Mukhtaṣar* 253.

1032 al-Bukhārī, *k. al-ḥajj, b. ṭawāf al-qārin.*

The place of slaughtering

It is not permitted to slaughter sacrificial animals except in the *Ḥaram.*[1033] Jābir reported that the Prophet ﷺ said: "All of Minā is a place for slaughtering, and the entire Muzdalifah is a place for spending the night; and all roads of Makkah are passageways and places to offer one's sacrifice".[1034]

The best way of slaughtering

The best way to slaughter camels is by *naḥr* (piercing the throat when they are standing) while for cows, sheep or goats it is by *dhabh* (cutting the throat).[1035] Ziyād ibn Jubayr reported that Ibn ʿUmar came upon a man who was slaughtering a camel while it was sitting. He said to the man: "Let it stand up, and tie its legs. This is the Sunnah of your Prophet ﷺ". [1036] Jābir reported that the Prophet ﷺ and his Companions used to slaughter their sacrificial camels with their left legs tied and standing on three legs.[1037]

Who should do the slaughtering

It is recommended that the one offering the sacrifice slaughter the animal themselves if they are able.[1038] If one is unable then one can instruct someone who is able or use specialised slaughter houses as is the case today.

The butcher should not be paid from it

One should give the sacrificed animal's covering, halter or reins away as *ṣadaqah* but should not pay the fee of the butcher from these things.[1039] ʿAlī said: "The Prophet ﷺ ordered me to take care of his camels that were to be slaughtered and to distribute their meat, skins and everything else

1033 al-Qudūrī, *al-Mukhtaṣar* 253.

1034 Muslim, *k. al-ḥajj, b. mā jā'a anna ʿArafah kullahā mawqif;* Abū Dāwūd, *k. al-manāsik, b. al-ṣalāh bi jamʿ.*

1035 al-Qudūrī, *al-Mukhtaṣar* 255.

1036 al-Bukhārī, *k. al-ḥajj, b. naḥr al-ibil muqayyadah*; Muslim, *k. al-ḥajj, b. naḥr al-budn qiyāman muqayyadah.*

1037 Abū Dāwūd, *k. al-manāsik, b. kayfa tunḥaru al-budn.*

1038 al-Qudūrī, *al-Mukhtaṣar* 254.

1039 ibid.

(among the needy), but he ordered me not to give any portion of it to the butcher".[1040] And then he said: "We shall give him from ourselves". ᶜAlī ibn Abī Ṭālib also narrated that: "Allāh's Apostle ﷺ put him in charge of his sacrificial animals, and commanded him to distribute the whole of their meat, hides, and saddle cloths to the poor, and not to give to the butcher anything out of them".[1041]

Eating from the meat of the *hady*

It is permitted to eat of the sacrificial animal offered voluntarily or for the *tamattuᶜ* or *qirān.*[1042] It is also permitted to give them away as *ṣadaqah* to the destitute of the *Ḥaram* and others.[1043] Allāh's command in regards the animals slaughtered in sacrifice is: *"Eat you thereof, and feed the contented and the beggars"*.[1044]. ᶜAlqamah says: "ᶜAbdullāh ibn Masᶜūd sent his *hady* with me, and commanded me when I sacrificed it, to give one third as *ṣadaqah,* to eat one third, and to send the other third to the family of his brother ᶜUtbah".[1045]

However, it is not permitted for one to eat from the meat of a sacrifice made for *kaffārah* (expiation).[1046] This has been narrated from ᶜAṭā', Ṭāwūs, Mujāhid, Ibrāhīm al-Nakhaᶜī and Saᶜīd ibn Jubayr.[1047]

The importance of sacrifice

Allāh, Exalted is He, says: *"Their flesh reaches not Allāh, nor does their blood, but it is your righteousness that reaches Him"*.[1048] Such sanctification is obtained only by ensuring that the offering is precious in quality whether it is great or little in quantity. The Messenger of Allāh ﷺ was once asked: "In what does the [true] piety of the pilgrimage consist?" He said "In ᶜ*ajj*' and in '*thajj*'."[1049] 'ᶜ*Ajj*' is the raising of the voice with the *talbiyah* and

1040 Muslim, *k. al-ḥajj, b. fī al-ṣadaqah bi luḥūm al-hady wa julūdihā wa jilālihā.*
1041 ibid.
1042 al-Qudūrī, *al-Mukhtaṣar* 252-3.
1043 ibid., 253.
1044 *al-Ḥajj* 36.
1045 Ibn Abī Shaybah, *al-Muṣannaf,* viii. 145.
1046 al-Qudūrī, *al-Mukhtaṣar* 252-3.
1047 Ibn Abī Shaybah, *al-Muṣannaf,* viii. 146.
1048 *al-Ḥajj* 37
1049 al-Tirmidhī, *k. al-ḥajj, b. mā jā'a fī faḍl al-talbiyah wa al-naḥr;* Ibn Mājah, *k. al-manāsik, b. rafᶜ al-ṣawt bi al-talbiyah.*

'*thajj*' is the shedding of the blood of a sacrifice". ʿĀ'ishah reported that the Messenger of Allāh ﷺ said: "No person does anything on the Day of Sacrifice that Allāh the Most High likes more than the shedding of the blood of a sacrificial animal, for the animal will appear on the Day of Judgment with its horns and hoofs, and the blood is spilt in the presence of Allāh, Exalted is He, even before it touches the ground; therefore, be pleased with it".[1050] Zayd ibn Arqam narrates that the Companions of the Prophet ﷺ asked: "O Messenger of Allāh, what are these sacrifices? He answered: 'They are Sunnah of your father Ibrāhīm'. Then they asked: 'What do we get from them, O Messenger of Allāh?' He answered: 'For every hair (of the sacrificial animal) there is a good deed'. They asked: 'What about the wool O Messenger of Allāh?' He answered: 'For every strand of wool there is a good deed'."[1051]

Imām Ghazālī says: "As for the *hady* offering. You should know that it is a devotion to Allāh, Exalted is He, by virtue of its compliance; so accomplish your *hady* and hope that Allāh, Exalted is He, will free every part of your body from Fire by virtue of the *hady*. The promise has arrived thus; therefore the bigger the *hady* and the fuller its parts the more comprehensive will be your release from the Fire".[1052]

5. SHAVING OR SHORTENING ONE'S HAIR

It is *wājib* to shave one's head or shorten it in order to come out from the state of *iḥrām* for both ʿ*umrah* and *ḥajj*.[1053] ʿAbdullāh ibn ʿUmar said: "Allāh's Apostle ﷺ and some of his Companions got their heads shaved in the Farewell *Ḥajj*, and others shortened their hair".[1054]

In another ḥadīth, ʿAbdullāh ibn ʿUmar also narrated: "The Messenger of Allāh ﷺ said: 'O Allāh! Be merciful to those who have their heads shaved'. The people said: 'O Allāh's Apostle, and (invoke Allāh) for those who get their hair cut short'. The Prophet said: 'O Allāh! Be merciful to those who have their heads shaved'. The people

1050 al-Tirmidhī, *k. al-aḍāḥī, b. mā jā'a fī faḍl al-uḍḥiyyah;* Ibn Mājah, *k. al-aḍāḥī, b. thawāb al-uḍḥiyyah.*

1051 Ibn Mājah, *k. al-aḍāḥī, b. thawāb al-uḍḥiyyah.*

1052 al-Ghazālī, *Iḥyā' ʿulūm al-dīn*, i. 378.

1053 al-Kāsānī, *Badā'iʿ al-ṣanā'iʿ*, iii. 98.

1054 al-Bukhārī, *k. al-ḥajj, b. al-ḥalq wa al-taqṣīr ʿinda al-ihlāl*; Muslim, *k. al-ḥajj, b. tafḍīl al-ḥalq ʿalā al-taqṣīr wa jawāz al-taqṣīr.*

said: 'O Messenger of Allāh, and those who get their hair cut short'. The Prophet said: (the third time), 'And to those who get their hair cut short'." Nāfiᶜ said that the Prophet had said once or twice: "O Allāh! Be merciful to those who get their head shaved," and on the fourth time he added: "And to those who have their hair cut short".[1055] Abū Hurayrah narrated: "The Messenger of Allāh ﷺ said: "O Allāh! Forgive those who get their heads shaved'. The people asked: 'Also those who get their hair cut short?' The Prophet said: 'O Allāh! Forgive those who have their heads shaved'. The people said: 'Also those who get their hair cut short?' The Prophet invoked Allāh for those who have their heads shaved and at the third time said: 'Also [forgive] those who get their hair cut short'."[1056]

Yaḥyā ibn al-Ḥusayn reported on the authority of his grandmother that Allāh's Apostle ﷺ invoked blessings on the occasion of the Farewell Pilgrimage three times for those who got their heads shaved and once for those who got their hair clipped. [1057] Imām Muḥammad says: "Shaving is better than shortening, and shortening suffices. This is the opinion of Abū Ḥanīfah and most of our jurists".[1058]

Timing

A pilgrim may shave or cut one's hair short right after throwing the first pebbles at *Jamrah al-ᶜAqabah* on the Day of *Naḥr* - the 10th of *Dhū al-ḥijjah.* If, however, a pilgrim has animals to slaughter then one can shave or cut one's hair short only after having slaughtered the animals.[1059] Anas ibn Mālik narrated that the Prophet ﷺ went to Minā, then to the *jamrah,* did *ramy,* then came to his place of stay in Minā and offered his sacrifice, and then called the barber to shave his head. [1060]

The time to shave or cut one's hair short while performing *ᶜumrah* is right after completing *saᶜy* between Ṣafā and Marwah. As for those who

1055 ibid.

1056 Muslim, *k. al-ḥajj, b. tafḍīl al-ḥalq ᶜalā al-taqṣīr wa jawāz al-taqṣīr.*

1057 ibid.

1058 Muhammad, *al-Muwaṭṭa'* 156.

1059 al-Samarqandī, *Tuḥfat al-fuqahā'* 201.

1060 al-Bukhārī, *k. al-wuḍū', b. al-mā' alladhī yughsalu bihi shaᶜr al-insān*; Muslim, *k. al-ḥajj, b. bayān anna al-sunnah yawm al-naḥr an yarmiya thumma yanḥara thumma yaḥliq.*

bring their sacrificial animals with them, they may shave right after they slaughter them.

At the time of shaving or cutting one's hair short, one must be in the *Ḥaram* and it must be during the Days of *Naḥr* - 10th, 11th, and 12th of *Dhū al-ḥijjah.*[1061]

The recommended way

It is liked that while shaving the head one should first shave the right half, then the left side, while facing the direction of the *Qiblah,* uttering *Allāhu Akbar,* and offering a two *rakᶜah* prayer at the end of it. Anas reported that: "The Prophet ﷺ called for the barber and started from the right half of his head, and he distributed a hair or two among the people and then asked the barber to shave the left side and he did similarly, and he the Prophet ﷺ said: 'Here is Abū Ṭalḥah' and he gave these (hairs) to Abū Ṭalḥah".[1062]

Wakīᶜ said: "Abū Ḥanīfah once told me: 'I was mistaken concerning five rites of *ḥajj* and a barber taught these to me and corrected me. This happened when I went to a barber and asked him: 'How much will you charge for shaving my head?' The cupper said: 'Are you from Iraq?' I said: 'Yes'. The cupper said to me: 'Sit down, this is a rite of *ḥajj,* and on it no conditions must be placed'. I sat down with my face slightly away from the direction of the *Qiblah.* At this he said: 'Turn your face towards the *Qiblah*'. I turned the left side of my head for him to shave it first, whereupon he said: 'Turn over the right side of your head (that I may shave it first)'. I turned the right side to him and he began shaving while I sat quietly. He again said: 'Say the *takbīr,'* which I did, until when I got up to leave, he said: 'Where are you going?' I said: 'I am going to my camp'. He said: 'Offer two *rakᶜah* prayers first, and then leave'. I asked him: 'Where did you learn all this?' He replied: 'I have seen ᶜAṭā' ibn Abī Rabāḥ doing this'."[1063]

1061 al-Kāsānī, *Badāʾiᶜ al-ṣanāʾiᶜ*, iii. 102.

1062 al-Bukhārī, *k. al-wuḍū', b. al-mā' alladhī yughsalu bihī shaᶜr al-insān*; Muslim, *k. al-ḥajj, b. bayān anna al-sunnah yawm al-naḥr an yarmiya thumma yanḥara thumma yaḥliq.*

1063 Ibn Khallikān, *Wafayāt al-aᶜyān,* iii. 261-2.

The ruling for a bald person

In the case of a bald man, who has little or no hair at all, it is compulsory to pass a razor over his head.[1064]

A woman may shorten her hair

Women do not shave their heads; rather they shorten their hair only.[1065] ᶜAlī and ᶜĀ'ishah both narrated that the Messenger of Allāh forbade women from shaving their heads.[1066] ᶜAbdullāh ibn ᶜAbbās narrated that the Prophet ﷺ said: "Women do not have to shave their heads; they may only shorten their hair".[1067] Ḥasan al-Baṣrī said: "A *muḥrim* woman will shorten (hair) from her forehead".[1068] In ᶜAṭā''s opinion, while cutting her hair, a woman should cut it off form the sides.[1069]

How much to shave or shorten?

It is better for men to shave their whole head. If someone shaves less than the quarter of his head then it will not suffice; but if one shaves at least a quarter of the head then this will suffice, though it is disliked, because the Sunnah is to shave the whole head. Those who shorten their hair must cut more than the length of the tip of a finger from all over the head.[1070]

Women should cut off the sides of the hair about the length of the tip of the finger.[1071] Ibn ᶜUmar said: "When a woman wants to cut her hair, she may hold her hair at the front and cut it off about the length of the tip of a finger".[1072] The same has been narrated from Ibrāhīm al-Nakhaᶜī.[1073]

1064 al-Kāsānī, *Badā'iᶜ al-ṣanā'iᶜ*, iii. 99.
1065 ibid., 100.
1066 al-Tirmidhī, *k. al-ḥajj, b. mā jā'a fī karāhiyat al-ḥalq li al-nisā'.*
1067 Abū Dāwūd, *k. al-manāsik, b. al-ḥalq wa al-taqṣīr.*
1068 Ibn Abī Shaybah, *al-Muṣannaf*, viii. 81.
1069 ibid.
1070 al-Kāsānī, *Badā'iᶜ al-ṣanā'iᶜ*, iii. 101.
1071 ibid., iii. 100.
1072 Ibn Abī Shaybah, *al-Muṣannaf*, viii. 81.
1073 ibid.

The wisdom

Shāh Walīullah writes: "The significance of shaving is that by it a method of coming out of the state of *iḥrām* is determined which is not opposed to dignity. If people were left to their own judgement everyone would be acting the way he liked. Besides, it marks the termination of the state of dishevelment that was desired earlier. It is like the turning of the face (*salam*) in *ṣalāh*".[1074]

6. *ṬAWĀF AL-ṢADR* (FAREWELL CIRCUMAMBULATION)

Ṣadr means returning. This *ṭawāf* is done before the pilgrim leaves Makkah to return home. It is also called *ṭawāf al-wadāᶜ*, (farewell circumambulation) as it means seeing of the House or saying farewell to the House and should be the last thing one does before departing Makkah. This *ṭawāf* is *wājib*[1075]. ᶜAbdullāh ibn ᶜUmar narrated that ᶜUmar said: "No pilgrim should return until he does the *ṭawāf* of the House. The last rite of *ḥajj* is *ṭawāf* around the House".[1076] ᶜAbdullāh ibn ᶜAbbās reported that the people used to return through every path, whereupon Allāh's Messenger ﷺ said: "None amongst you should depart until he performs the last *ṭawāf* round the House".[1077] ᶜAbdullāh ibn ᶜUmar narrated that the Messenger of Allāh ﷺ forbade the man to leave until he had contact with the House (he did *ṭawāf* as the last rite of the *ḥajj*).[1078]

However, this *ṭawāf* is not *wājib* on menstruating women, and those in a state of postnatal bleeding.[1079] ᶜAbdullāh ibn ᶜAbbās narrated: "The people were ordered to perform the *ṭawāf* of the Kaᶜbah (*ṭawāf-al-wadāᶜ*) as the last thing before leaving (Makkah), except the menstruating women who were excused".[1080] ᶜĀ'ishah narrated: "Ṣafiyyah bint Huyayy, the wife of the Prophet, got her menses, and the Messenger of Allāh

1074 al-Dihlawī, *Ḥujjatullāh al-bālighah*, ii. 94.

1075 al-Kāsānī, *Badā'iᶜ al-ṣanā'iᶜ*, iii. 104.

1076 Mālik, *al-Muwaṭṭa'* 198.

1077 al-Bukhārī, *k. al-ḥajj, b. wujūb ṭawāf al-wadāᶜ*; Muslim, *k. al-ḥajj, b. wujūb ṭawāf al-wadāᶜ wa suqūṭihī ᶜan al-ḥā'iḍ*.

1078 Ibn Mājah, *k. al-manāsik, b. ṭawāf al-wadāᶜ*.

1079 al-Samarqandī, *Tuḥfat al-fuqahā'* 203.

1080 al-Bukhārī, *k. al-ḥajj, b. wujūb ṭawāf al-wadāᶜ;* Muslim *k. al-ḥajj, b. wujūb ṭawāf al-wadāᶜ wa suqūṭihī ᶜan al-ḥā'iḍ*.

was informed of this. He said: 'Would she delay us?' It was said: 'She has already performed *ṭawāf-al-ifāḍah*'. He said: 'Therefore, she will not (delay us)'."[1081] ᶜIkrimah narrated: "The people of Madīnah asked Ibn ᶜAbbās about a woman who got her menses after performing *ṭawāf-al-ifāḍah*. He said: 'She could depart (from Makkah)'. They said: 'We will not act on your verdict and ignore the verdict of Zayd'. Ibn ᶜAbbās said: 'When you reach Madīnah, inquire about it'. So, when they reached Madīnah they asked (about it). One of those whom they asked was Umm Sulaym and she informed them of the narration of Ṣafiyyah'." [1082] Ibn ᶜAbbās said: "A menstruating woman is allowed to leave Makkah if she has done the *ṭawāf al-ifāḍah*".[1083] The same has been narrated from Saᶜd ibn Mālik and Ḥasan ibn ᶜAlī. [1084] Imām Muḥammad says: "*Ṭawāf al-ṣadr* is *wājib* on the pilgrim, and whoever leaves it has to offer a sacrifice, except a menstruating woman, and one in the state of post childbirth bleeding, they can leave Makkah without this *ṭawāf* if they want to. This is the opinion of Abū Ḥanīfah and most of our jurists."[1085]

Duᶜā' when leaving Makkah

The *ṭawāf al-ṣadr* is the last rite that one has to do before leaving Makkah. ᶜAṭā' ibn Abī Rabāḥ says: "One finishes everything, and when nothing is left other than riding home then one should ride, and do *ṭawāf* and leave". [1086] When departing, it is recommended that one should supplicate to Allāh expressing one's love for the House and asking His forgiveness. It is narrated that ᶜAbdullāh ibn ᶜAbbās used to say the following words upon his leaving:

اَللَّهُمَّ إِنِّي عَبْدُكَ، وَابْنُ عَبْدِكَ، وَابْنُ أَمَتِكَ، حَمَلْتَنِي عَلَى مَا سَخَّرْتَ لِي مِنْ خَلْقِكَ، وَسَتَّرْتَنِي فِي بِلَادِكَ حَتَّى بَلَّغْتَنِي بِنِعْمَتِكَ إِلَى بَيْتِكَ، وَأَعَنْتَنِي عَلَى أَدَاءِ نُسُكِي، فَإِنْ كُنْتَ رَضِيتَ عَنِّي

1081 al-Bukhārī, *k. al-maghāzī, b. ḥajjat al-wadāᶜ*; Muslim, *k. al-ḥajj, b. wujūb ṭawāf al-wadāᶜ wa suqūṭihī ᶜan al-ḥā'iḍ*.

1082 Muslim *k. al-ḥajj, b. wujūb ṭawāf al-wadāᶜ wa suqūṭihī ᶜan al-ḥā'iḍ*.

1083 Ibn Abī Shaybah, *al-Muṣannaf*, viii. 141.

1084 ibid.

1085 Muhammad, *al-Muwaṭṭa'*, 173.

1086 Ibn Abī Shaybah, *al-Muṣannaf*, viii. 622.

فَازْدَدْ عَنِّي رِضًا ، وَإِلَّا فَمِنَ الْآنَ فَارْضَ عَنِّي قَبْلَ أَنْ تَنْأَى عَنْ بَيْتِكَ دَارِي ، فَهَذَا أَوَانُ انْصِرَافِي إِنْ أَذِنْتَ لِي غَيْرَ مُسْتَبْدِلٍ بِكَ وَلَا بِبَيْتِكَ ، وَلَا رَاغِبٍ عَنْكَ ، وَلَا عَنْ بَيْتِكَ ، اللَّهُمَّ فَاصْحَبْنِي الْعَافِيَةَ فِي بَدَنِي ، وَالصِّحَّةَ فِي جِسْمِي ، وَالْعِصْمَةَ فِي دِينِي ، وَأَحْسِنْ مُنْقَلَبِي ، وَارْزُقْنِي طَاعَتَكَ مَا أَبْقَيْتَنِي ، وَاجْمَعْ لِي بَيْنَ خَيْرَيِ الدُّنْيَا وَالْآخِرَةِ ، إِنَّكَ عَلَى كُلِّ شَيْءٍ قَدِيرٌ

"O Allāh! I am your slave, son of your slave, son of your maid slave. You enabled me to mount what You subjected to my service of Your creation. You protected me in this land of Yours, until You, by Your grace, brought me to Your House. You helped me perform the rites of *ḥajj*. O Allāh! If You are pleased with me, increase Your pleasure with me. Otherwise, grant me Your pleasure before I depart from Your House. O Allāh! Now is the time for me to depart, by Your leave, without changing (my attitude) toward You and Your House, nor turning away from You or Your House. O Allāh! grant me health in my body, purity in my religion, bless my return, and help me to obey You as long as You cause me to live, and combine for me the good of this world and the world to come. You have power over all things". [1087]

7. THE ORDER OF THE ACTIONS

According to Abū Ḥanīfah, the order in which one does the *farḍ* and *wājib* actions are *wājib* in *ḥajj*.[1088] Anas ibn Mālik reported that: "Allāh's Messenger ﷺ came to Mina; he went to the *Jamrah* and threw pebbles at it, after which he went to his lodging in Minā, and sacrificed the animal. He then called for a barber and, turning his right side to him, let him shave him; after which he trimmed his left side. He then gave (those hairs) to the people".[1089]

1087 al-Ḥanbalī, *al-Mubdiʿ fī sharḥ al-muqniʿ, k. al-manāsik, b. ṣifat al-ḥajj.*

1088 al-Kāsānī, *Badāʾiʿ al-ṣanāʾiʿ*, iii. 147-8.

1089 al-Bukhārī, *k. al-wuḍūʾ, b. al-māʾ alladhī yughsalu bihī shaʿr al-insān;* Muslim, *k. al-ḥajj, b. bayān anna al-sunnah yawm al-naḥr an yarmiya thumma yanḥara thumma yaḥliq.*

According to Abū Yūsuf, Muḥammad and most scholars, the order of the actions is not *wājib*; rather it is Sunnah.[1090] ᶜAbdullāh ibn ᶜAmr ibn al-ᶜĀṣ narrated that: "The Messenger of Allāh ﷺ stood up in the Farewell *Ḥajj* in Minā for the people who were asking him questions. A man came and said: 'I did not realise and I shaved my head before sacrificing. The Prophet ﷺ said: 'Slaughter and there is no harm'. Another man came and said: 'I did not realise, and I sacrificed before doing the *ramy*'. The Prophet ﷺ said: 'Do *ramy* and there is no harm'. The Prophet ﷺ was not asked (about) anything brought forward or delayed from its place, but he said: 'Do and there is no harm'". [1091]

Today, the slaughtering is done by companies often organised through the travel operator. In such a situation, one should try one's best to obtain the timing of the slaughter and shave or shorten the hair accordingly. However, it may not be possible or is very difficult for the pilgrims to know the exact time of the slaughtering, in which case there is no harm for them if they shave or shorten their hair before slaughtering.

1090 al-Kāsānī, *Badāʾiᶜ al-ṣanāʾiᶜ*, iii. 148.

1091 al-Bukhārī, *k. al-ᶜilm, b. al-futyā wa huwa wāqif ᶜalā al-dābbah wa ghayrihā;* Muslim, *k. al-ḥajj, b. man ḥalaqa qabl al-naḥr, aw naḥara qabl al-ramy.*

CHAPTER 4: SUNNAHS OF THE *ḤAJJ*

THE FOLLOWING ARE Sunnah acts in the *ḥajj*:

1- *Ṭawāf al-qudūm*: This *ṭawāf* is the first thing that one does on arrival at Makkah for *ḥajj*, and it is a Sunnah. [1092]

2- Spending the night in Muzdalifah after leaving ᶜArafah is Sunnah; because the Messenger of Allāh spent the night there. It is disliked to pass by Muzdalifah and not spend the night there. [1093]

3- Leaving Muzdalifah for Minā after *Fajr* Prayer before the sun rise.[1094] It is reported that the Messenger of Allāh ﷺ said: "The people of *Jāhiliyyah* (pre-Islamic period) used to leave this place after sunrise, and we leave before the sunrise". [1095]

4- The sequence of the *ramy* of each *jamrah*. The order is Sunnah; it is confirmed that the Prophet ﷺ began with the first *jamrah* near Minā and then proceed to the middle *jamrah* further away, and finally he would go to *Jamrah al-ᶜAqabah*. Likewise, it is has come in a sound, well-known ḥadīth that he said: "Take your religious rites from me".[1096]

5- Spending the nights of the Days of Sacrifice in Minā. Spending three nights or two nights, the 11th and 12th of *Dhū al-ḥijjah*, at Minā is Sunnah. It is disliked to spend those days somewhere else other than Minā. [1097] The Prophet ﷺ spent those nights at Mina[1098] and allowed al-ᶜAbbās to spend the nights at Makkah. This is proof that spending nights in Minā is not *wājib*; rather it is Sunnah. ᶜAbdullāh ibn ᶜUmar reported that: "Al-ᶜAbbās ibn ᶜAbd al-Muṭṭalib sought permission from Allāh's Messenger ﷺ to spend in Makkah the nights (which he was required to spend) at Minā on account of his office of supplier of water, and the

1092 al-Kāsānī, *Badā'iᶜ al-ṣanā'iᶜ*, iii. 119.

1093 ibid., iii. 141.

1094 ibid., iii. 142.

1095 *Mishkāt al-maṣābīḥ, k. al-manāsik, b. al-dafᶜ min ᶜArafah* .

1096 Muslim, *k. al-ḥajj, b. istiḥbāb ramy jamrat al-ᶜaqabah yawm al-naḥr*; Abū Dāwūd, *k. al-manāsik, b. fī ramy al-jimār.*

1097 al-Kāsānī, *Badā'iᶜ al-ṣanā'iᶜ*, iii. 149.

1098 Abū Dāwūd, *k. al-manāsik, b. fī ramy al-jimār.*

Prophet ﷺ granted him permission".[1099] ᶜĀṣim ibn ᶜAdī reported that the Prophet ﷺ excused the shepherds from sleeping at Minā.[1100]

ᶜAbdullāh ibn ᶜAbbās said: "After you have thrown the pebbles you may spend the night wherever you want".[1101] ᶜAbdullāh ibn ᶜUmar disliked one sleeping the night in Makkah during the days of Minā.[1102] Mujāhid said: "There is no harm if one spends the first portion of the night in Makkah and the last in Minā, as there is no harm if one spends the first portion in Minā and the last one in Makkah".[1103]

ᶜAbdullāh ibn ᶜUmar narrated that ᶜUmar ibn al-Khaṭṭāb said: "No one among the pilgrims should spend the nights of Minā beyond ᶜAqabah". Imām Muḥammad says after narrating this: "We adhere to this, it is not appropriate for any pilgrim to spend the nights anywhere other than Minā. If one spends the nights anywhere other than Minā, it is disliked and there is no *kaffārah* on him. This is the opinion of Abū Ḥanīfah and most of our jurists".[1104]

One may return to Makkah before sunset on the 12th of *Dhū al-ḥijjah.* However, if one does not leave Minā before sunset, then it is disliked to leave before the sunrise of the 13th *Dhū al-ḥijjah.* After sunrise one must complete the *ramy* of all three pillars and then leave for Makkah.[1105]

1099 al-Bukhārī, *k. al-ḥajj, b. siqāyat al-ḥājj*; Muslim, *k. al-ḥajj, b. wujūb al-mabīt bi minā ....*

1100 al-Tirmidhī, *k. al-ḥajj, b. mā jā'a fī al-rukhṣah li al-riᶜā' an yarmū yawman wa yadaᶜū yawman.*

1101 Ibn Abī Shaybah, *al-Muṣannaf,* viii. 446.

1102 ibid., viii. 445.

1103 ibid., viii. 445.

1104 Muhammad, *al-Muwaṭṭa',* 168.

1105 al-Kāsānī, *Badā'iᶜ al-ṣanā'iᶜ*, iii. 149.

Chapter 5: A description of *Ḥajj*

When one intends to enter into *iḥrām,* one should makes *ghusl* or *wuḍū'* - although *ghusl* is preferable, then puts on two new or freshly washed cloths, the *izār* and the *ridā',* puts on perfume, prayers two *rakʿahs,* then says:

اَللَّهُمَّ إِنِّي أُرِيدُ الْحَجَّ فَيَسِّرْهُ لِي وَتَقَبَّلْهُ مِنِّي

"O Allāh, I intend to make the *ḥajj,* so make it easy for me and accept it from me".

One should then pronounce the *talbiyah*:

لَبَّيْكَ اللَّهُمَّ لَبَّيْكَ، لَبَّيْكَ لَا شَرِيكَ لَكَ لَبَّيْكَ، إِنَّ الْحَمْدَ وَالنِّعْمَةَ لَكَ وَالْمُلْكَ لَا شَرِيكَ لَكَ

If one intends only the *ḥajj,* one should make the intention for *ḥajj* with the *talbiyah.* One should thereafter often recite the *talbiyah;* at the end of each *ṣalāh* or every time one ascends a hill, descends into a valley, or meets riders, and in the last part of the night.

On entering Makkah, one commences with *al-Masjid al-Ḥarām* and on first sight of it, one should say: اَللَّهُ أَكْبَرُ، لَا إِلَهَ إِلَّا اللَّهُ "Allāh is greater" and "There is no god only Allāh". Then proceed to the Black Stone and facing it say: اَللَّهُ أَكْبَرُ "Allāh is greater", raising one's hands with the *takbīr* and لَا إِلَهَ إِلَّا اللَّهُ "There is no god, only Allāh". One should greet the Black Stone and kisses it if one is able to do so without molesting any other pilgrims. Then one should walk to the right by the door of the Kaʿbah having previously adjusted one's *rida'* to bare the right shoulder. Then one makes *ṭawāf* of the House seven times, ensuring that one goes around the Hatim, walking quickly in the first three rounds and at a calm and measured pace during the rest. One greets the Black Stone every time one passes by it if one is able and seals the *ṭawāf* with the greeting.

Following the completion of the *ṭawāf* one comes to the *Maqām* of Ibrāhīm and offers two *rakʿahs* of prayer there. If one is unable to offer the prayer at the *Maqām* then one should do so anywhere in the Mosque – and this *ṭawāf* is the *ṭawāf* of arrival.

Then one goes out to the hill of Ṣafā, climbs on to it, faces the House and says: اَللهُ أَكْبَرُ، لَا إِلَهَ إِلَّا اللهُ "Allāh is greater. There is no god, only Allāh", and invokes blessings on the Prophet ﷺ. One makes duʿā' to Allāh for his needs and then goes down towards the hill of Marwah walking at a calm and measured pace until one reaches the lower parts, where one walks at a brisk pace from the first green marker (lights) until one reaches the second. One continues upwards to Marwah, climbs up onto it and does the same as one did on Ṣafā – this will be one circuit. One then repeats the same back to Ṣafā and so on until one has completed seven circuits, which will end on Marwah.

One then stays in Makkah in *iḥrām* and makes *ṭawāf* of the House as much as one wants.

The day before the *Yawm al-Tarwiyah* i.e. Day of Watering (8th *Dhū al-ḥijjah*), the *imām* makes a speech in which he informs the pilgrims about going to Minā, about the *ṣalāh*, the stopping at ʿArafah, and the *ṭawāf.* After the pilgrims have made the *Fajr* Prayer on the Day of Watering in Makkah, they set out for Minā and stay there. Then on the Day of ʿArafah (9th *Dhū al-ḥijjah*), after offering the *Fajr* Prayer, and after sunrise the pilgrims set out for Arafah. When the sun has just gone past its zenith, the *imām* leads the people in the *Ẓuhr* and *ʿAṣr Prayers* – beginning, before the *ṣalāh*, with two *khuṭbahs* in which he informs the people of the *ṣalāh*, the stopping at ʿArafah and Muzdalifah, the stoning of the *jamrahs*, the sacrifice, the shaving of the head and the *ṭawāf* of the House. This will be done at the time of *Ẓuhr* with an *adhān* and two *iqāmahs*. Anyone who offers the *ṣalāh* alone offers each of the two *ṣalāhs* separately in their respective times according to Abū Ḥanīfah, while Abū Yūsuf and Muḥammad both say that one combines the two. Then the pilgrim finds a place to stay as near as possible to the mountain and offers *duʿā'* as much as one is able to. The whole of ʿArafah is a 'place of staying' except for its lower valley. For the pilgrims who travel with a group, the *imām* of the group should stop at ʿArafah and make *duʿā'* and inform the people of the rites. It is recommended that one takes a *ghusl* before standing at ʿArafah and make every effort to increase one's *duʿā's.*

When the sun has set, the *imām* and the people move down at their leisure until they reach Muzdalifah and make camp there. It is recommended they make camp near the mountain located there called Quzaḥ. The *imām* leads the people in the *ṣalāhs* of *Maghrib* and *ʿIshā'* with an *adhān* and one *iqāmah*, and it is not permitted for anyone to offer the *Maghrib Ṣalāh* on the way there, according to Abū Ḥanīfah and Muḥammad.

The pilgrims stay at Muzdalifah and at dawn, the *imām* leads the people in the *Fajr* Prayer when it is still dark, and stands with the people to makes *duʿā'*. All of Muzdalifah is a 'place of staying' except for the valley of Muḥassar.

Then the *imām* together with the people move on before sunrise until they reach Minā and then begin the stoning of the *Jamrah al-ʿAqabah* with seven pebbles saying: اَللّٰهُ أَكْبَرُ "Allāh is greater" for every pebble. The pilgrims will stop reciting the *talbiyah* after the first pebble is thrown. Then the pilgrims offers the sacrifices if he wishes, shaves his head or trims some hair, although it is better to shave, and then everything except sexual relation becomes permitted.

Then one goes back to Makkah on the same day, or the next morning, or the morning after that and makes *ṭawāf al-ifāḍah* of the House. If one had done *saʿy* between Ṣafā and Marwah at the end of one's [first] *ṭawāf* of arrival, then one does not do *ramal* in the first three rounds of this *ṭawāf* and does not have to do another *saʿy* ; if one had not made the *saʿy*, then one does *ramal* in this *ṭawāf* and makes *saʿy* after as we have mentioned earlier. After *ṭawāf al-ifāḍah* sexual relation also becomes permitted. This *ṭawāf* is *farḍ* and delaying it after this time is disliked; and if one does delay it, then one must offer a sacrifice according to Abū Ḥanīfah.

One then goes back to Minā and stays there. When the sun has gone past the zenith on the second day of the three Days of Sacrifice, one stones the *jamrahs* beginning with the one near the mosque. One stones it with seven pebbles, saying: اَللّٰهُ أَكْبَرُ "Allāh is greater" and then stands there making *duʿā'*; then one proceeds and stones the next *jamrah* and also stands by it; then one stones the last *jamrah* in the same way but does not stand by it.

The following day one stones the three *jamrahs* in the same way, after the sun has past its zenith. If one wants to leave early, then one leaves for Makkah, but if one stays, then one stones the three *jamrahs* on the fourth day after the sun has past its zenith – although it is permitted to perform the stoning after sunrise and before the sun has past its zenith, according to Abū Ḥanīfah.

After arriving in Makkah the pilgrims will make the final *ṭawāf* of the House without doing *ramal* and this is the *ṭawāf al-ṣadr* – the Farewell *Ṭawāf*.

Where women differ from men

The same applies to a woman as it does to a man in all of this -other than that she does not uncover her head but uncovers her face, does not raise her voice when declaring the *talbiyah,* does not do *ramal* in the first three circumambulations of the *ṭawāf* between the two green markers, and does not shave, but rather trims her hair. These details have been mentioned earlier in their relevant places.

THE *ḤAJJ* OF THE PROPHET

The Prophet ﷺ did one *ḥajj* only. That *ḥajj* is called *Ḥajjat al-Wadāᶜ* (the Farewell *Ḥajj*). It was attended by a large number of Companions, and many of them have described this *ḥajj* of the Prophet. Though they agree on most details, nevertheless they differ on some. I will present here a few well narrated descriptions which have come down through sound chains of narration.

Jaᶜfar al-Ṣādiq ibn Muḥammad al-Bāqir reported on the authority of his father: "We went to Jābir ibn ᶜAbdullāh and he began inquiring about the people (who had gone to see him) until it was my turn. I said: 'I am Muḥammad ibn ᶜAlī ibn Ḥusayn'. He placed his hand upon my head and opened my upper button and then the lower one and then placed his palm on my chest (in order to bless me.) I was, during those days, a young boy, and he said: 'You are welcome, my nephew. Ask whatever you want to ask'. And I asked him. He was a blind man. The time for prayer came. He stood up covering himself in his mantle. And whenever he placed its ends upon his shoulders they slipped off because they were short. Another mantle was lying on the clothes rack nearby (but he did not use it). He led us in the prayer. (After that) I said to him to tell me about the *ḥajj* of Allāh's Messenger ﷺ. He indicated nine with his fingers and said: 'The Messenger of Allāh ﷺ stayed in Madīnah for nine years but did not perform the *ḥajj,* then he made a public announcement in the tenth year to the effect that he ﷺ was going to perform the *ḥajj.* A large number of people came to Madīnah anxious to emulate the Messenger of Allāh ﷺ and follow his actions. We set out with him untill we reached Dhū al-Ḥulayfah. Asmā' the daughter of ᶜUmays gave birth to Muḥammad ibn Abū Bakr. She sent a message to the Messenger of Allāh ﷺ asking him: 'What should I do?' He (the Prophet) replied: 'Take a bath, bandage your private parts and put on *iḥrām*'. The Messenger of

Allāh ﷺ then prayed in the mosque and then mounted al-Qaṣwā' (his she-camel) and it stood erect with him on its back at al-Baydā'. And far as I could see in front of me, on my right, on my left, and behind me I saw riders and pedestrians. The Messenger of Allāh ﷺ was prominent among us and the (revelation) of the Holy Qur'ān was descending upon him, and it is he who knows its (true) significance. Whatever he did, we also did. He pronounced the Oneness of Allāh (saying): '*Labbayk*, O Allāh, *Labbayk, Labbayk*, You have no partner, praise and grace is Yours and the Sovereignty too; You have no partner,' and the people also pronounced this *talbiyah* which they pronounce (to this day). The Messenger of Allāh ﷺ did not reject anything of that (*talbiyah*), but he adhered to his own *talbiyah*'. Jābir (continued and) said: 'We did not have any other intention but that of *ḥajj* only, being unaware of the *ᶜumrah* at that time. When we came with him to the House, he touched the pillar and (made seven circuits) running three of them and walking four. And then going to the Station of Ibrāhīm, he recited: '*And adopt the Station of Ibrāhīm as a place of prayer*'. He stood at a place where the Station (of Ibrāhīm) was between him and the House. The Messenger of Allāh ﷺ recited in two *rakᶜahs*: '*Say: He is Allāh, One...*, and '*Say, O unbelievers...*' He then returned to *al-Ḥajar al-Aswad* (the Black Stone) and kissed it and (then) went out of the gate to al-Ṣafā; as he reached near it he recited: '*Al-Ṣafā and al-Marwah are among the signs appointed by Allāh,*' (and said) 'I begin with what Allāh began with (in the Qur'ān)'. He first mounted al-Ṣafā until he saw the House, and facing the *Qiblah* he declared the Oneness of Allāh and glorified Him, and said: 'There is no god but Allāh, One, there is no partner with Him. His is the Sovereignty, to Him praise is due, and He is Powerful over everything. There is no god but Allāh alone, Who fulfilled His promise, helped His servant and routed the confederates alone'. He then made supplication in the course of that saying such words three times. He thereafter descended and walked towards al-Marwah, and when his feet came down in the bottom of the valley, he ran, and when he began to ascend he walked till he reached al-Marwah. There he did as he had done at al-Ṣafā. When it was his last round of Marwah he said: 'If I had known beforehand what I have come to know afterwards, I would not have brought sacrificial animals and would have performed an *ᶜumrah.* So, he who among you who has not brought sacrificial animals with him should take off *iḥrām* and treat it as an *ᶜumrah*'. Surāqah ibn Mālik ibn Juᶜshum got up and said, 'Messenger of Allāh, does it apply to the present year, or does it apply forever?' Thereupon, the Messenger of Allāh ﷺ intertwined the fingers (of one hand) into the other and said twice: 'The *ʿumrah* has become incorporated into the *ḥajj*,' (adding) 'No (not just the present year), but forever and ever'.

ʿAlī came from the Yemen with the sacrificial animals for the Prophet ﷺ and found Fāṭimah to be one among those who had taken off *iḥrām* and had put on dyed clothes and had applied antimony. He (ʿAlī) showed disapproval of it, whereupon she said: 'My father has commanded me to do this'. (The narrator added that) ʿAlī used to say in Iraq: 'I went to the Messenger of Allāh ﷺ showing annoyance at Fāṭimah for what she had done, and asked the (verdict) of Allāh's Messenger ﷺ regarding what she had narrated from him, and told him that I was angry with her, whereupon he said: 'She has told the truth, she has told the truth'. (The Prophet then asked ʿAlī): 'What did you say when you undertook to go for *ḥajj*? I (ʿAlī) said: 'O Allāh, I am putting on *iḥrām* for the same purpose as Your Messenger has put it on'. He (the Prophet) said: 'I have sacrificial animals with me, so do not take off the *iḥrām*'.

He (Jābir) said: 'The total number of those sacrificial animals brought by ʿAlī from the Yemen and of those brought by the Messenger ﷺ was one hundred. Then all the people except the Messenger of Allāh ﷺ and those who had sacrificial animals with them, took off *iḥrām*, and had their hair trimmed; when it was the day of *Tarwiyah* (8th of *Dhū al-ḥijjah*) they went to Minā and put on the *iḥrām* for *ḥajj* and the Messenger of Allāh ﷺ rode and led there the *Ẓuhr*, *ʿAṣr*, *Maghrib*, *ʿIshā'* and *Fajr* prayers. He then waited a little till the sun rose, and commanded that a tent should be pitched at Namirah. The Messenger of Allāh ﷺ then set out and the Quraysh did not doubt that he would halt at al-Mashʿar al-ḥarām (Muzdalifah) as the Quraysh used to do in the pre-Islamic period. The Messenger of Allāh ﷺ however, passed on till he came to ʿArafah and he found that the tent had been pitched for him at Namirah. He stopped there until the sun had passed the meridian and commanded that Al-Qaswa be brought and saddled for him. Then he came to the bottom of the valley, and addressed the people saying: 'Verily your blood, your property are as sacred and inviolable as the sacredness of this day of yours, in this month of yours, in this town of yours. Behold! Everything pertaining to the

Days of Ignorance is under my foot, completely abolished. Abolished are also the blood-revenges of the Days of Ignorance. The first claim of ours on blood-revenge which I abolish is that of the son of Rabīᶜah ibn al-Ḥārith, who was nursed among the tribe of Saᶜd and killed by Hudhayl. And the usury of the pre-Islamic period is abolished, and the first of our usury that I abolish is that of ᶜAbbās ibn ᶜAbd al-Muṭṭalib, for it is all abolished. Fear Allāh concerning women! Verily you have taken them on the security of Allāh, and intercourse with them has been made lawful to you by words of Allāh. You too have (rights) over them, that they should not allow anyone to sit on your bed whom you do not like. But if they do that, you can chastise them but not severely. Their rights upon you are that you should provide them with food and clothing in a fitting manner. I have left among you the Book of Allāh, and if you hold fast to it, you would never go astray. And you would be asked about me (on the Day of Resurrection), (now tell me) what would you say?' They (the audience) said: 'We will bear witness that you have conveyed (the message), discharged (the ministry of Prophethood) and given wise counsel'. He (the narrator) said: 'He (the Prophet) then raised his forefinger towards the sky and pointing it at the people (said): 'O Allāh, be witness. O Allāh, be witness,' saying it thrice. The *adhān* was called and later the *iqāmah,* and he (the Prophet) led the *Ẓuhr* Prayer, then *iqāmah* was called (again) and he (the Prophet) led the *ᶜAṣr* Prayer and he observed no other prayer in between the two. The Messenger of Allāh ﷺ then mounted his camel and came to the place where he was to stay. He made his she-camel, al-Qaṣwā', turn towards the rocky side, with the pedestrian path lying in front of him. He faced the *Qiblah,* and stood there until the sun set, and the yellow light diminished somewhat, and the disc of the sun totally disappeared. He made Usāmah sit behind him, and he pulled the bridle of al-Qaṣwā' so forcefully that its head touched the saddle, and he indicated to the people with his right hand to moderate (their speed). Whenever he happened to pass over an elevated tract of sand, he slightly relaxed the bridle of his camel until she climbed up. This is how he reached al-Muzdalifah. There he led the *Maghrib* and *ᶜIshā'* Prayers with one *adhān* and two *iqāmahs* and did not glorify (Allāh) in between them (i.e. he did not observe supererogatory *rakᶜah*s). The Messenger of Allāh ﷺ then lay down until (it was) dawn and offered the *Fajr* Prayer with an *adhān* and *iqāmah* when the morning light was clear. He again mounted al-Qaṣwā', and when he came to al-Mashʿar al-Ḥarām, he faced the *Qiblah*, supplicated to Allāh, Glorified Him, and pronounced His Uniqueness and Oneness, and kept standing until the daylight was very clear. He then went quickly before the sun (fully) rose, and seated behind him was al-Faḍl ibn ʿAbbās and he was a man with beautiful hair, a fair complexion and handsome face. As the Messenger of Allāh ﷺ was moving on, there was also a group of women passing. Al-Faḍl began to look at them. The Messenger of Allāh ﷺ put his hand on (one side of) the face of al-Faḍl who then turned his face to the other side, and began to look, and the Messenger of Allāh ﷺ turned his hand to the other side and put it on the (other side of the) face of al-Faḍl. He again turned his face to the other side till he came to the bottom of Muḥassar. He urged her (al-Qaṣwā') a little, and, following the middle road, which comes out at the greatest *jamrah*, he came to the *jamrah* which is near the tree. At this he threw seven small pebbles, saying *Allāhu Akbar* while throwing each of them in the manner in which small pebbles are thrown (i.e. using the fingers) and this he did at the bottom of the valley. He then went to the place of sacrifice, and sacrificed sixty-three (camels) with his own hand. Then he gave the remaining number to ʿAlī who sacrificed them, and shared the sacrifice with him. He then commanded that a piece of flesh from each animal sacrificed should be put in a pot, and when it was cooked, both of them (the Prophet and ʿAlī) took some meat out of it and drank the broth. The Messenger of Allāh ﷺ again rode and came to the House, and offered the *Ẓuhr* Prayer at Makkah. He came to the people of ʿAbd al-Muṭṭalib, who were supplying water at *Zamzam*, and said: "Draw water, O Banī ʿAbd al-Muṭṭalib! Were it not that people might usurp this right of supplying water from you, I would have drawn it along with you'. So they handed him a bowl and he drank from it'."[1106]

ʿĀ'ishah narrated: "We set out with the Prophet ﷺ with the intention of performing *ḥajj* only. The Prophet ﷺ reached Makkah and performed *ṭawāf* of the Kaʿbah and between Ṣafā and Marwah and did not finish the *iḥrām*, because he had the *hady* with him. His Companions and his wives performed *ṭawāf* (of the Kaʿbah and between Ṣafā and Marwah), and those who had no *hady* with them finished their *iḥrām*. I got the menses and performed all the ceremonies of *ḥajj*. So, when the Night

1106 Muslim, *k. al-ḥajj, b. ḥajjat al-nabī ṣallallāhu ʿalayhi wa sallam.*

of Ḥaṣbah (Night of Departure) came, I said: 'O Allāh's Apostle! All your Companions are returning with *ḥajj* and *ᶜumrah* except me'. He asked me: 'Didn't you perform *ṭawāf* of the Kaᶜbah when you reached Makkah?' I said: 'No'. He said: 'Go to Tanᶜīm with your brother ᶜAbd al-Raḥmān, and assume *iḥrām* for *ᶜumrah* and I will wait for you at such and such a place'. So I went with ᶜAbd al-Raḥmān to Tanᶜīm and assumed *iḥrām* for *ᶜumrah*. Then Ṣafiyyah bint Ḥuyayy got the menses. The Prophet ﷺ said: '*ᶜAqrā ḥalqā*', 'you will detain us. Didn't you perform *ṭawāf al-ifāḍah* on the Day of *Naḥr* (slaughtering)?' She said: 'Yes, I did'. He said: 'Then there is no harm, depart'. So I met the Prophet ﷺ when he was ascending the heights towards Makkah and I was descending, or vice-versa'."[1107]

ᶜAbdullāh ibn ᶜUmar narrated: "During the *Ḥajjat al-Wadāᶜ* of the Messenger of Allāh ﷺ he performed *ᶜumrah* and *ḥajj*. He drove a *hady* along with him from Dhū al-Ḥulayfah. The Messenger of Allāh ﷺ started by assuming *iḥrām* for *ᶜumrah* and *ḥajj*. And the people, too, assumed *iḥrām* for *ᶜumrah* and *ḥajj* along with the Prophet. Some of them brought the *hady* and drove it along with them, while the others did not. So, when the Prophet arrived at Makkah he said to the people: 'Whoever among you has driven the *hady*, should not finish his *iḥrām* till he completes his *ḥajj*'. And whoever among you has not (driven) the *hady* with him, should perform *ṭawāf* of the Kaᶜbah and the *ṭawāf* between Ṣafā and Marwah, then cut short his hair and finish his *iḥrām*, and should later assume *iḥrām* for *ḥajj*; but he must offer a *hady*; and if anyone cannot afford a *hady*, he should fast for three days during the *ḥajj* and seven days when he returns home'. The Prophet performed *ṭawāf* of the Kaᶜbah on his arrival (at Makkah); he touched the corner (Black Stone) first of all and then did *ramal* during the first three rounds around the Kaᶜbah, and during the last four rounds he walked. After finishing *ṭawāf* of the Kaᶜbah, he offered two *rakᶜah* prayer at *Maqām* Ibrāhīm, and after finishing the prayer he went to Ṣafā and Marwah and performed seven rounds of *ṭawāf* between them and did not do any deed forbidden because of *iḥrām*, until he finished all the ceremonies of his *ḥajj* and sacrificed his *hady* on the Day of *Naḥr*. He then hastened onwards (to Makkah)

1107 al-Bukhārī, *k. al-ḥajj, b. kayfa tuhill al-ḥā'iḍ wa al-nufasā'*; Muslim, *k. al-ḥajj, b. bayān wujūh al-iḥrām.*

and performed *ṭawāf* of the Kaᶜbah and then everything that was forbidden because of *iḥrām* became permissible. Those who took and drove the *hady* with them did the same as the Messenger of Allāh ﷺ did'."[1108]

1108 al-Bukhārī, *k. al-ḥajj, b. man saqā al-budna maᶜahu;* Muslim, *k. al-ḥajj, b. wujūb al-dam ᶜalā al-mutamattiᶜ.*

Chapter 6: Types of *Ḥajj*

There are three types of *ḥajj*: 1- *ifrād*, 2- *qirān*, 3- *tamattuᶜ*.

Ḥajj al-ifrād is when one intends *ḥajj* only (not the *ᶜumrah*) at the time of *iḥrām*. According to Imām Shāfiᶜī this is the best type of *ḥajj*. It has been described in an earlier chapter and so we shall now describe the other two types of *ḥajj*.

QIRĀN

The *qirān* is better than the *tamattuᶜ* and *ifrād* according to Ḥanafīs. Imām Muḥammad says: "The *qirān* to us is better than the other types of *ḥajj*, and each of them is good; this is the opinion of Abū Ḥanīfah".[1109] It is also the opinion of Sufyān al-Thawrī.[1110] Many jurists consider that the *ḥajj* of the Prophet ﷺ was the *ḥajj* of *qirān*.[1111] Abū Wā'il says: "We went on *ḥajj*, and with us was al-Ṣubayy ibn Maᶜbad who did *iḥrām* of the *qirān*, and we came to ᶜUmar and al-Ṣubayy mentioned his intention of the *qirān*. ᶜUmar said to him: 'You are guided to the Sunnah of your Prophet ﷺ'."[1112]

A description of *qirān*

The *qirān* is to make intention of *ᶜumrah* and *ḥajj* at the same time from the *mīqāt*. At the end of the *ṣalāh*, one makes intention by saying: "O Allāh! I intend *ᶜumrah* and *ḥajj*, so make them easy for me and accept them of me". On entering Makkah, one begins with the *ṭawāf* of the House seven times, moving quickly in the first three but walking at a measured pace for the rest. After these circumambulations one then completes the *saᶜy* between Ṣafā and Marwah. These are the actions of *ᶜumrah*. Then he makes the *ṭawāf* of arrival after the *saᶜy*, and makes another *saᶜy* between Ṣafā and Marwah for the *ḥajj*, as we have explained

1109 Abū Ḥanīfah, *K. al-āthār* 81.
1110 al-Baghawī, *Sharḥ al-sunnah*, iv. 44.
1111 Ibn Abī Shaybah, *al-Muṣannaf*, viii. 423.
1112 ibid.

in the case of the *ifrād*. Then after stoning the *jamrah* on the Day of Sacrifice, one slaughters a sheep, cow or camel, or offers a seventh part of a camel or cow, and this is the sacrifice of the *qirān*. However, if one does not have anything to sacrifice, one should fast three days on the *ḥajj*, the last of them being the Day of ʿArafah; if one misses the fast and the day of Sacrifice begins, then only a sacrifice will do, and one is required to fast seven days when one returns home, although it is permitted for one to keep these fasts in Makkah after finishing the *ḥajj*.[1113]

Anas ibn Mālik narrated that the Prophet ﷺ did say *talbiyah* of both *ʿumrah* and *ḥajj* together. [1114] Ḥafṣah, the wife of Allāh's Apostle ﷺ said: "Messenger of Allāh, what about people who have taken off their *iḥrām* whereas you have not after your *ʿumrah*?' He said: 'I have put stuff in my hair to make it stick together and I have driven my sacrificial animal, and would not, therefore, take off *iḥrām* until I have sacrificed the animal'."[1115]

Ziyād ibn Mālik narrates that ʿAlī and ʿAbdullāh ibn Masʿūd said: "The *qārin* (one who is performing *qirān*) will do two *ṭawāfs*".[1116] Ḥasan ibn ʿAlī said: "When you do *qirān* then do two *ṭawāfs* and two *saʿys*".[1117] Similar narrations have also been recorded from al-Aswad, Shaʿbī, Abū Jaʿfar, Ḥakam, Ḥammād ibn Abī Sulaymān and Ibrāhīm al-Nakhaʿī.[1118] Imām Muḥammad narrates on the authority of Abū Ḥanīfah from ʿAlī ibn Abī Ṭālib who said: "When you make *iḥrām* of both the *ḥajj* and *ʿumrah*, then perform two *ṭawāfs* for them, and perform two *saʿys* of al-Ṣafā and al-Marwah for both of them". Manṣūr ibn al-Muʿtamir (one narrator of this ḥadīth) said: "I met Mujāhid who gave a *fatwā* of one *ṭawāf* for the one who does *qirān*, then I narrated to him this ḥadīth. He (Mujāhid) said: 'Had I heard it, I would have not given a *fatwā* but of two *ṭawāfs*. As for after this, I will not give *fatwā* but of two'." Imām Muḥammad said of this: "We adhere to this, and this is the opinion of Abū Ḥanīfah".[1119]

1113 al-Qudūrī, *al-Mukhtaṣar* 224-6.

1114 al-Bukhārī, *k. al-maghāzī, b. baʿth ʿalī ibn abī ṭālib…*; Muslim *k. al-ḥajj, b. ihlāl al-nabī…*

1115 al-Bukhārī, *k. al-ḥajj, b. al-tamattuʿ wa al-qirān bi al-ḥajj;* Muslim, *k. al-ḥajj, b. bayān anna al-qārina lā yatahallalu.*

1116 Ibn Abī Shaybah, *al-Muṣannaf*, viii. 430.

1117 ibid., viii. 431.

1118 ibid., viii. 431.

1119 Abū Ḥanīfah, *K. al-āthār* 81.

When the *qirān* becomes *ifrād*

If one does not begin the *qirān* by doing the *ᶜumrah* in Makkah but, instead, goes directly to ᶜArafah, then one has annulled the *ᶜumrah* that one intended. The sacrifice normally due as part of the *qirān* is no longer required, but one must sacrifice in expiation for annulling the *ᶜumrah*, and must also make up the *ᶜumrah* which one failed to do.[1120]

TAMATTUᶜ

Tamattuᶜ is better than *ifrād*.[1121] The one who intends to do *tamattuᶜ* enters a state of *iḥrām* for the *ᶜumrah* at the *mīqāt*. Then, once in Makkah, does the *ṭawāf*, the *saᶜy* after which one will shave or trim one's hair and thereby come out of the state of *iḥrām*.

One will remain in Makkah out of *iḥrām* until the Day of *Tarwiyah* (8th *Dhū al-ḥijjah*), when one will enter into *iḥrām* for the *ḥajj* from *Masjid al-Ḥarām* and does what the *mufrid* (one who has intended *ifrād ḥajj*) does, with the exception that one must sacrifice an animal for the *tamattuᶜ*. If one does not have anything to sacrifice, one fasts three days during the *ḥajj* time and seven days when one returns home.[1122]

Mujāhid says: ᶜAbdullāh ibn ᶜUmar and ᶜAbdullāh ibn ᶜAbbās used to do *ḥajj* of *tamattuᶜ*.[1123] Abū Maᶜn says: "I heard ᶜAbdullāh ibn ᶜUmar, ᶜAbdullah ibn al-Zubayr, Jābir ibn Zayd, Abū al-ᶜAlīyah and Ḥasan al-Baṣrī advising people to do *tamattuᶜ* in *ḥajj*". [1124] The same has been narrated from ᶜAṭā' ibn Abī Rabāḥ, Saᶜīd ibn Jubayr, Mujāhid and al-Ḍaḥḥāk. [1125] Mālik ibn Dinār says: "I asked eight people about *tamattuᶜ* in *ḥajj*, and all of them advised me to do that; (they were) Ḥasan al-Baṣrī, ᶜAṭā' ibn Abī Rabāḥ, Ṭāwūs, Jābir ibn Zayd, Sālim ibn ᶜAbdullāh, ᶜIkrimah, Mujāhid and al-Qāsim".[1126]

1120 al-Qudūrī, *al-Mukhtaṣar* 226.

1121 The person doing *tamattuᶜ* is of two kinds: one who brings the *hady* with him and the other who does not. I am discussing here only about the one who does not bring the *hady*; because the other type does not exist today especially among those people coming from outside.

1122 al-Qudūrī, *al-Mukhtaṣar* 227-8.

1123 Ibn Abī Shaybah, *al-Muṣannaf*, viii. 274.

1124 ibid., viii. 275.

1125 ibid., viii. 275-6.

1126 ibid., viii. 276.

For the residents of Makkah

There is no *tamattuʿ* or *qirān* for the people of Makkah; they have to perform the *ifrād* only.[1127]

1127 al-Qudūrī, *al-Mukhtaṣar* 229.

Chapter 7: Infractions committed during *Ḥajj/ᶜUmrah*

Most infractions committed during the *ḥajj* or *ᶜumrah* will be repaired by *ṣadaqah* or offering a sacrifice. Sacrifice refers to a goat or sheep, cow and camel. A goat or sheep suffices to compensate for every infraction except two instances: anyone doing *ṭawāf al-ziyārah* while in a state of major impurity (*janābah, ḥayḍ* or *nifās*) or anyone having sexual relations after staying in ᶜArafah.[1128] *Ṣadaqah* refers to half a *ṣāᶜ* of wheat.[1129]

These sacrifices, like the sacrifices of *tamattuᶜ* and *qirān* should be done in the *Ḥaram* as narrated from Ṭāwūs, ᶜAṭā', Ḥasan al-Baṣrī and Ibrāhīm al-Nakhaᶜī.[1130]

Applying perfume

Once in a state of *iḥrām,* if one applies perfume to a whole limb like the head, hand or thigh or more than that, then one must offer sacrifice; if one applies perfume to less than a limb, then one pays *ṣadaqah.*[1131]

Putting on sewn cloth

If someone in a state of *iḥrām* puts on sewn clothing or covers the head for a whole day, then he has committed an error and must offer a sacrifice; if less than a whole day, one gives *ṣadaqah.*[1132] ᶜAbdullāh ibn ᶜUmar said: "Whatever is above the chin, it is from the head; the *muḥrim* should not cover it". Imām Muḥammad states after narrating this: "We adhere to Ibn ᶜUmar's opinion; and this is the opinion of Abū Ḥanīfah and most of our jurists".[1133]

1128 al-Marghīnānī, *al-Hidāyah,* ii. 355.
1129 al-Samarqandī, *Tuḥfat al-fuqahā'* 208.
1130 Ibn Abī Shaybah, *al-Muṣannaf,* viii. 167.
1131 al-Qudūrī, *al-Mukhtaṣar* 232.
1132 al-Samarqandī, *Tuḥfat al-fuqahā'* 208-9.
1133 Muhammad, *al-Muwaṭṭa'* 144.

Shaving

If one in a state of *iḥrām* shaves a quarter of his head or more, then one must make a sacrifice; if less than a quarter, then one gives *ṣadaqah.* [1134]

If one applies perfume, or shaves, and wears sewn clothing due to some excuse, then one has the option to slaughter a sheep; or if one wishes, gives three *ṣāᶜs* of wheat in *ṣadaqah* to six destitute people; and if one wishes one fasts three days. [1135] This is based on His saying, may He be exalted: *"If any of you are ill or have a head injury, then the expiation is fasting, ṣadaqah or sacrifice"*.[1136] Kaᶜb ibn ᶜUjrah stated: "The Messenger of Allāh ﷺ came to me on the occasion of Ḥudaybiyyah and I was kindling fire under my cooking pot and lice were creeping on my face. Thereupon, he (the Prophet) said: 'Do the vermin harm your head?' I said: 'Yes'. He said: 'Get your head shaved and (in lieu of it) observe fasts for three days or feed six needy people, or offer the sacrifice (of an animal)'."[1137] Imām Muḥammad says after narrating this ḥadīth: "This is the opinion of Abū Ḥanīfah and most jurists". [1138]

Paring one's nails

If a person in a state of *iḥrām* cuts or trims the nails of his hands or feet, he must offer a sacrifice. If he pares the nails of one hand or one foot, he must also offer a sacrifice; but if he pares less than five nails, then he gives *ṣadaqah.* However, if he pares five different nails from his hands and feet, then he gives *ṣadaqah* according to Abū Ḥanīfah and Abū Yūsuf while according to Muḥammad, he offers a sacrifices. [1139]

Sexual desire

If one in a state of *iḥrām* kisses or touches a woman with desire, then he must offer a sacrifice.[1140] ᶜAbdullāh ibn ᶜAbbās said to someone who kissed his wife in a state of *iḥrām*: "Offer a sacrifice and your *ḥajj* is

1134 al-Qudūrī, *al-Mukhtaṣar* 232.

1135 al-Samarqandī, *Tuḥfat al-fuqahā'* 209.

1136 *al-Baqarah* 196.

1137 al-Bukhārī, *k. al-muḥṣar, b. al-itᶜām fī al-fidyah niṣf ṣāᶜ*; Muslim, *k. al-ḥajj, b. jawāz ḥalq al-ra's li al-muḥrim....*

1138 Muhammad, *al-Muwaṭṭa'*, 169.

1139 al-Qudūrī, *al-Mukhtaṣar,* 233.

1140 ibid. 234.

complete". Imām Muḥammad says after narrating this fatwā of Ibn ᶜAbbās: "We adhere to this … and this is the opinion of Abū Ḥanīfah, and this is what has come to our knowledge from ᶜAṭā' ibn Abī Rabāḥ".[1141] The same opinion has been narrated from ᶜAlī, Saᶜīd ibn Jubayr, Ḥasan al-Baṣrī, al-Zuhrī, Ibrāhīm al-Nakhaᶜī, Ibn Sīrīn, Saᶜīd ibn al-Musayyab, Qatādah, Shaᶜbī and ᶜAbd al-Raḥmān ibn al-Aswad.[1142]

If one has intercourse in one of the two orifices before the 'staying' at ᶜArafah, one has invalidated one's *ḥajj* and must offer a sacrifice. However, one carries on with the *ḥajj* as if it is not invalidated but must make up the *ḥajj*. He is not (as some authorities have claimed) obliged to part from his wife who will be accompanying him as she also has to make up her invalidated *ḥajj*.[1143] ᶜAṭā' and Mujāhid said about the couple who have intimate relations in a state of *iḥrām* before *ṭawāf al-ziyārah*: "Both will continue their *ḥajj*, and on each one is a sacrifice. If they offer one sacrifice that will suffice and they (will) have to do *ḥajj* (again) next year, and do not have to part from each other".[1144]

Whoever has intercourse after the standing at ᶜArafah does not invalidate his *ḥajj* but he must sacrifice a camel. ᶜAbdullāh ibn ᶜAbbās said: "If someone has intercourse after leaving ᶜArafah, then one has to offer the sacrifice of a camel, and complete the rest of one's *ḥajj*, and one's *ḥajj* is complete". Imām Muḥammad says: "We adhere to this, and this is the opinion of Abū Ḥanīfah".[1145]

Whoever has intercourse after the act of shaving their head, must offer a sacrifice of a sheep.[1146]

The ruling regarding the one who has intercourse out of forgetfulness is the same as the one who does so deliberately.[1147]

Impurity while doing *ṭawāf*

If one makes the *ṭawāf al-ifāḍah* without *wuḍū'*, then one must sacrifice a sheep, and if in a state of major ritual impurity which requires *ghusl*,

1141 Abū Ḥanīfah, *K. al-āthār* 85.
1142 Ibn Abī Shaybah, *al-Muṣannaf*, viii. 65-66.
1143 al-Qudūrī, *al-Mukhtaṣar* 234-5.
1144 Ibn Abī Shaybah, *al-Muṣannaf*, viii. 122.
1145 Abū Ḥanīfah, *K. al-āthār* 85-86.
1146 al-Qudūrī, *al-Mukhtaṣar* 235.
1147 ibid., 236.

then a camel - although it is better that one repeats the *ṭawāf* if still in Makkah, in which case one does not have to offer a sacrifice.[1148]

If one makes the *ṭawāf al-qudūm* without *wuḍū'*, then one is required to give *ṣadaqah*; and if in a state of major ritual impurity requiring a *ghusl*, then one must offer the sacrifice of a sheep.[1149]

Whoever makes the *ṭawāf al-wadāᶜ* without *wuḍū'*, must give *ṣadaqah*; and if one makes this *ṭawāf* in a state of major ritual impurity, then one offers the sacrifices of a sheep.[1150]

Missing *saᶜy*

Whoever misses the *saᶜy* between Ṣafā and Marwah must sacrifice a sheep and his *ḥajj* is valid.[1151]

Missing the stay in Muzdalifah

Whoever misses the stopping in Muzdalifah must sacrifice a sheep.[1152]

Missing the stoning

Whoever misses all the days of the stoning of the *jamrahs* must sacrifice a sheep, and if one misses stoning one of the three *jamrahs*, then he gives away *ṣadaqah*; if one omits the stoning of the *Jamrah al-ᶜAqabah* on the Day of Sacrifice, one must offer a sacrifice.[1153]

Delaying

Whoever delays shaving his head until the Days of Sacrifice are over, must offer a sacrifice according to Abū Ḥanīfah, and likewise if he delayed the *ṭawāf al-ifāḍah* according to Abū Ḥanīfah, he must sacrifice one sheep.[1154]

Killing game

Allāh, Exalted is He, says in the Qur'ān: *"If one of you kills any [game] deliberately, the reprisal for it is a livestock animal equivalent to what he has*

1148 ibid., 236-7.
1149 ibid., 236.
1150 ibid., 237.
1151 ibid., 237-8.
1152 ibid., 238.
1153 ibid.
1154 ibid., 238-9.

killed."[1155] If the person in *iḥrām* kills game or indicates its whereabouts to someone who as a result of this indication kills it, then he must pay compensation and this is irrespective of whether the person did it deliberately, out of forgetfulness, or whether the person did it for the first time or more than once.[1156]

The compensation, according to Abū Ḥanīfah and Abū Yūsuf, is that two just people estimate the worth of the game in the place (town, village etc) it was killed, or in the nearest place to it if in the wild. There are a few options. If the estimated value is equal to the price of a sacrificial animal, he buys one and slaughters it. Alternatively, he buys food to the same value and gives it away in *ṣadaqah*. It cannot all be given to one person; rather, it should be distributed as follows: half a *ṣāᶜ* of wheat, or a *ṣāᶜ* of dates or barley for each destitute person. Another way of doing the expiation is to fast a day for every half a *ṣāᶜ* of wheat, and a day for every ṣāᶜ of barley up to the estimated value of the animal. Imām Muḥammad said that one must pay compensation with something similar to what has been killed – if something similar exists – so for an oryx, a sheep; for a hyena, a sheep; for a jerboa, a four month lamb; for an ostrich, a camel.[1157]

There is no compensation to pay for crows, kites, wolves, serpents, scorpions, mice or dogs given to biting; there is also nothing to pay for killing gnats, midges or ticks.[1158] ᶜĀ'ishah narrated that the Prophet ﷺ said: "Five kinds of animals are harmful and could be killed in the *Ḥaram* (Sanctuary). These are the crow, the kite, the scorpion, the mouse and the dog with rabies". In another version, ᶜĀ'ishah said: "I heard Allāh's Messenger ﷺ say: 'Four are the vicious (birds, beasts and reptiles) which should be killed in a state of *iḥrām* or otherwise: the kite (and vulture), the crow, rat, and the voracious dog'." ᶜUbaydullāh ibn Miqsam who is one of the narrators of this ḥadīth said to Qāsim who heard the narration from ᶜĀ'ishah: "What about the snake?" He said: "Let it be killed with disgrace".[1159]

1155 *al-Mā'idah* 95.
1156 al-Qudūrī, *al-Mukhtaṣar* 239.
1157 ibid., 239-41.
1158 ibid., 242.
1159 Muslim, *k. al-ḥajj, b. mā yundabu li al-muḥrim wa ghayrihi qatluhu min al-dawābb fī al-ḥill wa al-ḥaram.*

Whoever kills a louse gives away *ṣadaqah* as he wishes; and "a date is better than a locust".[1160] Imām Muḥammad says: "The *muḥrim* should not hunt the locust; if he hunts then he should give *kaffārah*, and a date is better than a locust. This is what ᶜUmar ibn al-Khaṭṭāb said. This is the opinion of Abū Ḥanīfah and most of our jurists".[1161]

There is no harm if one in a state of *iḥrām* slaughters a sheep, a cow, a camel or a chicken.[1162]

There is no harm in someone in *iḥrām* eating the flesh of game hunted and slaughtered by someone not in *iḥrām* as long as the person in *iḥrām* did not indicate its location to him or instruct him to do it.[1163] Jābir narrated that the Prophet ﷺ said: "The flesh of game is lawful for you during the *iḥrām* as long as you did not hunt it or did not ask someone to hunt for you".[1164]

If a person in *iḥrām* sells game or buys it, then the sale is annulled.[1165]

If two people in *iḥrām* share in the killing of game from the *Ḥaram*, then each must pay the full compensation, whereas if two people not in *iḥrām* share in the killing of game from the *Ḥaram*, then they must pay the equivalent of a single compensation between them.[1166]

Cutting grass or trees

If one cuts any grass, trees or bushes of the *Ḥaram* which are not owned by anyone in particular nor of a kind planted by people, then one must pay what they are worth in compensation.[1167] Ismāᶜīl ibn Muslim narrated that al-Ḥārith and Ḥammād ibn Abī Sulaymān said about the one who cuts the tree of *Ḥaram* to pay in charity equivalent to its value.[1168]

1160 al-Qudūrī, *al-Mukhtaṣar* 242.
1161 Muhammad, *al-Muwaṭṭa'* 151.
1162 al-Qudūrī, *al-Mukhtaṣar* 243.
1163 al-Qudūrī, *al-Mukhtaṣar* 243-4.
1164 Abū Dāwūd, *k. al-manāsik, b. laḥm al-ṣayd li al-muḥrim;* al-Tirmidhī, *k. al-ḥajj, b. mā jā'a fī akl al-ṣayd li al-muḥrim;* al-Nasā'ī, *k. manāsik al-ḥajj, b. idhā ashāra al-muḥrim ilā al-ṣayd faqatalahū al-ḥalāl.*
1165 al-Qudūrī, *al-Mukhtaṣar* 245.
1166 al-Samarqandī, *Tuḥfat al-fuqahā'* 212.
1167 al-Qudūrī, *al-Mukhtaṣar* 244.
1168 Ibn Abī Shaybah, *al-Muṣannaf,* viii. 333.

Double *kaffārah* for the *qārin*

If any of the above mentioned things are committed by someone performing a *ifrād* - then one sacrifice would be owing. In the case of the person performing *qirān* who commits any of the above – then he must sacrifice two sacrificial animals, one for his *ḥajj* and one for his *ᶜumrah.*[1169] Ḥasan al-Baṣrī says about a *qārin* having relation with his wife that he has to sacrifice two she-camels.[1170]

1169 al-Qudūrī, *al-Mukhtaṣar* 244.

1170 Ibn Abī Shaybah, *al-Muṣannaf,* viii. 190.

CHAPTER 8: *IḤṢĀR*

IḤṢĀR MEANS BEING prevented from going on *ḥajj*. Nāfiᶜ reported that ᶜAbdullāh ibn ᶜAbdullāh and Sālim ibn ᶜAbdullāh said to their father ᶜAbdullāh ibn ᶜUmar in the year Ḥajjāj came to fight against Ibn Zubayr: "There will be no harm if you do not proceed for *ḥajj* this year, for we fear that there will be fighting among people which will cause obstruction between you and the House, whereupon he said: 'If there is to be obstruction between me and the (House), I will do as Allāh's Messenger ﷺ did. I was with him when the infidels of Quraysh caused obstructions between him (the Prophet) and the House. I call you as my witness that I have made ᶜ*umrah* essential for me'. He proceeded until he came to Dhū al-Ḥulayfah and pronounced the *talbiyah* for ᶜ*umrah,* and said: 'If the way is clear for me, I will then complete my ᶜ*umrah* but if there is some obstruction between me and that, then I will do what Allāh's Messenger ﷺ had done (on the occasion of Ḥudaybiyyah), and I was with him', and then (he) recited: '*Verily in the Messenger of Allāh, there is a model pattern for you*'. He then moved on until he came to the rear side of al-Bayda' and said: 'The matter of both of them (*ḥajj* and ᶜ*umrah*) is not but the same. If I am detained (in the performance) of ᶜ*umrah,* I am detained in the performance of *ḥajj* too. I call you as witness that *ḥajj* along with ᶜ*umrah* I have made essential for me'. He then bought sacrificial animals at Qudayd and then circumambulated the House and ran between al-Ṣafā and al-Marwah once, and did not put off *iḥrām* until the Day of Sacrifice'."[1171]

Definition of *iḥṣār*

Iḥṣār happens if a person in *iḥrām* is prevented from performing the *ḥajj* or the ᶜ*umrah* by the enemy or he is afflicted by an illness or any excuse which stops him from continuing. If one finds oneself in such as position, it is permitted to come out of a state of *iḥrām* on the condition

1171 al-Bukhārī, *abwāb al-muḥṣar, b. idhā uḥṣira al-muᶜtamir;* Muslim, *k. al-ḥajj, b. jawāz al-taḥallul bi al-iḥṣār...*

that one sends an animal for sacrifice in the *Ḥaram* and once the sacrifice is done, one can come out of *iḥrām.* In such a situation one does not need to shave one's hair or shorten it; though if one does, it is good.[1172] Al-Ḥajjāj ibn ᶜAmr al-Anṣārī narrated: "I heard the Prophet ﷺ say: 'Whoever's leg is broken then he has become *ḥalāl* (i.e. out of *iḥrām*), and he has to do another *ḥajj*'."[1173] ᶜAbdullāh ibn ᶜUmar narrated: "We went out with the Messenger of Allāh ﷺ and the unbelievers of Quraysh stopped us from the House. Then the Prophet ﷺ sacrificed his animals, shaved his head, and his Companions shortened their hair".[1174] ᶜAṭā' ibn Abī Rabāḥ said: "There is no *iḥṣār* except from illness or an enemy, or a preventing matter."[1175]

Iḥṣār of a *qārin*

If the *muḥṣar* (one who is prevented) is making the *qirān*, then he needs to sacrifice two animals, and he does not come out of *iḥrām* until both have been sacrificed.[1176]

The place of sacrifice for *muḥṣar*

The animal for the *iḥṣār* must be sacrificed in the *Ḥaram.*[1177] The Prophet ﷺ when he was prevented at Ḥudaybiyyah, sacrificed in a place in Ḥudaybiyyah which was within the boundary of the *Ḥaram.*

The time of sacrifice for a *muḥṣar*

The sacrifice of the *muḥṣar* of ᶜ*umrah* can be done any time.[1178]

The sacrifice for the *muḥṣar* of *ḥajj* is permitted to be done before the Day of Sacrifice, according to Abū Ḥanīfah, while Abū Yūsuf and Muḥammad say that it is not permitted to do the sacrifice before the Day of Sacrifice.[1179]

1172 al-Samarqandī, *Tuḥfat al-fuqahā'* 206.

1173 Abū Dāwūd, *k. al-manāsik, b. al-iḥṣār*; al-Tirmidhī, *k. al-ḥajj, b. mā jā'a fī alladhī yuḥillu bi al-ḥajj fayuksaru aw yuᶜraj.*

1174 al-Bukhārī, *k. al-muḥṣar, b. idhā uḥṣira al-muᶜtamir.*

1175 Ibn Abī Shaybah, *al-Muṣannaf,* viii. 237.

1176 al-Samarqandī, *Tuḥfat al-fuqahā'* 207.

1177 ibid.

1178 ibid.

1179 ibid.

Qaḍā' for _muḥṣar_

If the person prevented from *ḥajj* comes out of *iḥrām*, he must do *qaḍā'* of the *ḥajj* and *ᶜumrah*; and if a person is prevented from *ᶜumrah* he must do *qaḍā'* of the *ᶜumrah*; and the person performing *qirān* must do *qaḍā'* of a *ḥajj* and two *ᶜumrahs*.[1180] ᶜAbdullāh ibn ᶜAbbās narrated that when the Prophet was prevented from *ᶜumrah* at Ḥudaybiyyah, he did *ᶜumrah* the following year.[1181]

If _iḥṣār_ ends

When the person prevented from performing his *ḥajj* sends off his sacrificial animal and arranges for them to be slaughtered on a specified day but then the reasons for him being prevented ceases - and he is able to catch the *ḥajj* and with the sacrificial animal to amend its sacrifice date, then it is not permitted for him to come out of *iḥrām*; he must carry on his *ḥajj*.[1182]

If one can obtain the sacrificial animal but cannot catch the *ḥajj*, then the *iḥṣār* continues, because there is no benefit in getting the sacrifice if the *ḥajj* is missed. In this case the person comes out of *iḥrām* once the sacrifice is done.[1183]

Iḥṣār of residents of Makkah

If a resident of Makkah is prevented and hindered from the standing at ᶜArafah and the *ṭawāf*, then he is treated as someone who is prevented; while if he is able to perform one of these acts, then he is not considered to be someone who is prevented.[1184]

MISSING PART OF THE RITES

If one enters *iḥrām* for the *ḥajj* but misses the standing at ᶜArafah before dawn on the Day of Sacrifice - then one has missed the *ḥajj*. One must nevertheless continue and do the *ṭawāf* and *saᶜy*, then come out of *iḥrām* and make up the *ḥajj* the following year, but one does not

1180 ibid.
1181 al-Bukhārī, *k. al-muḥṣar, b. idhā uḥṣira al-muᶜtamir.*
1182 al-Samarqandī, *Tuḥfat al-fuqahā'* 208.
1183 ibid.
1184 al-Qudūrī, *al-Mukhtaṣar* 248.

have to sacrifice an animal.[1185] Sulaymān ibn Yasār narrates: "Habbār ibn al-Aswad came while ᶜUmar was sacrificing his camels, and said: 'O, Commander of the Faithful, we made a mistake in counting, we thought that today is the Day of ᶜArafah'. ᶜUmar said to him: 'Go to Makkah, do *ṭawāf* of the House, and *saᶜy* between Ṣafā and Marwah, and sacrifice a *hady* if you have it. Then shave your heads or shorten (your hair) and go back (home). Next year do *ḥajj* and sacrifice. And those who do not have *hady* should fast three days in the *ḥajj* and seven days when you go back'."[1186]

Imām Muḥammad says after narrating this ḥadīth: "We adhere to it; and this is the opinion of Abū Ḥanīfah and most of our jurists, except one thing, there is no *hady* on them next year and no fasting. This is what Aᶜmash narrated from Ibrāhīm al-Nakhaᶜī from al-Aswad ibn Yazīd, who said: 'I asked ᶜUmar ibn al-Khaṭṭāb about someone who misses the *ḥajj*, he answered: 'He will become *ḥalāl* with an *ᶜumrah*, and he has to do *ḥajj* next year'. ᶜUmar did not mention *hady*'. Al-Aswad says: 'Then after that I asked Zayd ibn Thābit and he said the same as ᶜUmar'."[1187]

ᶜUmrah is never considered as missed and is permitted throughout the year - except for five days in which it is disliked, which is explained in the following chapter. [1188]

1185 ibid., 249.
1186 Muhammad, *al-Muwaṭṭa'* 147.
1187 ibid., 147-8.
1188 al-Qudūrī, *al-Mukhtaṣar* 249.

Chapter 9: ᶜUmrah

ᶜUmrah means 'visit'. It is so named because it consists of a visit to the House. Abū Hurayrah narrated that the Prophet ﷺ said: "*ᶜUmrah* is an expiation for the sins committed between it and the previous one. And the reward of *ḥajj mabrūr* (the *ḥajj* accepted by Allāh) is nothing except Paradise".[1189]

The ruling about *ᶜumrah*

ᶜUmrah is a Sunnah.[1190] Ṭalḥah ibn ᶜUbaydullāh narrated that the Prophet ﷺ said: "*Ḥajj* is *jihād*, and *ᶜumrah* is voluntary".[1191] ᶜAbdullāh ibn Masᶜūd said: "*Ḥajj* is *farḍ* whereas *ᶜumrah* is voluntary".[1192] Shaᶜbī said: "*ᶜUmrah* is voluntary". [1193] Ibrāhīm al-Nakhaᶜī said: "*ᶜUmrah* is Sunnah, not *farḍ* ". [1194]

The timing of *ᶜumrah*

ᶜUmrah can be performed any time of year. There is no harm in performing *ᶜumrah* during *ḥajj*, or before it or after it.[1195] The Prophet ﷺ performed three *ᶜumrahs* in the month of *Dhū al-qaᶜdah.*[1196] Abū Maᶜn says: "I saw Jābir ibn Zayd and Abū al-ᶜAlīyah do *ᶜumrah* during the ten days of *Dhū al-ḥijjah.*"[1197]

Jābir ibn ᶜAbdullāh narrated: "ᶜĀ'ishah got her menses and performed

1189 al-Bukhārī, *k. al-ᶜumrah, b. al-ᶜumrah, wujūb al-ᶜumrah wa faḍlihā*; Muslim, *k. al-ḥajj, b. faḍl al-ḥajj wa al-ᶜumrah wa yawm ᶜArafah.*

1190 al-Qudūrī, *al-Mukhtaṣar* 250. According to some *Ḥanafī* scholars it is *wājib* like *ṣadaqah al-fiṭr* and *witr*, al-Kasani affirms that calling it sunnah does not contradict it being *wājib*, because the meaning is that it is a *wājib* proven by sunnah (*Badā'iᶜ al-ṣanā'iᶜ*, iii. 302).

1191 Ibn Mājah, *k. al-manāsik, b. al-ᶜumrah.*

1192 Ibn Abī Shaybah, *al-Muṣannaf*, viii. 263.

1193 ibid.

1194 ibid.

1195 al-Kāsānī, *Badā'iᶜ al-ṣanā'iᶜ*, iii. 304.

1196 Ibn Abī Shaybah, *al-Muṣannaf*, viii. 109.

1197 ibid.

all the ceremonies (of *ḥajj*) except the *ṭawāf*. So when she became clean from her menses, and she had performed the *ṭawāf* of the Kaᶜbah, she said: 'O Allāh's Apostle! Your (people) are returning with both *ḥajj* and *ᶜumrah* and I am returning only with *ḥajj*'. So, he ordered ᶜAbd al-Raḥmān ibn Abī Bakr to go with her to Al-Tanᶜīm."[1198]

Although *ᶜumrah* can be done at any time, it is not approved for one doing the *ḥajj* to do *ᶜumrah* on the Day of ᶜArafah or the Days of *Tashrīq*, because those are the busiest days of the *ḥajj*.[1199] ᶜĀ'ishah said: "*ᶜUmrah* is allowed all year except three days, the Day of Sacrifice and the two Days of *Tashrīq*".[1200] Ṭāwūs was asked about *ᶜumrah*. He answered: "When the Days of *Tashrīq* have passed, then do *ᶜumrah* whenever you like until the next year".[1201]

The mīqāts of ᶜumrah

ᶜUmrah has the same *mīqāts* as *ḥajj*, except for the person staying in *Ḥaram*, who should do *iḥrām* from al-ḥill like al-Tanᶜīm or other places.[1202] Al-ḥill, as mentioned earlier, refers to the area between *mīqāt* and the boundaries of *Ḥaram* of Makkah

Actions of *ᶜumrah*

ᶜUmrah has two *farḍ*s and two *wājibs*:

The two *farḍ*s are: *iḥrām* and *ṭawāf*.[1203]

The two *wājibs* are: *saᶜy* between Ṣafā and Marwah, and shaving or shortening the hair.[1204]

ᶜUmrah during Ramaḍān

ᶜAṭā' reported: "I heard Ibn ᶜAbbās narrate to us that Allāh's Messenger ﷺ said to a woman of the Anṣār (Ibn ᶜAbbās had mentioned her name but I have forgotten it): 'What has prevented you from performing

1198 al-Bukhārī, *k. al-ᶜumrah, b. ᶜumrat al-tanᶜīm*; Muslim, *k. al-ḥajj, b. bayān wujūh al-iḥrām*.

1199 al-Kāsānī, *Badā'iᶜ al-ṣanā'iᶜ*, iii. 304.

1200 Ibn Abī Shaybah, *al-Muṣannaf*, viii. 47.

1201 Ibn Abī Shaybah, *al-Muṣannaf*, viii. 47.

1202 al-Samarqandī, *Tuḥfat al-fuqahā'* 193.

1203 al-Kāsānī, *Badā'iᶜ al-ṣanā'iᶜ*, iii. 304.

1204 ibid., iii. 305.

ḥajj along with us?' She said: 'We have only two camels for carrying water. One of the camels has been taken by my husband and my son for performing *ḥajj* and one has been left for us for carrying water'. Whereupon, he (the Prophet) said: 'So when the month of Ramaḍān comes, perform *ᶜumrah*, for *ᶜumrah* in this (month) is equal to *ḥajj* (in reward)'."[1205]
Jābir narrated that the Prophet ﷺ said: "*ᶜUmrah* performed during Ramaḍān is equal to *ḥajj*'."[1206]

The *ᶜumrahs* of the Prophet
Qatādah narrated: "I asked Anas how many times the Prophet ﷺ had performed *ᶜumrah*. He replied: 'Four times. 1- *ᶜumrah* of Ḥudaybiyyah in *Dhū al-qaᶜdah* when the pagans hindered him; 2- *ᶜumrah* in the following year in *Dhū al-qaᶜdah* after the peace treaty with them (the pagans); 3- *ᶜumrah* from al-Jiᶜirrānah where he distributed the war booty (the booty of the battle of Ḥunayn). 4- *ᶜumrah* with his *ḥajj*'. I asked: 'How many times did he perform *ḥajj*?' He (Anas) replied 'Once'." [1207]

Mujāhid narrated: "ᶜUrwah ibn al-Zubayr and I entered the Mosque (of the Prophet) and saw ᶜAbdullāh ibn ᶜUmar sitting near the dwelling place of ᶜĀ'ishah and some people were offering the *Ḍuḥā* Prayer. We asked him about their prayer and he replied that it was an innovation. He (ᶜUrwah) then asked him how many times the Prophet had performed *ᶜumrah*. He replied: 'Four times; one of them was in the month of *Rajab*'. We disliked contradicting him. Then we heard ᶜĀ'ishah, the Mother of Believers cleaning her teeth with *siwāk* in her dwelling place. ᶜUrwah said: 'O Mother, O Mother of the Believers! Don't you hear what Abū ᶜAbd al-Raḥmān is saying?' She said: 'What does he say?' ᶜUrwah said: 'He says that the Messenger of Allāh ﷺ performed four *ᶜumrahs* and one of them during the month of *Rajab*'. ᶜĀ'ishah said: 'May Allāh be merciful to Abū ᶜAbd al-Raḥmān. The Prophet ﷺ did not perform any *ᶜumrah* except that he was with him, and he never performed any *ᶜumrah* in *Rajab*'."[1208]

1205 al-Bukhārī, *k. al-ᶜumrah, b. al-ᶜumrah fī ramaḍān;* Muslim, *k. al-ḥajj, b. fī faḍl al-ḥajj wa al-ᶜumrah.*
1206 Ibn Mājah, *k. al-manāsik, b. al-ᶜumrah fī ramaḍān.*
1207 al-Bukhārī, *k. al-maghāzī, b. ghazwat al-ḥudaybiyyah*; Muslim, *k. al-ḥajj, b. bayān ᶜadad umar al-nabī ṣallallāhu ᶜalayhi wa sallam…*
1208 Muslim, *k. al-ḥajj, b. bayān ᶜadad ᶜumar al-nabī ṣallallāhu ᶜalayhi wa sallam.*

Repeating ᶜ*umrah*

It is allowed to perform more than one ᶜ*umrah* in the same year. ᶜIkrimah says: "Do as many ᶜ*umrahs* as your head can be shaved".[1209] ᶜAlī ibn Abī Ṭālib allowed an ᶜ*umrah* in a month.[1210] ᶜAṭā' ibn Abī Rabāḥ was asked about ᶜ*umrah* twice in a month. He said: "There is no harm in it".[1211]

However, some scholars disliked one to perform more than one ᶜ*umrah* in a year. Ibn ᶜAwn states that Muḥammad ibn Sīrīn did not consider ᶜ*umrah* except once in a year.[1212] Ibrāhīm al-Nakhaᶜī says: "They did not perform ᶜ*umrah* in the year except once".[1213] Ḥasan al-Baṣrī also considered one ᶜ*umrah* a year as being appropriate.[1214]

1209 Ibn Abī Shaybah, *al-Muṣannaf*, viii. 47.

1210 ibid.

1211 ibid., viii. 48.

1212 ibid., viii. 48.

1213 ibid., viii. 48.

1214 ibid., viii. 48.

CHAPTER 10: VISITING MADĪNAH

THE CITY OF Madīnah is of great importance in Islam; it is a city only second to Makkah in sacredness. It is the place where the Prophet ﷺ did *hijrah*, spent the last ten years of his life and where he died and was buried. Many parts of the Qur'ān were revealed there. It is the place where the Islamic conquests started and it remained the capital of the *khilafah* during the caliphates of Abū Bakr, ʿUmar and ʿUthmān.

Ghazālī says: "No other place after Makkah is more excellent than Madīnah, (the city) of the Apostle of Allāh ﷺ. All deeds are counted as double there. (The Apostle of Allah) ﷺ said: 'A prayer performed in this mosque of mine is more meritorious than a thousand prayers offered in any other mosque save the Sacred Mosque (*Masjid al-Ḥarām*)'. Likewise, every good deed in Madīnah is equal to a thousand deeds (elsewhere); then after the city (of the Apostle) comes the Holy Land where every prayer is equal to five hundred prayers (performed) in other places save the Sacred Mosque; and this is the case with all other deeds. Ibn ʿAbbās has reported that the Prophet ﷺ said: 'A prayer performed in the Mosque of Madīnah amounts to ten thousand prayers, and a prayer performed in the al-Aqsa Mosque amounts to one thousand prayers, and a prayer performed in the Sacred Mosque amounts to one hundred thousand prayers'. He ﷺ (also) said: 'To him who endures patiently its (i.e. Madīnah's) hardship and severity, I will be an intercessor on the Day of Resurrection'. (Still again) he ﷺ said: 'He who is able to die in Madīnah let him do so for no one dies in it for whom I will not be an intercessor on the Day of Resurrection'. All places after these three are equal save the frontiers where abiding for the sake of defense has a great merit. Consequently, he ﷺ said: 'Do not set off on a journey unless to the three mosques: the Sacred Mosque, My Mosque, and the al-Aqsa Mosque'."[1215]

1215 al-Ghazālī, *Iḥyā' ʿulūm al-dīn*, i. 342-343.

Ḥaram of Madīnah

Madīnah is a *Ḥaram* as Makkah is a *Ḥaram.* Abū Saʿīd al-Khudrī reported that Allāh's Messenger ﷺ said: "Ibrāhīm ﷺ made Makkah *Ḥaram* (Sacred), and I declare Madīnah and what lies between its two black tracts *Ḥaram.* No blood should be shed in it, no weapon should be carried in it, no tree should be cut except what is required for feeding animals".[1216]

ʿAlī reported that the Prophet ﷺ said: "Madīnah is *Ḥaram* and its Sacred Precincts extend from ʿAyr to Thawr".[1217] (ʿAyr is a mountain at the *mīqāt* for Madīnah, and Thawr is a mountain near Uḥud to the north.)

The meaning of Madīnah being *Ḥaram* is that it should be respected and loved. Though killing the game or cutting down the trees in Madīnah carries no penalty nor does it require any compensation.[1218]

Some *aḥadīth* on the virtues of Madīnah

Here are a few *aḥadīth* which speak about the virtues of this city:

Abū Hurayrah narrated that the Prophet ﷺ said: "I have made Madīnah a sanctuary between its two mountains". [1219]

ʿAbdullāh ibn Zayd ibn ʿĀṣim reported Allāh's Messenger ﷺ as saying: "Verily Ibrāhīm declared Makkah sacred and supplicated (for blessings to be showered) upon its inhabitants, and I declare Madīnah to be sacred as Ibrāhīm had declared Makkah to be sacred. I have supplicated (to Allāh for His blessings to be showered) in its *ṣāʿ* and its *mudd,* doubling what Ibrāhīm asked for the inhabitants of Makkah".[1220]

Nāfiʿ ibn Jubayr narrates that: "Marwān ibn al-Ḥakam addressed people and made mention of Makkah and its inhabitants and its sacredness, but he made no mention of Madīnah, its inhabitants and its sacredness. Rāfiʿ ibn Khadīj called him and said: 'What is this that I hear you making mention of Makkah and its inhabitants and its sacredness, but you did not make mention of Madīnah and its inhabitants and its sacredness, while the Apostle of Allāh ﷺ also declared sacred (the area) between its two lava lands. And (we have record of this) with us written

1216 Muslim, *k. al-ḥajj, b. al-targhīb fī suknā al-madīnah.*

1217 al-Bukhārī, *k. faḍā'il al-madīnah;* Muslim, *k. al-ḥajj, b. faḍl al-madīnah...*

1218 Ibn ʿAbidīn, *Radd al-muḥtār*, vii. 476.

1219 Muslim, *k. al-ḥajj, b. faḍl al-madīnah...*

1220 ibid.

on *khawlanī* parchment. If you like, I can read it out to you'. Thereupon, Marwān became silent, and then said: 'I too have heard some part of it'."[1221]

In a narration Anas ibn Mālik reports that the Messenger of Allah ﷺ said about Madīnah and Uḥud: "This is the mountain (Uḥud) which loves us and we love it. And as he came close to Madīnah he said: 'O Allāh, I declare (the area) between the two mountains of it (Madīnah) sacred just as Ibrāhīm declared Makkah as sacred. O Allāh, bless them (the people of Madīnah) in their *mudd* and *ṣāᶜ*".[1222]

Ibrāhīm al-Taymi reported on the authority of his father that ᶜAlī ibn Abī Ṭālib reported Allāh's Apostle ﷺ as saying: "Madīnah is sacred from ᶜAyr to Thawr; So if anyone makes an innovation or accommodates an innovator, the curse of Allāh, the angels, and all persons will fall upon him, and Allāh will not accept any obligatory or supererogatory act as recompense from them".[1223]

Abū Hurayrah reported Allāh's Messenger ﷺ as saying: "A time will come for the people (of Madīnah) when a man will invite his cousin and any other near relation: 'Come to (a different place) where living is cheap, come to where there is plenty'. But Madīnah will be better for them, if only they knew. By Him in Whose Hand is my life, none amongst them would go out (of this city) with a dislike for it, but Allāh would make his successor in it someone better than him. Behold! Madīnah is like a furnace which eliminates impurities. And the Last Hour will not come until Madīnah banishes its evils just as a furnace eliminates the impurities of iron."[1224]

The virtue of death in Madīnah

ᶜAbdullāh ibn ᶜUmar narrated that the Messenger of Allāh ﷺ said: "Whoever from among you can die in Madīnah, he should die there. For

1221 Muslim, *k. al-ḥajj, b. faḍl al-madīnah...*

1222 ibid.

1223 al-Bukhārī, *k. faḍā'il al-madīnah, b. ḥaram al-madīnah, k. al-jizyah wa al-muwādaᶜah, b. ithm man ᶜāhada thumma ghadar, k. al-farā'iḍ, b. ithm man tabarra'a min mawālīh, k. al-iᶜtiṣām bi al-kitāb wa al-sunnah, b. mā yukrahu min al-taᶜammuq wa al-tanāzuᶜ wa al-ghuluww fī al-dīn wa al-bidaᶜh;* Muslim, *k. al-ḥajj, b. faḍl al-madīnah...*

1224 Muslim, *k. al-ḥajj, b. al-madīnah tanfī shirāraha.*

whoever dies there, I will intercede for him".[1225] Zayd ibn Aslam reports from his father that ᶜUmar said: "O Allāh! Grant me martyrdom in Your cause, and let my death be in the city of Your Apostle".[1226]

The mosque of the Prophet ﷺ

Abū Hurayrah narrated that Allāh's Apostle ﷺ said: "A prayer in my mosque is a thousand times more excellent than a prayer in any other mosque, except *Masjid al-Ḥarām*.[1227] Abū Hurayrah also reported that the Prophet ﷺ said: "Prayer in the mosque of Allāh's Messenger ﷺ is more excellent than a thousand prayers in other mosques except the *Masjid al-Ḥarām*, for I am the last of the Prophets, and my mosque is the last of the mosques".[1228] Ibn ᶜUmar reported Allāh's Apostle ﷺ as saying: "Prayer in this mosque of mine is better than a thousand prayers (observed in other mosques) besides it, except that of *Masjid al-Ḥarām*".[1229]

Ibn ᶜAbbās reported that a woman fell ill and she said: "In case Allāh cures me I will certainly go and observe prayer in *Bayt al-Maqdis*." She recovered and so she made preparations to go out (to that place). She came to Maymūnah, the wife of Allāh's Apostle ﷺ, and after greeting her she informed her about it, whereupon she said: "Stay here, and eat the provision (which you had made) and observe prayer in the mosque of the Messenger ﷺ, for I heard Allāh's Messenger ﷺ say: 'Prayer in it is better than a thousand prayers observed in other mosques except the mosque of the Kaᶜbah'."[1230]

ᶜAbdullāh ibn Zayd al-Māzinī reported Allāh's Messenger ﷺ as saying: "That which is between my house and my pulpit is a garden from the gardens of Paradise." Abū Hurayrah reported Allāh's Messenger ﷺ as saying: "That which exists between my house and my pulpit is a garden from the gardens of Paradise, and my pulpit is upon my cistern."[1231]

Abū Hurayrah reported it directly from Allāh's Apostle ﷺ that he

1225 al-Tirmidhī, *k. al-manāqib, b. fī faḍl al-madīnah.*

1226 al-Bukhārī, *k. al-ḥajj, b. karāhiyat al-nabī ṣallallāhu ᶜalayhi wa sallam an tuᶜrā al-madīnah.*

1227 Muslim, *k. al-ḥajj, b. faḍl al-ṣalāh bi masjiday makkah wa al-madīnah.*

1228 ibid.

1229 ibid.

1230 ibid.

1231 Muslim, *k. al-ḥajj, b. mā bayna al-qabr wa al-minbar rawḍatun min riyād al-jannah.*

said: "Do not undertake a journey but to three mosques: this mosque of mine, the Mosque of *al-Ḥarām* and the Mosque of al-Aqṣā."[1232]

Virtue of Uḥud

Abū Ḥumayd reports: "We went out along with Allāh's Messenger ﷺ on the Expedition of Tabuk. We proceeded until we reached the valley of Qura; and Allāh's Messenger ﷺ said: 'I am going forth, so he who among you wants to move fast with me may do so; and he who likes to go slowly may do so'. We proceeded until Madīnah was within our sight, and he (the Prophet) said: 'This is Taba (another name of Madīnah); this is Uḥud, the mountain which loves us and we love it'."[1233]

Anas ibn Mālik reported Allāh's Messenger ﷺ as saying: "Uḥud is a mountain which loves us and which we love".[1234]

Visiting Qubā Mosque

The Messenger of Allāh used to come to the mosque of Qubā every Saturday riding or walking and used to pray two *rakᶜahs* there. The Prophet used to encourage people to do that, He said: "Whoever does purification in his house, then comes to the mosque of Qubā, and prays there it will be like the reward of an *ᶜumrah*".[1235]

ᶜAbdullāh Ibn ᶜUmar reports that Allāh's Messenger ﷺ used to go to the mosque at Qubā riding and on foot, and he observed two *rakᶜahs* of (*nafl* prayer) in it.[1236] ᶜAbdullāh ibn Dīnār mentions this narration and states that ᶜAbdullāh ibn ᶜUmar used to do the same as the Prophet ﷺ did.[1237]

WHAT THE PILGRIM SHOULD DO IN MADĪNAH

The pilgrim (man or woman) should pray in the mosque of the Prophet, say *salām* to him, his Companions Abū Bakr and ᶜUmar who are buried next to him, visit Baqīᶜ where many other Companions were laid to rest,

1232 Muslim, *k. al-ḥajj, b. lā tushaddu al-riḥāl illā ilā thalāthat masājid.*

1233 Muslim, *k. al-ḥajj, b. uḥud jabalun yuḥibbunā wa nuḥibbuhu.*

1234 al-Bukhārī, *k. al-maghāzī, b. uḥud jabalun yuḥibbunā wa nuḥibbuhu*; Muslim, *k. al-ḥajj, b. faḍl al-madīnah.*

1235 Ibn M ājah, *k. iqāmat al-ṣalawāt, b. mā jā'a fī al-ṣalāh fī masjid qubā'.*

1236 Muslim, *k. al-ḥajj, b. faḍl masjid qubā....*

1237 ibid.

and say *salām* to all who are buried there, visit the mosque of Qubā, Uḥud and other places which have an attachment or retain a memory of the Prophet ﷺ. One does so out of love and respect for the Messenger of Allah ﷺ. It is reported that a man from the family of al-Khaṭṭāb narrated that the Prophet ﷺ said: "Whoever visits me, intending (just) that, he will be in my neighbourhood on the Day of Judgement.[1238] ʿAbdullāh ibn ʿUmar narrated that the Prophet ﷺ said: "Whoever performs (the) *ḥajj*, then visits my grave after my death, he is like someone who (has) visited me during my life.[1239] In another ḥadīth, the Prophet ﷺ is reported to have said: "Whoever came to me as a visitor, having no need other than visiting me, it will be a right upon me to be his intercessor on the Day of Resurrection".[1240] The three *aḥadīth* just quoted are categorised by ḥadīth experts as weak.

Muḥammad ibn Sīrīn once said to ʿAbīdah al-Salmānī: "We have some hair of the Messenger of Allāh ﷺ which we got from Anas ibn Mālik." On hearing this ʿAbīdah said: "If I (could) get one single hair from those hairs, it will be more beloved to me than all the gold and silver on the face of the earth".[1241] Dhahabī commenting on this story says: "This statement of ʿAbīdah is a measure of perfect love, whereby he prefers one hair of the Prophet to all the gold and silver that is in the hands of the people. This is a statement of this *imam* fifty years after the Prophet ﷺ. So what would we say in our (own) time if we got some of his hair with sound proof, or his shoe lace, or a nail of his, or a piece of a pot from which he used to drink? If a rich person spent most of his wealth in acquiring any of this, will you consider him a waster or (say he is) stupid? Never! So spend whatever you own in visiting his mosque which he built with his (own) hands, and greet him in his room in his city. Enjoy looking at his Uḥud, and love it, because your Prophet ﷺ loved it. Feel comfort in getting off at his garden and place where he sat. You can not be a believer unless this master becomes more beloved to you than yourself, your children, your goods and all the people".[1242]

1238 al-Bayhaqī, *Shuʿab al-īmān, b. fī al-manāsik.*

1239 ibid.

1240 al-Haythamī, *Majmaʿ al-zawāʾid, k. al-ḥajj, b. ziyārat sayyidinā rasūlillāh ṣallallāhu ʿalayhi wa sallam.*

1241 al-Dhahabī, *Siyar aʿlām al-nubalāʾ* iv. 42.

1242 ibid.

Dhahabī also writes that Ḥasan ibn Ḥasan ibn ʿAlī saw a man stopping where the grave of the Prophet ﷺ is and made *duʿā'* saying *ṣalāh* and *salām* to the Prophet ﷺ. Thereupon, he said to the man: "Don't do this because the Messenger of Allāh ﷺ said: 'Do not make my house a place of celebration, do not make your houses as graves, and say *ṣalāh* and *salām* to me wherever you are, for your *ṣalāh* reaches me".[1243] Commenting on this Dhahabī says: "This is a disconnected chain of narration, and Ḥasan did not provide much useful argument. How good it is for someone to stop at the sacred room in humility saying *ṣalāh* and *salām* to his Prophet ﷺ. He has done well in visiting and done well in his humility and love, and has done an additional act of worship compared to the one who send prayers and salutations to him from his own land; for the visitor has the reward of the visit and reward of the *ṣalāh* on him, while the one who says *ṣalāh* to him from anywhere else has the reward of *ṣalāh* only; anyone who says *ṣalāh* to him once Allāh has mercy on him 10 times. If someone visits him ﷺ and commits a mistake in the manner of his visit, or does a *sajdah* (prostration) to the grave, or does what is not allowed, then this person has done good and bad, and he should be taught what is right with gentleness, and Allāh is All-Forgiving and All-Merciful. By Allāh, the impatience, crying, kissing of the walls and weeping don't happen to the Muslim, but that he loves Allāh and his Messenger. Now love of him is the measure and distinction between the people of Paradise and the people of the Fire. Visiting his grave is among the best acts of closeness to Allāh. If we accept that travelling to the graves of the Prophet and saints is not allowed because of the generality of the word of the Prophet ﷺ: "Do not travel but to three mosques," then at least we will say that travelling to our Prophet ﷺ necessitates travelling to his mosque, and that is allowed without any dispute. And because one cannot reach his room without entering his mosque, one should start with the greeting of the mosque, then greeting of the man of the mosque".[1244]

Imām Ghazālī says: "As for the visit to Madīnah: when your eyes catch sight of its walls, remember that it is the town that was chosen by Allāh, Exalted is He, for His Prophet ﷺ and made the destination of his Flight (*hijra*); that it was his dwelling-place, in which he promulgated

1243 ibid., iv. 483-484.

1244 ibid., iv. 484-485.

the Laws of his Lord Most High and the Sunnah, fought His enemy and proclaimed His religion, until the time when Allāh, Exalted is He, caused him to die; then Allāh established in it a burial ground for him; and for his two ministers who maintained the truth after him. Next, imagine to yourself the places where the feet of the Apostle of Allāh ﷺ have trodden as he went about the city, and (consider to yourself) that wherever your feet have trodden there too have his dear feet trodden; therefore, take each step with tranquility and with awe. And remember his walking (around) and traversing upon the (city's) roads; picture to yourself his humility and tranquility while walking, despite what Allāh, Exalted is He, has entrusted to his heart, such as his great knowledge (about God), the exaltation of his name alongside the name of the Most High to the extent that (God) has joined him to the remembrance of Himself, and the rendering vain of the deeds of those who vilify him even by way of raising their voice higher than his. And remember the Grace that Allāh, Exalted is He, bestowed on those who enjoyed his companionship and were fortunate to have been with him and to have listened to his speech. Be exceedingly sorrowful over been denied (the opportunity to be) his Companion or the Companion of his Companions. Remember that it has not been given to you to see him in this life, and that to see him in the life to come is to place yourself in jeopardy; for it may be that you will grieve when you see him, having been barred from him (after) he blamed you for bad deeds, as he said ﷺ: 'God will bring before me (on the Day of Resurrection) some people (who will call on me) saying: 'O Muḥammad. O Muḥammad! Then I will say: 'My Lord! They are my Companions'. And Allāh will say: 'You do not know what they have introduced after you (had died). Then I will say: 'Go away'. Therefore, if you neglect the sanctity of his law, even of a minute thing, you have no guarantee that you will not be barred from him because of you straying from his right way. Nevertheless, have great hope that you will not be barred from him, for you have been blessed by Allāh, Exalted is He, with faith and have been brought hither from your home country in order to visit him, (being motivated), not by any (concern with) commerce or worldly gain, but only by your love of him and your longing to see his traces and the wall of his tomb. Since, having not been (privileged to) see the Prophet (in this world), you have been prompted to travel by these considerations alone; you are most worthy to be looked upon by Allāh, Exalted is He, with (His) Gracious Eye.

When you reach the mosque (of the Prophet at Madīnah), remember that it is the place that has been chosen by Allāh, Exalted is He, for His Prophet ﷺ and for the first band of Muslims and the best of all, that the laws of Allāh, Exalted is He, were the first thing to be established in that place and that (this mosque) contained the best of all the creatures of God, living or dead. Increase your hope in Allāh Most High, that He will forgive you for entering it. Enter with solemnity and reverence. How deserving it is (of solemnity and reverence) from the hearts of every believer, as Abū Sulaymān is reported to have said: "Uways al-Qarni ؓ had performed the pilgrimage and entered Madīnah. When he stopped by the gate of the mosque, it was said to him: 'This is the grave of the Prophet ﷺ'. Thereupon, he fainted. When he awoke, he said: 'Let me go out, it is not proper for me to be in a town where Muḥammad ﷺ is buried'."[1245]

Ghazālī further says: "As for the visit to the Apostle of God ﷺ, it is befitting to stand in front of him – as we have already described – and to visit him in death as you would visit him alive; do not approach his grave except as you would approach his noble person, were he alive. And as you would have believed it unseemly to touch his body or to kiss him, but would have stood back to be seen by him, likewise do (now), for the touching and kissing of shrines are a custom of Christians and Jews. Know that he is aware of your presence, your standing and your visit, and that your greetings and prayers reach him. Therefore, picture in your mind his noble likeness laid out in the grave by your side, and reflect on his exalted position. The Prophet ﷺ is reported to have said: 'God Most High has appointed (a special) Angel as an agent to his grave in order to convey to him the greeting of anyone among his community'. This being true of one who has not visited his grave, what then, of the one who has left his home country and passed over desert after desert longing to meet him, but content with seeing his shrine, since he has missed seeing his noble face? He ﷺ has said: 'Whoever prays for me once, Allāh prays for him ten times'. If this be his reward for his verbal prayer, what of his coming in person to visit him? Then, proceed to the pulpit of the Apostle ﷺ, and imagine the Prophet to be ascending into it ﷺ, picture in your mind his beautiful appearance, as though he were in the pulpit surrounded by the Migrants and Helpers

1245 al-Ghazālī, *Iḥyā' ʿulūm al-dīn*, i. 379.

urging them through preaching to obey Allāh Most High. And (finally) ask Allāh, Exalted is He, not to separate you and him on the Day of Judgement. These are the duties of the heart throughout the acts of the pilgrimage'."[1246]

Departure

Imām Ghazālī says: "When (the pilgrim) finishes them all, he should keep his heart in (a state of) sadness and fear; (it is proper that) he remain uncertain whether his pilgrimage has been accepted, (in which case) he has been confirmed as belonging to the group of (the) beloved ones; or not, (in which case) he has been included among the banished ones. Let him find this out through (the testimony of) his heart and his actions; if he finds that his heart is more disenchanted with the Abode of Vanity (i.e. the world), and more inclined toward the Abode of Fellowship with Allāh, Exalted is He, to the Law, let him be certain that (he is) accepted; for Allāh accepts only him whom He loves. And whomever He loves He helps, showing to him the effects of love; such a one He protects against the power of his enemy, 'Iblis, Allāh curse him. If this is apparent (from the pilgrim's piety and lawful behavior), then it is an indication of his acceptance. If the opposite is the case, then it is certain that toil and trouble will be the reward of his journey. We seek protection from Allāh, Exalted is He, from that".[1247]

The *duʿā'* of returning back

ʿAbdullāh ibn ʿUmar reported that whenever Allāh's Messenger ﷺ came back from battle or from expeditions or from *ḥajj* or *ʿumrah*, as he reached the top of the hillock or upon the elevated hard ground, he uttered:

اَللّٰهُ أَكْبَرُ، اَللّٰهُ أَكْبَرُ، اَللّٰهُ أَكْبَرُ، لَا إِلَٰهَ إِلَّا اللّٰهُ وَحْدَهُ لَا شَرِيكَ لَهُ، لَهُ الْمُلْكُ وَلَهُ الْحَمْدُ، وَهُوَ عَلَىٰ كُلِّ شَيْءٍ قَدِيرٌ، آئِبُونَ، تَآئِبُونَ، عَابِدُونَ، سَاجِدُونَ، لِرَبِّنَا حَامِدُونَ، صَدَقَ اللّٰهُ وَعْدَهُ، وَنَصَرَ عَبْدَهُ، وَهَزَمَ الْأَحْزَابَ وَحْدَهُ

1246 ibid., i. 379-380.

1247 al-Ghazālī, *Iḥyā' ʿulūm al-dīn*, i. 380.

('Allāh is greater, Allāh is greater, Allāh is greater. There is no god but Allāh. He is One, there is no partner with Him, His is the sovereignty and His is the praise and He is Potent over everything. We are returning, repenting, worshipping, prostrating before our Lord, and we praise Him, Allāh fulfilled His promise and helped His servant, and routed the confederates alone'.)[1248]

One should inform his family of his expected arrival time, and should not come to them suddenly. After entering into the locality, one should start with the masjid and pray there two *rakᶜahs* if it is not a disliked time, then enters into his house, pray two *rakᶜah*s there, praise and thank Allāh for the favour that He has bestowed upon him of completing this important act of worship and coming back safely, continues thanking and praising Him all the time, making effort to avoid anything that can destroy his reward for the rest of his life. The sign of accepted *ḥajj* is that one becomes better than what one has been.[1249]

1248 Muhammad, *al-Muwaṭṭa'*, 173.

1249 See: Ibn ᶜĀbidīn, *Radd al-muḥtār ᶜalā al-durr al-mukhtār,* vii. 482-483.

GLOSSARY

adhān	– the call to *ṣalāh* (prayers)
ᶜArafah	– (pl. ᶜArafāt) a pilgrimage site, about 25 kilometres east of Makkah. Staying there on the 9th of *Dhū al-ḥijjah* is the most important pillar of the *ḥajj.*
ᶜawrah	– parts of the body that must be covered
duᶜā	– supplication
Fajr	– the dawn *ṣalāh*
farḍ	– a definitive obligation proved by a firm evidence, as distinguished from a mere obligation or *wājib*
fitnah	– persecution, a situation in which the believers are harassed and intimidated because of their religious beliefs or practices.
ghusl	– ritual bath, the complete washing of the body which removes major impurity
ḥadīth	– (pl. *aḥādīth*) lit.; account of a saying, act, or approval of the Prophet, or of a Companion
hady	– a camel, cow, sheep or a goat that is offered as a sacrifice by a pilgrim
Ḥajj	– major pilgrimage, one of the five pillars of Islam
ḥanīfī	– follower of *ḥanīfiyyah,* one who devotes himself fully to Allāh and completely surrenders to His will. This is the name of the religion of Prophet Ibrāhīm
Ḥaram	– Sanctuary, usually used with regard to the sanctuaries of the *Masjid al-Ḥarām* in Makkah and *Masjid* of the Prophet in Madīnah. Both are referred to as '*al-Ḥaramayn al-Sharīfayn,*' the two Holy Sanctuaries
Ḥaṭīm	– known as *Ḥijr.* it is the half-walled area attached to the Kaᶜbah which is also called *Ḥijr Ismāᶜīl* and *Ḥijr al-Kaᶜbah*

ḥayḍ	– menstruation
Ḥijr	– see: *Ḥaṭīm*
al-Ḥill	– the area between *mīqāt* and the boundaries of *Ḥaram* of Makkah
iḍṭibāᶜ	– to wrap the right side of the *ridā'* (the upper garment) underneath the right arm and over the left shoulder leaving the right shoulder uncovered. This is done in any *ṭawāf* which is followed by *saᶜy*
ᶜīd al-aḍḥā	– lit.; the feast of the sacrifice; festival that completes the rites of *ḥajj* and takes place on the 10th-13th of *Dhū al-ḥijjah*
ᶜīd al-fiṭr	– festival marking the end of Ramaḍān. It takes place on the 1st of Shawwāl, the 10th month of the Islamic calendar
ifṭār	– breaking of the fast immediately after sunset
iḥrām	– the state of consecration which is required for performing *ḥajj* and *ᶜumrah*
iḥṣār	– lit.; being prevented; when one in *iḥrām* is prevented from performing the *ḥajj* or the *ᶜumrah* by the enemy or one is afflicted by an illness or any excuse which prevents one from continuing the pilgrimage
ijmāᶜ	– the consensus of all qualified jurists of an age
iᶜtikāf	– lit.; devotion; spending days and nights while fasting in a mosque so as to devote oneself exclusively to worship. In this state one may go out of the mosque only for absolutely necessary requirements of life, but one must stay away from gratifying one's sexual desire. The minimum period for *iᶜtikāf* is one day and one night. *Iᶜtikāf* of the last 10 days of Ramaḍān is Sunnah
Istilām	– lit.; to touch with the hand or the mouth. *Istilām* of the Black Stone means kissing it or touching it or pointing to it
izār	– lower garment; one of the two sheets that the male pilgrim puts on in the *iḥrām*
jamāᶜah	– congregation
Jamrah al-ᶜAqbah	– One of the three pillars at Minā

jamrah – (pl. *jamarāt, jimār*) three pillars built of stone at Minā. One of the rites of *ḥajj* is to throw pebbles at these stone pillars

jihād – lit.; to strive or to exert to the utmost. It signifies all forms of striving, including armed struggle to defend Muslims or Muslim land and to remove any obstacle in the path of Islam

janābah – major impurity, which makes *ghusl* obligatory

Kaᶜbah – the House of Allāh built by Ibrāhīm in Makkah. It is the direction faced in *ṣalāh,* and *ṭawāf* is done around it

kaffārah – expiation

kuḥl – a black powder applied in a line on the eyelids of both the eyes

maḥram – a woman's close relative with who she can never marry, e.g. father, son, brother, etc.

Marwah – a hill in Makkah

mīqāt – (pl. mawāqīt), the points which an outsider coming for pilgrimage cannot cross except in the state of *iḥrām*

miswāk – a stick used for brushing the teeth

mithqāl – a weight mentioned in sources in the context of zakāh; the minimum amount of gold on which zakāh is obligatory is 20 *mithqāl* which equals 87.480 grams

muḥrim – a pilgrim in the state of *iḥrām*

muᶜtakif – one performing *iᶜtikāf*

Muzdalifah – A site between ᶜArafah and Minā where the pilgrims spend the night of the 10th of *Dhū al-ḥijjah* during *ḥajj* –

nafl – supererogatory, a voluntary act

nifās – postnatal bleeding

niṣāb – specific amount on which zakāh become due

qaḍā' – performance of an act of worship after its prescribed time

Qadr – lit.; destiny; the night of destiny, which is more probably one of the last ten nights of Ramaḍān. It is better than one thousand months as mentioned in

	sūrah 97 of the Qur'ān
qiblah	– the direction of the Kaᶜbah
Quraysh	– the most noble Arab tribe living in Makkah, to which the Prophet ﷺ belonged
Ramaḍān	– the ninth month of the Islamic calendar; fasting is obligatory during this month on Muslims
ramal	– walking speedily, during the *ṭawāf*, taking short steps whilst moving the shoulders as if one was trotting
ridā'	– upper garment; one of the two sheets that the male pilgrim puts on in the *iḥrām*
ṣāᶜ	– a measure equalling 4 *mudd*s. 3,3 kg
ṣadaqah	– charity for the pleasure of Allāh
ṣadaqat al-fiṭr	– a charity paid at the end of the month of Ramaḍān.
Ṣafā	– a hill in Makkah
ṣalāh	– (pl. *ṣalawāt*) prayer
ṣawm	– fasting
saᶜy	– walking seven times between the hills of Ṣafā and Marwah; a compulsory (*wājib*) rite of *ḥajj* and *ᶜumrah*
sharīᶜah	– divine law based on the Qur'ān and the Sunnah
shawṭ	– circling of the Kaᶜbah once during the *ṭawāf*; each *ṭawāf* consists of circling of the Kaᶜbah 7 times
Shawwāl	– the tenth month of the Islamic calendar
suḥūr	– a meal taken before dawn to begin fasting
sujūd/ sajdah	– prostration
Sunnah	– practice of the Prophet, less than a *farḍ* and *wājib*
tahlīl	– uttering *lā ilāha illallāh*
takbīr	– uttering *Allāhu Akbar*
talbiyah	– the pronouncement pilgrims make during *ḥajj* and *ᶜumrah.*
tarāwīh	– supererogatory *ṣalāh*s during the nights of Ramaḍān
tashrīq	– it refers to 3 days when fasting is forbidden: 11th, 12th and 13th *Dhū al-ḥijjah*
ṭawāf	– the circling of the Kaᶜbah; *ṭawāf* is done in sets of seven
tayammum	– a substitute ablution by striking upon pure earth with one's hands and then wiping over one's face and hands

ᶜumrah	– minor pilgrimage; it consists essentially of *iḥrām*, *ṭawāf* around the Kaᶜbah (seven times), and *saᶜy* (i.e. running) between Ṣafā and Marwah (seven times), then shaving or shortening the hair
ūqiyyah	– a weight mentioned in sources in the context of zakāh; the minimum amount of silver on which zakāh is obligatory is 5 *ūqiyyahs* which equal 200 *dirhams*
ᶜushr	– ten percent of the agricultural produce payable by a Muslim as part of his religious obligation, like zakāh
wājib	– a compulsory act, less than a *farḍ*
wasq	– a measurement for agricultural products; a *wasq* equals 60 *ṣāᶜs*
wiṣāl	– continuous fasting even after the sunset; it can continue until the sunset of the next day, or even further
wuḍū'	– ablution
wuqūf	– staying at ᶜArafah or Muzdalifah as part of the *ḥajj*
zakāh	– lit.: purification, obligatory charity, as a means of purifying the person concerned and the remainder of his property. It is among the five pillars of Islam
zawāl	– decline of the sun at mid-day, when the sun passes its zenith, i.e. highest point

BIBLIOGRAPHY

Abū Ḥanīfah, al-Nuʿmān ibn Thābit (d. 150): *Kitāb al-Āthār*, narration of Muḥammad ibn al-Ḥasan al-Shaybānī, Multan, Maktabah Imdādiyyah, n.d.

Abū Dāwūd, Sulaymān ibn al-Ashʿath (d. 275): *al-Sunan*, ed. Muḥammad ʿAbd al-ʿAzīz al-Khālidī, Beirut, Dār al-kutub al-ʿilmiyyah, 1416/1996.

Abū Yaʿlā, Aḥmad ibn ʿAlī al-Mawṣilī (d. 307): *al-Musnad*, ed. Ḥusayn Salīm Asad, Damascus, Dār al-thaqāfah al-ʿarabiyyah, 1412/1992.

Aḥmad ibn Ḥanbal (d. 241): *al-Musnad*, al-Maṭbaʿah al-maymanīyyah, 1313; Maṭbaʿat al-maʿārif, 1365.

al-Baghawī, Abū Muḥammad al-Ḥusayn ibn Masʿūd (d. 516): *Sharḥ al-Sunnah*, Beirut, Dār al-kutub al-ʿilmiyyah, 1412/1992.

al-Bayhaqī, Abū Bakr Aḥmad ibn al-Ḥasan (d. 458): *al-Sunan al-kubrā*, ed. Muḥammad ʿAbd al-Qādir ʿAṭā, Beirut, Dār al-kutub al-ʿilmiyyah, 1414/1994.

al-Bukhārī, Muḥammad ibn Ismāʿīl (d. 256): *al-Jāmiʿ* al-ṣaḥīḥ, printed with its commentary *Fatḥ al-Bārī*, Beirut, Dār al-kutub al-ʿilmiyyah, 1410/1989.

al-Dāraquṭnī, ʿAlī ibn ʿUmar (d. 385): *al-Sunan*, ed. Majdī ibn Manṣūr ibn Sayyid Shurā, Beirut, Dār al-kutub al-ʿilmiyyah, 1417/1996.

al-Dārimī, Abū Muḥammad ʿAbdullāh ibn ʿAbd al-Raḥmān (d. 255): *al-Sunan*, ed. Muṣṭafā Dīb al-Bughā, Damascus, Dār al-qalam, 1417/1996.

al-Dhahabī, Shams al-dīn Muḥammad ibn Aḥmad (d. 748): *Siyar aʿlām al-nubalā'*, Beirut, Mu'assasat al-risālah, 1413/1993.

al-Dihlawī, Waliullāh Aḥmad ibn ʿAbd al-Raḥīm (d. 1176): Ḥujjatullāh al-bālighah, ed. Sayyid Sābiq, Beirut, Dār al-jīl, 1426/2005.

al-Ghazālī, Muḥammad ibn Muḥammad (d. 505): Ihya ulum al-din, Beirut, Dār al-kutub al-ʿilmiyyah, 1423/2002.

al-Ḥākim, Abū ʿAbdillāh Muḥammad ibn ʿAbdillāh al-Naysābārī

(d. 405): *al-Mustadrak ᶜalā al-ṣaḥīḥayn*, ed. Muṣṭafā ᶜAbd al-Qādir ᶜAṭā, Beirut, Dār al-kutub al-ᶜilmiyyah, 1415/1995.

al-Ḥanbalī, Burhān al-dīn, al-Mubdiᶜ fī sharḥ al-muqniᶜ, Beirut, al-Maktab al-Islami, 1421/2000.

al-Haythamī, Nūr al-dīn ᶜAlī ibn Abī Bakr (d. 807): *Majmaᶜ al-zawā'id*, ed. ᶜAbdullāh Muḥammad al-Darwīsh, Beirut, Dār al-Fikr, 1414/1994.

Ibn ᶜĀbidīn, Muḥammad Amīn (d. 1252): *Ḥāshiyat radd al-muḥtar ᶜalā al-durr al-mukhtār sharḥ tanwīr al-abṣār*, ed. Dr Ḥusām al-dīn Farfūr, Damascus, 1421/2000.

Ibn Abī Shaybah, Abū Bakr ᶜAbdullāh ibn Muḥammad (d. 235): *al-Muṣannaf*, ed. Muḥammad ᶜAwwāmah, Jeddah, Dār al-*qiblah*, 1427/2006.

Ibn Ḥibbān, Abū Ḥātim Muḥammad (d. 354): *al-Ṣaḥīḥ*, Beirut, Dār al-Fikr, 1417/1996.

Ibn Mājah, Muḥammad ibn Yazīd al-Qazwīnī ((d. 273): *al-Sunan*, ed. Maḥmūd Naṣṣār, Beirut, Dār al-kutub al-ᶜilmiyyah, 1419/1998.

Ibn al-Qayyim, Muḥammad ibn Abī Bakr (d. 751): *Zād al-maᶜād fī hady khayr al-ᶜibād*, ed. Shuᶜayb al-Arnāwūṭ and ᶜAbd al-Qādir al-Arnāwūṭ, Mu'assasat *al-risālah*, Beirut, 1409/1989.

al-Kāsānī, Abū Bakr ibn Masᶜūd (d. 587): *Badā'iᶜ al-ṣanā'iᶜ*, ed. al-Shaykh ᶜAlī Muḥammad Muᶜawwid and al-Shaykh ᶜĀdil Aḥmad al-Mawjūd, Beirut, Dār al-kutub al-ᶜilmiyyah, 1418/1997.

Mālik ibn Anas (93-179): *al-Muwaṭṭa'*, narration of Yaḥyā ibn Yaḥyā al-Laythī, Beirut, 1425/2004.

al-Marghīnānī, Burhān al-dīn Abū al-Ḥasan ᶜAlī ibn Abī Bakr (d. 593): *al-Hidāyah*, Karachi, Maktabat al-Bushra, 1428/2007.

Muslim ibn al-*Ḥajj*āj al-Naysābūrī (d. 261): *al-Jāmiᶜ* al-ṣaḥīḥ, printed with the commentary by Imām al-Nawawī, Beirut, Dār al-kutub al-ᶜilmiyyah. 1415/1995.

Nadwī, S. Abū al-Ḥasan ᶜAlī (1333-1420): The Four Pillars of Islam, translated into English by Mohammad Asif, Qidwai, Lucknow, 1978.

al-Nasā'ī, ᶜAbd al-Raḥmān ibn Aḥmad ibn Shuᶜayb (d. 303): *al-Mujtabā*, Beirut, Dār al-kutub al-ᶜilmiyyah. 1416/1995.

al-Qudūrī, Abū al-Ḥusayn Aḥmad ibn Muḥammad (d. 428): *al-Mukhtaṣar*, Karachi, Maktabat al-Bushra, 1429/2008.

Raḥmānī, Khālid Sayfullāh: *Jadīd fiqhī masā'il*, Karachi, 2005.

al-Samarqandī, ᶜAlā' al-dīn Muḥammad ibn Aḥmad (d. 539), *Tuḥfat al-fuqahā'*, Beirut, Dār al-Fikr, 1422/2002.

al-Ṣanᶜānī, ᶜAbd al-Razzāq ibn Hammām (d. 211): *al-Muṣannaf.* ed. Ḥabīb al-Raḥmān al-Aᶜẓamī, 2nd edn. Beirut: al-Maktab al-islāmī, 1403/1983.

al-Shaybānī, Muḥammad ibn al-Ḥasan (d. 189): *al-Muwaṭṭa',* published with its commentary *al-Taᶜlīq al-Mumajjad,* Azamgarh, 1419/1999.

al-Ṭabarānī, Abū al-Qāsim Sulaymān ibn Aḥmad (d. 360): *al-Muᶜjam al-kabīr; al-Muᶜjam al-awsaṭ; al-Muᶜjam al-ṣaghīr,* Matbaᶜah al-anṣārī, Delhi, 1311.

al-Tabrīzī, Muḥammad ibn ᶜAbdillāh al-Khaṭīb (d. 741): *Mishkāt al-maṣabīḥ* ed. Muḥammad Nizar Tamīm and Haytham Nizār Tamīm, Beirut, Dār al-araqm, n.d.

al-Ṭaḥāwī, Abū Jaᶜfar Aḥmad ibn Muḥammad (d. 321): *Sharḥ maᶜānī al-āthār,* Beirut, Dār al-kutub al-ᶜilmiyyah. 1416/1996.

al-Ṭayālisī, Abū Dāwūd (d. 204), *al-Musnad,* Dā'irat al-Maᶜārif, Hyderabad Deccan, 1321.

al-Tirmidhī, Muḥammad ibn ᶜĪsā (d. 279): *al-Sunan,* ed. Aḥmad Shākir, Beirut, Dār iḥyā' al-turāth al-ᶜarabī, 1415/1995.

al-Fatāwā al-hindiyyah (known as *al-Fatāwā al-ᶜālamgīriyyah*), Pakistan, 1403/1983.

INDEXES

Index of Qur'ānic *Āyāt*

A

B

But touch them not [that is, your wives] while you are in retreat (*iʿtikāf*) in the mosques 136
By no means shall you attain righteousness unless you spend (in charity) of that which you love 61-62, 66

E

Eat you thereof, and feed the contented and the beggars 228

F

Fear Allāh. and let every soul consider that which it sends forth for tomorrow and fear Allāh 64

I

If any of you are ill or have a head injury, then the expiation is fasting, *ṣadaqah* or sacrifice 254
If one of you kills any [game] deliberately, the reprisal for it is a livestock animal equivalent to what he has killed 256
If you publicise your almsgiving, it is alright, but if you hide it and give it to the poor, it will be better for you 75
Indeed, We sent the Qur'ān down during the Night of Decree 127

L

Let those who disobey his orders beware, lest some trial befall them or a painful punishment be inflicted on them 168

O

O Messengers, eat of the good things, and do good deeds; verily I am aware of what you do 75
O our Lord, accept (this service) from us, Verily, You are the All-Hearing, the All-Knowing 141, 145, 147
O our Lord I have made some of my offspring dwell in a valley without cultivation, by Your Sacred House 141, 142
O people, fear your Lord, Who created you from a single being 64
O you who believe, do not invalidate your *ṣadaqah* by reminders of your generosity or by injury, like those who spend their property to be seen by men 74
O you who have believed, decreed upon you is fasting as it was decreed upon those before you 78, 80, 88, 97

S

T

U

V

W

Y

Z

Index of Aḥādīth

A

F

G

H

I

Now listen. Allāh's Messenger ﷺ sent 16 sacrificial camels with a man whom he put in charge of them 226
No woman is allowed to go on a journey of three days except with her son, or 158

O

O Allāh! Be merciful to those who get their head shaved 229-30
O Allāh! Forgive those who get their heads shaved 229-30
O Allāh's Apostle! All your Companions are returning with *ḥajj* and *ʿumrah* except me 246
O Allāh's Apostle, we used to perform *ṭawāf* between Ṣafā and Marwah 208
Observe *iʿtikāf* (i.e. spend a night or a day near the Kaʿbah) and fast 132
O family of Muḥammad, who so among you intends to do ḥajj must raise his voice uttering the *talbiyah* 172
Of the dīnar you spend in Allāh's path, or to set free a slave, or as a *ṣadaqah* given to one in need 71
O Messenger of Allāh ﷺ is there a reward if one satisfies his passion? 68
On a land irrigated by rain water or by natural water channels or if the land is watered due to a nearby water channel, one-tenth is compulsory 31
One of you comes with all his property to make *ṣadaqah,* then after [giving all he had] he sits [by the road] begging from the people 70
On no other day does the Satan feel so belittled, humiliated, and angry 187
O people, Allāh has made ḥajj obligatory for you; so perform ḥajj 156
O people, Allāh is Good and He therefore accepts only that which is good 75
O people, calm down; obedience (does not consist in) rushing 193
O People! Do not kill each other when you stone the pillar 217
O people of *Anṣār,* did I not find you erring and Allāh guided you through me, and in a state of destitute and Allāh made you free from want through me, and in a state of disunity and Allāh united you through me? 45
O people, the ḥajj has been made obligatory upon you 155
O Qabīṣah, *ṣadaqah* is justified only for the following three 40
O women give alms even from your ornaments 39
O Yazīd! You will be rewarded for what you intended. O Maʿn! Whatever you have taken is yours' 55

P

R

S

T

U

V

W

Y

Index of Narrators and Persons mentioned

A

I

J

K

M

N

Q

R

S

T

U

W

Y

Z